In Search of Fulfillment

The Quest of Psychologist/Educator Arthur W. Combs

AN AUTOBIOGRAPHY

ARTHUR W. COMBS, Ph.D.

edited and with an Epilogue by

Anne C. Richards, Ed.D.

FREEPERSON PRESS

Novato, California

Anne C. Richards, Ed.D. Trustee,
THE FIELD PSYCH TRUST
301 Dixie Street, Carrrollton, GA 30117

Printed in the United States of America
First Edition

Cover Design: Debby Holcombe, University of West Georgia

Freeperson Press
1516 Grant Avenue
Novato, CA 94945
www.somaticsed.com

Table of Contents

With each person you meet
there's a special gift for you to have.
It's another piece of the puzzle
that will help you sort out your place in the circle.

Tadodaho Chief Leon Shenandoah
(cited in Wall, 2001, p. 86)

The more of everyone's story, of the human story,
that we hold inside our hearts and minds,
the stronger we become.

(Gopin, 2004, p. 274)

Introduction

Students of perceptual-experiential psychology and students in humanistic education often ask me: "How did it come about that you got these ideas?" Frequently, too, I am interviewed by students assigned to "find out what you can about Arthur Combs." I am generally flattered by such requests except when callers wake me in the night because they have forgotten about time zones or when such calls come at a time when I am in the garden or at the dinner table. "We are studying your work in our seminar," such callers typically say, "and I'm supposed to find out more about you personally. Can you tell me about yourself?" "Has a summary of your life experiences been published anywhere?" Always I have to say, "I'm sorry. There is no published record of my personal life." Some of my own students and friends have asked similar questions and suggested I write my autobiography.

In order to write one's autobiography, one must begin with the assumption that one is important enough to matter. For someone who began life with deep feelings of rejection, that thought seems downright presumptuous. Accordingly, I have generally resisted the notion. Besides I do not feel that my life is yet a finished product. I am still in the process of becoming. On several occasions, students have written about me as a topic for dissertations in psychology or education, but these efforts have been restricted to explorations of my professional contributions (see, for example, Russell, 1969; Print, 1978*). Once, at the request of a journal editor, I tried to write a brief piece about the highlights of my career, but at the last moment withdrew it for fear people would regard it as unseemly. So, until now, I have always resisted the idea of telling my own story.

In the Fall of 1988, I was talking with my good friend, Richard Usher,† about the concept of self-actualization and its significance for education and psychotherapy. "We have lots of stuff," Dick said, "about the development of

* Editor's note: References to publications authored by Arthur W. Combs or written about him will be found in the chronological list of publications beginning on p. 378. Publications used by the editor or referred to in discussion of various topics throughout the text will be listed at the end of each chapter.

† Editor's note: Richard H. Usher, one of Art's students in the doctoral program at the University of Florida in the 1960s, subsequently taught at the University of Northern Colorado and Murray State University before retiring in 1998. He currently resides in Benton, KY.

the self in children but almost nothing about fulfillment in adults." We agreed that was a pity and that someone ought to do something about it. Later in our conversation, Dick suggested, "Why don't you do an autobiography and show how the search for fulfillment expressed itself in your own life? I think that would be interesting and informative."

As I got to thinking about the matter, it appealed to me more and more. I had been toying with the idea of a book on fulfillment. Why not "A psychologist/educator looks at his life as a case study in human fulfillment?" This would serve a larger purpose and offer an acceptable context for disclosing the personal stuff some people wanted to know. I could also provide an object lesson in perceptual psychology and, at the same time, illustrate the process of self-actualization. Besides, some day my children might read it and be glad to know more about who their Dad was.

That is how this book came to be. I have tried to tell the story of my adult life as one man's search for self-fulfillment. Side by side with salient aspects of my life story, I have interpreted their meaning from the perspective of the perceptual-experiential psychology that Don Snygg and I formulated in 1947. Establishing, refining, and implementing that humanistic frame of reference is my most significant professional contribution. I have also proposed a perceptual field approach to human fulfillment or self-actualization and have explored its implications for education and psychotherapy in many previous publications and presentations. It seems fitting that I should apply this thinking to my own life story.

I have begun this book with a brief discussion of self-fulfillment from a perceptual-experiential orientation for readers who may not be familiar with that point of view. In each of the remaining chapters, I have tried to (a) set forth significant features and events of some period in my life, and (b) show how these contributed to the growth and development of this human being's quest for self-fulfillment. For those who would like to pursue the professional aspects of my life more fully, I have added an appendix containing a listing of my publications to date.

It has been fun writing this autobiography. I have learned things about myself in the process. Gordon Allport, a noted psychologist, once said, "Psychologists keep busy looking at people's lives backward, while people are busily living them forward." I hope this backward glance at my life may prove interesting to others. In the meantime, I resume living my life forward. Who knows what may lie around the next corner?

Arthur W. Combs
4/1/91

Editor's Preface

Writing in 1981 as an analyst of social trends and public attitudes, Daniel Yankelovich maintained that the search for self-fulfillment was a force to be reckoned with in American society, a phenomenon that would serve as a catalyst for cultural change of revolutionary proportion (p. xx). Not all he understood to be associated with this force appealed to him. There were the problems inherent in self-centeredness, self-indulgence, and the lack of a social ethic, for example. But Yankelovich (1981) contended that excesses, conflicts, and contradictions could be expected to occur in any significant process of social change (p. 37).

Arthur W. Combs was born in 1912, long before this period of cultural turbulence, experimentation, and transformation got underway. He became an adult and began his professional career living by the ethic of self-denial and deferred gratification that permeated our society and contributed to survival through the years of the Great Depression. He was educated at a time when established psychological theories were found to be inadequate for dealing with the practical problems of clinical practice. He became a contributor to the humanistic movement that fueled the development of self-psychology and sought to define and describe the nature of optimally-human being. His life story thus captures the transition from a focus on self-improvement in a more material sense to fulfillment through more meaningful personal relationships and commitments to the well-being of individuals, societies, and the global world.

Art Combs wrote this autobiography over an extended period of time while giving considerable thought to the developmental process he had undergone. He began sketching out an account of his personal and professional life in his early 60s, and continued revising and reworking this into his 86th year. In many ways, Art's life comes full circle in this project. His doctoral dissertation (completed in 1945) explored the usefulness of autobiographical material for an understanding of personality. Some forty-five years later, he returned to this medium, using his own autobiographical history to further clarify what he had come to understand about human psychology.

He undertook this project with great enthusiasm and interest, and shared early drafts of what he had written with several colleagues, friends, and family members. He hoped to produce a book other adults would find meaningful at a personal level—a book that might prompt them to reflect on and assess the nature and quality of their own pursuit of self-fulfillment.

Many may pick up this book out of curiosity—to learn more about a man who achieved distinction in his professional career, a person who has been a significant contributor to the improvement of American education and co-founder of one of the pioneering efforts to formulate theory in the humanistic movement in psychology. Beyond this, readers may find far more than they bargained for in these pages. For this is a very human story about a man much like many of us who long to experience ourselves positively, to feel "at home" with ourselves and the world that surrounds us, to be at one with other people in our lives, to have the personal resources that enable us to thrive in the midst of whatever life brings our way, and to experience a "good death" (as we individually understand this) when we have reached the end of life as we know it.

Malcolm Cowley (1984) has written: "Every man, every woman, is not only a person but also a representation of the age in which he has lived" (p. 18). In this sense, Art's story is also the story of a person who grew into adulthood during the Great Depression and in the shadow of World War II. Writing about other persons of this "greatest generation," Tom Brokaw (1998) shared ways in which they distinguished themselves as persons of substance and integrity in the midst of hardship, turmoil, and a momentous war. Art was not among those who went off to fight in this war, yet he fought many a battle for educational reform in his lifetime and, as you will discover in reading the pages that follow, his contributions certainly reflect a spirit of working collaboratively with others toward a common good that Brokaw considered characteristic of his generation (p. 232).

Art long had a talent for writing clearly, plainly, and effectively about ideas—in such a way that one can readily find personal meaning in whatever topic he is addressing in professional articles. Here, too, he writes clearly, plainly, and effectively—about his life, his professional perspectives, and his experience of self across nearly eight decades. Art was well aware of the distortions in memory that can occur over time and, in a book we co-authored, several pages are devoted to pointing out this principle (Combs, Richards, & Richards, 1976, pp. 214–222). Having lived into his 80s, he also had considerable opportunities to revisit and revise earlier perceptions, and he shares a number of these transformations in the pages that follow.

Discussing an effort to write his own memoirs at age 85, Malcolm Cowley (1984) takes issue with memoirs that are written before the author has sufficient self-awareness and experience to identify significant turning points in life. While acknowledging that sharpness and richness of detail may fade from one's memories as the years go by, Cowley sees an advantage in the memoirs of elders. As he explains this:

> I used to hear college students asking, "Who am I?" They were genuinely distressed in those days about the questions of their personal identities. I listened to them with sympathy, but also with a measure of disdain. "When I was your age," I wanted to tell them, and didn't, "I knew damned well who I was." Now I am not so certain. Since I am 85, the question comes back to me, if in a slightly different form. "Who was I?" and the answer isn't always what I expected.
>
> . . .To search for one's past is a fascinating occupation and one that may be appropriate to the older memoirist, it is among the privileges that partly compensate for his handicaps. In earlier years he had been too busy living among others to think much about himself, but now at last he has an opportunity, if not always the time, to discover the shape of his life. He has the perspective of years, in which crucial events continue to stand out, while much that is trivial fades into the background. (p. 18)

As Atwood and Stolorow (1984) have explained so eloquently, in the human sciences, "the investigator is an experiencing individual, situated personally and historically," which means his or her

> quest for knowledge is accordingly subject to the influence of all those historical, personal, and circumstantial factors that come into play in every human action. These factors inevitably relativize the investigator's understanding and threaten to subvert the aim of arriving at conclusions possessing general validity. (p. 3)

For narratives of this type to "bridge the gulf between the concrete particularity of an individual life and the experience of being human in universal terms," the author must succeed at "unveiling the experiences of that life in a form to which others can relate their own personal worlds in empathic dialogue" while "describing the pattern of the individual's life as the realization of shared human possibilities" (p. 7).

For Cowley, "every human life is a drama, brief or prolonged, commonplace or astounding, and different in detail from every other human life. . . ."; but "[i]f the protagonist has truly depicted himself, then others will recognize their own features in the portrait" (p. 18). If a writer can achieve this, writes Cowley (1984), a reader is in a position to gain insight into his or her own life journey. I believe Art has achieved this kind of authenticity, writing an autobiography that not only enables others to understand him and his theory better, but also provides them with the means of finding themselves in these pages as well.

My First Meeting with Art

I first met Art Combs, almost by happenstance, at the suggestion of Dr. Sidney M. Jourard. In a class taught by Abraham H. Maslow that I had taken while an undergraduate student majoring in psychology at Brandeis University (1961–1965), I had read the first edition of Jourard's (1964) *The Transparent Self,* and found it intriguing. After earning my B.A. at Brandeis University and a master's degree in education at the University of Chicago and teaching seventh-graders in public school in New Jersey, I consulted with Maslow about where I might further explore the humanistic ideas to which I had first been introduced in his classes. Maslow recommended several possibilities, including the doctoral program in the Department of Psychology at the University of Florida, where Jourard was on the faculty.

I applied to and was accepted into a Ph.D. program in psychology at the University of Florida. Early in 1968, I made a trip to Gainesville, FL to look for housing and to talk with Jourard about studies I could pursue under his direction. In the course of this meeting, I learned for the first time that my master's degree in education would not be accepted as sufficient preparation for doctoral work in the psychology department at the University of Florida. As a result, before I could actually begin doctoral work in that department, I would be required to earn the equivalent of another master's degree in psychology, a program that did not include independent study options. Somehow, I had missed any indication of such guidelines in the catalog or the application process. In addition, once I began the doctoral program, the structured introductory coursework that was a prescribed part of the first-year experience would postpone still further the possibility of my taking independent study courses under the direction of Dr. Jourard.

I was not at all pleased at this news, realizing that at least three years would go by before I would be able to work with Jourard! In those days that seemed like an eternity. I must have somehow conveyed my disappointment and dismay at learning all this and Jourard suggested I go across campus to talk with a fellow named Art Combs about getting into a doctoral program in psychological foundations, housed in the College of Education. In that context, my master's degree would readily be accepted and Jourard thought the program had an elective component that would enable me to take coursework under his direction in the psychology department very soon after launching my studies.

I immediately got an appointment with Art. Though I now recall little of what we talked about that day, I distinctly remember that I experienced Art as a thoughtful, attentive, gracious, welcoming, and supportive individual. Where I had been anxious in Sid's presence, because I knew him to be a nationally known contributor in psychology, I felt very comfortable interacting with Art because I had no knowledge of his professional writings, contributions, or national reputation. Beyond this, he was so kind, helpful, and approachable that I felt very much at ease in his presence. At the time, I think my understanding was that Art was a person who handled administrative matters for the department, a department chair. I had a naïve and limited grasp of academia and how it was organized back then; I don't think it even occurred to me that Art was among the teaching faculty in the department.

Art readily clarified options in the foundations department program that would enable me to work with Jourard as soon as I wished to, and found doctoral students I could talk with about their experience of the Ed.D. program in the foundations department. These students had nothing but praise for the quality and substance of the program in which they were enrolled, which was encouraging. Shortly thereafter, I withdrew my application from the Ph.D. program in psychology, where I had already been accepted, and applied to the Ed.D. program in the foundations department. I was accepted there as well and arrived in Fall, 1968 to begin my doctoral studies. During my first quarter on campus, I enrolled in a course described by the students I had spoken with previously as an excellent point of departure. Unbeknownst to me at the time, it was taught by Arthur W. Combs himself.

On the first day of class, as I chatted with my fellow students before the teacher arrived in the room, I discovered that Dr. Combs was going to be the professor. Not only that, virtually everyone I spoke with was well acquainted with Art's professional contributions and reputation and had been eagerly anticipating the chance to study with someone they regarded so highly, even revered!

I was first stunned, then mortified. Here I was, a brand new doctoral student, taking this "great man's" class, but how had I treated him during our initial interaction? Certainly not as a person of consequence in the program I was talking about entering. From my limited memories of our meeting, it seemed I had just rushed into his office preoccupied with a desire to study with Sidney Jourard. Had I insulted him? Spoken too frankly? Been incredibly disrespectful? I fretted about not having been, at the very least, more inquisitive about Art's interests and professional contributions. Since my overt priority at the time was how I might use the program in Art's department to get to work with someone in another department across campus, I marveled that I had gotten into the program at all.

My embarrassment and self-doubts were short-lived, however. The course Art taught was both meaningful and stimulating. The program proved all I could have hoped for at a doctoral level—and then some. I took additional coursework with Art, and when it came time to do my dissertation, chose to work with him as my major professor. Sidney Jourard was also a member of my dissertation committee, along with Donald L. Avila, Walter Busby, and Robert Blume.

My doctoral dissertation was intended to serve as a bridge between humanistic psychological theory and educational practice. It involved development of a resource manual of curriculum materials addressed to the classroom teacher who wished to foster self-development in students of junior high school age and beyond. It was designed to promote greater actualization in both teacher and students of the capacity for openness to experience. It also contained a wide variety of materials that illustrated fundamental postulates and principles of perceptual psychology.

Perhaps because of this, as well as the significant relationship my husband Fred and I developed with Art Combs, he invited us to collaborate with him on the revision of perceptual psychology in the early '70s (Combs, Richards, & Richards, 1976, 1988). This formed the beginning of a professional collaboration and personal friendship that has lasted over thirty years.

The Autobiography Project

Prior to his death in 1999, Art asked me if I would be willing to take responsibility for posthumously publishing an autobiography he had begun. I understood that this was a manuscript he was actively working on and would be continuing to develop to the end of his days. I knew many who would be interested in learning more about the man whose professional writings and speeches held profound meaning for them. When I agreed to undertake this project, I envisioned my role as a rather minimal one, focused primarily on securing a publisher for an essentially complete and well-polished manuscript. I also agreed to organize and sustain Art's intellectual property and to become administrator of a small trust (known as the Field Psych Trust) that he was in the process of establishing to cover expenses related to the foregoing and to provide grant funding for promising graduate students conducting research in perceptual or field psychology.

When I first received a copy of Art's original draft of this manuscript, I realized the project was going to require some further work. This initial draft contained factual and chronological summaries of significant events in his life, which were interesting in and of themselves to someone wanting to know more about this noted psychologist/educator but offered a limited glimpse of the meanings these events held for him. I offered some editorial suggestions, as did others, and Art took most of them.

As this project evolved, and the years went by, Art provided greater substance to the manuscript until physical limitations associated with the aging process, a couple of accidents, and bouts of ill health began to take their toll on his energy level and capacity to capture his experience more completely in writing. Over time he wrote less often and in less detail about his experience until he stopped writing anything further—nine days before his death at age 86. I didn't discover this, however, until I received the copy of the latest draft of his autobiography that he arranged to be sent to me after his death.

The "work" involved in preparing this manuscript for publication has been a labor of love. It has enabled me to deepen my own understandings of perceptual theory while learning much about a significant mentor figure that I hadn't known previously. At the same time, I could readily identify with Noël Bennett's description of how editing another's story can be a "precarious" undertaking (Bighorse & Bennett, 1990, p. xxii). Bennett learned weaving among the Navajo (principally from Tiana Bighorse) while her (Bennett's) physician-husband provided public health services to this population. Subsequently, she undertook the task of educating others about the weaving arts (see, for example, Bennett & Bighorse, 1971) and edited stories illustrating the ideals and values of traditional Navajo people.

Speaking about restoration of woven art, Bennett explains some of the risks inherent in this process while reminiscing about the first time she was asked to restore an historic Navajo blanket.

> Twenty years ago a dealer brought me a hundred-year-old serape. Would I reweave it? I was wary. Reweaving meant taking out some of the old yarn and putting in new—sheer folly in a rare fabric of cochineal yarn. Yet gaping holes despoiled its beauty. (Bighorse & Bennett, 1990, p. xxii)

Bennett restored this serape to the satisfaction of the trader who brought it to her, but was dismayed by what she had done. As she saw it, the serape's historic integrity was lost in the process. This experience taught her an important lesson that she considered relevant to and carried over into her work as an editor:

> Stretched sections told how a fabric had been worn. Raveled ends showed where a blanket had been held tightly closed. Thin areas implied repeated leaning—perhaps against the trading post or hogan wall. But blankets that had been restored down to their thin warp and frayed edges showed nothing. Pertinent cultural information, lost forever because the restorer didn't distinguish damage from wear, didn't know what to weave and what to leave, didn't know when to stop. (Bighorse & Bennett, 1990, p. xxiii)

This lesson came home to me time and again as I worked with the manuscript Art left in my care. For example, Art planned for this book to include a comprehensive listing of his publications (see p. 378). He had organized his numerous publications in chronological order and had even compiled a master list of same (one of which was published previously in the *Person-Centered Review*; see Combs, 1986). In reviewing this material, however, I discovered numerous typos, errors, oversights, and omissions. Determined not to pass these on to new generations of those who might be interested in Art's work, I decided to locate a copy of each and every publication Art had ever contributed to the literature so I could verify the accuracy of citations regarding these. I began this process in the summer of 1999, and regret to report that it is still a work in progress.

Because Art was such a prolific and long-lived professional, his writings span six decades, beginning in the 1940s. Despite sometimes Herculean efforts to locate earlier works, I have been unsuccessful in securing copies of all of them. Rather than hold up publication of this manuscript until I achieved a level of 100% accuracy (assuming this is even a realistic possibility), I eventually decided that the reading public would be better served by having the opportunity to read this manuscript sooner rather than later, even if it were incomplete in some aspects. The bulk of Art's publications have been verified and are presented accurately and completely here. In cases where I was not able to secure and verify references, these are indicated with an asterisk. If anyone reading this manuscript is in possession of copies of asterisked items, or knows how to locate any of them, I would very much appreciate being informed of this.

During the time Art was sharing early drafts of this material, the question of photographs that might be included in the text never came up. After his death, his daughter, Carol, mentioned that he had set aside several photographs for possible use for the book. Most of these were photos taken in the latter years of his life. I got the impression Art thought some photograph of him might be expected, and he had set aside several from which to choose one. After reviewing the manuscript in its final form, and learning that family photographs existed from nearly all phases of Art's life, I made a decision as editor to include a broad range of these photographs in this book. In addition, I sought out photographs of particular persons with whom Art had significant interactions. For me, these enhance the presentation of his life history in meaningful and sometimes particularly engaging ways. Given that the selection presented here came about through my choices rather than Art's, however, they may say more about my personal perspectives regarding highlights of Art's life than Art's identification of events he would have regarded as highlights.

The inclusion of sections labeled "Heart-Warmers" in several chapters is also my doing. In Chapter 5, Art himself made only passing reference to this collection of messages from others who found him to be a significant presence in their lives. I thought readers would have a more detailed picture of his legacy across time, and of the nature of the recognition he treasured, if excerpts from this collection were included. Accordingly, I've inserted a section labeled "Heart-Warmers" in chapters 5 through 13.

Art began his career when it was customary to use male pronouns exclusively whenever one intended to speak generally about humankind. In later decades, when this was no longer acceptable in professional writing, he struggled with how best to convey in writing an inclusive reference to persons of both sexes. He addressed the issue by (a) using plural terms where appropriate, (b) alternating male and female pronouns in his publications, and (c) avoiding sexual stereotypes in references to occupations of men and women. As editor, I have chosen the first and fourth of these options in my own writing, but have left any direct quotes from Art's writings in the wording in which they were originally written.

Aside from these personal choices, the reader will find numerous editorial comments throughout the text. These are typically presented in the form of footnotes, or appear in bracketed text. While doing background research for this book project, I came across information in Art's files or elsewhere that I thought would provide the reader with a more complete or substantive view of given passages and decided to share with others what I learned along the way.

It has been an honor and a privilege having the opportunity to work so closely with this material and to bring it before a larger audience. And I have no doubt it will prove to be a continuing educational experience for me. As indicated in the Epilogue, from the point of view of those of us who have occasion to reflect on Art's life, this book remains a work in progress—and probably will be so to the end of our own days.In the years that have passed since Art's death, some facets or dimensions of his life story that only seemed part of the background or periphery earlier on have emerged into clearer light for me, while others that seemed initially to have major significance have paled in comparison with their earlier importance. Continued growth, maturity, and aging on my part will undoubtedly influence my discovery of new meaning in particular passages and experiences. The same is likely to be true for other readers as well. Knowing Art as I did, I expect he'd have been pleased about this.

Anne C. Richards
8/10/06

References

Atwood, G. E., & Stolorow, R. D. (1984). *Structures of subjectivity: Explorations in psychoanalytic phenomenology.* Hillsdale, NJ: Analytic Press.

Bennett, N., & Bighorse, T. (1971). *Working with the wool: How to weave a Navajo rug.* Flagstaff, AZ: Northland Press.

Bighorse, T., & Bennett, N. (1990). *Bighorse the warrior.* Tucson, AZ: University of Arizona Press.

Brokaw, T. (1998). *The greatest generation.* New York: Random House.

Cowley, M. (1984, June 17). Looking for the essential me. *New York Times Book Review,* pp. 1, 18.

Gopin, M. (2004). *Healing the heart of conflict: 8 crucial steps to making peace with yourself and others.* Emmaus, PA: Rodale.

Jourard, S. M. (1964). *The transparent self. Self-disclosure and well-being.* New York: Van Nostrand Reinhold.

Wall, S. (2001). *To become a human being: The message of Tadodaho Chief Leon Shenandoah.* Charlottesville, VA: Hampton Roads Publishing Co.

Yankelovich, D. (1981). *New rules: Searching for self-fulfillment in a world turned upside down.* New York: Random House.

Voyager *by Richard Kirsten-Daiensai*

Acknowledgments

Richard Kirsten-Daiensai's *Voyager*—on facing page—captures well the sense of connection or relationship that has sustained and given me forward momentum during the seven years I have worked to bring the manuscript of this book into published form.

The assistance and support of Art's children and extended family have been invaluable. I turned often to Carol Hole, Peter Combs, Lynn Combs, and Erin Combs for answers to questions only close family members were in a position to know and gained access through them to photographs of their father taken across the many years of his life. Photographs were also provided by Art's first wife Mildred Mitchell Combs, before she died, and Art's second wife, Susan J. Kannel. Art's sister Dorothea C. Lamson also shared anecdotes and photographs that have been incorporated in this book. Art's brother, Charles (Chuck) Combs, though deceased by the time I began working on this project, had compiled an informative and detailed history of his extended family that offered clarifying and helpful information on particular passages in this publication.

I am grateful for the group of men whose companionship and support meant so much to Art when he was alive (Jim Fittz, Tom Flower, David Gonzalez, Marc Ringel, Roy Wardell), and who have continued to hold him in their hearts as the years have gone by. Along with family members, colleagues and close friends Robert (Bob) Blume, David Cain, Larry Kerrigan, Fred Richards, George and Ann Rader Tate, and Dick and Mary Usher, men's group members were among those who read preliminary drafts of this book, offered critical assistance in assuring the accuracy of the book's content, and shared thoughtful commentary about Art's life and the perspectives he articulates herein.

I am grateful to Eleanor Criswell-Hanna, a pioneer in humanistic psychology in her own right, and a former student of Art's as well, for making publication of this book possible through Freeperson Press. It has been a joy working with her and the team of talented and caring individuals she assembled for editing, designing, and printing this book: Marsha Calhoun, Hassan Herz (TBH Typecast), Satri Pencak, and the personnel at McNaughton & Gunn.

Locating some of the photographs included in the text was a challenging and sometimes discouraging process. Since Art's life spanned decades long gone by, many institutions and individuals were unable to assist me in securing photographs I had hoped existed. Several photographs included in these pages were taken years ago, making it difficult, if not impossible, to determine the identity or current whereabouts of the photographers who took them. If anyone reading this book happens to recognize names and has information regarding the whereabouts of these individuals, I would very much appreciate knowing this.

Synchronicity and good fortune were with me on several occasions, however. I discovered in casual conversation, for example, that a colleague of mine, Karl Steinen (professor of anthropology, University of West Georgia), had grown up in the neighborhood where Donald Snygg and his family lived in Oswego, NY. (Art Combs and Don Snygg together formulated the theoretical position known as perceptual psychology that was foundational to Art's professional contributions from the mid-forties to the end of his life.) Snygg's daughter Fran had even been Karl's babysitter when Karl was a child. Karl was instrumental in my contacting the family of Donald Snygg, without whose assistance and cooperation a photo of Art and Don would not have appeared in this book.

On another occasion, when it seemed as if I would be unable to find a photograph of Art's former colleague and good friend, Dan Soper, Walter Busby took it upon himself to pursue the matter, knew just the person to turn to for assistance, and was readily successful in accomplishing what I had begun to believe was out of my reach. And when, despite the professional courtesy and best efforts of Roberta Wespiser, executive secretary of university relations at the Union Institute and University, I was unable to make contact with a graduate of that institution, Roy Fairfield's commitment to maintaining contact with his former students at Union Graduate School enabled me to reach John Fowler and subsequently to secure his permission for inclusion of material from an interview he conducted with Art Combs in 1974.

I owe an immense debt of gratitude to librarians at the University of West Georgia, and elsewhere, for assisting me patiently, mindfully, helpfully, and resourcefully over several years as I sought to compile a more accurate and complete list of Art's publications. Special thanks in this regard go to the following members of the library staff at the Ingram Library, University of West Georgia: Nancy Farmer, Angela M. Mehaffey, Laura Hartman and Melissa Gearhart (Reference/Interlibrary Loan Department); Carol Goodson (Library Access Services); Myron House (Special Collections/reference librarian); Charles Beard (former director, Ingram Library); as well as Michael Aldrich, Betsy Griffies, Chris Huff, Brian Kooy, Shirley Lankford, Lori Lester-Wilson, Monica Ollendorff, and Jan Ruskell. I was also helpfully assisted by John B. Straw, Archives & Special Collections librarian, Ball State University; Timothy Driscoll, archivist/records manager, Harvard Business School; Mary O'Brien and Edward L. Galvin (Archives and Records Management), and Joan Recusaro and David L. Prince (Art Collection), Syracuse University. And the following individuals went to some lengths to assist me in locating key information about Art's publications that were translated into Japanese: D. J. Amis, Yuriko Azuma and her family, Mai Hiraoka, Hiroshi Ishii, and Aki Matsushima.

Several persons provided technical assistance in the preparation of this book. David Payne of Carrollton Photographic Services creatively and skillfully brought new life to time-worn photographs (which appear throughout the text). Deborah B. Holcombe (Publications and Printing, University of West Georgia), created the cover design for the book. Blake Adams (Information Technology Services, University of West Georgia) provided support services for my computer that enabled me to move forward with vital word-processing operations on countless occasions. Rolanda Farmer (Learning Resources, University of West Georgia) prepared electronic data-bases for the photographs to be included in this book.

Ellen Foust Dodson, C. G. Prado, and George Sherman, although unfamiliar with Art's writings and professional contributions, read the manuscript in draft form and were encouraging about its significance to a wider audience. Tanya Morehead has literally walked with me through the tough times and the uplifting moments as this project has moved toward completion. I am also indebted to the following individuals for their support and assistance (a) in the work of the Field Psych Trust (Renate Nummela Caine, Don Dellow, Fred Richards, M. Mark Wasicsko, David Welch, and Dick Usher); and (b) with matters large and small that contributed to the accuracy and significance of portions of this book: Shirley Avila, Dee Blume, Bruce Brewer, David Cain, Louise Chinn (Robert Ducas Literary Agency), John Cleare, Mitchell Clute, Eva Carney Cohen, Alan L. Cohen, Nicole DiBlasi (Getty Images), Richard Kirsten-Daiensai, Mary B. Landsman, Bonny McNerney, Anne McNaughton, Vicki Soper Marsh, Natalie Rogers, Betty and Joel Siegel, John Snygg, Charles Snygg, Sandra Štetić (first secretary, Embassy of the Republic of Croatia), Katherine Ward, Hannelore Wass, and Alan Wilkes.

Last, but by no means least, Fred Richards, my husband, life companion, and colleague, has been a continual source of strength and inspiration throughout our 37-year marriage, and his intellectual camaraderie and encouragement have been invaluable as this book moved ever so slowly but steadily toward publication.

I also wish to acknowledge the following organizations and/or individuals for granting permission to use protected and/or previously published material in this volume.

Excerpts from *Tuesdays with Morrie. An Old Man, a Young Man, and Life's Greatest Lesson* by Mitch Albom (Doubleday edition). Copyright © 1997 by Mitch Albom, reproduced by permission of Random House, Inc.

Excerpts from *Structures of Subjectivity: Explorations in Psychoanalytic Phenomenology* by George E. Atwood & Robert D. Stolorow, reproduced by permission of The Analytic Press and doctors Atwood & Stolorow.

Excerpts from *Bighorse the Warrior* by Tiana Bighorse, edited by Noël Bennett. Copyright © 1990 by The Arizona Board of Regents. Reprinted by permission of the University of Arizona Press.

Excerpt from *My Son . . . My Son . . . A Guide to Healing after Death, Loss, or Suicide* by Iris Bolton with Curtis Mitchell, reproduced by permission of Bolton Press, Atlanta.

Excerpts from *Being and Becoming: A Field Approach to Psychology* by Arthur W. Combs, copyright © 1999 by Springer Publishing Company, Inc. Published by Springer Publishing Company, Inc., New York 10036. Used by permission.

Excerpts from "Looking for the Essential Me" by Malcolm Cowley, reprinted by permission of Robert W. Cowley, Literary Executor for the Estate of Malcolm Cowley.

Excerpts from *The View from 80* by Malcolm Cowley, copyright © 1976, 1978, 1980 by Malcolm Cowley. Used by permission of Viking Penguin, a division of Penguin Group (USA) Inc.

Excerpt from *Voluntary Simplicity. Toward a Way of Life that is Outwardly Simple, Inwardly Rich* (rev. ed.) by Duane Elgin, copyright © 1981 by Duane Elgin. Reproduced by permission of HarperCollins Publishers.

Excerpts from 1974 interview with Arthur W. Combs (under the pseudonym "Bill Rose") reprinted with permission of John Fowler, who conducted this interview.

Quotation by Marc Gopin from *Healing the Heart of Conflict. 8 Crucial Steps to Making Peace with Yourself and Others* by Marc Gopin, reproduced by permission of Zachary Schuster Harmsworth.

Excerpt from *Looking in the Distance. The Human Search for Meaning* by Richard Holloway, copyright © by Richard Holloway, 2004, reproduced by permission of Canongate Books, Ltd.

Excerpts from *The Right to Die. Understanding Euthanasia* by Derek Humphry & Ann Wickett, reproduced by permission of Derek Humphry.

Excerpts from *Let Me Die Before I Wake. Hemlock's Book of Self-Deliverance for the Dying* by Derek Humphry, reproduced by permission of Derek Humphry.

Excerpts from *Evolution in Action* by Julian Huxley © 1953 by Julian Huxley, reprinted by permission of PFD on behalf of the Estate of Julian Huxley.

Excerpts from *Suicidology: Contemporary Developments.* Copyright © 1976 by Harcourt Assessment, Inc. Reproduced with permission. All rights reserved.

Excerpt from Giampaolo Moraglia, *Journal of Humanistic Psychology* (Vol. 44, No. 3), pp. 337–357, copyright © 2004 by Sage Publications, Inc., Reprinted by permission of Sage Publications, Inc.

Excerpts from *Awakening the Heroes Within. Twelve Archetypes to Help Us Find Ourselves and Transform Our World* by Carol S. Pearson, copyright © 1991 by Carol S. Pearson, reprinted by permission of HarperCollins Publishers.

Excerpts from *The Last Choice. Preemptive Suicide in Advanced Age* by C. G. Prado. Copyright © 1990 by C.G. Prado. Reproduced with permission of Greenwood Publishing Group, Inc., Westport, CT.

Quotation by Tadodaho Chief Leon Shenandoah, from *To Become a Human Being* by Steve Wall, reproduced by permission of Hampton Roads Publishing Company, Inc.

Photo Credits

(Cover) "Bow of Boat on Lake." Jorg Greuel/Photonica/Getty Images.

(Acknowledgments) *Voyager* by artist Richard Kirsten-Daiensai. Reprinted with permission of Richard Kirsten-Daiensai.

(1.1) "Bow of Boat on Lake." Jorg Greuel/Photonica/Getty Images.

(2.1) Charlotte H. Vyse Combs (Arthur's mother) with Arthur and Dorothea (Newark, NJ, circa 1917). Reprinted by permission of Dorothea Combs Lamson.

(2.2) Arthur's paternal grandmother, Miriam J. Wright Combs, circa 1945. Photo courtesy of Susan J. Kannel.

(2.3) Arthur Combs, Sr., a veterinary officer in WWI, 1917. Photo courtesy of Susan J. Kannel.

(2.4) Arthur (at left) with his neighborhood buddies (circa 1922). Photo courtesy of the Estate of Arthur W. Combs, reproduced by permission of the Estate of Arthur W. Combs.

(2.5) Charles (Chuck) Combs, 1920. Photo courtesy of the Estate of Arthur W. Combs, reproduced by permission of the Estate of Arthur W. Combs.

(2.6) Arthur W. Combs on graduation from eighth grade, 1926 (with grandmother Miriam Combs in background). Photo courtesy of the Estate of Arthur W. Combs, reproduced by permission of the Estate of Arthur W. Combs.

(2.7) Arthur's college dorm room, circa 1932. Photo courtesy of the Estate of Arthur W. Combs, reproduced by permission of the Estate of Arthur W. Combs.

(2.8) Arthur in his ROTC uniform, September, 1930. Photo courtesy of the Estate of Arthur W. Combs, reproduced by permission of the Estate of Arthur W. Combs.

(3.1) Arthur W. Combs, 1935, Alliance, OH. Photo courtesy of Mildred Mitchell Combs, reproduced by permission of the Estate of Mildred Mitchell Combs.

(3.2) Millie and Arthur, circa 1933. Photo courtesy of Mildred Mitchell Combs, reproduced by permission of the Estate of Mildred Mitchell Combs.

(4.1) Arthur W. Combs in Syracuse, NY (circa 1950). Photo courtesy of Dorothea Combs Lamson.

(4.2) Arthur W. Combs (circa 1945-1950). Parent Interview, Psycho-educational Clinic, Syracuse University. Photo courtesy of the Estate of Arthur W. Combs, reproduced by permission of the Estate of Arthur W. Combs.

(4.3) *St. Jerome* by Ivan Meštrović. Photo by Nadya S. Lutz, reproduced courtesy of Nadya S. Lutz and the Embassy of the Republic of Croatia, Washington, DC.

(4.4) Peter, Millie, and Carol (1945). Photo courtesy of the Estate of Arthur W. Combs, reproduced by permission of the Estate of Arthur W. Combs.
(4.5) Millie, Peter, Carol, and Arthur (Christmas, 1949). Photo courtesy of Mildred Mitchell Combs, reproduced by permission of the Estate of Mildred Mitchell Combs.
(4.6) Millie, Arthur, and dog Sparkie behind their new home with flagstone patio, Fayetteville, NY (circa 1951). Photo courtesy of Mildred Mitchell Combs, reproduced by permission of the Estate of Mildred Mitchell Combs.
(4.7) Ted Landsman (standing at back of photo) and Arthur (with suit on, sitting at table) in Syracuse, NY (circa 1950). Photo by Gene Logan Photographic Studio, Syracuse, NY. Photo courtesy of the Estate of Arthur W. Combs, reproduced by permission of the Estate of Arthur W. Combs and Mary B. Landsman.
(4.8) Arthur Combs as a young married man (circa 1950). Photo by Fryer Studio, Syracuse, NY. Photo courtesy of Mildred Mitchell Combs, reproduced by permission of the Estate of Mildred Mitchell Combs.
(5.1) Donald Snygg and Arthur W. Combs at summer family picnic (circa 1948). Photo courtesy of the Donald Snygg family. Reproduced by permission of the Donald Snygg family.
(5.2) Donald Snygg with Trapezoidal Window, circa 1960s. Photo courtesy of Special Collections of Penfield Library, State University of New York (SUNY) at Oswego.
(5.3) John Snygg, Peter Combs, Arthur Combs, Fran Snygg, Charles Snygg, and Elaine (Mrs. Donald) Snygg (circa 1948). Photo courtesy of Mildred Mitchell Combs, reproduced by permission of the Estate of Mildred Mitchell Combs and the Donald Snygg family.
(5.4) Arthur W. Combs (circa 1950). Photo courtesy of Mildred Mitchell Combs, reproduced by permission of the Estate of Mildred Mitchell Combs.
(6.1) Arthur W. Combs in Florida (circa 1955). Photo courtesy of Mildred Mitchell Combs, reproduced by permission of the Estate of Mildred Mitchell Combs.
(6.2) Arthur W. Combs (circa 1950). Photo courtesy of the Estate of Arthur W. Combs, reproduced by permission of the Estate of Arthur W. Combs.
(6.3) Arthur W. Combs (circa 1952). Photo courtesy of Mildred Mitchell Combs, reproduced by permission of the Estate of Mildred Mitchell Combs.
(6.4) Millie, Carol, Peter, and Arthur (1953). Photo courtesy of Mildred Mitchell Combs, reproduced by permission of the Estate of Mildred Mitchell Combs.
(7.1) Arthur W. Combs conducting workshop (circa 1961). Photo courtesy of the Estate of Arthur W. Combs, reproduced by permission of the Estate of Arthur W. Combs.
(7.2) Arthur W. Combs (circa 1962). Photo courtesy of Mildred Mitchell Combs, reproduced by permission of the Estate of Mildred Mitchell Combs.
(7.3) Dan Soper with his daughter Vicki (circa 1960s). P. K. Yonge Laboratory School, Gainesville, FL. Photo courtesy of the D. W. Soper family.
(7.4) Mr. and Mrs. Arthur W. Combs (Art's parents, circa 1960). Photo courtesy of Susan J. Kannel.
(7.5) Dan Soper (circa 1960), Gainesville, FL. Photo courtesy of the D.W. Soper family.
(8.1) Arthur W. Combs with unidentified individual at meeting of the American Society of Personnel Administration (ASPA), forerunner to the Society for Human Resource Management (SHRM). Photo taken circa late 1960s. Photo

courtesy of Mildred Mitchell Combs, reproduced by permission of the Estate of Mildred Mitchell Combs.

(8.2) Peter, Millie, and Art (1961). Photo courtesy of Dorothea Combs Lamson.

(8.3) Art with daughter Carol on her wedding day (December 27, 1959). Photo courtesy of Dorothea Combs Lamson.

(8.4) Art Combs (1963). Photo courtesy of Mildred Mitchell Combs, reproduced by permission of the Estate of Mildred Mitchell Combs.

(8.5) Millie Combs (1963). Photo courtesy of Mildred Mitchell Combs, reproduced by permission of the Estate of Mildred Mitchell Combs.

(9.1) Arthur W. Combs (1972). Photo by Susan J. Kannel, reproduced courtesy of Susan J. Kannel.

(9.2) Millie and Art in Hawaii, 1967. Photo courtesy of Mildred Mitchell Combs, reproduced by permission of the Estate of Mildred Mitchell Combs.

(9.3) Art Combs teaching (1972). Photo by Susan J. Kannel, reproduced courtesy of Susan J. Kannel.

(10.1) Arthur W. Combs in Greeley, CO (circa 1977). Photo by Monte Clute. Reproduced by permission of the Estate of Monte Clute.

(10.2) Arthur W. Combs lecturing in class (circa 1975). Photo by Susan J. Kannel, reproduced courtesy of Susan J. Kannel.

(10.3) Charles Horn, Art, Susan, Ted Landsman, Mary B. Landsman, and Mary Horn (Micanopy, FL. Photo taken by tripod circa 1975). Reproduced courtesy of Susan J. Kannel and by permission of Susan J. Kannel, Mary B. Landsman, and Charles and Mary Horn.

(10.4) Arthur W. Combs in Allenspark, CO (circa 1975). Photo courtesy of Susan J. Kannel.

(10.5) Arthur W. Combs (circa 1977). Photo by Monte Clute. Reproduced by permission of the Estate of Monte Clute.

(10.6) Chuck Combs (left) and Art (right) with their mother (circa 1980). Photo by Susan J. Kannel, reproduced courtesy of Susan J. Kannel.

(10.7) Arthur W. Combs (circa 1986). Photo courtesy of the Estate of Arthur W. Combs, reproduced by permission of the Estate of Arthur W. Combs.

(10.8) Lynn, Arthur, Erin, and Susan (1985). Photo by Tony Wu, Contemporary Studios, Greeley, CO, reproduced courtesy of Susan J. Kannel.

(10.9) Daniel Bruns, Barbara Porter, George Tate, Art Combs, and David Welch, Community Counseling Associates, 1987. Photo by Daniel Bruns (on tripod), courtesy of the Estate of Arthur W. Combs, reproduced by permission of the Estate of Arthur W. Combs and former members of Community Counseling Associates.

(10.10) Susan and Art (1983). Photo by Nancy Campbell, courtesy of Susan J. Kannel, reproduced with permission of Nancy Campbell and Susan J. Kannel.

(10.11) Erin, Art, and Lynn (1988). Photo by Susan J. Kannel, reproduced courtesy of Susan J. Kannel.

(11.1) Arthur W. Combs (1994). Photo by Katherine Ward, reproduced by permission of the Estate of Dr. Katherine Ward.

(11.2) Arthur W. Combs, Mary Hart, Anne C. Richards (sitting), Katherine Ward, and Fred Richards (standing), Carrollton, GA (1994). Photo by Tobin Hart, reproduced courtesy of Anne C. Richards with permission from Tobin Hart, Mary Hart, the Estate of Dr. Katherine Ward, and Fred Richards.

(11.3) Anne C. Richards, Lynn Combs, Art Combs, and Erin Combs, Greeley, CO, July, 1993. Photo by Fred L. Richards, reproduced courtesy of Fred L. Richards, Lynn Combs, and Erin Combs.

(11.4) Lynn, Carol, Peter, and Erin (1995) in Greeley, CO. Photo by Susan J. Kannel, reproduced courtesy of Susan J. Kannel.

(11.5) Art with Walter Busby, Greeley, CO (July, 1993). Photo by Anne C. Richards, reproduced courtesy of Anne C. Richards and Walter Busby.

(11.6) Arthur W. Combs talking with his daughter Erin during visit to Carrollton, GA, 1994. Photo by Anne C. Richards, reproduced courtesy of Anne C. Richards.

(11.7) Dick and Mary Usher (1999). Photo by Anne C. Richards, reproduced courtesy of Anne C. Richards, Richard Usher, and Mary Usher.

(12.1) Arthur W. Combs hugging a dinosaur at Swetsville Metal Sculpture Garden, 1997—the occasion of Arthur's 85th birthday (near Ft. Collins, CO). Photo by Alan Wilkes, reproduced courtesy of Alan Wilkes, Freestyle Images.

(12.2) Art Combs Get-Together, October 4–6, 1996. Big Canoe, GA. Photo courtesy of Anne C. Richards. From left to right:

Front row: Katherine Ward, Will Neville, Mary Usher, Shirley Avila, and Marie Welch

Second row: Terry Jennings, Walter Busby, Betty Siegel, Art Combs, David Welch, Richard Usher, Joel Siegel, and Fred Richards

Back row: Gerald Jennings, LaVerne Glover, Anne C. Richards, Dee Blume, and Bob Blume. (Others present but not pictured included Scott and Mary Busby).

(12.3) David Welch, Chris Breier, and Art Combs (Greeley, CO, 1996). Photo by Anne C. Richards, reproduced courtesy of Anne C. Richards.

(12.4) The Men's Group (1997), taken at Swetsville Metal Sculpture Garden. From left to right: Marc Ringel, David Gonzalez, Roy Wardell, Tom Flower, Art Combs, and Jim Fittz. Photo by Alan Wilkes, reproduced courtesy of Alan Wilkes, Freestyle Images.

(12.5) The Day after Dick Usher's 60th birthday party (March 1998). From left to right: Fred Richards, Art Combs, Mary Usher, Dick Usher, Shirley Avila, David Welch, Ron Chesley, and Lynn Combs. Photo by Anne C. Richards, reproduced courtesy of Anne C. Richards.

(13.1) Arthur W. Combs (Gainesville, FL, February, 1999). Photo by Anne C. Richards, reproduced courtesy of Anne C. Richards.

(13.2) Arthur W. Combs, Anne C. Richards, Franz Epting, and Bob Blume (Gainesville, FL, February, 1999). Photo by Fred L. Richards, reproduced by permission of Fred L. Richards, Franz Epting, and the Estate of Robert A. Blume.

(14.1) Photo of "Lone Oarsman" by John Cleare, reproduced by permission of John Cleare, Mountain Camera Picture Library.

(15.1) The Art Combs Memorial Deck, Allenspark, CO (1999). Photo by Mary Usher. Reproduced courtesy of Mary Usher.

(16.1) Publications of Arthur W. Combs. Photo by Anne C. Richards, reproduced courtesy of Anne C. Richards.

BACK COVER. Anne C. Richards and Arthur W. Combs (1994). Photo by Katherine Ward, reproduced by permission of the Estate of Dr. Katherine Ward.

"Bow of Boat on Lake" Jorg Greuel/Photonica/Getty Images

CHAPTER ONE

What Is Self-Fulfillment?

Every human being is engaged in a never-ending search for personal fulfillment and shares this need with every other living thing. The need for fulfillment is a built-in characteristic of protoplasm, the stuff of life itself. Even the simplest form of life, like a single cell amoeba floating about in a drop of water, moves toward food and away from danger. It seeks to maintain itself as best it can. So does every other living thing. Plants grow toward light. Trees scab over their injuries. A cat that has lost a leg immediately walks on the remaining three. Grasses trampled by footsteps struggle back upright. Animals hunt for food, defend themselves and their young. Every living thing seeks to maintain and enhance itself. This same drive exists in every cell of a human body and provides a basic or underlying motivation for life.

While the need for self-fulfillment in human beings is rarely a topic of daily conversation, it is always there. Its force is enormous. We see it illustrated in the courage and fortitude with which people somehow manage to crawl back from disaster and pick up the pieces of their shattered lives once again. We may see its effects closer to home as we watch relatives or friends rebuild their lives after radical surgery, an accident, divorce, or the death of someone near and dear. "How could they do it?" we ask. The need for fulfillment is insatiable. It provides the motive power for every behavior. Without an understanding of this fundamental, natural force, it is difficult to make sense of human achievements or to appreciate the resources each of us may have internally for coping with life circumstances.

A number of professions depend upon the basic need for fulfillment. The practice of medicine is one. Doctors do not cure us. They help our bodies cure themselves. They may remove the blocks that lie in the path of a patient's move toward fulfillment by prescribing an antibiotic to kill or impede the growth of an invading organism or by removing a sick or offending organ. Physicians may also nurture a patient's basic need by prescribing rest, proper diet, or exercise. But in the final analysis, if recovery is achieved, it is achieved by the person's own resources.

Other helping professions are equally dependent upon the need for fulfillment. Counselors, teachers, social workers, and the clergy can help their clients, students, and parishioners see things differently, but persons, themselves, must take the necessary steps to move toward greater health and achievement. As a psychotherapist, I am continually fascinated as I watch my clients struggle with monumental personal problems. I stand in awe as I see them, slowly but surely, find their ways to new and more fulfilling lives and relationships. The fundamental need for fulfillment is a powerful force.

What is more, human beings are overbuilt. When engineers build a bridge, for safety's sake they put into it materials and designs with capacities to hold up under stresses and strains much greater than the bridge is ever projected to withstand. Likewise, human beings possess enormous resources for dealing with life's problems. Had we not possessed such resources, in the course of evolution the human race would have died out long ago. We are survivors, and it is our fundamental need for fulfillment that makes us so.

The Special Nature of Human Fulfillment

Though we share a basic drive for fulfillment with all living things, this drive takes special form in human beings. For one thing, because of our complex sense organs and brains, we have possibilities available to us in our search for fulfillment that other species lack. Animals without sight, smell, or hearing can only respond to events that somehow touch them physically. The possession of sight, smell, and hearing immensely increases the types of events to which we can respond. Such capacities, for example, make it possible to deal with matters at a distance before they actually reach us and so enable us to plan for or anticipate events in the future.

Even more important, our marvelous brains make it possible for us to be aware of ourselves. That drastically affects the very nature of the fundamental need we share with other living things. Because we are aware of ourselves, we do not seek to maintain and enhance our physical selves alone. We seek the fulfillment of a much larger self, the self as person—the self of which we are aware, the one we refer to when we speak of "I" or "me." Psychologists refer to it as the phenomenal self or self-concept.

The Self-Concept

The self-concept of any person is a highly complex mix, consisting of countless personal definitions dealing with every aspect of human being. Here are but a few of the myriad definitions that Helen Cole differentiates as she sees herself: "I am a woman, wife, mother, lawyer. My name is Helen Cole. I am 35 years old. I play tennis and piano and I swim. I am a brunette, a Democrat, Catholic, driver of a Ford. I am someone accustomed to standing up for my beliefs. I am interested in the future of my community." Some of Helen's definitions are highly important to her. Others are less so and some are trivial in the total organization of ways in which she sees herself. The self that each person seeks to maintain and enhance goes far beyond self-definitions, however. It includes values, relationships, and judgments about self. So Helen may see herself also as a good mother, fair tennis player, miserable skater, smart shopper, concerned citizen, etc., etc., etc.

Because of our human capacity for awareness of self, any conceptualization of the basic need for fulfillment in human beings must refer to much more than mere maintenance and enhancement of our physical bodies. Earl Kelley once described the body as only "the meat house we live in." It is the self-concept, ourselves as persons that we want to fulfill. Some of us will even place our bodies at risk in order to enhance ourselves as persons. We do it every day. Knowing what we do about the dangers of smoking, bad diet, alcohol, traffic hazards, and the transmission of disease, we would never smoke, overeat, drink too much, drive too fast, or kiss other people if all we focused on was fulfillment of our physical beings. People may even deliberately choose to destroy their bodies in order to die for a cause, to save another person, to achieve anticipated fulfillment in heaven, or to avoid real or imagined humiliation or disgrace.

The self we seek to fulfill may also extend beyond our physical beings to include those we love, care for, or with whom we feel a sense of identity, like family, fellow workers or fellow citizens, friends, lovers, team members, or colleagues. Our self-concepts can include such people in our reach for personal fulfillment. Parents, for example, behave as though they were personally affronted when their children are unappreciated or mistreated by outsiders. Many share the belief that our selves are more than our bodies and go on after our bodies have turned to dust. The desperate client considering suicide in the course of therapy almost always explores the question, "But what will people think?" This concern to keep the self beyond reproach even after death is often enough to prevent a suicidal act.

The Nature of Self-Fulfillment and Health

Because of the immense importance placed upon the self-concept in modern psychological thinking, many people have equated self-esteem, feeling good about self, with the self-concept. Self-esteem, however, is but a symptom of a far larger, deeper constellation of human experience. The self-concept is a dynamic organization of perceptions of self and is involved in every human behavior. Self-esteem is a more limited concept having to do with a person's feelings of personal adequacy. Preoccupation with self-esteem has led to an extensive body of literature about the concept and the invention or advocacy of methods and techniques by which it presumably can be achieved. There are even national organizations "for the advancement of self esteem." Unfortunately, much of this preoccupation centers attention upon form rather than essence, on symptoms rather than causes. While deeply fulfilled persons probably feel good about themselves, it does not follow that helping folks feel good about themselves will assure self-actualization or fulfillment. What, then, is the nature of human fulfillment and how is it related to psychological health?

Over the past thirty years* a number of persons in the helping professions have been exploring the nature of self-fulfillment. They have asked such questions as: "What does it mean to be supremely healthy?" or "What is the nature of human fulfillment at the highest possible levels?" They have referred to this peak of fulfillment by many names. In medicine, it has been referred to as "high-level wellness." Psychologists, sociologists, and anthropologists have spoken of it as self-fulfillment, self-actualization, the fully functioning person, the adequate personality, even the wise and beautiful person. Whatever the name, investigators have sought to understand the nature of the supremely healthy, fulfilled human being.

Attempts to study fulfillment have generally taken one or the other of two approaches. Some researchers have tackled the question externally, that is to say from the objective viewpoint of an outside observer. They have asked "What are self-actualizing people like? What are their characteristic traits or behaviors?" Other students of the problem have sought to understand self-actualization internally or phenomenologically from the point of view of self-actualizing persons themselves. They have asked, "How do self-actualizing persons see themselves, others and the world?" or "What are the perceptions, purposes, needs, hopes, aspirations, or beliefs of self-actualizing persons?"

Editor's Note: Art wrote this passage in 1991 and died in 1999 before the Positive Psychology movement gained national recognition (see, for example, Seligman, 2002). Art was referring here to persons like Carl Rogers, Abraham Maslow, Earl Kelley, Ted Landsman and others associated with the humanistic movement in psychology, some of whom (along with himself) addressed these questions in 1962 (see Combs, 1962, *Perceiving, Behaving, Becoming*).

An Objective View of Self-Actualizing Persons

Approaching fulfillment from the external perspective has produced a long list of traits or behaviors characteristic of self-actualizing persons. Here is a sample compiled from the lists presented by various writers:

accurate and efficient relationships with reality
acceptance of self, others, and nature
spontaneity
optimistic view of the world
efficiency in problem-centeredness
detachment from social and physical forces and a desire for privacy
autonomy, independence of culture
compassion
empathy
freshness of appreciation
capacity for mystic or oceanic experiences
feelings of identification and oneness
deeper interpersonal relationships
openness to experience
democratic character structure
sensitivity to others
unhostile sense of humor
creativity
integration, integrity, is all of one piece
resistance to enculturation
trusts in the organism—one's own and that of others
sees personal stake in others
sees self as part of the world
sees self as becoming
thinks well of self and others
sees value of mistakes
experiences living as a process, in a more existential fashion
behaves more effectively and efficiently
can live comfortably with unsolved problems
develops and holds humane values
makes clear discrimination between means and ends
lives in keeping with his/her values.

This is a formidable list. Looking it over, one has the feeling, "Yes, I would like most of such descriptors to be true of me." Unfortunately, such a list is more useful for helping us understand self-actualizing persons in general than for helping us to become so. Behaviors, after all, are only outward expressions or symptoms of what is going on inside people. Knowing a person's symptoms often tells us very little about why or how he or she behaves in a particular way. For example, the fact that self-actualizing persons typically show "freshness of appreciation," are "living as a process," or have an "unhostile sense of humor" leaves us with the difficult question: Just how do you go about developing such traits? The origins of traits or behavioral characteristics are extremely diverse and merely cataloguing and describing them tells us very little about how they came into being.

A Perceptual Approach to Self-Actualization

Searching for more dynamic understanding, some workers have tried to examine self-actualization by looking more deeply for the causes of behavior. Perceptual-experiential psychologists, for example, believe the primary causes of behavior lie in people's perceptions, that is to say, in their personal meanings or experience. As a consequence, these psychologists have tried to look beyond symptomatic behaviors and to examine the perceptions or belief systems of self-actualizing persons that underlie or are expressed in these behaviors. This is my own preferred approach to the question.

Looked at from a perceptual-experiential orientation, the perceptions of self-actualizing people consistently seem to reveal four basic and distinguishing characteristics: They are: (a) a positive view of self, (b) openness to experience, (c) identification with others, and (d) perceptual fields that are rich, extensive, and available when needed.*

A Positive View of Self

Self-actualizing persons see themselves in essentially positive ways: as liked, wanted, acceptable, able persons of dignity and integrity. Having a positive self-concept provides enormous advantages. It is like going sailing with a vessel you can feel sure about; you can sail with confidence and may travel

---

Editor's note: During the course of most of his professional life, Art Combs described this fourth characteristic in the language used here. This was also the language he used in one of the last books he wrote summarizing the perceptual-experiential orientation (Combs, 1999). While writing latter chapters of this autobiography, however, he began to use other terminology, i.e., fields that are "rich, comprehensive, integrated, and available when needed."

far from a port or harbor. When you are unsure of your boat, however, sailing is a very different business. You are more likely to proceed cautiously, staying close to harbor or shore. In similar fashion, people with positive views of self have deep feelings of personal security and so can operate in more relaxed fashion and with greater latitude and certainty. They can also be more creative and courageous. If we relate perceptual characteristics such as this to the above list of behavioral traits obtained from objective observation, they do, indeed, appear to be underlying causes of the behavioral characteristics of self-actualizing persons. For example, a positive view of self seems absolutely essential if one is going to be autonomous, creative, resist enculturation, or have trust in one's own organism.

Acceptance and Openness to Experience

Self-actualizing persons are able to accept themselves and events around them. They perceive themselves and the world with greater freedom and clarity. They do not feel it necessary to defend themselves against experience or life. They are less threatened by what goes on about them and perceive life more richly and broadly than other people. The use of the term "acceptance" here should not be confused with resignation. Self-actualizing persons are not resigned to events or to things simply remaining as they are. Acceptance for them involves a willingness to confront themselves and events just as they are and to deal with them straightforwardly in whatever fashion is appropriate. Such openness to self and the world gives self-actualizing persons the capacity to cope with events with greater ease and efficiency than less fulfilled people. It is also likely to lead to many of the behaviors catalogued in the behaviors list above. For example, openness seems essential to such traits as accurate and efficient perceptions of reality, problem centeredness, democratic character structure, integration, seeing the value of mistakes, and developing and holding values.

Identification and Oneness

Self-actualizing persons typically perceive themselves as "one with" a broad spectrum of humankind. They have deep feelings of identification with other people of whatever race, creed, color, or persuasion. They feel that "the bell tolls" for everyone. This capacity for identification makes them deeply compassionate, responsible, sensitive, and loving persons. Referring again to the list of behavior characteristics above, identification seems a necessary prerequisite for acceptance of self and others, feelings of oneness, sensitivity, seeing one's stake in others, compassion, and an unhostile sense of humor.

Rich and Available Fields of Meaning

Self-actualizing persons possess highly integrated belief systems that are rich, extensive, and available when needed. They are knowledgeable people with pertinent and varied experience to draw upon. We are not speaking here of academic knowledge, although that too can certainly be enriching. The information self-actualizing persons possess is whatever is required to deal with the problems they confront in the course of their life situations. In addition to information, the belief systems of self-actualizing persons include values or generalized perceptions that give consistency and direction to their behavior. The possession of such integrated belief systems acts as a kind of personal theory that provides trustworthy guidelines for making choices and taking action. Like the perceptual characteristics in the paragraphs above, integrated belief systems produce such behaviors as more accurate and efficient relationships with reality, an ability to solve problems, resistance to enculturation, and knowing no other way to live but in keeping with one's values.

These four primary categories of experience involved in self-fulfillment are by no means discrete. Instead, they are but divisions of convenience for discussion purposes. Actually, all four are closely interrelated aspects of a unique personality and each aspect affects and is influenced by all of the others. A positive view of self, for example, determines in large part whether a person is likely to be self-accepting or open to experience. Likewise, a feeling of identification is both part and product of a positive view of self. And, certainly, a positive view of self plays an important role in an integrated system of personal beliefs. The organism's reach for fulfillment includes growth in all four aspects.

The perceptual approach to self-actualization has a number of advantages over approaches that operate from a more behavioral frame of reference. For example, it results in a much shorter and more dynamic list of characteristics. Understanding self-actualization in terms of a positive view of self, openness to experience, identification, and a comprehensive, available, and integrated belief system is far more convenient than the much longer lists composed by externally oriented theorists. Even more important, the shorter perceptual list provides immediate clues to action. For example, with respect to positive views of self, teachers (or parents) need only ask themselves such questions as, "How can a student (or child) feel liked unless someone likes her?" "How can someone feel able unless somewhere he has some success?" "How can one define oneself as a person of dignity and integrity unless someone treats one so?" "How can one discover significant ways to influence students (or children) toward greater self-actualization?" Similar questions can be asked about each of the other major characteristics of self-actualization to produce effective guidelines for action either in the classroom, in planning curricula, or in parenting. If self-actualization is, indeed, the essence of health and fulfillment, these four dynamics must also serve as goals and guidelines for all manner of human relationships and institutions.

Maslow's Hierarchy

Whereas the need for fulfillment is universal, self-actualization is generally achieved in stepwise fashion. In his study of self-actualization Abraham Maslow (1970) suggested a hierarchy of needs through which most people pass on the road to self-actualization or fulfillment. Here is the hierarchy he proposed:

> Level one: Physiological needs (e.g., for food, water, shelter, oxygen etc.).
>
> Level two: Safety needs (e.g., for security, stability, freedom from fear, the need for structure and limits).
>
> Level three: Belongingness and love needs (e.g., for affectionate relationships and the feeling that one is rooted in or an integral part of some social context).
>
> Level four: Esteem needs (e.g., for achievement, adequacy, recognition, or significance).
>
> Level five: Self-actualization, fulfillment: to actualize one's idiosyncratic potential, to become all that one is inherently capable of becoming (Maslow, 1970, pp. 35–47).

In this hierarchy, basic requirements like food, air, and water are so fundamental that all else is dependent upon their acquisition. Without these, life itself is at stake and the person's total attention must be concentrated on gaining satisfaction with regard to such requirements. With these goals fulfilled, persons are able to turn attention to higher order matters such as safety, belonging, esteem, and finally self-actualization. On the other hand, deprivation at lower levels is threatening to fulfillment and focuses attention and energy on their satisfaction. This preoccupation also forestalls the achievement of higher order goals. After all, one is unlikely to spend much time contemplating the fine points of democracy on an empty belly. That is probably a major reason why democracy is so difficult to establish in most have-not nations. Fulfillment at each level in Maslow's hierarchy frees the individual to spend increasingly larger portions of energy on the fulfillment of higher order goals.

Some Societal Effects of Fulfillment

While deprivation at lower levels in Maslow's hierarchy impedes a person's progress toward self-actualization, fulfillment has the effect of opening new horizons. With basic requirements for food, air, water, and safety sufficiently fulfilled, people are able to turn attention to the search for love, self-esteem, and eventually self-actualization. One important reason for the current growth of interest in self-actualization and human fulfillment in the United States and other industrialized nations is probably linked to the success of these countries in supplying the goods and services required to fulfill the basic needs of larger and larger groups of people. It has even been suggested that the advances of industry and technology in filling basic requirements have within them the seeds of their own demise as primary goals for humankind. With every step forward our culture makes in providing need satisfaction at basic levels, more and more people are freed to long for and to work toward a myriad of personal and social goals.

For example, a consequence of the success our society has had in fulfilling the basic needs of its citizens can be seen in the burgeoning of all sorts of self-enhancing interests among our citizens. With maintenance levels of need secured, thousands of people are seeking physical enhancement through such endeavors as holistic health, nutrition, and exercise programs of a thousand varieties. They also give indications of widespread interest in consciousness-expanding activities like education, meditation, encounter groups, self-hypnosis, and experimentation with drugs. For many citizens, the search for self-enhancement finds expression in participation in all sorts of causes: religious and spiritual explorations, conservation of natural resources, civil rights, child care, women's lib, social security, mental health, or the struggles of have-not nations.

The ways people seek self-enhancement in their new levels of freedom are not always socially desirable. The use of drugs, sexual promiscuity, unbridled ambition, irresponsibility, and the breakup of marriages have caused many people to castigate an entire generation as "the me generation." Setting people free to seek personal fulfillment at higher and higher levels can, indeed, produce selfish and self-destructive forms of behavior. Self-destructive patterns are also common in persons who have not achieved higher levels of self-fulfillment, however. They are not inevitable consequences of the quest for personal fulfillment.

As Maslow's hierarchy suggests, fulfillment is achieved by moving from level to level up the ladder of self-actualization. The hierarchy, of course, is not a map or a formula for self-fulfillment. Rather, it is a diagram or approximation useful for thinking about the growth of persons toward fulfillment. There are no universal roads to self-fulfillment. Everyone seeks it in his or her own way. Neither does anyone ever achieve fulfillment "in one fell swoop." Quite the contrary, self-actualization is not a finite goal but a process, a life-long quest. The steps by which it is achieved are unique and personal to the individuals who experience them.

Health and Ill Health

While self-fulfillment represents the supremely healthy condition psychologically, its obverse, deprivation, is the source of much human unhappiness, immaturity, and mental distress. Just as self-actualizing persons are characterized by (a) a generally positive view of self, (b) openness to experience, (c) identification with others, and (d) possession of a rich, available, and integrated belief system, unhappy, maladjusted, and mentally ill persons are burdened with (a) a generally negative view of self, (b) lack of acceptance or openness, (c) feelings of alienation, and (d) inadequate or conflicting personal theories. Children who feel good about themselves do not cause severe problems for parents, schools, and communities. It is the ones who feel negatively about themselves who are unhappy and disruptive as children and who grow up to fill our jails and institutions. Similarly, the adults who come to psychotherapy are, almost without exception, people who feel unloved and unable to accept themselves and the world, or are operating from inadequate frames of reference.

The parameters of self-actualization not only define the nature of self-fulfillment for individuals, they must also represent the goals of our society and its institutions. People join groups to find support and facilitation of their need for fulfillment. Societies and the institutions they invent also exist for this essential purpose. Whatever we decide is the nature of human fulfillment must simultaneously become the goal of our schools, industries, families, and society itself.

How Self-Fulfillment Comes About

I have described self-actualization as a consequence of four dynamics: a positive view of self, acceptance or openness to experience, identification with others, and a rich, available, and integrated system of beliefs. For those who wonder how these conditions come into being, I maintain that people are not born with these characteristics. They must learn them from two primary and interactive sources: from experience in the world and from personal processes of perception.

Learning from Experience—The Importance of Opportunities

People learn who they are and what they are, what they can and cannot do, and what sorts of values to place upon themselves and their performance from the opportunities they have, including the ways in which they are treated in the processes of growing up. So children learn that they are lovable from being loved, that they are able from success experiences, and that they are acceptable from being accepted by those around them in their early years. This process continues through adolescence, adulthood, and even into old age. Adolescents learn that they are acceptable or unacceptable from experience with their peer groups. Similarly, adults define and redefine themselves and their relationships as they confront the worlds they inhabit. The process never ceases and extends to all aspects of human growth. We learn who we are, what to trust and avoid, what to value and reject in large part from personal experience in the course of our interactions with the world around us and especially with the significant persons we encounter.

We are all products of the cultures in which we live. Some of these cultures are very large, like the primary religious orientation of the portion of the world we live in, and some are very small, like the particular family or work group we inhabit. Some are fleeting, some are of long duration. Some are dramatic or traumatic, some are subtle and indefinable. Whatever their nature, the opportunities or environments we confront contribute to our perceptions about ourselves, our relationships, and the world.

In speaking of opportunities to learn about self and the world, it is necessary to remember that we are talking about *experienced* opportunities. Mere exposure to events is not enough. Many a child goes through school exposed to the curriculum, yet fails to assimilate knowledge for any of a thousand personal reasons. We are surrounded by events in our complex modern society and each of us is constantly engaged in making choices about what to attend to, value, or reject. Opportunities that other people think we have are irrelevant and immaterial in the evolution of our personal belief systems. The opportunities that affect us are *psychological* opportunities, those that effect some change in personal meanings or beliefs.

Integration of Personal Beliefs—The Capacity to Give Meaning

The second dynamic for personal growth occurs entirely within the person. It has to do with the personal discovery of meaning and its formulation into a belief system capable of providing trustworthy guidelines for action. This occurs in our marvelous brains and nervous systems. Although experts are not yet sure about how it happens, everyone in the course of development constructs a phenomenal field of meaning, a personal system of perceptions or beliefs upon which he or she depends for making the myriad choices necessary to live successfully. The belief systems of self-actualizing persons are comprehensive, orderly, internally consistent, and adaptable to changing needs and conditions. The belief systems of less healthy persons are narrower, filled with inconsistencies, rigid, and inflexible. The content or subject matter for such personal theories may come from experiences or opportunities similar to those of other persons, but the organization of meanings into which they are formed is unique to each individual.

The Stepwise Nature of Change

As Maslow's hierarchy suggests, the search for fulfillment occurs in phases or at different levels. The five steps of his hierarchy, however, are far too few to adequately define the growth of any individual. Nor do people jump quickly from stage to stage. Indeed, many in our society never achieve satisfying levels of fulfillment in their entire lifetimes. People simply do not change quickly. Instead, the growth of persons towards self-actualization generally occurs in a long series of individual steps, sometimes up, sometimes down. Occasionally, growth may occur in sudden or dramatic fashion. More often it comes about piecemeal, bringing about change so subtly that the person may be quite unaware that change is happening.

There is good reason for this step-by-step pattern of growth. The development of a personality is cumulative and many aspects of personal discovery are dependent upon previous ones. For example, before one can feel very positively about self, one must first be rid of essentially negative definitions, achieve self-acceptance, and attain some positive experiences. Likewise, in order to be open to experience, one must first feel positively enough about self to be challenged rather than threatened by events. This dependence of later steps upon previous ones produces a stair-step sort of progression for the growth of a personality in which a critical perception is confronted, assimilated, then subjected to a period of testing before being consolidated into the individual's personal belief system. Mostly, growth proceeds by acquiring some new insight, followed by a period of living with the new concept and exploring its meaning. In my own life, I can trace eighteen to twenty such turning points or shifts. Sometimes these insights may seem to the person like clear breaks with the past or startling new concepts. More often, new perceptions of self and the world come about slowly, often so gradually that persons may be surprised to find themselves behaving differently before they are consciously aware that a significant change in their belief system has occurred.

This step-by-step pattern of change can often be observed in the protocols of psychotherapy. When examining the transcript of a series of counseling sessions, it is often possible to trace in the client's own words small shifts in personal meanings from session to session. Sometimes these are so subtle that the counselor, too, is unaware of the change in meaning that is occurring. Even when clients appear to experience sudden insights, sometime called "Aha moments," careful examination of the counseling transcripts usually demonstrates that the new insight is but the culminating expression of a series of more subtle changes over a period of time. There is a common misconception about psychotherapy that persons involved in treatment reach a point where everything falls into place and the client emerges totally transformed. Actually, for most persons who come for treatment, it has taken a long time to reach the state they are in and reversing the process is also likely to be time-consuming.

Self-Actualization and Authenticity

The growth of persons toward ever greater degrees of self-actualization is mirrored in the individual's behavior by more profound levels of personal authenticity. Highly self-actualizing persons are genuine. They are who they are, what they are, wherever they are. They engage in a minimum of acting or role-playing in all phases of their lives. Maslow (1954) has pointed out that everyone engages in two basic forms of behavior: what he called "coping behavior" and "expressive behavior" (pp. 179–186). Coping behaviors are the effortful things we do to contend with life circumstances, to deal with events we confront. These include the things we do to manage life, the roles we play, and the strategies we apply to the events and people around us.

Coping behaviors are always aimed at accomplishing something or getting something done. Expressive behaviors, on the other hand, are the things we do simply to express what we are feeling or thinking at any moment. They are our spontaneous reactions to events, mostly effortless manifestations in action of our fundamental belief systems. Maslow also points out that self-actualizing persons cope effectively with their environments but tend to do so unwittingly, without premeditated exertion of effort. Just by expressing, they cope! That is the very essence of authenticity.

It is a fascinating scenario to observe the movement of clients in psychotherapy from doubt and confusion to greater self-actualization and authenticity. Brought up in a things-oriented culture, they have been thoroughly indoctrinated with a manipulation-of-forces approach to life, including themselves. Their lives are full of "oughts" and "shoulds," what they must do or be. Feeling they are not enough, they spend their lives trying strenuously to be what they feel they need to be. So clients begin by describing their frustration with the world and persons they encounter and their own inadequacies in coping.

As therapy progresses they define their inadequacies more precisely and become more keenly aware of where and how they learned them. When therapy is successful, this stage is followed by the discovery that "It's all right to be me! I don't have to be what others think I should, I can live successfully being who I am." This revelation is often accompanied by a deep sense of wonder and relief, generally followed by an intense period of exploration about "Who am I really, what are my potentialities, and what do I want for myself?" This sequence of events is so characteristic of client experience as to seem almost universal, opening the way for deeper and deeper discovery of personal meaning and progress toward greater self-actualization and personal authenticity.

The Rationale for This Book

My own search for fulfillment has passed through a number of steps forward and backward in the course of my adult life. Some of these steps were sudden and dramatic; some were very gradual. Often I was aware of changes as they occurred. But sometimes I did not realize that I had moved to a new perspective until long after the change took place. My journey continues, for human need satisfaction is insatiable and no one is ever completely fulfilled. Self-actualization is a process to be achieved only more or less. Always, there are new heights to scale, new challenges to meet.

The pages that follow illustrate the principles of self-actualization as reflected in my personal autobiography. In this book I have tried to show

how one adult made his way, step by step, from an inadequate self in childhood to a highly fulfilled adult human being. Of course, one person's manner of progression never duplicates another's. And yet, there are parallels, ways in which contemplation of one person's life may prove helpful to someone else. The story told here is not meant to be a model but an illustration. It provides a glimpse into the dynamics of one man's reach for fulfillment as interpreted from a perceptual-experiential frame of reference.

References

Maslow, A. H. (1954). *Motivation and personality*. New York: Harper & Brothers.

Maslow, A. H. (1970). *Motivation and personality* (2nd ed.). New York: Harper & Row.

Seligman, M. E. P. (2002). *Authentic happiness: Using the new positive psychology to realize your potential for lasting fulfillment*. New York: Free Press.

Charlotte H. Vyse Combs (Arthur's mother) with Arthur and Dorothea (Newark, NJ, circa 1917)

CHAPTER TWO

Childhood and Youth

How different a family looks from the perspective of an outside observer as compared with that of a child who grows up in it. Seen from the point of view of a social worker or psychologist, the Combs household was not far different from millions of other middle-class American families in the first half of the 1900s. My father, Arthur Combs, and Charlotte Helene Vyse fell in love, married, and slipped easily into the traditional roles of husband and wife, breadwinner and homemaker, father and mother. They worked hard at their customary tasks, and adapted readily to the demands and expectations of society as caring, responsible citizens. Although they came from quite different backgrounds and had very different personalities they, nevertheless, found ways of living and being together that satisfied many of each other's needs. They truly loved one another, survived the stresses and strains of their times and maintained their relationship for more than sixty years until my father's death at 85. From any external assessment their marriage would have to be rated as reasonably successful. Yet, from this union came three offspring, two boys and a girl, who grew up with serious personal problems.

Some Family Background

My paternal grandfather, Charles F. Combs, was intensely proud of being a self-made man. With limited education he was, nonetheless, a keen observer of what went on around him and a canny businessman. He retired from his successful fish business in Brooklyn at 50 and built an imposing home in Lynbrook, Long Island, NY. He retired again at sixty or so from a feed and grain business just as horses were being supplanted by motor cars. He retired a third time ten years later from a real estate operation. He was a skilled planner and foreman who quietly but firmly made his wishes known and generally achieved his objectives. He was proud of his achievements and of his financial success. He was proud, too, of being a native-born American. Once, he was tempted to find out more about his origins and hired a researcher to dig up the family history. He must not have been very happy with what he

Arthur's paternal grandmother, Miriam J. Wright Combs, circa 1945

discovered, for when the genealogy was delivered, he burned the documents in the fireplace and thereafter never spoke of the matter. Despite their curiosity, no one in the family had nerve enough to ask him what he found out.

His wife, my grandmother, Miriam J. (Wright) Combs, was a high-strung, tight-lipped woman who knew without doubt what was good and right and brooked no nonsense from those about her in adhering to her standards. She was an officer in the Women's Christian Temperance Union and years later enrolled my children as "White Ribbon Recruits" without so much as asking my permission. During its resurgence in the twenties she was also an officer in the Ku Klux Klan.

Both grandparents were pillars of their fundamentalist church, which they faithfully attended three times during the week and three more times on Sunday. Their son, Arthur (my father), wanted to be a professional baseball player but had to give up those aspirations because his parents would not permit him to play on Sunday. They wanted him to be a minister of the gospel. My father resolved this dilemma by opting to become a veterinarian.

We visited these grandparents often when I was growing up. I loved playing in the barns among the piles of feed bags or bales of sweet-smelling hay. It was great fun. too, to ride the load while making deliveries by horse and wagon with my great uncle Wilbur, who worked for my grandfather.* The enormous attic of "grandpop's house" was a wonderful place to play on rainy days. But, oh how I hated going to church!

When I was four years of age, at Thanksgiving at my paternal grandparents' home, my grandmother had invited an elderly man who lived in the back room of a nearby store. At dinnertime the old man showed up in a tail

* Editor's note: Arthur's son, Peter, also recalled a story Art once told him about how Art liked to run along beside the wagon at times when his grandfather was driving. One time, however, he tied a rope to the wagon, accidentally got entangled in it, and was dragged for a distance because his grandfather was hard of hearing and didn't hear his cries (personal communication, October 4, 2004).

coat. Naturally, I was fascinated. The table setting included a gravy boat with a ladle (standard practice). When my grandmother handed the boat to our guest, I was astounded to see him ignore the ladle and pour gravy from the spout. Seeing this, my grandmother served herself in the same manner and removed the ladle from the plate on which the boat rested. Noticing all this was new behavior for me. Then, it hit me—of course, the gravy boat was designed to be used in the way our guest had employed and, of course, grandma removed the ladle and we all followed suit.

I know very little of my mother's family. Charlotte was an only child, born in Saxony in Germany. Her father, Richard Vyse, a man much older than her mother, died when she was three. Shortly after, her mother, Helene Loebel Vyse, brought her to the United States to live with relatives in Brooklyn. When Charlotte was twelve, her mother died, too, leaving her in the care of her grandmother, Carolyn Hoyer Loebel, whom I came to love as "Grossmama" when I was a child. Mother never got through high school but went to work early in a delicatessen where, I was told, folks stood in line on Fridays to buy her famous clam chowder. What with losing her parents early, moving to a new country, living in an immigrant culture, it is not surprising that Charlotte acquired deep feelings of inferiority and doubts about her acceptability. These doubts were only made worse when she married my father, a young student just out of Cornell. She was intimidated by her father-in-law, a stern and wealthy businessman, and by her mother-in-law, who was intensely proud of coming from "an all-American family." Charlotte never felt accepted by her husband's family. They made it clear that they felt their son had "married beneath his station." Even as a young child I sensed my grandparents' disapproval and the pain and humiliation my mother suffered.*

Mother was a conscientious, self-effacing housewife: an excellent cook, seamstress, and housekeeper. She had enormous respect for her husband's

---

* Editor's note: In a history of the Combs family that Arthur's brother Chuck wrote circa 1998, he reports Charlotte had told her children her mother died in 1902, but this was not actually the case. Instead, extensive interviews Chuck conducted with family members suggest that once in the United States, Charlotte's mother just "took off" from her family home at age 32 to avoid living under her own mother's strict rules, essentially abandoning her daughter. She also allegedly believed that having a daughter was "restricting her social life" and future "marriage eligibility." Several years later, according to Chuck's account, Helene remarried, had two baby boys, and sought to take "Lottie" back. Believing that all Helene wanted was to have an unpaid servant on hand to care for these new babies, Charlotte's grandmother went out of her way for years to evade Helene and successfully thwarted any of her efforts to reclaim her daughter (C. F. Combs IV, n.d., pp. 100–101).

Chuck further writes that when Arthur Combs, Sr., brought Charlotte home to meet his parents they disapproved of her as a prospective bride. Because he loved her so much, Arthur kept his continued dating and subsequent marriage to Charlotte a secret for some time (p. 102).

education and intellect and generally deferred to his judgment in matters outside the household. Although my father was "Daddy" or "Arthur" at home, I remember being puzzled when she referred to him in public as "Doc" or would speak of him deferentially as, "I'll see what Dr. Combs thinks about that."

The Seeds of Inadequacy

Mother suffered agonies making sure that she and her children did the right thing in public. She was always fearful of upsetting people. "What will people think?" was a frequent expression in our house. In public, mother was anxious to please and self-effacing in the extreme. Once, during a visit to a friend's home, she was severely bitten by her hostess's dog. For fear of upsetting the dog's owner, she somehow managed to keep her wounded hand out of sight for two days until she returned home. Even when I was in my fifties, she chided me one day for going to a meeting without a tie. "What will people think?" she asked. When I told her I did not care what they thought, she broke out in tears that she "had raised me so badly"! Mother longed for social acceptance and had deep feelings of inferiority around women of wealth and power. When she died, she left behind a drawerful of beautiful handmade leather gloves—symbols of elegant female attire in her day. The gloves had never been worn, sad relics of dreams unfulfilled.

My father was a quiet, kindly man, thoroughly content to enjoy the comfort and fulfillment provided by his loving and respectful wife. He was also a cautious man who valued security and avoided confrontation whenever possible. On graduation from Cornell as a veterinarian, he chose the security of being an inspector in the Federal Meat Inspection Service over the risks of private practice. He was a scholarly, meticulous worker and kept a handwritten digest of professional information up to date in a set of looseleaf notebooks. He probably knew more about the details of meat inspection during his working years than anyone in the country. Dad was not one to make waves. After eighteen years of service as an inspector in Newark, he finally got around to making a trip to Washington to inquire why he had not been promoted. His bosses were astounded. "We thought you never wanted to leave Newark," they said, and promoted him a week later.

Dad was an inveterate reader and gathered a considerable library. In addition, he spent much time in the summer months growing giant dahlias in our small back yard or doing his own maintenance on whatever car we owned. His way of dealing with most things was to just let them happen.

This was sometimes maddening to his high-strung workaholic wife. His distaste for confrontation, however, extended to family matters as well. He usually handled such friction by "letting Charlotte have her way" or by ignoring the matter altogether. One consequence of this life style was to make him a friendly but remote influence on his children. My childhood memories of him are, for the most part, of a shadowy figure in the background of the family who left everything up to my mother.

Arthur Combs, Sr., a veterinary officer in WWI, 1917

One of my earliest memories of my father has to do with his involvement in a traumatic treatment for polio when I was about four. A common treatment for polio at the time was to "tap the spine." I have a vivid memory of this procedure being performed on me on our dining room table by some strange men all dressed in white. Especially, I remember my feeling of shock and despair that "my own father" was holding me down and letting them do this to me. I also recall the joy of my parents, physicians, and nurses when I was able to walk across the room after months of illness with polio.

Dad served two years as a veterinary officer in the first World War. I have a vague memory of seeing him in uniform and marching in a parade. A less pleasant memory has to do with his departure for overseas service. During the war, mother took my sister, Dorothea, and me to live with "Grossmama" in Valley Stream, Long Island. Grossmama lived alone in a house without gas or electricity at the edge of a woods. The house was heated by a big old wood stove and going to the bathroom meant using a "slop jar" or the outhouse. Grossmama was tiny, less than five feet tall, and spoke only halting English. I felt very important to split kindling for the stove or to dig a garbage pit. Often I was sent to the bakery for "tsen cents crumb cake and tsen cents strudel," favorite snacks for afternoon "kaffee klatches." Grossmama was a remarkable woman who gave up "taking in washing" at the age of 95 and died just before her 100th birthday. She truly loved children and provided a much-needed feeling of unconditional love for me during the war years.

When I was six, I disgraced myself at my own birthday party. The war was still on and my grandmother, my aunts, and my mother decided to have a birthday party for me in the big house in Lynbrook. They also thought it a great idea to celebrate the birthday of the young son of grandmother's fundamentalist preacher. The arrangements for the party involved a beautiful dining room table set with a tent full of goodies, streamers, party favors, etc. There must have been twenty kids invited, but the only person there whom I had ever seen before was my sister Dot. I was overwhelmed and refused to join in the games the adults proposed and was sent to my room, where mother came to talk with me after a while and finally convinced me to go downstairs and join the rest of the children as they sat down to eat.

Mother suffered deeply during and after the war. The anti-German hysteria of the times only added further to her feeling of being an outsider in her husband's family. After the war, her mother-in-law became a chapter head in the Ku Klux Klan and pressed my father to join. I sensed my mother's feelings of rejection and I remember being very proud of my father who "refused to join any group that Charlotte could not be in."

Early Feelings of Rejection

Most of my childhood memories are dominated by my mother. Later, as a psychologist, I came to understand the origins of her erratic behavior. As a child, I experienced her unpredictability as rejection and disapproval, resulting in deep feelings of being unloved, inadequate, or not being enough. Within the family, Charlotte was capricious, vacillating between openhanded generosity and service to others on one hand and searing condemnation for picayune or imagined faults on the other. She sought to control or teach her children by put downs that cut deeply (e.g., "Well, I can certainly do that—Even I know better than that and I never went to college" or "Here, let me do that right!"), by guilt ("I'd be ashamed . . ." or "How could you do that to me?"), or by the silent treatment (not speaking to you for a day or two). When I was six or seven, she heard me shouting "cuss words" at a boy who was tormenting me. Rushing toward me in the street and in a rage, she dragged me into the house and ground laundry soap into my teeth. As a consequence of her temperament, I was ever-anxious not to upset her.

I spent a great deal of time trying to please my mother and feeling guilty for not being a better son. Although I was desperate to please, it seemed like everything I tried turned out badly. Once I thought I would help her by sharpening the kitchen knives on the curb in front of the house. In the process I cut my thumb badly. Mother was terribly frightened at the sight of my bleeding and "lost it." She spanked me in a fury, all the time impressing upon me what a bad boy I was. This incident produced a phobia for knives that lasted far into my adult years. Even today I feel uneasy around someone carelessly waving a knife.

One day, when I was about five and had committed some indiscretion, mother flew into a rage, packed a suitcase with my clothes, and pushed me out the back door, all the while telling me to be gone, she never wanted to see me again. To this day I can recall my utter feelings of desolation and despair as I sat sobbing uncontrollably on the back steps. I do not know what brought on this event, nor do I remember how it turned out, but the feeling of utter desolation is easy to call up again.

Many of mother's fears were passed unconsciously to me. In her youth she had been traumatized when some boys threw a snake at her as she climbed a ladder in the barn to follow them. The snake wrapped around her neck and she was seriously injured as she fell from the ladder. One day when I was three or four, mother and I were walking beside a brook when suddenly she screamed, "A snake!", picked me up in a panic, and ran for the road. For many years after I had a phobia for snakes. That caused me no end of embarrassment in later years when I was a biology teacher and students would hand me a snake and ask, "Mr. Combs, what kind of snake is this?"

As with many an oldest child who sees himself displaced by a new arrival in the family, my feelings of rejection were heightened when my sister, Dorothea, was born. "Dot" was 18 months younger than I, but did not escape her own dogged feelings of rejection and inadequacy. She had real talent as a dancer and mother tried to live out her own need for recognition and self-esteem through my sister's success. She placed Dot under enormous pressure to succeed at tap, ballet, acrobatic, and ethnic dances, leaping at every opportunity for Dorothea to perform. For years our home seemed always full of costumes and weeks before a performance everything else was ignored. Mother's preoccupation with Dot and her talent only confirmed my feelings of inadequacy and rejection.

Any sign of weakness or self-indulgence was anathema to mother. No one was allowed to be sick unless it was a true emergency. When that happened, mother was caring and compassionate to a fault. Ordinary aches and pains, however, were treated with scorn or derision. From this, I learned to ignore my body's messages and to bear pain stoically. It has often happened during my lifetime that people around me would remark that I had a cold, was hoarse, tired, or the like, and I would be surprised to realize that, indeed, I was.

Despite the negative effect of my mother's treatment of her children, she loved us deeply, which I did not understand until I was long into being a grownup. She worked very hard at feeding, clothing, and caring for us physically. Indeed, serving others was her forté. She had a delightful sense of humor, was comforting and supportive at moments of crisis, and was generous to a fault when the spirit moved her. I did not appreciate these facts, however, until long after my childhood. As a child, I loved my mother but her unpredictability and the impossibility of pleasing her left me with persistent feelings of rejection and inadequacy. I also resonated to feelings of being an outsider and throughout my life found it easy to identify with persons suffering repression or disapproval.

School Days

The first five years of public school were a godsend for me. An intelligent child, I quickly learned to read. I was an eager student and my teachers began to supply some much-needed praise and encouragement. Things went well in my school years. Then, in fifth grade, my teachers decided to skip me to sixth. What a disaster! I was already having trouble being accepted among my fifth-grade peers because I was light of frame, short, and maturing more slowly than any of my classmates. Pushing me ahead only heightened the contrast with my peers. I now found myself the last one chosen or left out entirely when boys were choosing up teams. I began to feel rejected and inadequate among my peers as well as at home. The few friends I made were generally other boys on the fringes of adolescent society.

I remember hanging out with David, an extremely bright oddball like myself. Together we floated about the neighborhood getting into mischief like taking off people's screen doors. In those days, houses often had small cast-iron doors into their coal bins. A favorite prank we invented was to save up firecrackers from the fourth of July to use late in the year. We thought it great fun to throw one into someone's basement and watch their consternation from a hiding place nearby.

Once we got in serious trouble on a construction site, when, after hours, we experimented with the workers' tools by sawing down through a pile of cement bags and other unacceptable stunts. Fortunately, our parents and the workers agreed to payment for the damage we had done instead of sending us off to juvenile court.

Another time, I was harassed by an older boy in the neighborhood, who had me on the ground and was hurting me badly. Suddenly, I became sure he was going to kill me. My panic released enormous energy and I threw him off, landed on top of him, and began to beat his head on the sidewalk. Fortunately, a passer-by separated us. My disregard for Marquis of Queensbury

Arthur (at left) with his neighborhood buddies (circa 1922)

rules shocked the playground boys who saw the incident. Thereafter they warned other boys, "Watch out for Combsy! He's crazy!"

When I was twelve, my brother Charles Franklin (named after my grandfather) was born. Unfortunately, the difference in our ages inhibited much close interaction during my youth. I left home for college when he was only five. Our respective life patterns brought us together for only short periods later in life, so I never got to know my brother as intimately as I would have liked, a fact I have always regretted.

In my pre-teens, I discovered my father's library and immersed myself in a frenzy of reading everything I could lay hands on. When I had devoured what I could of Dad's collection, I turned to the public library. Someone there gave me a list of "the world's best novels" and I set out to read every one. This reading binge started a lifelong enjoyment of reading. While enormously increasing my general field of knowledge, it also helped to assuage my feelings of aloneness. I was particularly charmed by Dumas' works and fantasied myself as "the Viscount of Vaildburg" (the section of Newark in which we lived), complete with a home-made coat of arms.

Some indication of the strains I was living under in those years may be inferred from the fact that I developed "a nervous condition" diagnosed as Saint Vitus' Dance, which was treated with arsenic. Over a period of time I was required to take arsenic before meals. The dosage began with a few

Charles (Chuck) Combs, 1929

drops and increased periodically until I was taking "enough to kill a grown man." I vividly recall a meal at which I complained of the bitter taste of the arsenic. My father insisted, "That's nonsense. Arsenic is tasteless." "Then you take it," I replied, and immediately was overcome with guilt. The stuff would kill him! I am sure that I was suffering from hypertension and psychological distress. Today, my condition would probably be treated with sedatives and psychotherapy.

On a more positive note, my father seemed aware of my difficulties in relating to my peer group and enrolled me in the boys' division of the National Turn Verein, a German gymnastics club. Gymnastics proved a natural for a small boy with a light frame and good coordination. Soon I was able to perform with considerable skill. I began to show off on the school playground's horizontal bar well enough to elicit "oohs" and "ahs" from my schoolmates, an oasis in the desert for a child thirsting for peer acceptance. Involvement in gymnastics continued throughout my school years thereafter. It laid a foundation for a healthy physique.

The Maypole Dance: Birth of a Rebel

One other event in elementary school had a critical effect on my personality for many years after. Early one autumn, the teachers at Lincoln School held a meeting to decide when each grade would be responsible for the auditorium programs throughout the year. My seventh grade teacher, Miss Riley, drew May first. Bubbling with enthusiasm, Miss Riley reported to our class, "Aren't we lucky? I know just what we will do. We will put on a Maypole dance." This plan was met with coos of delight from the girls in the class. Nobody noticed that the boys sat in stunned silence. At noon that day, we met in a corner of the school yard for an indignation meeting. The idea of a maypole dance with girls was unthinkable. The boys were incensed. We swore a holy oath ("cross my heart, hope to die") that we would not participate. By early April, however, most of the boys had forgotten the pact. We were caught by surprise when Miss Riley announced it was time to prepare for the big event. As she read out the names of couples for the dance, not a single boy demurred. Then she came to me. When she assigned my partner, I said, "I'm very sorry Miss Riley, I can't participate." "Why not?" she asked. "I'm not at liberty to say," I replied. The room became deathly quiet. Miss Riley was astounded. The more she pushed for an explanation, the more firmly I stood my ground. Finally, in desperation, Miss Riley sent me off to the cloakroom to "think it over."

Resuming the discussion after school got her no further. I refused to explain. As I entered the room the next day, Miss Riley asked, "Arthur, will you be in the Maypole dance?" To which I responded, "I'm sorry Miss Riley, I can't be in the dance and I can't tell you why." So, off I went to spend the day in the cloakroom. This went on every school day for two weeks. Imagine the bewilderment of the teacher at this ordinarily nice boy's defiance. But what a glory for me! Here I was, desperately longing for status and acceptance by my peers, and the only boy who dared to stand by his word. Every boy knew it and had his nose rubbed in it day after day as Arthur, the martyr, marched off to the cloakroom. I spent my time in the cloakroom savoring my newly found notoriety and railing against the system. The only decoration in the cloakroom was a framed copy of "The American's Creed," a defense of minorities and the downtrodden of society. I remember dissecting it, line by line, with irony and an emerging consciousness of injustice in the world. A lifelong rebel was being born.

Three days before the scheduled auditorium event, Miss Riley took me to the principal, who sent me home, "not to return without your father." After listening to my story, my father advised me, "Look, it's two days before the program and you can't possibly learn the steps in that time. Why don't you just apologize and let it go at that?" I followed his advice when we went to school together. But Miss Riley was not satisfied. She insisted I must be part of the program in some way. The only place she could find for me on such short notice was to make me the announcer. What a climax! On the day of the performance, I remember announcing, "We will now have a maypole

Arthur W. Combs on graduation from eighth grade, 1926 (with grandmother Miriam Combs in background)

dance by the girls AND THE BOYS of the seventh grade." With that I stepped back into the wings to watch the final degradation of my classmates.

The pleasures of "bucking the tide" or beating the system continued through my school years. I began to enjoy the aspects of being different. My high school sponsored an exclusive fraternity called FMD, which made much to-do about its secret name and activities. One day I discovered that FMD stood for "Faire Mon Devoir," to do my duty, and I took great glee in spreading the word. On another occasion I got in trouble for entering the elevator control room on the roof of the school and shutting off the power, leaving a car full of students stranded between floors. Under my picture in the high school year book is the quotation, "There is more faith in honest doubt, believe me, than in half the creeds." In later years Susan [Art's second wife] was to exclaim, "My god, that's just as true today!"

For about three years between grade school and high school, I operated a neighborhood distributorship for Curtis Publishing Company magazines: *The Saturday Evening Post*, *Ladies Home Journal*, and *The Country Gentleman*. The *Post* sold for a nickel and the salesman earned two cents. The profit on the *Journal*, which sold for ten cents, was four cents. My job involved recruiting youngsters to sell these publications door to door and to build up regular customers. Since the staying power of my salesmen was not very great, I was kept busy recruiting new ones constantly.

When I was fourteen, I had a second traumatic experience with the medical profession. I needed a circumcision, which was carried out in my room at home. Dad was working at that time in a kosher slaughter house. The men at work treated the occasion of my misery as a celebration, showering Dad with bottles of wine and other gifts. I only wanted to get the matter over as quickly and quietly as possible. While I was still healing, a fellow student kneed me in the groin during the passage of classes. When I doubled up in pain, I was surrounded by students asking, "What's the trouble?" As if I could tell them!

Peer Relationships

The few friends I made in high school were, for the most part, boys like myself who felt themselves to be outsiders but who refrained from expressing their frustration in confrontation or violence. I enjoyed the companionship of a black classmate in my early high school days, unusual in those days before desegregation and civil rights. Later there were friendships with Wayne and Dallas, built around a common interest in gymnastics at the YMCA. These were boys like me, not physically equipped for competition in football or basketball. I tried out for football in high school but the coach took me aside and explained that I was too light to make the team. Instead, he talked me into being manager, a job I did pretty well except for one embarrassing incident. We were playing at Asbury Park. As our bus rolled into the stadium, the coach called from the front of the bus, "Art, throw me a ball." To my utter chagrin, I had everything we needed—but no football! To add to my humiliation, I had to borrow several from our opponents.

I was certainly not an exceptional student in high school. With the amount of reading I had accumulated, I could pass most courses with comparatively little effort, except for languages. Somehow I managed to gain three years credit in Latin and one year of Greek The most auspicious happening in those high school years came about as a consequence of not doing my homework. When I was age 14, Hazel Poole, my English teacher, had required her class to memorize a selection from Milton's *L'Allegro*. Next day, she unexpectedly passed out papers and told us to write what we had memorized. While the rest of the class was writing, I used my paper to compose a plea for mercy in verse. I did not intend for her to see my production, but the student collecting the papers whisked mine off my desk with all the rest. Next day, Ms. Poole returned my paper, graded A, and had written a poem of her own, entitled, "An Ogre By Profession." Here is the interchange, which I published many years later:

A SCHOLAR'S LAMENT

Rather than cheat as others might do,
I'll write this little poem to you
To tell you just how sad I am,
That I can't memorize like Lamb,
And rattle off at a lively gait
The words of a poet whose blind state
Kept him from the beauteous sights
That we see on moonlit nights.
I wish that I might yell and call
"My homework isn't done at all."

Sad but true,
What I tell to you,
Have pity on me,
And I'll tell to thee,
These words at a later date.
A. W. COMBS

AN OGRE BY PROFESSION

Lest, overcome by rash despair,
You think Medusa's snaky hair,
With power to strike its victims dead,
Grows now upon your teacher's head,
I hasten to accept with glee
Your rhythmical apology.
Fierce monsters in the days of old
Had lenient moments, we are told—
Dread Pluto's tears drowned out his ire
When pleading Orpheus played his lyre;
And Cerberus would his post forsake
When gentle fed with honey-cake.
I, too, an ogre by profession,
Am touched by your unique confession;
Renouncing Milton's words sublime,
I take instead your honest rhyme.—
And if you wish to learn him yet,
Some extra credit you may get.
HAZEL B. POOLE
[Combs, 1974, p. 363].

This incident launched me into a spate of poetry writing that lasted several years. Unfortunately, my poems have long since disappeared in the processes of moving.

My relationships with females during my school years were hopelessly naïve. From experience with my mother, I learned to treat women cautiously. I placed them on a pedestal as superior beings to be admired and served. On a trip to the World's Fair in Chicago with a group of boys, we went to see Sally Rand do her shocking (in those days) fan dance. I remember being appalled by the smirking reactions of my colleagues. I thought she was absolutely beautiful. On another occasion, a group of us went to Toledo to take in a burlesque show. I felt ashamed rather than titillated watching the female performers seeming to denigrate themselves. My experience was also not helped by the people sitting next to me (a man, a woman, and a young boy), all quite drunk. In the middle of the show, the young boy threw up while I desperately tried to escape the results. I have a similar aversion to pornographic movies and to this day I am deeply distressed to see a woman abused or humiliated.

Because of my feelings of rejection, I very much doubted that any woman would ever care for me anyhow. I was surprised when now and then some female showed any sign of interest in me. Under no circumstances would I ever have been able to make the first move, however. Rejection can be taken in stride if one has not asked to be cared for. To hold out one's hand or ask for affection and be rejected is more than one can bear. With such feelings, it is not surprising that I had little or no romantic contact with girls in the course of growing up. It was not until my senior year in high school that I began to discover the pleasures of female company.

In 1929 in the midst of the Great Depression, my father received a promotion and the family moved from the big city of Newark, New Jersey to the small town of Fostoria, Ohio. Once again I made friends with boys on the fringes but discovered a totally new world with girls. Because I was the "new boy in town," several girls made advances strong enough to overcome my shyness. One of these, Rosie, invited me to join her while baby-sitting and let her friends know when and where we would be. I nearly died of embarrassment when half a dozen of them came to check us out. Humiliated as I was by Rosie's betrayal, the incident cracked my shell. I began to reach out for female companionship, but so tentatively and fearfully that I must have been a great disappointment to my occasional partners.

Off to College

Graduation from high school in 1930 made it necessary to confront the question, "What next?" I did not want to go to college right away. Instead, I wanted to stay out a year and find out who I was and what I wanted to do. But the Depression was on and my parents were fearful that, if I did not go now, I never would. Not having any other options that appealed to me, I followed my father's admonition: "Scientific agriculture, Son. It's the field of the future." I enrolled at Cornell University, my father's alma mater, to major in plant pathology.

Once the decision was made, I was anxious to be on my way. I had no regrets at leaving my family. Indeed, one of the more positive aspects of feeling rejected is that one learns self-reliance. That summer I went to work for my grandfather immediately after graduation from high school. I spent the summer painting and repairing some of the houses he owned on Long Island. When autumn came, I boarded the train for Ithaca. On the trip I met another freshman student. We discovered that each of us had no prearranged place to stay and would have to look for housing on arrival. We decided to team up as roommates and look for a place together. We rented a room in a house full of freshmen like ourselves and settled in for our first year at college.

The other men in the house could hardly believe my naiveté. On one hand, they ignored me. On the other, they thoroughly enjoyed introducing me to the pleasures of alcohol and carousing. I remember the night I came home from the library to find most of them seated on the floor of one of the rooms, drinking. Never having had a drink, I asked to try it. They gave me a tumbler of gin to chug and when I said, "I don't feel anything," they gave me another. All I remember after that is seeing the room tilt up so that it looked like all the men and furniture were about to slide down on me. I woke up in the morning in my own bed with a very sore head, wishing I was dead.

In the midst of Prohibition, drinking had an additional thrill of lawbreaking. One would call a particular number and shortly a man with a suitcase would arrive at your room, open his case, and display his selection of booze. Or we would drive out into the country to a farmhouse where you would be admitted IF you knew the password. Or you could visit a place in town where you were examined through a peephole before getting past the locked door. All this really heightened the adventure of drinking and I did my share that first year at Cornell.

After a few months my roommate joined a fraternity, as did a number of others in the house. I declined to be rushed because I could not afford it and because I considered fraternities rich men's territory in which I would be sadly out of place. Once again I felt like an outsider, a feeling made more intense by the disdainful attitude of liberal arts and engineering students toward those of us in the College of Agriculture. Ag students were generally derided as "hicks" and "country boys."

An amusing incident occurred in our freshman health class. I sat in the front row at the foot of a banked-up lecture hall. On the demonstration table just in front of me was a life-size model of the male body to which the instructor frequently referred for illustration. One day, in the course of his lecture, the professor said, "Now, if we take a cross section about here . . ." and drew his scalpel across the model's scrotum. I passed out cold, to the amusement of all and excruciating embarrassment to me.

During my second semester, I got special permission to take a course on the liberal arts campus in psychology. The course I was assigned was a study of perception. The professor spent six weeks on the color pyramid. I was bored to death and had great difficulty grasping what it was all about. I managed to pass the course by the semester's end and swore I would never take another course in psychology as long as I lived. It was not until four years later that I discovered I was color-blind.

The College of Agriculture required summer farm work for all students who had not worked extensively in agriculture. Accordingly, at the close of my first year, I went to work on the Cornell University Farms with twenty other students like myself. The work was hard but I enjoyed being out of doors and the experience of living, working, and playing with a group congenial young men.

During my second year at Cornell I found a new roommate, Bill Vougatsis. Bill was a loner, like me, but infinitely worse off. The child of Greek immigrants, he grew up in Hell's Kitchen in New York City, where he had worked as a Western Union delivery boy. He, too, was a student in the College of Agriculture and was as strapped for funds as I was. Though we roomed together, we were never very close, for in addition to our studies, we each held one or more jobs and I spent increasing amounts of time with my girlfriend.

In my sophomore year my sister Dorothea also came to Cornell. With the Depression in full swing, the family could not afford two children in college. Accordingly, I began to earn my way with a variety of jobs held at one time or another as dishwasher, waiter, short order cook, house cleaner, windowwasher, head waiter, and even, for a very short time, as butler in a wealthy home. One day, during my butler experience, my very prim, proper, and imposing dowager employer ordered some tea. As I returned to the sitting room with the tray, I tripped over the extended rockers of a Lincoln rocker and went crashing down at the lady's feet. As I fell, I cried, "Jesus Christ!" When I dared to raise my eyes, she had drawn herself up to full height, was staring at me and saying, "Well!" in a shocked and horrified tone. I apologized, left the premises as quickly as possible, and never went back for my wages. The work experience was good for me but took more and more time to make ends meet.

I Fall in Love

Near the end of my second year, I fell in love with Mildred Mitchell, a twin whose family lived in Ithaca. Millie, too, had led a very sheltered life and our needs complemented each other neatly. Millie was meek and affectionate, providing the kind of secure and undemanding relationship that I could handle. In turn, I provided an adoring and respectful relationship that Millie needed. Betty, Millie's twin, was seeing Fred Kinder, a pre-med student, and

Arthur's college dorm room, circa 1932

many a night after seeing the girls home, Fred and I lingered over coffee and an order of toast in the "Ideal Coffee Shop" comparing notes, critiquing the state of the world, and dreaming of life in the future. We were full of high ideals and commitment to serving humanity.

My second summer I was assigned to work on a farm near Trumansburg, New York. The owner was a very sick man who died a few weeks after I started work, leaving me to handle the entire farm by myself with occasional help from neighbors. One weekend I arranged to have a neighbor do my chores so that I could spend a few days in Ithaca with Millie. Several weeks later he asked that I return the favor while his family went to the state fair. What a nightmare! Years before I had frozen my hands one cold winter morning while delivering early morning newspapers. As a consequence, my hands never toughened up to the milking task. Now, in addition to my own six cows, I was responsible for my neighbor's ten as well! Milking all those cows was torture. It took me hours and hours to milk the two herds. I never again asked to trade time off.

At the beginning of my third year at Cornell, I signed up for officer's training in ROTC. I needed the stipend the government paid and the uniforms were sharp, complete with jodhpurs and riding boots. During this junior year, Millie and I spent more and more time with each other. Years later, Millie told me that the dean of my college, who was a friend of her family, called her in one day and warned her, "Don't get involved with that young man. He's too unstable." The warning did little good, however, for Millie kept the advice to herself and our relationship continued to deepen.

Arthur in his ROTC uniform, September, 1930

At the same time, I found it necessary to devote increasing amounts of time to working at one job and another in order to pay my expenses. It was also becoming painfully clear to me that I did not really want to be a plant pathologist. As a consequence of all these factors, my grades rapidly declined. Finally, near the end of my third year, I found myself out of funds, physically exhausted, and in imminent danger of academic suspension. I decided to withdraw from the university, left Ithaca one jump ahead of the registrar, and returned home to Fostoria.

Recapitulation

As I have indicated in the previous chapter, it is my intention to use my life history as an illustration of one adult's search for fulfillment. One of my contributions to psychological theory has been the formulation of a theory of psychological health that holds that self-actualization is a function of at least four basic characteristics:

1. A positive view of self,
2. Acceptance or openness to experience,
3. Deep feelings of identification, and
4. A comprehensive, available, and integrated or internally consistent belief system.

Accordingly, each chapter in this volume concludes with a Recapitulation in which I have tried to show how each of the above factors was affected by the events and growth of my personal history. The experiences of these first 21 years laid the baseline for my growth as an adult.

Views of Self

The outstanding sense I had about myself in the spring of 1933 was that I experienced intense feelings of rejection and inadequacy firmly established from my family experience and attitudes passed along from my mother's own personal problems. The dean was right in his assessment of me as an unstable person. I desperately needed the love and approval of my family but I was not at all certain where I stood with them. I worked very hard at trying to please them but always seemed to fall short of achieving it. I felt guilty that I was not a better son. Having to leave the university was only the latest example of my inability to meet their expectations. I felt unworthy, continuously experienced myself as inadequate, and believed that I was letting my parents down. I lacked confidence in myself.

I was fearful of angry confrontation and avoided it at all costs. Rather than risk disapproval, I would defer to the needs of others. The simplest choices were difficult or impossible. When asked where to go, what to do, even what to eat, I would become confused and unable to voice a preference. I was certain I would not be accepted by my peers. That made me shy and unlikely to seek out relationships. I was keenly aware that I was smaller and less mature than most men of my age and woefully less experienced. The slightest miscue in social relationships would cause me to feel guilty and apologetic. Whenever I was successful at something, approbation came as a surprise. I was sure it was an accident. Praise or commendation caused me to feel embarrassed, for I was sure it was undeserved. I was certain that, if anyone ever knew what I was really like, they would surely be disapproving of me—an almost universal characteristic of persons suffering from rejection.

Clinicians know that the consequences of rejection are not entirely negative. Some good things can be learned from such experiences. One thing rejected children often learn is this: if you are going to make it, you have to do it on your own. I learned that lesson well. As a consequence, I developed strong but carefully shielded feelings about what was right and wrong in the world: the groundwork for rebellion and innovation. I did not expect outside help. Indeed, I was surprised and embarrassed when it was offered. Such feelings also made possible intense levels of concentration on tasks I chose to throw myself into. I knew how to work hard.

Acceptance and Openness to Experience

The negative feelings about self that I experienced produced the belief that it was not "all right to be me." I was full of "oughts and shoulds." As a consequence, I tended to be introverted and unlikely to push myself forward, thus cutting myself off from important growth experiences. I ignored the messages from my own body and missed out on social experiences for fear I did not belong. I avoided confrontation, seeking ways to solve problems with a minimum of acrimony or hard feelings. Feelings of inadequacy made me shy and reserved, thus reducing the number of my friends and acquaintances. I had no close friends. It never occurred to me to work at seeking some. My fear of rejection kept me from reaching out to others. The few friends I did have were those I met at work.

On the other hand, I was beginning to discover myself as an intelligent human being. My voracious reading was opening horizons to a wider world. Similarly, the diversity and extent of my work experience were adding new dimensions to my store of experience, as did three years of basic and technical studies at college. While fear of rejection and feelings of being an outsider restricted my experience in many areas, they also led to an acceptance of being different and so to a greater likelihood of valuing innovation.

Feelings of Identification and Oneness

When I left Cornell, I was primarily a loner. I was still longing for the love and support of my family. Like my mother, I felt I was an outsider, someone who really did not belong. Feelings of rejection made me hesitant to reach out for intimate relationships. My feeling of alienation also had a positive side. It produced deep sympathy for the less fortunate of the world and feelings of oneness with outcasts or persons struggling for acceptance. These are valuable attributes for persons in the helping professions.

My relationships with women could only be described as naive. I had had little or no significant relationships with the opposite sex throughout childhood and adolescence. My relationship with Millie was the only intimate one I had ever known, a relationship born of great longing. My relationships with males were hardly much better. While I had more contacts with them, they were largely limited to topics considered appropriate for males at the time. Our society raises its males to deal with things, not feelings, to be objective rather than subjective, and I learned to repress my sensitivity very well along with the rest of the male half of the population.

A Comprehensive, Available, and Integrated Belief System

The wide-ranging reading habit I developed in adolescence and during my studies at Cornell laid the groundwork for an expanding belief system. My scientific studies at Cornell gave me a basic understanding of the physical world that would prove invaluable in years to come. I was discovering that I could hold my own in intellectual circles. I was becoming knowledgeable. Likewise, my personal experiences, both positive and negative, were shaping my personality toward an appreciation of order and values, fundamental bases for the construction of a more comprehensive, internally consistent belief system.

References

Combs, C. F. IV. (circa 1998). *History of the Combs family* (unpublished photocopied manuscript circulated within the family).

Arthur W. Combs, 1935, Alliance, OH

CHAPTER THREE

Awakening

I returned home to Fostoria with mixed reactions. On one hand, I felt relieved that I was no longer on the road to being a plant pathologist, a field I never really wanted in the first place. It was also good to be free of my financial worries and to relax in the comfort of my old home. I had feared my parents would regard my failure to make it at Cornell as a family disgrace but they treated my return with surprising acceptance. On the other hand, I felt under great pressure to go to work, and that was not easy. The Depression was hanging on in Fostoria and jobs were scarce. I also missed Millie. Having given up plant pathology, I was faced once again with the question, "What are you going to do with yourself?"

Several months after returning home, I found a job as a nickel plater in a local household appliance factory. Later, I worked as proof reader and copy writer in a printing establishment and had my first experience of being fired. One of my tasks was to prepare the annual report of the local superintendent of schools for typesetting. I was appalled at the organization and grammar of the superintendent's manuscript and made the mistake of commenting in public about his command of the English language. When news of this indiscretion reached my boss, he was furious and I was summarily fired. I felt very badly that I had lost my job but I learned a good lesson about public relations.

Deciding to Teach

Being unemployed much of the time, I spent many hours hanging out or practicing gymnastics at the YMCA. At Cornell, I had taken a course in economics where I learned about the "Balanced Dollar," a concept advocated by President Roosevelt's cabinet to help cure the Depression. A group of businessmen at the Y found out I knew something about this and asked me to lead a series of discussions. I was glad to oblige. In the process, I discovered that it was great fun to teach and I could do it rather well. I decided to become a teacher. I could go to Ohio State on a tuition I could afford and I

Millie and Arthur, circa 1933

could use my Cornell training in biology and chemistry as content areas for teaching. The decision was a great relief. When my application was accepted at OSU I began to make plans for the new year.

A Hasty Marriage

Just before leaving for Ohio State, I hitchhiked back to Ithaca to see Millie. We had been apart for five months and were about to separate for another year with Millie at Cornell and me at Ohio State. After two days together, it was clear to both of us that if we did not marry now we probably never would. This thought was so upsetting that we decided to get married at once. A ceremony was hastily arranged at the Mitchell home with Millie's twin, Betty, and her friend, Fred, as our attendants. I spent my last cash on a ring and borrowed ten dollars and a car from Fred for a honeymoon. After the ceremony two virgins in a daze rode off to Elmira, New York, for a night in a hotel. Somehow, we made it through an awkward night and returned to Ithaca next day. A day later, I said goodbye and hitchhiked my way to Ohio State, still reeling from a torrent of emotions and a whole new set of problems. All of a sudden I had become a married man, a role I was poorly equipped to fill.

Millie and I only saw one another at Christmas and Easter breaks that year. When Millie graduated from Cornell in June of 1935, she joined me in Columbus and we began our life together. It was tough going financially but we each found part-time jobs. Millie handed out towels at the women's gym and I had a National Youth Administration job assisting a faculty member with a research project.

A few weeks after the beginning of the fall semester, I got a notice to report to the commandant of OSU's ROTC. The commandant wanted to know why I had not registered to continue my officer-training program that I had begun at Cornell. When I explained that I was married and needed to graduate as soon as possible and wanted to put all my energies into completing my degree, the commandant said, "Well, you can do that." Then, turning to his sergeant aid, he said further, "Sergeant. bring me Mr. Combs's record and let's see how much he owes the government." If I did not continue the training to completion, I owed Uncle Sam the stipends paid me at Cornell. I do not remember the figure the sergeant came back with, but it seemed gigantic and I said, "Sir, please sign me up!"

During the summer, Millie and I were chaperons for a fraternity house, which included making beds and keeping out of sight. A special recreational treat was sharing a pint of ice cream and a twenty-cent movie. Despite the handicaps, little by little we worked out a loving, caring relationship.

A Challenge to the Status Quo

My first contact with the issue of integration came in 1935 when I was inducted into the honorary education society Phi Delta Kappa. PDK was then exclusively for white males and the liberal educators at Ohio State decided to force the national organization to face the problem of its segregationist attitude by admitting a black man and an Asian man to its Ohio State chapter. I was invited to join the chapter as well and was asked if I had any reservations about being involved in the test. I agreed at once and was initiated standing between the black and Asian individuals. I do not remember what I felt at the time, but I suspect I was pleased to be involved in the confrontation and to be making a stand for what I believed. Sure enough, the chapter was censured and its charter withdrawn. That action confronted Phi Delta Kappa with the necessity to bring the matter to light and publicly debate the issue, however. Several years later, the constitution of the group was amended to open its membership to men without regard to race or ethnicity. It was not until much later, however, that the organization was opened to women.

Teacher Training

On arrival at Ohio State, I discovered that a major requirement for the education program was a course in educational psychology. Remembering my experience with psychology at Cornell, I tried every dodge I could invent to avoid the course, all to no avail. Much to my surprise, the course dealt with people. It provided a wealth of new understandings, many of which related directly to myself, especially such matters as child development, learning, motivation, adjustment, and maladjustment. I began to discover new meanings about myself and how I came to be like I was. In the course of a class demonstration, I also discovered that I was color-blind, which explained a great deal about the troubles I had with the course in perception at Cornell. I was so excited by these new insights that I signed up for additional courses in psychology not required in the teacher preparation sequence.

Ohio State in the mid-thirties was an exciting place to be for people interested in education. The Progressive Education movement was in full swing. The Laboratory School was experimenting with ways to put John Dewey's philosophy of "learning by doing" and concern for the learner into practice. I enjoyed the time I spent observing there as well as my classes with such liberal thinkers as Boyd Bode, Gordon Hullfish, Horace English, Ross Mooney, and Sidney Pressey. Pressey employed me as a research assistant and encouraged me to think about graduate work. I was thrilled at this recognition and enrolled in several graduate courses.*

I planned to go right on for graduate work as soon as I completed my undergraduate degree. Unfortunately, lack of money and my new responsibilities as a married man would not permit such luxury. Millie wrote to her mother in 1935 thanking her "fervently" for sending us a dollar, telling her proudly that she spent fifteen cents on our dinner. She wrote: "Arthur and I are so well versed in the art of getting along on nothing that we can live indefinitely on 85 cents." But we simply ran out of funds. So, a month after graduating in December of 1935, I reluctantly turned my back on graduate work and accepted a high school teaching position in Alliance, Ohio.

First Days as a Teacher

It was a cold, gloomy day late in January when I arrived in downtown Alliance. Piles of soot-blackened snow were everywhere. Alliance was a heavy-industry town still reeling from the Depression and looked it. It certainly was not a glamorous place to begin one's career. I was employed without an interview to replace a teacher who was leaving in mid-year to accept a position elsewhere. The job I had accepted was to teach general science in the town's only high school for the magnificent salary of twelve hundred dol-

---

* Editor's note: As part of an assistantship he held during this period of time, Art taught in a "how to study" program. One of his students in that program was Jesse Owens, the internationally renowned track and field athlete who went on to win four gold medals and break three world records in the 1936 Olympics held in Nazi Germany. According to the website established in Owens's honor by his estate, Jesse Owens was born James Cleveland (J. C.) Owens in Alabama in 1913. His family moved to Cleveland, Ohio, when J. C. was age 8. On the first day he attended school there, his new teacher misunderstood his pronunciation of "J. C." as "Jesse." She listed him as Jesse Owens in her record book, and this became the name by which he was known from then on.

lars a year—minus 10 per cent "because of the Depression." I spent the day hunting for a place to live and settled on a dark and dingy furnished apartment within walking distance of the high school. I was unhappy at having to give up graduate work, but the idea of being a full-time teacher was exciting and the promise of a regular paycheck was a welcome security.

The next day I reported to the high school, signed the necessary employment papers, and was shown to the room I was to occupy. The teacher whose shoes I would be filling was silently packing up her belongings. She impatiently acknowledged our introduction as I took a seat at an empty classroom desk. I remember feeling very inadequate and awed by what I had been told about the wonderful teacher I was replacing. I tried several times to make conversation, with no luck whatever. Then, trying once more, I asked with humility and heartfelt admiration, "How long have you taught here?" She turned on me in a flash and snapped, "Young man! That's a question you *never* ask a teacher!" So much for my introduction to the profession.

Millie arrived a few days later and we moved into our apartment feeling discouraged and depressed. We agreed to make the best of it for now and to find better quarters in June. I went to work on my plans for the first day of school. When opening day came, I set out for school early, with my stomach churning and my heart in my mouth. I wanted to get there in time to prepare my room for what I foresaw as "the big encounter." When I arrived, I found the room was locked, so I set out in search of the janitor. I found him sweeping a hallway and asked politely, "Please, could you open room 126 for me?" "I'm sorry, Sonny," he said, "You'll have to wait till the teacher comes!" Blow number two.

The morning went well. When I set out for lunch at noon, the halls were filled with students making their way out of the building. Suddenly, a very large woman grabbed me by the shoulder and spun me around. "Where's your locker?" she yelled above the noise. As I stood there speechless with embarrassment, another teacher saved the day. "He's a teacher," she said. It was my attacker's turn to be embarrassed. The slow pace of my physical maturation embarrassed me often in my early adult years. It contributed further to my feelings of not being acceptable and I regarded my youthful appearance as a handicap. When I grew older, it became an advantage. Despite this inauspicious beginning, I enjoyed my ninth graders and my first day on the job, and began to think I had found my profession.

Later that week I was assigned to proctor a study hall with 120 students during the last period in the day. Monitoring so many students was bad enough. The fact that I had this responsibility during the last period, when everyone was tired and ready to escape, made it no task for a beginner. I had more than I could cope with. What a nightmare! After three days, the principal relieved me of the task despite my objections. "I don't think you're ready to handle it, Arthur," he said. "But tell you what, when you're ready, let me know and I'll give it back to you." Blessed man! A year later I asked to have the study hall assignment again. That time I was ready and salved my wounded pride.

My youthful appearance continued to plague me. The school was overcrowded. Regular classes with empty seats had students assigned to the back of the room for study. In one of my classes these free riders included a huge football player. One day, five minutes before dismissal, he slammed his book shut and began to talk to his neighbor across the aisle. I walked to the back of the room and informed him the period was not yet over. "It is for me!" he said defiantly. With everyone watching, I made a fatal mistake. "You are disturbing my class. Open your book!" I commanded. The moment the words were out of my mouth, I thought, "Oh my God, what if he stands up?" For someone fearful of confrontation, I had really put my foot in my mouth. We maintained this stance, glaring at each other for what seemed to me like hours. Then, praise be! he slowly opened his book and I quickly retreated to the front of the room. I learned another important lesson in basic human relationships that day.

I thoroughly enjoyed teaching and threw myself enthusiastically into everything I did. I became a popular and innovative teacher. When the head of the biology department retired during my second year at the school, I was assigned to that department, then headed by his daughter. Teaching biology was great fun for me, in spite of the run-ins with my boss. The department head was a living caricature of the tight-lipped spinster schoolmarm. She thoroughly disapproved of my innovations. I objected, for example, to a curriculum that dealt with plants, animals, and birds in mid-winter when there were none available for observation, and indoor laboratory studies of animals and plants in spring and fall when field trips would be possible. She disapproved of my early-morning bird hikes in the spring. Though our textbook treated reproduction up the evolutionary scale from protozoa to lower order mammals, it totally ignored the question when it came to human beings. She was horrified at my insistence that I would deal with the matter in my classes. Our office adjoined the classroom and on the day I dealt with that subject, I noticed the door was ajar and in the course of my teaching, I sauntered over and closed it firmly. She never forgave me for carrying out my plan.

After school one day, I was standing at the lab table in the front of our classroom setting up a demonstration for next day's classes when a beautiful girl came in to talk to me. After a few remarks she moved closer and closer, then reached out to put her arms around my neck. I was totally flabbergasted and retreated faster and faster around the lab table until I reached the classroom door, then bolted for the safety of the hallway.

I Become a Father

During the first years after our arrival in Alliance, Millie put her home economics training to work as an assistant county agent in a small town thirty miles away. We bought a used car. Each of us lived in rented rooms in our respective towns during the week that year and lived together at my place on weekends. The second year, we moved to a small house in Alliance, and began to accumulate some furniture and think about having a child. Times were still hard. We were barely making it financially. There was no money left to carry us over the summer, so each year we borrowed from Household Finance against the next year's income. To supplement our income, during two summers I organized a play school for young boys, collecting a small fee from parents who wanted to get their children out from underfoot.

Getting pregnant proved more difficult than we had anticipated. After a year we sought help from an obstetrician in Akron and in 1939 Carol Andrea was born on August thirty-first, the day Hitler marched into Poland. Becoming a father was both a thrill and an awesome experience. I enjoyed my new role and shared much of the work of caring for an infant. On the other hand, like many a new father, I was also aghast at my new responsibilities.

Introduction to Counseling

During these years I was faculty sponsor of HI Y, a student service club at the high school. As one of our fund-raising activities, we put on a yearly spoof of faculty and students. This was very enjoyable for me. Sponsoring these youngsters also put me in closer touch with students and gave me opportunities to learn of many who were coping with difficult personal problems. I felt great empathy for them even as I felt inadequate to assist. As a consequence of these experiences, I decided to return to OSU for counselor training and so started my life-long interest in counseling. During two summers I returned to Ohio State to work toward a master's degree with a specialty in school counseling.

During one of these summers, it was my misfortune to be assigned a front-row seat in a statistics class where I was the daily target of the professor's jokes and jibes. Every day I braced myself for a new onslaught. Then, one day, just after a particularly vicious assault, he said to me, "Combs, do you know why I pick on you?" "No sir," I replied. "Because you can take it!" he said. I could not believe my ears. Inside, I was a quivering mass of jelly, and he thought I was brave. The incident reveals how frail I was and how skilled I had become at covering up my feelings. It may also explain, in part, my continued distaste for statistics. Happily, my other classes renewed my determination to continue graduate work in psychology.

The high school where I worked had a part-time counselor. I began helping with his caseload. The popularity of our service kept growing. Each year we would make a request for more release time from teaching to counsel with students. By the time I left Alliance, we were each spending half our time in such activities. I had found what I wanted to do.

My course work in psychology also turned my attention inward to the stresses in my own personality and how they had come to be. This was a painful, upsetting experience that aroused in me great feelings of anger toward my mother. I was in a no-win situation, however. I had no way to incorporate my new insights. From my earliest days I had thoroughly learned, "You do not confront Mother." I also had a neurotic desire for her love. I suffered greatly as I began to face up to this and other problems in my psyche. At one point I grew so desperate that I sought the help of my counseling colleague. I remember calling him late one night. We sat on a log in the woods behind his home while I tearfully poured out my unhappiness and despair. After a while, I began to feel better, whereupon Walter proceeded to tell me of the dreadful problems his uncle was experiencing! This threw me back into my own despair and I went home with two problems, mine and Walter's uncle's!

Scouting Experience

For three or four years during our time in Alliance, I was scoutmaster for a troop in our local school.* One of the parents attached to our troop had a

---

* Editor's note: Although he makes no mention of it in his autobiography, according to records in the national office of the Boy Scouts of America, Art earned the Eagle Scout Award on December 13, 1939 while Scoutmaster of Troop 53 in Alliance, OH. Until the late 1940s both scouts and scoutmasters could earn this award. After that, only scouts through age 17 could earn the award (personal communication, Boy Scouts of America, November 12, 1999). Art's scouting sash indicates that he was also awarded Life Scout Rank and earned merit badges in Botany, Camping, Zoology, Cycling, Civics, First Aid to Animals, Hand Craft, Carpentry, Hiking, Personal Health, Athletics, First Aid, Firemanship, Public Health, Wood

cabin in the woods and offered it to us for a winter campout. One winter day, then, 10 boys and I set out for the cabin expecting to spend a couple of nights there. The cabin was very rustic, set in the bottom of a small valley in the woods and heated with a small pot-bellied stove. We had a great time that day and all turned in after a late supper. During the night I woke to find a couple of my charges crying because they were cold. I found out later that overnight the temperature had dropped to 10 below zero. I got out of bed to comfort the boys and to build a fire in the stove. This commotion woke the rest of the group, who now added to the complaints and tears over being cold. Because of the location of the cabin in a draw, we were at the bottom of a mass of cold air and I could not get a fire started in the stove because of the cold air in the stove pipe. I was frightened by our dilemma, yet trying not to show my concern, while more and more boys joined in the sobbing and complaint. After what seemed like an eternity, I got the stove going and we warmed up the cabin. This was a nightmare experience I have never forgotten.

Meeting Carl Rogers

In the period since my earlier studies at Ohio State, Carl Rogers had arrived on campus. Clinical psychologists were much impressed with his book, *Clinical Treatment of the Problem Child* (Rogers, 1939). He came to Ohio State from Rochester, New York, where he had been director of the Child Guidance Center. For a psychologist to head a mental health service in those days was almost unheard of. Such positions were almost exclusively the prerogative of psychiatrists. Rogers was also in the process of inventing nondirective counseling, a revolutionary approach to psychotherapy based upon absolute respect for the dignity and integrity of clients.

Nondirective Counseling

Nondirective counseling was predicated upon a firm belief that people can find their own best ways to deal with personal problems. It relied upon a technique of responding to client feelings that Rogers called "recognition and acceptance of feeling." This required counselors to respond to client feelings

Work, Pioneering, Bird Study, Swimming, Farm Home and Its Planning, Cooking, Farm Layout and Building Arrangement, Physical Development, Pathfinding, Painting, Electricity, Book Binding, Scholarship, Basketry, Reptile Safety, Stalking, Safety, Weather, Chemistry, Life Saving, Animal Industry and Forestry.

about the events their clients were reporting rather than to the events themselves. This innovative approach to therapy was destined to change the face of American psychology in three vital ways:

1. Until then, most clinical psychology was preoccupied with diagnosis, explaining why clients behaved as they did. Nondirective therapy challenged that focus, forcing attention to the problems of treatment.
2. Rogers opened the whole question of psychotherapy to public scrutiny. Through the use of phonograph recordings at first, and tape recordings later, the protocols of therapy were courageously thrown open to examination and critique. He said in effect, "Therapy is not magic. It can be explored and understood like any other human phenomenon."
3. In addition to opening up the protocols of therapy, Rogers began to subject them to careful research, something that had never been done before.

I enrolled in one of Carl's courses during my second summer at OSU and before long decided I wanted to work with him. This was not unusual. Indeed, it seemed like every graduate student I met sought the same thing. The flocking of students to a new standard-bearer was not altogether appreciated by the majority of professors in the Psychology Department, however. Graduate students are the "coin of the realm" for graduate faculties. They can be symbols of prestige and status for professors as well as providers of man- or womanpower for pet research projects. The admiration and respect students show for their mentors can also be a potent source of ego enhancement. Resentments produced by the loss of graduate students to a colleague may be carefully masked—professors can be "oh so polite" about it—but the underground rumblings and faculty in-fighting can be vicious and destructive.

Rogers was one of the most popular professors on campus with almost everyone but the members of his own department. We students did not help matters. We were thoroughly delighted to be working with him and unaware of the hidden antagonisms. Among ourselves we thought it was funny to talk about his book as "The Bible," or raise our eyes to the skies and bow at mention of his name. Such horseplay must surely have added to his difficulties.

During my second summer at Ohio State I settled on a master's thesis. I would administer the Mooney Problems Checklist to our entire high school and analyze the results. Little did I know what I was getting into. Ross Mooney had developed a checklist of adolescent problems, upon which students were asked to indicate those they had experienced. He was in need of subjects to provide standardized norms. I set out to provide some of those data by applying the test to the 1700 students in the high school in which I was teaching and to analyze the data as my master's thesis. The checklist contained 320 items organized in 16 problem areas. I proposed to discover the frequencies for each item and category, class by class, for boys and for girls and to show the trends for each classification throughout the four-year high school period. Our students reported experiencing 38,353 of the problems included in the checklist, requiring an enormous number of calculations. Since electronic calculators did not exist, I painstakingly cranked them out on a Marchant hand-operated machine. The task absorbed most of my spare time for more than two years.

In academic circles, a master's thesis is supposed to be an exercise in research and to make a contribution to the literature. My thesis was certainly an exercise in research, far more than I anticipated. It also made a small contribution to the literature. The human cost, however, in time away from family and broader interests was excessive. I remembered this experience long after and made a point of protecting graduate students I worked with from biting off more than they could comfortably chew.

A Teaching Assistantship

After five years in Alliance, I decided to go full-time for graduate work and applied for a graduate assistantship in the Psychology Department at OSU. Carol was a year old and Millie was pregnant with our second child. At work I had finally achieved a salary of 1800 dollars a year. Nevertheless, when word came that I had been granted an assistantship, we were delighted. Immediately after school was out in June, we packed up and headed for Columbus to take up graduate work on a stipend of 900 dollars a year.

In Columbus we rented a house some distance from the campus and I set out to find a job that would carry us to our first stipend check in the fall. Jobs were scarce, but after several weeks I found one on the packaging line of a company that manufactured a substitute for mother's milk. Because this was an agricultural industry, it was not required to comply with usual wage and hour regulations. Accordingly, workers were subject to the vagaries of the vacuum machines that dried the milk. Whenever a batch was ready, morning, noon, or night, it had to be packaged immediately. Workers could be called in at any time, kept waiting for hours to start work, then required to work without overtime until a batch was canned, no matter how long that took. It was grueling work if batches were ready without time between. I once worked 32 hours with only two hours off. I felt lucky that I would soon be able to quit. My fellow workers had no such relief. I was incensed at such unfair and arrogant treatment. I have never forgotten my assembly line experience or what it is like to be stuck in a dead-end job.

Teaching at OSU

When the fall semester opened, I went to work as a teaching assistant in Psych 407, Sidney Pressey's course in educational psychology. This was the very course I had tried so hard to avoid taking seven years earlier. The many class sections of this course were taught by graduate assistants like myself and Pressey gave us great freedom to structure things in our own way within the generous constraints of the syllabus.

Teaching 407 was a delightful experience. Pressey was breaking new ground in educational psychology, shifting from traditional concentration on learning to a developmental approach concerned with the growth of students and an emphasis upon learning by doing. In place of standard lectures, classes were limited to about thirty students and included interesting demonstrations, school observations, opportunities for individuals to pursue matters of special interest, and the like. We were seldom denied opportunity to test out our innovations. Pressey, who had a delightful sense of humor, enjoyed our group of graduate students as much as we enjoyed each other.

I had enormous respect for Sidney Pressey. I got to know him well because he hired me for library documentation and research during holidays and between semester breaks. He was deeply interested in gerontological research, especially on knowing more about the age range when people are most likely to be productive. After I had compiled all the data for one of his projects he invited me to participate in a joint article, on "Acceleration and Age of Productivity" (Pressey & Combs, 1943), my very first publication. The article dealt with the effect of acceleration through school upon the age of greatest productivity.

Somehow, Pressey seemed to know when I was against the wall financially. At least four times while I was at Ohio State, he called me in to ask if I was free to work for him. Then, in an off-hand way, he would suggest, "Why don't I write you a check right now?" I could not have made it through graduate school without his help and I have tried to emulate his example with some of my own students over the years.

Pressey was a great kidder. It was fun to banter with him. The only time I ever saw him nonplussed was one day when he walked into the office and found me sitting in his chair. "What are you doing there, Art?" he asked. "Just trying out the seats of the mighty," I replied. He blushed with embarrassment, speechless for a moment. One Christmas season, he invited all of us to his home. During the evening he took us to his well-stocked cellar and invited us to choose whatever we liked. As a poverty-stricken graduate student, I was especially incredulous at a bottle of Geltwasser, a German cordial with flecks of gold leaf floating about in the liqueur. The thought of drinking gold was simply beyond comprehension, the ultimate in decadence.

Family Problems

In contrast to such opulence, our family lived continuously on the brink of financial disaster. We stretched my graduate stipend to the limit, padded out occasionally with contributions from Fostoria. But Mother and Dad were, themselves, trying to recover from the financial burden of maintaining two kids at college. We walked a mile or so to attend a ten-cent movie and occasionally splurged on a shared pint of ice cream, still our primary form of recreation. The first Christmas in Columbus I made a toy train and a set of blocks for Carol out of wood scraps from the Psychology Department shop.

Shortly before Christmas that first year in Columbus, Pearl Harbor was attacked and the country was plunged into World War II. That brought a whole new set of problems. While at Cornell I had enrolled in the advanced Reserve Officers' Training Corps to take advantage of the stipend that went with the program. Receiving my commission on graduation at OSU, I was so involved in teaching and subsequently starting graduate work that I made no attempt to keep it current in the ensuing years. After five years it became inactive. Now, with the outbreak of hostilities, I was torn by the necessity for some sort of decision. Millie was pregnant. Our second baby was due in January. We were contributing to the maintenance of Millie's folks. What would happen to my family and hers if I enlisted? On the other hand, the country was at war and I felt conscience stricken at the thought of not joining up. What to do? After much anguish, I decided to postpone enlistment. I reasoned that the war was going to be a long one. Accordingly, I would put off military duty at least until I had passed my qualifying exams and the babies were a little older. I later regretted my decision and felt guilty long after for not joining up immediately.

My son, Peter Arthur, was born in January. To make ends meet, we sold our car to pay for the delivery and I began walking to the university. This was so time-consuming for me, and so disrupting for the family, that after a month or two we moved to a new home on the edge of the campus. While savoring my experiences in professional growth, I was also learning to enjoy two very small children. Nurturing a family of four on a graduate stipend was a constant worry but I managed to spend considerable time with our toddler, Carol. I learned to make various toys from scraps and built a two-wheeled cart to take her to an experimental nursery school each day. Together we made "explorations" of bus rides, visits to the fair grounds and the University Farms, to fire stations, parks, and trips downtown. I enjoyed these times immensely and once toyed with the idea of writing a book for fathers on how to play with young children.

On graduation from high school in 1942, my brother, Charles, came to live with us while studying for a degree in engineering. Chuck is twelve years younger than I. As a consequence, I had already left home by the time he was six, so we had never had a real opportunity to get to know one another. He, too, suffered feelings of rejection, perhaps even more than I did. His coming to live with us might have been a time when we became more closely acquainted. Unfortunately, that did not happen. I was caught up in the excitement and discipline of teaching and working on my doctorate. In addition, Millie and I were absorbed in the problems of a young family with an infant and a toddler. For his part, Chuck was caught up in the trauma of breaking away from home, dealing with his own psychological problems, and the expectation of being drafted at any moment. As a result, he only stayed with us for a quarter and then decided to enlist. I have always regretted that we did not have more opportunity to find each other in those days.

Experiencing Counseling

During my first quarter of graduate work I began to worry about my own mental health. This was brought to a head one day when I took my educational psychology class on a field trip to Columbus State Hospital. As we toured the wards, I had an overwhelming feeling that I, too, should be a patient there. This is not an unusual reaction for students in clinical psychology, but I did not know that then. As my anxiety increased, I sought counseling from Carl Rogers. The five or six sessions we had laid the foundations from which further growth could proceed. During our sessions I explored relationships with my parents and came to understand the origins of many of my difficulties. I became aware of the source of my feelings of rejection and inadequacy. More importantly, I began to give up my unrealistic expectations of affirmation from my parents. Someone has said, "Sooner or later each of us must give up hope of having a better past." That is essentially what I accomplished. Counseling set me free to experience vital new growth.

Working with Carl Rogers

In the early forties Rogers was preoccupied with the nondirective technique for counseling and research in the dynamics of the counseling process. This was enormously significant work. It not only opened the practice of psychotherapy to discussion and research; it gave a giant stimulus to the humanistic movement just then getting underway. Psychology up to that time was primarily experimental and diagnostic. Psychologists were heavily behavioristically oriented. The training of clinical psychologists was overwhelmingly concerned with testing and diagnosis. Rogers turned attention to the question of treatment. This new emphasis for psychology was destined to change the profession by encouraging the growth of applied psychology, a shift in emphasis the profession is still trying to digest.

In seminars with Rogers we learned the nondirective approach and put these ideas to work in various practica. I became so nondirective in those days that if you had asked me "What time is it?" I probably would have replied, "You're wondering what time it is." We had no tape recorders. Instead, we recorded sessions on dictaphones or phonograph records and played these back in our seminars. Someone would report on his or her sessions with a client. The rest would discuss and critique the counselor's responses. We would listen to what a client said as it was recorded on a phonograph disk, then lift the needle before hearing the counselor's comment to ask, "What would you say?" Or, we would ask, after hearing the counselor's response, "Was that a good thing to say?" or "How could you respond better?" We also listened with special interest to Carl's own recordings and tried to emulate his example. Carl's revolutionary book, *Counseling and Psychotherapy* (Rogers, 1942), came out while I was at OSU. In fact, he paid me for doing the index for it.

One evening all Carl's graduate students were invited to a barbecue in Rogers's backyard. After eating we sat around talking. I chose to lie on the grass. I was so interested in the conversation that I was unaware of being invaded by chiggers. That night I was awakened by itching all over my body. At the clinic the next day, the doctors told me it was the worst case of chiggers they had ever seen. I was in misery for a week. I resolved from the experience that I would never again prostrate myself at the feet of any master!

Several of Rogers's students at that time became interested in the theoretical aspects suggested by nondirective practice. Most notable among these was Victor Raimy, who included as part of his dissertation a theory of the self-concept. Rogers was so engrossed with research and the nondirective technique, however, that he did not recognize Vic's contribution and recommended that it not be included in Raimy's dissertation. Raimy included it anyhow and subsequently it was acknowledged to be an early and definitive exploration of the self-concept and its dynamics for human behavior. Vic never published his dissertation. Years later, however, the document was in such demand that the Ohio State University library took it upon itself to publish the study and I was honored to write a foreword for it (Combs, 1971; Raimy, 1971). I, too, was intrigued with the theoretical issues raised by nondirective practice and began to see its broader implications for education and social action. These ideas were beginning to germinate and found early expression in my dissertation and my approach to teaching.

Counseling was not the only subject of my studies. In those days no clinician worth his salt could ignore the fields of psychological testing or research methodology. I paid my dues in those matters like everyone else. I have never forgotten the first time I tested a mental patient. As part of our training, we were required to administer tests to persons in all sorts of settings. One day I was assigned to test a patient in the mental ward at Fort Hayes Hospital. When I arrived, the sergeant in charge led me down the hall to a padded cell. He looked through the peep hole, then opened the door. "Here's your man," he said. With fear and trembling, I stepped into the room and was aghast to hear the door clang shut behind me. I turned around. The peep hole was closed. I was trapped with a patient in a padded room. The patient was seated on the edge of his cot, a veritable giant with a great black beard. He began to stand up and it seemed to me he would never stop unfolding. In a moment, he towered over me. I was scared to death. Fumbling for something to say, I stammered, "Why are you here?" The moment it was out of my mouth, I realized how stupid the question was. Suddenly, however, my client broke into tears. Much to my relief, I heard him sob, "The fellers have been pickin' on me." With that, I realized I had nothing to fear and we got along fine through the tests I was scheduled to perform.

For a time during this period, I was employed on weekends as a substitute for the psychologist in the Huntington, West Virginia induction station. My task was to administer a test to determine if men with little education were sufficiently intelligent to be acceptable for military service. This was a weird experience. The test was administered totally in pantomime to groups of totally naked men—hardly the most salutary conditions for taking a test! The hundred-dollars-a-day fee was a windfall for our family budget, however. And because I had to ride a bus all night on these trips, I taught myself

self-hypnosis. I would take my seat on the bus, put myself under, and wake up in Huntington or Columbus. The ability to do this has been a valuable relaxation technique that has served me all my life.

We Leave Ohio State

Finally, it came time for my prelims and doctoral oral. Graduate students in the department were honor-bound to write down the questions on the exams and pass them along to the next generation of students. With the help of these gifts from my predecessors, I passed the written exams with flying colors. After the oral exam, however, Professor Dockeray, a kindly behaviorist, took me aside to chide me that "even a clinical psychologist ought to know the difference between the fovea and blind spot in the human eye." In those times, Ohio State's Psychology Department was predominantly oriented toward stimulus-response psychology, but I was already feeling dissatisfied with that explanation of human personality.

It was time to leave Ohio State, and shortly after completing my exams I accepted an assistant professorship at Syracuse University. Sidney Pressey's last words were, "Art, you've been starving long enough. Now that you are going to be making some money, ($2400 a year!) don't be afraid to spend it!" We took his advice and traveled to Syracuse in a parlor car.

Recapitulation

View of Self

The period 1932 to 1943 was a time of awakening, of tentative steps towards greater personal fulfillment. The process began with my experience in counseling with Carl Rogers. Carl was a warm and caring counselor and the nondirective technique was just what I needed to help me explore the relationships of my childhood home. That experience made it possible for me to cut loose from my neurotic expectations of my parents. Giving up those hopes set me free to pursue fulfillment elsewhere. It paved the way for the further growth of my self.

Rejected children learn very early to rely upon themselves and are often driven to succeed in the hope that "if I can only work hard enough or be good enough, perhaps someone will notice and care." It was like that with me. The experience in counseling was like casting off the moorings that held my boat to the dock. Once I gave up hoping to fill my childhood needs from my family, I was free to devote my energies to other arenas. I still felt basically inadequate. I was still a long way from being a fulfilled adult. But, at least, I now felt free to direct my energies in more promising directions.

I was also beginning to discover my self as an intelligent human being. My success as a student at Ohio State overshadowed my record during the last year at Cornell. I was becoming intrigued with ideas and the joy of innovation. My interest in non-violent rebellion found congenial outlets in progressive education and liberal politics. The discovery of psychology afforded by the courses I took at Ohio State opened a whole new world. It also began to make me aware of my own personality problems.

Other factors were contributing in important ways to the growth of a healthier self. For one thing, I was growing older and taking on adult responsibilities. I was also looking more mature. After an inauspicious beginning, my marriage was becoming a source of love and security. Though we lived a hand-to-mouth existence, ever on the brink financially, I was finding real satisfactions in being a husband and a father. At work, I was a successful and innovative teacher. That brought with it the fringe benefits of admiration and respect from students and the approval of supervisors. Added to this, the successful completion of a graduate program and the encouragement of mentors at Ohio State were building blocks for a more positive view of self. My self was beginning to grow more stable. However, a self-concept manufactured over a 20-year period is not rebuilt overnight. I was still unsure that anything had really changed and certain that, if anyone *really* knew me, they would know I was living a lie.

Acceptance and Openness to Experience

One effect of more positive feelings about self was to broaden my base of security. Things are less threatening when you feel better about yourself. And so it was with me. Making the break from my family of origin made possible tentative steps toward greater self-acceptance. I was beginning to learn that being different has its positive features. The innovations I experimented with while teaching high school in Alliance and educational psychology at Ohio State provided success experiences in breaking with tradition and finding my ways to do things.

Two other factors contributed to greater openness during this period. One of these was the sheer excitement of new ideas. It was fun being part of Rogers's revolution in psychology. The group of graduate students I was a part of under Rogers's mentorship was a stimulating one. "We had the feeling we were on to something big, at the cutting edge of an idea and a process destined to change the field of therapy" (Combs, 1995, p. 159). Being part of such a movement put a further premium on pioneering ideas. The rebel let loose by Miss Riley in seventh grade was becoming more sophisticated but no less a rebel. Many other new sources of ideas were opened for me in the study of philosophy, psychology, sociology, research, and education. Each of these presented unlimited vistas for exploration.

The second factor came from the discipline of nondirective therapy itself. The prime essential for success in this kind of treatment lies in the counselor's capacity to listen, to be empathic. The practice of nondirective counseling was, itself, an exercise in openness to experience. Rogers once said that the experience of psychotherapy was like the discovery of the X-ray in medicine. It made it possible to see inside the human organism to the very essence of being. I did not know it in 1943, but the regimen of intent listening and the empathy I learned to employ as a counselor were to contribute greatly to my own growth as an individual, as a therapist, and as a contributor to psychological theory in years to come.

Identification and Oneness

By now my marriage had long settled into the expected roles of "normal" married life. Millie was housewife, mother, and nurturer of her family. She loved her husband and was content to follow his lead. I, too, fell into the accepted role of husband, provider, and head of the household. I loved my wife and children. My eagerness to serve others made certain that I would respond to their necessities without reservation. Later in life it became clear to me that they often experienced longings to which I was totally oblivious. I was so excited by my work and studies at Ohio State, such a workaholic, that I missed many priceless opportunities for close relationships with my children, which I regret today. At that time, however, I am sure that our family looked to outsiders as though we fitted each other like a hand in a glove. I was treating my family as I was treating my profession—giving and serving but rarely sharing my deepest feelings. I was there in the crises but too often preoccupied with the challenges of my professional life to give much energy to day-to-day interactions. I know now that I treated my wife like I treated my mother; I loved her deeply, needed her desperately, and tried as best I knew how to serve and deserve her. At the same time, I was guarded about communicating more openly for fear of being rebuffed.

During this period I made no close friends. I was too busy exploring the delights of my chosen profession. Besides, my history of rejection left me apprehensive about initiating contact with others that might lead to my being spurned. Students often chided me for passing them somewhere outside of class: "You never said 'Hello.'" This always came as a surprise to me. I never believed I was important enough for them to care. My experience in counseling made me increasingly aware of the origins of my problems and I was becoming more and more alienated from my family of origin. Primarily a loner, I felt as my mother did, like an outsider, someone who did not really belong.

At the same time, I was experiencing deep sympathy for outcasts or unfortunates of the world, and a growing sense of oneness with the human condition. News of the war and the atrocities against the Jews in Germany saddened and horrified me. I felt intense alliance with my nation, compassion for the victims of war, and guilt for not being more involved. The assembly-line experience at the milk-processing plant opened my eyes to the plight of workers, adding further to my feelings of concern for people in trouble.

Many people who have experienced childhood rejection learn to give themselves in service to others but are often unable to accept love from others without embarrassment. I am sure this "serving others" syndrome was largely responsible for leading me into teaching and counseling. This was a growth experience for me. Since clients generally come to counseling because they believe a therapist can assist them, I did not fear rejection. I could be open and genuine in the role of "helper," while keeping myself from being at risk. The experience of successful teaching and counseling deepened my feelings of oneness with people in general. With tongue in cheek, counseling has sometimes been defined as: when two people get together to help each other. The observation is more truth than fiction. I was learning much from my experiences as a counselor. One cannot walk hand-in-hand with a client through the dark spaces of his or her life without developing a strong sense of compassion toward and oneness with the human condition.

A More Trustworthy Belief System

Little by little my experiences were laying the groundwork for an internal guidance system. My early joy at rebellion and successful innovations as a teacher were resulting in a fascination with change and impatience with the status quo. These attitudes were enhanced by the liberal thinking symbolized nationally by Franklin Roosevelt, and stimulated by the atmosphere at Ohio State. The philosophy of John Dewey and the attempts to implement it represented by the Progressive Movement in education struck a responsive chord. The thrill of innovation was making an idea person of me. I was becoming more interested in strategy than tactics, in basic assumptions than details, more excited by the initiation of projects than their maintenance. In later years my wife would often complain that I was more interested in engineering projects, like building an office or putting in a sprinkler system, than in washing cars or windows.

Experience as a nondirective counselor was influencing my belief system in two other ways that were to play vital parts in the development of my personal theory in years to come. One of these was the practice of empathy, the capacity to put oneself in someone else's shoes, to understand how things seem from the point of view of another. Nondirective counseling required the counselor to zero in on the feelings of the client, rather than on behavior or objective information. This discipline was teaching me how to approach the understanding of people from an internal or phenomenological frame of reference.

A second fundamental lesson I was learning from nondirective therapy was the power of the organism's basic drive toward health. Watching my clients move insatiably forward while I was being, almost exclusively, nondirective led to an awesome recognition that here was a drive so strong that a whole system of therapy could be built upon it and could encourage it. Later this principle was to become a fundamental assumption for perceptual-experiential psychology.

Like many counselors and therapists before me, I was originally drawn to psychotherapy in large part because of my own unresolved problems. Many people look with deep suspicion upon such reasons for becoming a therapist, but it has always seemed to me an intelligent thing to do. Being attracted to a profession that can foster one's personal growth while helping others seems an ideal reason for such a vocational choice. I have never been able to understand the distressingly large numbers of psychologists I have encountered who have never experienced therapy from the client's viewpoint. That seems to me to constitute gross lack of confidence in the helpfulness and validity of one's own profession.

References

Raimy, V. C. (1971). *The self concept as a factor in counseling and personality organization.* Doctoral dissertation, Ohio State University, 1943. Columbus, OH: Ohio State University Libraries.

Rogers, C. R. (1939). *Clinical treatment of the problem child.* New York: Houghton Mifflin.

Rogers, C. R. (1942). *Counseling and psychotherapy*. Boston: Houghton Mifflin.

Arthur W. Combs in Syracuse, NY (circa 1950)

CHAPTER FOUR

Growing Pains

My first assignment at Syracuse University was to teach classes in educational psychology. I enjoyed every minute of my teaching duties and began to discover that I had much to contribute to a college of education. One of my colleagues at Syracuse had received his bachelor's degree at Ohio State at the same time that I had. When we were students together, I remember being very envious that he could go right on for graduate work while I had to postpone graduate work and take a job teaching. Now, six years later, here we were on the same faculty. I was surprised to find how much better prepared I was to deal with problems of teacher education than he was. My work experience had given me firsthand knowledge of the problems of education. I knew what would and would not fly on the firing line. This made it possible to understand and communicate with my students more effectively. I was also less prone to the arrogance of many on teachers' college faculties who frequently assume superior knowledge of what is good for teachers and administrators in the field based solely on theoretical understandings.

A Dissertation Topic

While I was learning the ropes as a college instructor, I was also seriously involved in working on my doctoral dissertation. The Thematic Apperception Test (TAT) had just appeared and was making a stir in clinical circles. The TAT is a projective test composed of a number of purposely vague pictures that are presented one at a time to the test taker with instructions to tell a story about what seems to be occurring in the picture. Since the pictures were vague, the test assumed that whatever the subject expressed came from his or her own experience and must therefore reveal significant aspects of the person's personality. The inventor of the test had also contrived a complex scoring system for analyzing the protocols of a person's responses to the pictures.

I was intrigued by the idea that personality could be explored projectively through people's responses to pictures and I set out to validate the TAT against autobiography as my dissertation. I would determine to what extent information about a person's personality, obtained from the TAT, could be corroborated by the subject's experience as revealed in his or her autobiography. The task turned out to be much bigger than I anticipated. Before any validation could be attempted, it was necessary to develop a method of analysis that could be used with protocols of both TAT and autobiographies. Tackling that problem, I took my first step toward phenomenological research, finding a way to explore human experience through the eyes of the behaver.

I reasoned that people's behavior represents an attempt to solve personal problems. To understand the dynamics of such activity, it is necessary to know: (a) what the person is trying to accomplish (the goal), (b) the nature of the obstacles between the person and the goal, and (c) the strategy chosen to surmount the barrier. To study problem-solving behavior in such terms, it was necessary to make inferences about the person's intent, that is, to seek to understand the individual and his or her world from the viewpoint of the behaver. Though I did not realize it at the time, I was carrying over to research the empathic or phenomenologic view I was using in nondirective therapy.

From such thinking, I devised a scoring system involving a list of commonly sought goals, perceived barriers, and strategies for surmounting them. Using this system, I then analyzed the story plots from the TAT and life situations reported in the same person's autobiography. I hoped from this data to be able to validate the TAT against autobiography. Although I worked on it every available moment, it took more than two years to complete the analysis. How that worked out is another story to be told in a subsequent chapter.

Arthur W. Combs (circa 1945–1950) Parent Interview, Psycho-educational Clinic, Syracuse University

Building a Clinical Program

Among my colleagues in the College of Education were Lance Hunnicutt, whose specialty was in reading, and William Cruikshank, whose expertise was in special education. Together we established a psychoeducational clinic open to the community. My part in this project was to supervise the clinical-counseling aspect of the program. The clinic served a dual purpose. On the one hand, it provided a service to children and adults in the community. On the other, it provided a practicum setting where graduate students could observe educational and counseling problems in the flesh and participate in diagnostic and treatment activities.

The establishment of the psychoeducational clinic provided a steady source of clients for the practice of counseling. It also created a demand for new courses to prepare students for clinical work. To that end, I began teaching courses in therapy and diagnostic testing. I would add a new course to our graduate offerings and carry it as an overload. When it enrolled enough students to justify its existence, I would go to the administration and make a case for additional help. Over the next five years this procedure resulted in the development of a program for the preparation of clinical psychologists. I never sat down to plan for such a goal. It just happened. As I saw a use for a particular course, I created it, taught it myself, then passed it on to someone else. Among these were courses entitled Tests and Measurements, Individual Testing, Personality and Intelligence Tests, Introduction to Clinical Psychology, Individual Differences, Educational Psychology, Personality Theories, Human Growth and Development, Psychology of Adjustment, Introduction to Counseling, Seminar in Clinical Practice, Clinical Internship, and Seminar in Counseling and Psychotherapy. In time, this resulted in a full-fledged graduate program in clinical psychology with five full-time clinical psychologists.

Once, after six or seven years at Syracuse, the dean of the college showed me the record of one of my graduate students. "Art," he asked, "How is this? Bob has ten courses, all taken with you?" When I explained that the record was correct, that I had, indeed, taught all of them, he chided me, "Ten courses with Art Combs? Or one course, under twelve different names? That doesn't look good." I had to admit that the dean had a point and promised to limit my requests for new courses in the future. That was easy to agree to because, by that time, we had all the courses we considered relevant for a clinical program already in place.

Without realizing it at the time, I had stumbled upon a valuable approach to innovation. One quietly fills a vacuum. Then, by the time people get around to questioning what you are up to, the innovation is well established and producing so well it cannot be handily dismantled. Lance Hunnicutt called it "using your wriggle room." In every situation there is always room to wriggle. If one takes up the slack in the same direction, people get used to your being there and give you more room to wriggle. In this way it is possible to move a long distance before anyone becomes aware how far out you have really traveled. The technique is also a natural for a shy person anxious to avoid rejection.

From an outsider's point of view, this approach looks like a cynical strategy to gain one's personal goals. Actually, it was not. The only long-term goal I have ever purposely planned for was earning my doctoral degree. Whatever I have accomplished in my career is more typically the result of the accumulation of small efforts or decisions made in response to current events or opportunities. It is only in recent years, while looking at my life more objectively, that I have become aware of the process as a strategy for change and innovation.

The Specter of the Draft

The war was still on and the possibility of being drafted was an ever-present worry. I wanted desperately to finish my dissertation before being called up, and thus I spent every available moment pushing it forward. Then, my father-in-law lost his job. Since he had no retirement benefits, my sister-in-law's husband and I began to provide as much financial support as we could. I was appalled at what would happen to my in-laws and to my family if I were drafted. How could they live on a private's pay of $80 dollars a month? It was too late to reinstate the commission I had earned in the ROTC. Anxiously, I cast about for possible ways to serve in the armed forces as a psychologist. Only the Navy showed any interest and I was called to Washington for an interview. The talks went well until the lieutenant commander who interviewed me discovered I was color-blind. "I'm sorry," he said, "We would like to use you but regulations do not permit us to accept a color-blind officer."

"But what you want me for is a desk job here in Washington," I protested. "How can my color-blindness make any difference for that?" I asked.

This was his reply: "I'm sorry Dr. Combs, but the fog gets pretty thick here in Washington. You need to be able to discriminate the riding lights of an approaching desk!" I was crushed and returned home to prepare for my impending induction.

A few weeks later I was classified 1A and reported for my physical examination. Being in fine shape, I was ordered to report for induction several weeks later on a Monday. We notified our landlord that we would be leaving, arranged for Millie and the children to move in with her folks in Ithaca, notified the university, and began to pack or dispose of our belong-

Saint Jerome—by Ivan Meštrović. Photo by Nadya S. Lutz

ings. Then, on the Friday before my induction, President Roosevelt proclaimed that no more married men would be called up. What a reprieve! We began to put our lives back together, only to find that our house had already been rented to someone else. Housing in the city, as almost everywhere at the time, was practically unavailable. After we searched desperately without success for a place to live, the university put us up, temporarily, in one of the houses they owned on the edge of the campus.

The house we occupied backed up to an alley, across which was the studio of Ivan Meštrović, a Croatian sculptor brought to America by the university and installed as an artist in residence.* His sculptures had a powerful spiritual quality, full of love and serenity. They moved me and I enjoyed standing in the open door of his studio to watch him work when the weather permitted.

The End of Graduate Work

The threat of the draft behind me, I went back to work, redoubling my efforts to finish my dissertation. Several months later, working late in the

* Editor's note: Ivan Meštrović (1883–1962) was a professor of sculpture in the School of Art at Syracuse University from 1947 to 1955. Described by Auguste Rodin as "the greatest phenomenon among sculptors" (http://archives.syr.educ/arch/faculty/mestbio/htm), he was internationally known, exhibiting work in Vienna, Paris, Zagreb, and Rome. He also worked on several commissions for the Vatican. A biography of Meštrović can be found on the Syracuse University website. (See also Meštrović, 1948.)

quiet house, I reached the end of the crucial calculations. I realized, with horror, that my fundamental assumption was in error; the TAT could not be validated against autobiography! I was devastated. In despair, I called Maurice Troyer, a colleague and friend in psychology. It was midnight, but he told me to "bring it over and let's see what we can do." I have never forgotten his kindness and understanding. We worked all night. As dawn was breaking, we discovered a way to save the study by making it a comparison of the two personality instruments instead of a validation. Carl Rogers had left Ohio State to develop a counseling program for returning veterans for the USO. Accordingly, Horace English had become my advisor. He gave approval to the new format and I finally completed the document in the spring of 1945.

William Snyder, who had taken Carl Rogers's place at Ohio State, invited me to stay with him when I arrived in Columbus for my final oral examination. Meantime, the war in the Pacific was winding down and I arrived in Columbus amidst excitement over the impending Japanese surrender. My exam was set for VJ Day! The university was closed for the holiday but my doctoral committee agreed to hold the examination anyway. No one was in a mood to quibble or debate. Like most graduate students, I expected a grueling adversarial session. Instead, I thoroughly enjoyed the experience. The committee treated me with respect and dignity and my work with appreciation. The exam was what the capstone of a doctoral program ought to be—a celebration among peers for a job well done. With proper attention to protocol, we held the examination, signed the necessary papers, shook hands all around, and left the dark and silent halls of the building. My long ordeal was over!

Yet I felt it as a let down! The end of the war and the end of my long and tortuous struggle on the same day! In a daze, I returned to Bill Snyder's apartment. No one was home, so I lay on the floor and listened to radio reports of the surrender. I was exhausted and soon fell asleep. A cold breeze blew over me while I slept. When I awoke I was weak and dizzy with the flu. Next morning, I stumbled onto a bus and headed for Fostoria, where my mother put me to bed. I stayed in bed for three days and I might have stayed forever had Millie not called to say that Carol had broken off the end of her finger in a door accident. That got me going again and I took the train for Syracuse. For weeks afterward I did not know what to do with myself with no dissertation to fill up my days. Millie said, "Good Lord! You're like a man who has retired!" In a sense, I had.

We Move to Slocum Heights— A Time of Growth and Expansion

With the war over, the university entered upon an exciting period of expansion. Thousands of GI's were coming home to pick up the tangled threads of their disrupted personal lives. Congress enacted the GI Bill to provide veterans tuition and to support higher education. Chancellor Tolley established a policy that the university would not turn down any veteran who could meet our entrance requirements. A whole village of temporary housing units from vacated military bases was moved onto land about half a mile from the campus. Shortly after, our family moved into one of these converted barracks, a four-room apartment in Slocum Heights.

For months, the project had no paved streets and we lived in a quagmire of mud. I recall one day looking out the window to see my mother plodding up the street to our apartment, ankle deep in sticky mud. Our quarters were cramped. The rooms were small and there was no way to get away from each other. My desk was a board laid across the arms of a chair. I wrote on a typewriter resting on my knees. Despite the crowded quarters we got along very well, thanks largely to Millie, who quietly managed most household affairs. I, on the other hand, was a typical workaholic father; I was there for my children in emergencies but left most parenting responsibilities to Millie. Looking back, I have real regrets that I was not more deeply involved with Carol and Peter in those times.

During this period I was invited to conduct a workshop and speak about counseling with several classes at Goddard College. I thought I was to work over a weekend, so I planned to be there for three or four days and made reservations for a return home on Sunday. On arrival, I found I was scheduled for only a three-hour session on Friday morning and that was all that was expected of me. Most of the faculty and many students left for New York City for the weekend, leaving me at loose ends on a strange campus.

After lunch, I wandered out on the campus and sat down under a tree, wondering what to do with myself. Soon a group of bare-footed students arrived and began English folk dancing on the lawn. They looked like they were having fun and I enjoyed watching them. I was astounded when one of the young women came to ask me to join them. Despite my embarrassment at their attention and my protests about not knowing how to dance, they said they would teach me and I permitted myself to be pulled into the group. Soon I, too, was dancing with the rest. After several hours we went to dinner together and then to a party that lasted well into the next morning.

When I awoke Saturday morning I looked out my window and saw a group of students washing a car in front of the building. Among them was a woman I recognized as having met the day before. I walked out to chat with them and soon found myself helping to wash the car too. This was a totally new experience for me, but I enjoyed myself thoroughly. In a few minutes, more of last night's participants arrived and we took up the party where we left off, with alcohol flowing freely until time for me to leave.

We were all feeling no pain and, with much hugging and regrets at parting, my newfound friends delivered me to my plane. Arriving home, I remember sitting on the back steps of our Slocum Heights apartment, smoking a cigarette and reliving the experience. I recall thinking with astonishment that "This, too, is me—this person who can be free and uninhibited. I am not just a hard-working college professor. I am a man with unexplored capacities for life, love and joy that I never knew existed." It was a revelation! I was not sure why, but I felt I had moved as a person to another dimension. I began to ask myself, what else is there to discover?

We Build a Home

Among other faculty members in Slocum Heights were the families of Virgil and Lois Cover and George and Ruth Chaput. During the second year there we bought adjacent lots in Fayetteville, a suburb of Syracuse, and began to plan for building new homes. This was something else to pour my energies into. George Chaput was a draftsman/supervisor in the university's buildings and grounds department who provided invaluable aid in drawing up plans and helping us locate a reliable builder. Building a house is a great joy and a great hassle. I thoroughly enjoyed clearing the lot, formulating the plans, lending a hand with the actual building, and landscaping the place when building was completed. Fayetteville did not feel like a suburb. Instead, it was a delightful small town with a character all its own. Our house was only a block from the children's school. If you wanted information, you simply called the local operator, who generally knew everything and everyone in town. Over the next six years, I spent many happy hours landscaping the property and tending to its upkeep.

Our house-warming was a topic of conversation for years after. Being woefully ignorant about alcohol, I found a recipe for artillery punch in one of Millie's cookbooks. This turned out to be a concoction of unbelievable power, loosening inhibitions and contributing to a party few of the guests would soon forget. Even the dean shed his dignity. At one point, he gallantly rushed out to help a guest who was stuck in the mud. Getting behind the car

Peter, Millie, and Carol (1945)

to push, he shouted to the driver "Gun the engine!" She did—and splattered the dean from head to foot with several inches of mud.

Millie, Peter, Carol, and Arthur (Christmas, 1949)

Building our home and living in Fayetteville was an inspiriting time for all of us. The area was a dead-end street consisting of a large circle with about thirty homes. Our neighbors were pleasant, friendly people and there were lots of children in the same age range as Carol and Peter. Our backyard was a great place to play "capture the flag." I worked out a deal with a local nursery to supply at reduced cost two or more Japanese cherry trees to anyone in the area who wished to participate. Everyone in the circle planted them. Years later, when the trees were grown,

Millie, Arthur, and dog Sparkie behind their new home with flagstone patio Fayetteville, NY (circa 1951)

people drove through the area in the springtime to admire the spectacle of a neighborhood awash in cherry blossoms.

Expanding Professional Programs

The thousands of ex-servicemen admitted to the university in these years made possible greatly expanded budgets, which, in turn, facilitated the expansion of programs, employment of staff, and a general feeling of progress and excitement throughout the university. The influx of such mature and experienced students also changed the tone of the campus and the character of instruction everywhere in the institution.

Throughout the country, large numbers of veterans with psychological struggles created a pressing demand for counselors and clinical psychologists both in and out of hospital settings. The government responded by making funds available for veterans counseling programs and subsidies for the training of counselors and clinical psychologists. Hunnicutt, Cruikshank, and I proposed the expansion of our psychoeducational clinic into a Psychological Services Center that would provide counseling services for veterans in upper New York state. The idea was accepted and our services were expanded to include a very large section devoted to psychological testing and vocational and personal counseling for returning veterans. Milton Hahn was hired to act as overall director of the center while Hunnicutt, Cruikshank, and I continued our original services. My responsibility in the new center was the Personal Counseling Service designed to serve both the campus and community. Our clinic building was expanded to three times its original size. We now had a comprehensive Psychological Services Center that incorporated five separate but cooperating services largely funded by providing service to veterans.

It is always exciting to live in an expanding economy and I thoroughly enjoyed these days of program building and innovation. In the clinical training program, we responded to the times by admitting more students, increasing our offerings, and employing more staff. Before long I found myself director of clinical training, supervising a staff of clinical psychologists and several part-time professors. Our clinical staff—Leon Gorlow, Ernst Beier, and Kenneth Peterson—were a marvelous team: young, enthusiastic, and committed to building a humanistically oriented program. From hundreds of high-quality applicants we selected only 15 graduate students a year. To meet their needs, we expanded our offerings, developed internship relationships with hospitals and clinics, and applied for program accreditation from the American Psychological Association. By 1951 we had 45 of the brightest, most committed group of doctoral students with whom it has ever been my pleasure to work enrolled in our program.

Our graduate students were discerning, mature, hard-working, sensitive, and fully engaged in the program. They were a close-knit group who enjoyed each other's company socially as well as professionally. I thoroughly enjoyed the occasional parties and outings to which I was invited. Traditional barriers between student and professor, however, exacerbated by the fact that I was also director of the program and shy about initiating relationships, made close friendships difficult. Besides, I was too busy and absorbed with the professional events in my life at the time to make room for friends. In later years, I came to regret missing this opportunity to develop more friendships among this beautiful group of people.

Less happy was my relationship with my brother, Charles, who came into our program for graduate work after finishing his bachelor's degree at Ohio State. Chuck was fiercely independent and leaned over backwards to make sure that other students found no grounds for claiming that he either wanted or accepted special favors from his brother. I felt it necessary to honor his decision and wanted to avoid any question of favoritism as well. As a consequence, we had little contact with each other outside classes or

Ted Landsman (standing at back of photo) Arthur (with suit on, sitting at table) Syracuse, NY (circa 1950)

graduate student parties. Each of us overdid it. I lost yet another priceless opportunity to get to know my brother more intimately and have regretted this ever since.

Some Lifelong Friends

I acquired three close friends in the Syracuse years who were destined to have important bearings upon my later life. One of these special friends was Ted Landsman. Ted came to our program after the war and quickly attained a leadership position among our students. He was a warm and sensitive human being and a fine counselor. I valued his skill so much that I sought him out as my counselor when I was experiencing an especially rough time. Those sessions stimulated a chain of growth that continued for many years. Ted, in later years, came to the faculty at the University of Florida after I moved there and so we had opportunities to work together once again.

A second friend was Daniel Soper. Dan had a magnificent capacity for positive criticism and was an exceptional counselor. We soon recognized his talents and appointed him supervisor of our graduate student aides in the Counseling Center. I deeply appreciated his ability to size up a situation and cut to the heart of the matter. I often dropped into his office to talk about personal and professional problems. After receiving his degree, Dan joined the faculty at the University of Florida and some years later was largely responsible for my own move to Florida.

Earl Kelley came from Michigan State to teach a class one summer. He and I found we were kindred souls on many matters in education and human relationships. Our friendship began with an invitation to a "clambake" at his home. Millie and I thought this was an invitation to dinner and spent a very hungry evening. A clambake for Earl was an invitation to drop in for a drink! Later Earl and I became deeply involved in the Association for Supervision and Curriculum Development. Our friendship lasted for twenty years and I missed him sorely when he died.

Searching For a Theory of Counseling

In the early phases of this growth at Syracuse, Carl Rogers invited me to head the Counseling Center he was establishing at the University of Chicago. I was deeply honored at the invitation and thought about it long and hard. I turned it down, however, because it seemed to me that I was embarked on a promising career in my own right. If I went to Chicago, I feared I would always be regarded as Rogers's disciple. I had great respect for Carl and I was profoundly grateful for his part in launching me on a career in counseling. I was too excited, however, by my own growth as a person and as a professional helper to live in anyone else's shadow.

As nondirective counseling was catching hold with psychologists, I began to be invited to speak on the subject. People were debating directive versus nondirective therapy and I was surprised and delighted to find that I could successfully participate in such jousts, even with highly respected psychologists. I was flattered at an invitation to address the New York Academy of Science on the subject (see Combs, 1947). Several appearances at New York State Psychological Association meetings added further to my feelings of professional competence. These signs of success encouraged me to deepen

Arthur Combs as a young married man (circa 1950)

my inquiries into theory and I began to search for the factors that made counseling work and explore their applications to teaching.

During this period I began to find myself in demand as a speaker/ consultant for schools and colleges. I joined the New York State Psychological Association and participated in its conferences and activities. I enjoyed these activities immensely. Unfortunately, they only added to the workload I was carrying and the stress started to take its toll. About 1948, I began having migraine seizures, usually on weekends. Like a typical workaholic, while I was keyed up and working hard during the week, I got along fine. But when I let down and sought to relax after a week of high-pressure activity, the attacks were severe and excruciatingly painful. Often I was unaware that attacks were commencing until someone asked if I had a cold, and I knew a siege was about to start. The pain was dreadful, made worse by bright light. Accordingly, many a Saturday or Sunday I would hole up in a darkened bedroom waiting impatiently for the pain to cease.

Important Lessons from Counseling Practice

About this time I had several experiences in counseling that made memorable and lasting impressions upon me. One day one of my students brought a disheveled-looking young man to my office. She reported that the young man was living like a hermit in a filthy shack in the woods near her home. She had struck up a conversation with him, discovered he had talents as an artist, and brought him to me in the hope that I might be able to help him. He had been diagnosed by psychiatrists as schizophrenic and had been deteriorating for several years. At that time, nondirective counseling was being severely criticized by many psychologists and psychiatrists as unsuited for serious cases of mental illness. They maintained that it might be useful for minor maladjustments but was totally inadequate in the treatment of psychosis. I was, therefore, intrigued with the possibility of testing whether nondirective counseling could, indeed, work with a person this seriously troubled. I asked if he would like to give it a try. He agreed and we began treatment.

My client had real artistic talent but otherwise had great difficulty communicating. I therefore set up a table beside my desk with an ample supply of paper, color markers, pens, and pencils and encouraged him to draw as he talked. He did this with great lack of restraint. After each session, I would note on his drawings what he had been talking about as he drew or sketched. I soon had a pile of priceless artifacts full of the dynamic symbolism characteristic of therapy in progress. As the weeks went by, he began to talk more freely and his drawings became more structured and precise. After 6 weeks, he moved into town and got a job as a sweeper in a local appliance factory. After 12 weeks, he became a furniture polisher on the production line. Several months later he was employed as assistant to a carpenter. After that, he got a job as an overhead garage-door installer. Three months later he began work as a draftsman. At this point he gave up drawing while he talked. "I don't think I need that any more," he said, and turned his chair to face me during our sessions. Months later, he was hired as an art instructor at the university. Soon after he ceased therapy. Last I heard of him, he was working in advertising to make a living but concentrating his primary energies as a serious creative artist.

I learned a great deal from this client. For one thing, I satisfied myself that client-centered therapy could, indeed, work effectively with psychotic clients. I began to depart from the rigidities of strictly nondirective procedure to experiment with a wider range of technique. I also began to seek more adequate theory to explain what I saw happening in the counseling hour and illustrated in my client's drawings. I thought about publishing a book around his priceless illustrations. Unfortunately, while I was on a sabbatical leave, the custodian in our building cleaned my office and disposed of what he thought was "just a pile of old papers!"

The second client who vitally affected my thinking was a social worker who brought her two children to our clinic. It immediately became clear from our workup that her children experienced her as deeply rejecting towards them. In our report to the mother, we tried very hard not to say so directly, but the mother was aware that we knew her secret. That night she took the children to the kitchen and turned on the gas. When one of the children toppled over, she decided she could not carry out her plan. When she told me the story next day, I was appalled at the consequences of our report and offered to take her on in therapy. Because I felt guilty and responsible for her, I assured her I would personally see her through in therapy.

Our sessions soon produced a full-blown transference, a condition in which the client becomes intensely attached to and dependent upon the therapist. This happened to my client. Wherever I went to speak, she would be sitting in the front row. In our counseling sessions she would yell, "You S.O.B.! You got me into this and you're going to get me out!" You can imagine that I was not exactly appreciated by her husband! It took two years before we were able to bring counseling to a happy conclusion. That is the longest I have ever worked with a client and the only time I have ever experienced such a transference. I am convinced that a transference of this nature is neither natural nor desirable for therapy. I believe it is a consequence of therapist error in accepting responsibility for solving the client's problems and encouraging client dependence. It is a product of the counselor's insecurity, lack of faith in the process, and acceptance of responsibility for the client's actions. A further consequence of my experience with this client was to turn my attention to exploration of the nature of the counseling relationship and personal dynamics within the therapist.

An Expanding Self

Despite my obvious success in developing our clinical program, and my increasing popularity as a speaker and consultant, I had a gnawing feeling that I was really not enough, that I was somehow living a lie, that if people ever really knew me they would find out how inadequate I really was. My personal vulture was eating at my guts. One day, when these feelings were especially poignant, I sought out Ted Landsman and asked him to take me on in therapy.

Over the next few weeks I poured out my heart in a way I had never done before, holding nothing back. Then one day, in a moment I still recall in sharpest detail, I said to Ted, "Ted, you're an awfully nice guy." Then, almost at once, I was astounded to hear myself say, "But, you know, so am I," and I burst into tears. It felt like a huge load had rolled off my back and I sobbed my heart out with wonder and relief. When I calmed down a bit, I went on to explore the up-to-then unbelievable notion that it was "all right to be me." I was overwhelmed by the experience. As we continued to talk, a sense of peace and contentment spread over me. When the hour was over, I returned to my office, canceled everything for the rest of the day and went out for a walk. Everywhere I looked I saw the world with different eyes. The grass was greener than I had ever seen it, the sky bluer, bricks were redder, buildings sharper, images clearer, sounds more crisp. I was walking in a whole new world. I was beginning to accept myself. The scales were falling from my eyes.

I continued these sessions with Ted for some time after, savoring the wonder of this revelation and exploring its meaning for every aspect of my life. I had taken another large step toward fulfillment, the likes of which I have seen duplicated in many of my own clients over the years. Before building a new self, one must begin from an acceptance of who one is. I was coming to terms with myself and opening the doors for further growth.

Recapitulation

These early days at Syracuse were times of enormous personal and professional growth. I was charging headlong into all kinds of new experiences.

Building our clinical training program by teaching all its courses, then turning them over to others was a fabulous learning experience. Experienced teachers know that teachers learn more than their students when starting new courses. Teaching, practicing, and thinking about therapy also taught me much. The saying that psychotherapy is when two people get together to help each other certainly was proven true for me. These years were heady times of beginning professional and personal growth. They saw the end of my years of preparation and were filled with numerous instances of success, marred only by the impending threat of war and the draft. Whatever I turned my hand to turned out well: the essential diet for buttressing a weak self-concept or encouraging growth and fulfillment. I was becoming aware of talents and capacities I had never dreamed of.

A Positive Self

By all odds, the most important developments happening for me in this period were the changes in my concepts of self made possible by an accumulation of professional successes culminating in my counseling experience with Ted Landsman. My workaholic character, driven by feelings of inadequacy and the sense of urgency to prove myself was a two-edged sword. On one hand, it left little time for more meaningful relationships with family and friends. On the other, it provided the hard work necessary for achievement. And achievement I had in abundance as teacher, counselor, program builder, manager, speaker and family provider.

My sense of self was also beginning to expand into areas I never anticipated. The experience at Goddard College, for example, suggested that I could be more than successful professionally; there were other aspects of life to be explored, other facets of self to try out. Having discarded some neurotic constraints learned from my family of origin and discovering it was all right to be me, I was beginning to explore what else I might be or become.

Clients in psychotherapy often seem to make progress toward greater fulfillment in four basic steps: (a) giving up wanting fulfillment in relation to one's family of origin, (b) accepting self—feeling "this is who I am and it's all right to be so for now," (c) discovering new dimensions of self, and (d) coming at last to believe, "It's good to be me." I experienced the first of these stages in counseling with Carl Rogers. At that time I gave up my unrealistic expectations related to my family of origin and my dependence upon them. That set me free to seek fulfillment elsewhere. Now, in the early Syracuse years, I was learning to accept myself, to believe that it was okay to be Art Combs. On the surface such acceptance seems like a simple achievement, but its consequences are far-reaching. For one thing, it makes possible a basic shift in life style from a defensive stance to a proactive approach to reality. Perception changes. Events are seen as less threatening, in truer perspective. Coping with life requires less effort when things are perceived more clearly and unencumbered by a compulsion to prove oneself. Even more important, acceptance opens the door to wholehearted exploration of who or what one is or would like to be.

Little by little I was developing a more positive view of self, especially in my professional life. Success experiences were adding basic support to my concepts of self as teacher, counselor, psychologist, and professor. These, in turn, were adding to the likelihood of further growth. Nothing succeeds like success, the old saying goes, and it is certainly apt for the growth of human personality. I was starting to grow in remarkable ways, but there was still a long road ahead.

Acceptance and Openness

A major contribution of a more positive self is its effect upon one's capacity for openness and acceptance. When one feels less need to defend the self, there is less interference with or contamination of the perception of reality. One is able to confront events with greater equanimity, perceive them more accurately, and so deal with them more appropriately. During this period at Syracuse, I was learning to accept myself and beginning to expand my horizons. I was making friends. My successes at innovation were leading to greater self-confidence and opening the doors to still more areas for exploration and discovery. Successes in teaching and counseling encouraged the rebel in me. I was beginning to value even more the exploration of ideas, an essential attitude for innovation.

Expanding Beliefs

The success I was having in my professional life was laying the foundation for an expanding belief system. I was becoming increasingly dissatisfied with the behavioristic thinking of traditional psychology that I had learned at Ohio State. It did not fit my experience as therapist or teacher and I began to cast about for better explanations. It seemed to me that therapy and teaching were fundamentally alike as applied aspects of learning. In my judgment, they ought, therefore, to be more similar than disparate in practice. What worked in one ought surely to apply somewhere in the other. Yet theories of learning current at that time had little to offer in either practice. I was gripped by doubts about the adequacy of the positions I had been exposed to and so became ripe for something better: a mixture aboil only waiting for a catalyst.

Feelings of Identification

The satisfactions and enthusiasm I was experiencing professionally those first years at Syracuse had a mixed effect upon my personal life. Because I was happy at work, I asked little of my home life. I was a good husband and father in all the traditionally desirable ways. I loved my wife and my children, but they were not my primary concerns. I was so busy with my professional life that I had limited time for family affairs. When a crisis occurred, I was there, but day to day I was only minimally involved in family life. Millie handled most of those everyday matters and did so very well. The family accepted me as I was, making few demands upon me. They thought, "This is the way life is," and so did I. As a consequence, there was nothing to prod us into a different way of life or cause us to reach for something better and more fulfilling. Like millions of other American families, we did not know there were other, more meaningful, ways of sharing life as a family.

References

Meštrović, I. (1948). *The sculpture of Ivan Meštrović*. Syracuse, NY: Syracuse University Press.

Donald Snygg and Arthur W. Combs at summer family picnic (circa 1948)

CHAPTER FIVE

An Intellectual Conversion

Throughout my graduate training I had a gnawing feeling that the behavioristic thinking then current in psychology was somehow inadequate. It provided all sorts of answers to problems of behavior but seemed to me to be superficial and full of inconsistencies. It left me feeling chock full of information, much of which was irrelevant to the questions I was asking or the practices in which I was engaged. The prevailing behavioral approach characteristic of most American psychology emphasized diagnosis and explanations for how clients got this way, but provided few clues for action in my work as therapist, teacher, or consultant. I was intrigued with the processes I observed in counseling and teaching but could find no satisfying relationships between these and most of the psychology I had learned. I was ready for something new.

On one of his visits to teach a class on our campus, Donald Snygg, a professor at New York State University at Oswego, handed me a reprint of an article he had written in 1941. The paper was entitled, "The Need for a Phenomenological System in Psychology," hardly an exciting title. It lay on my desk for months among things I would one day get around to reading. In 1946, I was invited to speak on nondirective counseling at the American Orthopsychiatric Convention in New York City. This was my first experience in addressing a national meeting. I prepared for it carefully and fearfully. I was beginning to think more broadly about the link between human behavior and meaning, the significance of focusing empathically on the way things appear to a given individual, as I had learned from the practice of psychotherapy. When it came time to leave for the conference, I stuck Snygg's reprint in my briefcase, thinking I might get to it on the train.

When I arrived at the conference, I was dismayed to discover that I was scheduled to share the platform with Carl Rogers, the inventor of nondirective therapy, and Peter Blos, a psychoanalyst and the most virulent critic of the movement. I was traumatized by the realization that I was caught between the national expert and the enemy. I made the talk on "Phenomenological Concepts in Nondirective Therapy" [later published as Combs,

Donald Snygg with Trapezoidal Window, circa 1960s Courtesy of Special Collections of Penfield Library, State University of New York (SUNY) at Oswego

1948]. Thankfully, I found it well accepted. I remember Carl congratulating me at the close of the meeting but I recall nothing else until I woke up sprawled across the bed in my hotel room five hours later!

Next evening, I took the train for Syracuse. Still high from the previous day's events, I removed Don's article from my briefcase and began to read. What an experience! It struck me like a bolt of lightning. Suddenly, I found clear answers to many of my unanswered questions about psychology. So much began to fall into place. I was astounded. What had seemed so confusing and inconsistent in current psychology now fell neatly into an orderly, systematic whole. I sat there playing with ideas like a child putting a puzzle together, then tearing it apart for the fun of putting it back together again. "What about learning?" I would ask and the answer would come, "Well, of course!" "What about emotion, motivation, stimuli, perception, consciousness, counseling, teaching?" The solutions came flowing to mind, fitting neatly into an integrated whole. I was thrilled beyond belief.

When the train reached Syracuse I went immediately to a phone and, despite the late hour, called Don in Oswego. "I've got to see you tomorrow," I said. "It is terribly important." We made an appointment and the next day I drove to Oswego. I walked into his office and exclaimed, "Don! This is the most amazing thing I have ever read! Do you know what you've done?" I remember his reply: "What the hell are you talking about?" With that, I began to lay out what I saw of the implications of his paper. He had, indeed, laid the groundwork for a whole new psychology. As I talked, he, too, began to catch fire. Before the day was over we had agreed to write a book together. A few days later we met again and outlined the first edition of *Individual Behavior: A New Frame of Reference for Psychology* (Snygg & Combs, 1949). It took another two years of writing, research, and editing before the project was completed but we never changed the basic outline we laid out that first afternoon. Over twenty years later I reported this origin of *Individual Behavior* in an article in *Theory Into Practice* as part of a compilation of reports by many authors on "Moments that Made a Difference" (Combs, 1969).

Product of and Stimulus for the Humanistic Movement

For more than fifty years the dominant frame of reference in American psychology was behaviorism and its off-shoots. Most psychologists typically examined behavior externally, from the point of view of an outside observer. The interaction of stimulus and response was the primary dynamic by which psychology sought to explain behavior and personality. For a young science eagerly straining for recognition as a legitimate discipline, that frame of reference had much to commend it. Stimuli and responses could be observed directly and measured with high degrees of precision. Unfortunately, however, total commitment to a behavioral approach severely limited the scope and contributions of the profession. It produced a depersonalized science narrowly restricted to externally observable events.

A discipline limited to external observation cannot deal effectively with such matters as emotion, motivation, feelings, attitudes, hopes, fears, desires, aspirations or personal experience, the very qualities that make us human. Mainstream psychology in 1946 had settled down to polishing and repolishing the external frame of reference. It was time to look for a new and more adequate theoretical base. As Donald Snygg put it, "Sometimes you can sell more papers by shouting louder on the same corner but, sometimes, you need to move to a better corner."

By 1947, increasing numbers of psychologists were becoming dissatisfied with behavioral approaches. This was particularly true of people in the helping professions, whose daily practice made it necessary to deal with problems of human experience. Little by little they were groping toward a more humanistic psychology, one more applicable to human beings as persons rather than objects, one capable of dealing with human experience. Similar stirrings toward a more humanistic approach to human problems were occurring in other disciplines as well, especially in anthropology, sociology, political science, theology, and medicine. In time, this broad search for more adequate understandings of persons became known as the humanistic movement. The phenomenological or perceptual psychology of Snygg and Combs was both a product of this early movement and a stimulus to its advance.

The Position of Individual Behavior

The perceptual-experiential psychology Snygg and I proposed was the first attempt to provide a comprehensive, systematic, and internally congruent psychology of persons from an internal perspective, that is, from the point of view of the behaver rather than an outsider. We began our proposal with two postulates or assumptions:

1. That all behavior is lawful. This is an essential postulate; any science must assume there is order in its subject matter capable of being observed or discovered.
2. That all behavior, without exception, is a direct outgrowth of the phenomenal or perceptual field of the organism at the moment of acting. That is to say, people behave in terms of their perceptions or personal meanings about themselves and the situations in which they find themselves. If we can understand these, we can hope to comprehend personality and behavior.

From these basic assumptions we proceeded in *Individual Behavior* to outline an entire psychology. Part I of the book began with a discussion of three factors determining personality and behavior familiar to behavioral psychology; namely, the effects on behavior of:

1. the person's physiology,
2. the time of exposure to events, and
3. the stimuli or environmental forces acting upon the individual.

Beyond those traditionally-accepted influences upon personality and behavior, Don and I proposed five more. These included:

4. the effect of need on motivation and behavior,
5. the nature and dynamics of perception or personal meaning,
6. the origins and function of the self-concept,
7. the influence of goals and values on perception and behavior, and
8. the effects of the existing perceptual field on behavior and experience.

Part II attempted to show how the above principles applied to the practical problems of:

- social structure and action,
- educational goals,
- teaching,
- research in a phenomenological system, and
- the nature and practice of counseling and psychotherapy.

John Snygg, Peter Combs, Arthur Combs, Fran Snygg, Charles Snygg, and Elaine (Mrs. Donald) Snygg (circa 1948)

Part III concluded with a section on the phenomenological approach as a valid method of science.

Writing Individual Behavior

Don and I worked well together. He was very much into the literature and establishing the details while I was especially intrigued with ideas and the implications of our theory for education, therapy, and social action. We would get together weekly to outline a chapter, then one of us would take it home to write it up. After that we would read the chapter together, critique it, and revise and edit it. Then one of us would take it home to rewrite once again until we were satisfied with the product. In the process, we became such fast friends that we vacationed together with our families. Some psychologists found that hard to believe. One well known clinician said to Don, "I can't believe you two wrote a book together and you are still friends."

One day, during the time we were working on the manuscript, we visited Carl Rogers at his summer home on Seneca Lake. Carl was intrigued by our ideas and borrowed the manuscript for three or four months. When he returned it, he wrote the following commendation for the dust jacket:

"An original and distinctive contribution to psychological thinking, built on a fortunate combination of insights gained from practical clinical work, and from informed theoretical analysis. It is a book which no psychologist, 'pure' or 'applied,' can afford to overlook." In addition, he graciously referred to our book twice in his presidential address to the American Psychological Association in 1947. Gardner Murphy and Gordon Allport also read the manuscript and provided favorable comments for the cover. Needless to say, Don and I were immensely pleased at the endorsement of such giants in the field.

Don and I agreed the book would be published with his name first in consideration of his original paper. To emphasize the true nature of our partnership, however, we agreed that any revision would carry my name as senior author. Working on the book was an exciting time for me. I had a keen sense of being involved in something that was much bigger and more important than either of us. It was good to feel I was on the cutting edge of my profession. I was aware, however, that any theory only supplies a framework for what we already know. Sooner or later, it will be superseded by a better, more comprehensive frame of reference. I wanted to be awake to that eventuality. I did not want to hang on to our view when the next one appeared upon the horizon or be so preoccupied with our view that I would defend it long after it was outmoded. I once expressed this fear to Don, but he only replied, "Hell, Art. It will take them thirty years to catch us. By then I won't care." I felt that was a pretty cocky attitude and I was not so sure of that conclusion then. It seems apparent today, however, that he was right.

There are three very common responses to innovations in science. One is to dismiss them with the statement, "Why, we've known that for twenty years." Another is to ignore the new idea with the comment, "It's just a fad. It will pass." Both these objections to innovation were frequently leveled at *Individual Behavior* in the early years after publication. A more insidious error is to attempt to stretch the old frame of reference to cover new concepts unreasonably. It seems to me that is what happened with psychoanalysis. Confronted with events that did not readily lend themselves to psychoanalytic terms, some theorists were led to such bizarre interpretations as fear of falling is, in reality, fear of a moral fall: the subject really wants to go to bed with his mother. I wanted most especially to avoid that kind of error.

When the manuscript was almost complete we came across the work of three authors who had published similar ideas. One of these was Gardner Murphy (1947), who had a chapter in one of his books entitled, "The Maintenance and Enhancement of the Self," a fundamental concept in our theory. A second was Earl Kelley's (1947) *Education for What Is Real*, a book with many of the same implications for education as we were proposing. Most astonishing, however, was our discovery of Prescott Lecky's (1945/1961) book, *Self Consistency*, in which we found whole paragraphs almost word for word like our own. The fact that other thinkers had arrived at conclusions similar to our own was welcome corroboration for our work. Such coincidences in scientific literature often set off strenuous efforts to discover who first discovered an idea or to determine who learned from whom. When the time is ripe, however, it's been my experience that similar ideas occur to persons in widely separate places who often have no prior knowledge of each other.

When *Individual Behavior* finally appeared in 1949, it was largely ignored by most mainstream psychologists. One reviewer was so incensed by its ideas that he referred to it as "a book by a couple of upstate New York teachers," then reprinted the review the next month! Our publisher, Harper and Row, also found difficulty in marketing *Individual Behavior* because it did not fit any established patterns or existing college courses. Despite this inauspicious start, it gradually began to find acceptance, primarily among counselors, educators, social workers, pastoral counselors, and guidance personnel. Experimental and theoretical psychologists were, almost exclusively, attached to behavioristic ways of thinking and experimenting that they equated with true science. Accordingly, most academic and research psychologists regarded our perceptual-humanistic stance as suspect. Workers in applied fields, however, found our perceptual view of persons and behavior to be helpful. It resonated with their experience and had immediate application to the practical problems with which they had to deal.

While we were working on the manuscript for *Individual Behavior*, I was much impressed with the ways in which phenomenological thinking helped to explain what was going on in the process of therapy. Accordingly, I began to apply perceptual concepts to nondirective counseling. Two of my papers, for example, deal with the implications of phenomenological thinking for nondirective therapy: "Some Dynamic Aspects of Non-directive Therapy" (Combs, 1947) and "Phenomenological Concepts in Nondirective Therapy" (Combs, 1948). A third paper, on "A Phenomenological Approach to Adjustment Theory," was prepared for the 1947 American Psychological Association meeting. On the day of my presentation, Carl Rogers, who was in the audience, congratulated me on the paper. He also said that his presidential address would deal with the same question.

Sure enough, his speech next day included a number of similar conclusions. Because he was president of APA, Carl's paper was published at once (Rogers, 1947). Mine, on the other hand, had to pass through the usual hurdles for journal acceptance: peer review, editing, and proof reading, before publication. As a consequence it did not appear until 1949. This was an occasional source of embarrassment to me in later years. Some people assumed I had drawn my ideas from Carl without acknowledging his authorship.

The Importance of Assumptions

The experience of writing *Individual Behavior* and applying it to the practical problems of teaching and counseling taught me the crucial importance of assumptions. The simple shift in mode of observation from external (behavioristic) to internal (perceptual-experiential) had enormous ramifications. It produced a whole new psychology reducing behavior to symptom and locating the "causes" of behavior in personal meaning. Likewise, the application of this different way of thinking to teaching and therapy transformed approaches to the problems of education and human growth and fulfillment. I was endlessly fascinated with the ways in which this elemental change in a basic assumption led to revolutionary concepts in theory and productive strategies for practice.

Most people in our "things-oriented" culture deal pragmatically with the problems they confront and search for solutions by manipulating the forces that seem to be involved. Only rarely do they question or consider the fundamental assumptions behind their activities. Accordingly, in the search for solutions to problems, they often go round and round on the same track. An unhappy example can be seen in the widely accepted assumption that good teaching is a matter of knowledge and methods. As a consequence, educational reform is trapped in a never-ending cycle of efforts directed at curricula, gadgets, methods, gimmicks, and administrative or legislative fiats that keep the profession polishing and repolishing the same old only partly-true assumptions. Attacking problems from the same assumptions restricts the sources of solutions, keeping one preoccupied with variations on old themes or tired answers wrapped in new packages. This error seems to me responsible for many of our failures to bring about important social reforms. For those struggling with human problems, the new perspective that perceptual thinking offers accounts for much of its appeal and success.

Working on our book and applying its premises to the practical problems I confronted taught me a way of thinking that has proven invaluable throughout my life. During my remaining years at Syracuse, I began to search for the underlying reasons that counseling practices worked. I also tried to implement perceptual theory in the practice of counseling and teaching. It seemed to me that both counseling and teaching are essentially learning processes. Accordingly, they must be grounded in some common conception of the nature of learning. Likewise, the practice of each of these applied professions ought to have relevance to the other. In later years I was to extend this hypothesis to make a case for the essential unity of all helping professions (Combs, 1963).

Experiments in Teaching

While *Individual Behavior* was still in process, I began to teach a course based upon its concepts. The course was a great success. Within a short time it required a number of sections to accommodate all who wanted to take it. The concepts of perceptual psychology are comparatively simple. The idea that people behave according to how they see themselves and the situations they are in has a feeling of reality to most people. It fits their personal experience. The same can be said for most of the basic concepts in perceptual-experiential thinking. For many students, the ideas seem like only a systematic way of thinking about things they already know. Years later, after Don's untimely death, I wrote to his children. In my letter, I tried to tell them what a great contribution their father had made to psychology. One of them replied to my letter, "We were surprised at some of the things you said about Dad's importance in psychology. When he talked about those things, we always felt it just made good sense."

I believe it was this very simplicity and "of course" quality that made it difficult for many traditional psychologists to accept perceptual psychology as a valid contribution to the profession. It smacked too much of common sense. For some psychologists, science ought to be complex and difficult. Furthermore, it is threatening to spend a large part of one's life becoming an expert in a particular field of study only to realize that there is a simpler, more efficient way of understanding the issues under consideration.

The basic principle of learning from a perceptual view is: "Any information will affect a person's behavior only in the degree to which the person has discovered its personal meaning to the self." Applying this to education, it seemed to me that teachers were experts at providing students with information but did very little to help students discover personal meaning. Accordingly, I sought ways to reduce my time as lecturer and to find ways to facilitate student discovery of meaning.

I experimented with contract grading as a means of putting responsibility for learning in the student's own hands. This involved establishing criteria for grades in terms of what the university had a right to expect for each grade, then entering into a contract with each student for the grade he or she wished to attain. These contracts generally required students to describe: (a) what their purposes were, (b) what resources they planned to utilize, (c) how they intended to go about their projects, and (d) how they proposed to demonstrate the completion of those projects. This placed control of performance in the student's hands, involved students in their own learning, and greatly reduced the authoritarian role of the instructor.

In an attempt to involve students in thinking about the *meaning* of events or ideas rather than merely knowing or describing them, I introduced weekly "Reaction Reports." In these reports students were required to write a page or more about their *reactions* to events rather than descriptions or objective analyses. The reports also opened communication between instructor and student. Many students used their reaction reports to explore deeply personal problems as well.

Applying Therapy to Teaching

Examining the basic assumptions of teaching and counseling from a perceptual-experiential perspective, I began to see both practices as ways of facilitating learning (the discovery of personal meaning). Both teaching and therapy are designed to help students or clients to discover new and better ways of perceiving self and the world. Their differences lie primarily in the data to be confronted. Education is designed to help students explore and discover additional relationships between self and the world. Accordingly, it concentrates on providing opportunities to expand one's understandings of the world through curricula, subject matter, laboratories, demonstrations, etc. Therapy, too, seeks to help its clients discover novel meaning, especially about relationships between self and others.

While they differ in areas of content, both teaching and therapy are based upon the fundamental principles of learning. If that is so, I reasoned, these fields are far more alike than different and teachers and therapists have much to learn from each other. Based upon this thinking, I broke my classes into small "discussion groups" and treated these sessions in much the same fashion as "group therapy" sessions. I also reduced the number of my lectures, converting them from formal presentations closely following a syllabus into problem-solving or question-focused sessions around topics requested by my students.

Some Unsolved Problems in Teaching

In graduate classes, I began to experiment with the application of counseling techniques to classroom practice. I reasoned that if counseling is, indeed, a helpful way of learning about self and the world, then the methods of therapy ought to have application to other kinds of learning, including that facilitated in teaching. I was surprised to find that even when I was completely nondirective, giving no information or direction whatever, good things happened for many students. In one experiment, with Ted Landsman and Ken Peterson as colleagues, we carried the nondirective philosophy to its extreme. In both traditional and nondirective fashions, we "taught" classes in "How to Study," offered for undergraduate students at risk of failing. One section was given instruction in standard study techniques, e.g., time management, reading skills, etc. The other was treated nondirectively with the instructor helping students to explore whatever they expressed a need for. Some of the students in the latter group never got around to asking for anything. They spent their time reading the paper or chatting with other students while the instructor maintained a nondirective stance. Much to our surprise, more of the students in the "nondirective" group became successful enough to stay in college than in the class taught specific skills. Though we speculated at great length on the reasons for this finding, we never arrived at a satisfying answer. The results were so intriguing, however, that we were encouraged to experiment further.

Although I have learned a great deal from these experiments, one problem continues to be incompletely resolved, i.e., how to reconcile the role of authority figure and facilitator effectively. On one hand, students want, and often require, information and direct guidance. In fulfilling these expectations, however, the instructor becomes an information provider or answer person in the eyes of students. This puts the instructor in the role of authority, encourages dependence, and gets in the way of a truly therapeutic process of facilitation. On the other hand, exclusive maintenance of the facilitator role robs students of the experience or information the instructor has the expertise to provide. So, the instructor must find ways to supply information and guidance without being cast in the role of authority, a knotty problem with which I continue to struggle.

Some Outcomes of Teaching Experiments

Even when my classes became very large, I sought ways to break them up into small groups where students could interact and discuss ideas with maximum freedom while I went about from group to group as a consultant rather than an authority. Here are some excerpts from a letter written to someone inquiring about our program in those times:

> This has been an exciting and rewarding experience. The research we have done on these methods demonstrates that our group discussion methods produce people who do not know any more than traditionally taught classes when given the same tests at the end of the semester. Months later, however,

> they remember much more and behave differently as a result of their experience. Even more important, from the point of view of human relationships, are the gains these people make, quite aside from the learning of subject matter, in greater liking for each other, improved abilities to communicate with others, to more democratic and less autocratic dealings with other people, greater respect for themselves, increased acceptance both of themselves and of other people, less prejudice, and the development of personal convictions.
>
> At the University we have applied these methods to all kinds of classes in Education, Mental Hygiene, Dynamics of Behavior, Mathematics, Sociology, School Administration and even in Engineering and Advanced Electrical Wiring. Though we have not worked out our techniques in all areas at the same levels, we get very much the same outcomes in the values mentioned above.

In the midst of these experiments, the dean of the college one day informed me that I was the subject of complaints from some on the faculty that I was undermining student confidence in more traditionally oriented professors by advocating the elimination of lecturing. Despite my best efforts to carry on these experiments quietly, enthusiastic students were creating problems by criticizing their more orthodox instructors. I was unhappy to hear of these reactions but not enough to suspend our experiments. Though universities tout themselves as centers for progress and ideas, they are, in fact, more often than not extremely conservative bureaucracies intent upon the maintenance of the status quo. Often, they do not take kindly to innovators.

I continued these experiments throughout my career, keeping the solutions that worked and dropping off those that did not. Other instructors, even outside the College of Education, became interested and tried to emulate our thinking and techniques in their classes. Now and then, we attempted to measure the outcomes of one or another of our experiments. I wish we had done so more often. One reason we were so lax in this regard is that finding ways to measure change in personal meaning is a difficult problem in its own right. We had piles of proof of the effectiveness of our efforts in the form of student testimonials, reaction reports, contract demonstrations, and personal evaluations. These were more than enough to convince us we were on the right track, but difficult to reduce to statistical summaries.

Experiences in Professional Writing

Another area in which I engaged in experimentation was in the field of professional writing. Charles Taylor, one of our clinical students, and I carried out two experiments, one on "The Effect of the Perception of Mild Degrees of Threat on Performance" (Combs & Taylor, 1952) and another on "Self Acceptance and Adjustment" (Taylor & Combs, 1952). The first was a clear demonstration that even mild feelings of threat had upsetting effects upon a person's ability to work with a simple code. The second supported the hypothesis that healthy personal adjustment is a function of positive beliefs about self. Both studies produced neat and significant results supporting perceptual concepts. I was pleased by the results but, even more, with the write-ups. So much professional writing at the time was painfully strained and obscure. Psychologists were obsessed with being "scientific" and psychological journals were dreadfully dull. In writing up these studies, I tried to be as straightforward as possible in the presentation, using the simplest possible style and organization.

Among the most quoted and reprinted articles I have done is "Intelligence from a Perceptual Point of View" (Combs, 1952), published while I was at Syracuse. Most psychologists in those days conceived of intelligence as innate, something people were born with. In my paper, I examined human capacity as a function of the richness, extent, and availability of the perceptual field. I discussed some of the factors determining such a condition. Since the perceptual field is primarily a function of experience, I concluded in this paper that intelligence is far more open to modification than had previously been assumed. Nearly ten years later J. McV. Hunt (1961) expressed a similar position in his book, *Intelligence and Experience*.

Growth as a Speaker

The security and consistency provided by a fundamentally congruent theory was also contributing to my growing success as a speaker and consultant. The internal understanding of people and behavior provided by perceptual theory had the feeling of familiarity to audiences. What I had to say often found immediate response in the experience of listeners. They could easily relate to perceptual concepts. From experience as a counselor, I had learned the importance of empathy. Counseling techniques of careful listening and attempting to understand clients from their own points of view impose a valuable discipline on speakers and consultants. This in turn keeps them in touch with audiences and attuned to feedback, and makes them more likely to respond to audience concerns with respectful attention. Who has not suffered at the hands of speakers insensitive to their captives' wish that they would quit?

Arthur W. Combs (circa 1950)

A further value of counseling experience for teaching, consulting, and speaking is the practice it provides in expressing ideas simply and straightforwardly. Interacting with hurting and sensitive clients requires that counselors speak with care and simplicity. Because one does not want to be misunderstood, counselors learn to say things with an eye to how they are being perceived by the client. I believe that much of my success as a speaker and consultant is due to the discipline I have learned as a therapist. I pride myself on being able to take a complex psychological concept and translate it into simple, straightforward language easily grasped by another person. A speech specialist once told me, "Art, you break all the rules for effective public speaking. You never tell a joke and you never spend time softening up the audience. You are totally intellectual. You plunge right into your subject like you were sure they wanted to hear it." One reason that I do not tell jokes is because I can't. I never seem to remember them and I always seem to foul up the punch line. I think the speech professor's analysis is essentially true. What this specialist missed, however, were the dynamics referred to above.

I have never been able to remember jokes or to tell them successfully. Instead, as a speaker I found it helpful to intersperse anecdotes illustrative of the points I was making. Several of these seemed to have special power to move persons in the audience and I often found someone waiting at the foot of the stage to tell me: "Thank you for that story. It was just what I needed!" Following is one story that seemed particularly to touch the members of my audiences.

To illustrate that we behave in terms of what we believe and why this is important, I often used the story of a first grade teacher in one of the suburbs of Atlanta. On the first three days of school she wore her beautiful hair in a pony tail that hung clear down to her waist. Then, on Thursday that first week, she decided to do it up in a knot on her head. This changed her appearance so much that one of the little boys in her class didn't recognize his teacher and he wandered the halls looking for the right room. The bell rang and still he had not found where he belonged. He was lost and had begun to cry when a supervisor came along and tried to comfort him. "What's the matter?" she asked.

"I can't find my teacher," the little boy replied.

"Well, what's your teacher's name?" asked the supervisor.

"I don't know," the child sobbed.

"Well, what room are you in?"

He did not know that either. He had looked in the room but decided it was the wrong place because the teacher was not his.

"Never mind," said the supervisor. "We'll find your teacher."

And the two started down the hall, hand in hand, opening one door after another without much luck. Finally, they came to the right room.

When they opened the door, the teacher was in the midst of explaining to the class their next assignment. As the door opened, she turned, saw the supervisor and the little boy in the doorway, and said, "Why Joey! It's so good to see you. We have been wondering where you were! Come in! We've missed you so!"

With that, Joey pulled loose from the supervisor's hand, and threw himself into the teacher's arms. She gave him a hug, patted him on the fanny, and he took his seat.

The supervisor who told me this story said to me, "Art, I said a prayer for that teacher. She knew what was important. She thought little boys were important." We were riding somewhere in a car at the time and we began to play a game, imagining what would have happened if the teacher had thought something else was important. Suppose she had thought that supervisors were important. In that case she might have said, "Good morning, Ms. Johnston. We've been hoping you would come and see us, haven't we boys and girls?" And Joey would have been ignored. But she hadn't; she thought little boys were important.

Or, she might have thought that the lesson was important. In that case she might have said: "Joey, for heaven's sake where have you been? Get out your book and get to work!" But she hadn't. She thought little boys were important.

Or, she might have thought that discipline was important. In that case she might have said, "Joey! You know very well when you are late you must go to the office and get a permit. Now run right on down there and do that." But she hadn't. She thought little boys were important.

I have had more heartfelt responses to this anecdote than to any other I have ever shared. At least a hundred teachers have told me at one time or another how deeply moved they were and how important the story was for them. On more than one occasion I have even heard it used by other speakers.

It is a sad thing that our approach to education has converted the teaching profession into a mechanistic function in too many places. So many teachers feel unimportant and suffer from feelings of inadequacy. As a consequence I have tried whenever possible to help them see their tasks as truly significant, even enobling. I often concluded a talk to teachers with this observation: "Ever since Freud, psychologists have known that each of us is the product of all the things that have happened to us in the course of our lives. Each of us here is a product of all our experiences to date. Do you know what that means to us teachers? Any good thing you do for a child is forever! People cannot unexperience what they have experienced, so any good thing you do for a child is forever." This simple observation, I found, has enormous impact on many teachers. Often they have sought me out after a speech and told me with tears in their eyes, "Thank you, Dr. Combs, you have no idea how much I needed to hear that."

Once I accepted an invitation to do a commencement address and picked a topic I thought the audience would like to hear about. What a disaster! No one wanted a message. They came to see Bill or Jane get a diploma. My earnest attempt to share an important idea fell flat as a pancake. I am not an entertainer. The few occasions when I have tried to be proved so embarrassing that I have given it up altogether. My way of speaking is to assume my audience wants to hear about my topic and I share straightforwardly what I think and believe about the matter in as honest a fashion as I know how. All these factors were making me a more and more effective speaker. I was beginning to be in some demand as a consultant in New York State and beyond.

Speaking is a creative, therapeutic experience for me. Over the years I have learned to give of myself in public speaking in the same fashion in which I approach my counseling practice. I learned to share myself and my thinking—warts and all—with maximum authenticity. People often write to me saying such things as, "You seemed so relaxed," or "I thought you were speaking right to me." At the same time, speaking, like counseling, is an intense and exhausting experience for me. So much so that I am sometimes embarrassed after a talk when someone asks me for an address or an autograph. Often, I am so shaky that I cannot write legibly. After the high of a speech into which I have thrown myself without reservation comes a period of letdown. I am sure my hosts must sometimes be puzzled to find that on the way to the airport, their speaker, who was so communicative on stage, is hard to engage in lively conversation.

Applications to Industry and the Military

During these halcyon days at Syracuse, I sought every opportunity to try out the implications of perceptual psychology in every arena to which I had access. I welcomed the chance to try its applications to industry when it came my way. One of these occasions involved setting up a program in human relationships for employees being prepared for management positions at a nearby General Electric plant. During this effort, the plant experienced a strike that, after some weeks, began to turn nasty. As time passed, tempers grew shorter and shorter, accompanied by the development of threat and counterthreat and the breakdown of communication.

I had opportunity to observe the picket lines and to talk with the workers in the morning and meet with management in the afternoon. It was fascinating to perceive firsthand how things looked from the point of view of each side, not only at the plant but in the community as well. For example, a few weeks before the strike began, the union called a meeting at a local theater. Only a handful of workers showed up and they voted to give their negotiators the right to call a strike. This action brought indignant cries from the community and editorials in the local papers condemning the authorization of a strike before negotiations even started. They also decried the way "the workers were being led around by the nose" and hinted at nefarious communist plots. From the workers' viewpoint, giving their negotiators the right to strike was a foregone conclusion. You don't send your soldiers into battle without the very best weapons you can supply.

I also had an opportunity to apply perceptual thinking in a military setting. The Air Force was discovering that the proliferation of technical weaponry made it necessary to use many more non-commissioned officers in highly responsible roles. Accordingly, a nearby air base asked my assistance in designing a program of human relations training for non-commissioned officers. I suggested a perceptual-experiential program to be taught by a nucleus of non-commissioned trainees, with my help as consultant. The base commander agreed and I began with a group of "non-coms" to design a course, write a training manual (Mroz, Dahlquist, DeLany, DiIanni, Gardner, Overstreet, & Combs, 1954), and show the team how to teach it. The course was then introduced into the base training program. It was made self-perpetuating by selecting two or three promising teachers from each class to teach the next. The program continued to operate successfully for several years.

The Seduction of Consulting

One of the ways in which the Veterans Administration was encouraging the training of clinical psychologists after the war was to open their hospitals as internship facilities for clinicians in training. As our clinical program grew, we had increasing numbers of students doing internships in the half dozen hospitals and domiciliaries in upper New York State. To supervise these students and maintain relationships with the hospitals, I began making regular visits to the various installations—for a substantial honorarium and expenses each time. Often these trips involved little more than paying respects to the director of the institution and chatting with our students about their experiences. Without being aware of it, my standard of living was insidiously becoming dependent upon this extra income.

After several years, I met one of my fellow students from Ohio State days at an American Psychological Association convention. We took the afternoon off for some sightseeing and reminiscing. While at Ohio State, I had regarded my friend as one of the most brilliant thinkers among Rogers's students. He was now a department head at one of our larger universities. In the course of sightseeing we stopped on top of a mountain, enthralled with the view. Suddenly, my friend poured out his frustration. "Art," he said, "I feel like I have sold out. I'm not writing or counseling. I'm making so much money as a consultant to the Veterans Administration and have raised my standard of living so high that I can't afford to stop." As I listened to his anguish, I was horrified at his dilemma and began to examine whether I, too, was being seduced by easy money. I could see the treacherous effects of raising the family standard of living to a height where maintaining it became important in its own right and I resolved to give up consulting at the hospitals. The decision was painful financially, but I have never forgotten how easy it is to surrender one's integrity by valuing things above principles. Though I have enjoyed a comfortable life style in the years since, I have never permitted possessions to outweigh values and humanity in the important decisions of living.

Recapitulation

*View of Self**

A Comprehensive Belief System

By all odds, the most important event of my early years at Syracuse was the formulation with Donald Snygg of perceptual-experiential psychology. Writing *Individual Behavior* opened a whole new world for me. It would be hard to overestimate the effect of this experience upon my personal and professional self. Professionally, it gave order and sequence to my thinking, theoretical bases for research, and guidelines for the practice of teaching, counseling, and administering. It laid the foundations for a comprehensive, systematic, and internally consistent belief system. It gave me a feeling of significance and a solid base from which to tackle all kinds of questions. That, in turn, made possible a lifetime of writing, research, and teaching. Possession of a trustworthy theory provides a person with vast reserves of strength and security. I did not know this in the early days at Syracuse, but over the years since it has become more and more apparent to me. As a psychologist, it has given me a theoretical base capable of synthesizing both behavioristic and humanistic thinking in a single frame of reference. This makes it possible to avoid the confrontational stance often adopted by adherents of these two schools of thought and to see both positions as complementary within a broader, more encompassing perspective.

For my personal life, it provided a secure frame of reference for examining the world and for approaching life's problems. Over the years it has become more and more a part of me, affecting every aspect of my personality and relationships. The basic psychology that Don and I introduced expanded into a personal belief system that gave unity and direction to my life both personally and professionally. I found that what I believed, psychologically, made sense when put to work in professional practice and provided trustworthy guidelines for living my personal life as well. Perceptual-experiential views were also consistent with my theological beliefs and with my beliefs about democracy and government. To find one's professional thinking congruent with the personal facets of one's life is an endlessly comforting and fulfilling experience.

* Editor's note: Missing as a separate section, but addressed in following sections.

Openness to Experience

A comprehensive, systematic theory makes another tremendous contribution. It opens vast new areas to exploration. When you begin to look at matters from a new frame of reference, all sorts of previously unexamined facets and relationships become clear. It becomes possible to question old assumptions and to attack problems from emergent and more fertile hypotheses. Innovation becomes easy and exciting. Perceptual-experiential thinking, for example, made possible innovations in teaching, counseling, administering, and speaking as well as applications to industry and the military. When one is among the first in one's field to look at events through a fresh frame of reference, solutions to many problems often seem strikingly simple and clear. Conveyed to persons still thinking in traditional terms, this looks like a remarkable capacity to penetrate to the heart of matters and suggest workable solutions. This is what was happening to me as I dove deeper and deeper into the implications of perceptual thinking. Perceptual-experiential theory made it possible to look at old problems with new glasses, to find answers that readily fit the personal experience of students, clients, and audiences. The approbation that process generated provided numerous experiences of success, resulting, in turn, in an increasingly stable and positive self-concept.

Growing personal security and openness also make possible increased tolerance of ambiguity. Working with theory and assumptions makes one keenly aware of the temporary nature of events, while an empathic attitude provides constant proof of the existence of many realities. As a consequence, openness is increased and the barriers to innovation and growth are pierced. Very early in my development I became a rebel. Now, acceptance of self and openness to experience were channeling those energies into constructive and innovative directions.

The internal strength and direction of a comprehensive, systematic, and congruent theory makes it possible to explore hitherto unexamined territory with joy and abandon. Events encountered are seen as challenges rather than threats, as areas for exploration rather than frightening jungles. Just so, my emergent professional growth and security opened the opportunity to apply perceptual thinking in all sorts of areas. I became, at once, more open to life experiences and more capable of dealing with them.

Feelings of Identification

The publication of *Individual Behavior* also made an immense contribution to my search for personal fulfillment. The feeling of being involved in something much bigger than myself contributed to a spiritual sense of oneness with the world. On a more immediate plane, these feelings of identification were enhanced by the close friendship I had with Don Snygg during our close collaboration over a two-year period. We shared everything so closely that we began to write and think alike. Often, one of us would comment about something we were reading together from the manuscript, "Hey! That's good stuff!" only to have the other reply, "It should be. You wrote it!" Don was a beautiful human being whom I loved very much. At that stage in my psychological growth, however, you can be assured I never told him so. I believed then, as we males are indoctrinated from birth in our society, that men do not express such feelings for men. Besides, with my entrenched fear of rejection, such expressions would have been much too risky.

While the stability of my family life was slowly deteriorating during this period, tentatively I was reaching out to others. I was making friends among students and colleagues, some of whom were destined to remain friends for life. I was also beginning to receive strong indications from students, clients, and others that I had made a difference in their lives. I opened a new file in my cabinet, entitled "Heart-Warmers," in which to accumulate notes and letters that deeply moved me. [See section below for some examples.] These are among the fringe benefits of teaching and counseling, indications that one has not lived in vain. It is a profoundly fulfilling experience to know that one has touched another human being from heart to heart in ways that truly matter.

Heart-Warmers*

Excerpts from cards, letters, and notes that Art preserved in a file bearing this title.

DECEMBER, 1944

My admiration for your own achievement is great. Lately I have read a piece from Goethe's Wilhelm Meister's Apprenticeship called The Indenture which perfectly expresses my impression of you and your work. (No known address.)

* Editor's note: Many years have gone by since most of the statements in this section have been written. As a consequence, it seemed futile to attempt to locate or identify those who had authored given pieces in order to secure their permission for publication of what they wrote to Art. Yet I thought this material would be of interest to many readers. For this reason, I have chosen to present all excerpted material anonymously, only indicating, where the information was available to me, the part of the country or the world from which each piece originated.

JANUARY, 1945

If you don't mind a word of praise from an ex-student, I'd like to tell you again how much I enjoyed working with you. Your courses are the kind which "stick" long after most other lecture notes have been forgotten. (No known address.)

NOVEMBER, 1945

I really can not express in words how grateful I am to you for all that you have done for me—You helped make life a great deal brighter for me and I only hope that in the future I can in some way repay you for everything. I sincerely hope that you can help more unstable and bewildered students in Syracuse, so that they may enjoy the real fruits of life. . . . Regards and once again, thanks from the bottom of my heart. (somewhere in "sunny" California)

JANUARY, 1952, *from a student writing about her experience of Ed. Psych. 151.(Individual Behavior)*

What a wholly new thing it is to find warmth and love instructing a class . . . to find a heart instead of merely a mind-larynx . . . to see eyes and lips that transcend word power; that silently say: "Here is part of me—will you take it and may I have some of you?" I am excited. . . . I feel my heart pounding. . . . my body cannot withhold all that is there. . . . I weep just a little. . . . I thank you for presenting the sole course of my college studies that I shall remember long after graduation!

JULY, 1953

I want to thank you personally for the very fine job which you did in my class last Monday afternoon. I can honestly say I know of no other Psychologist who is able to make teachers able to feel that psychology is not some mythical science which they can never hope to know. All the people in the class were so enthusiastic about the practical suggestions you gave them and the way that you made us all feel that we could all help children by applying simple principles and techniques. (Syracuse, NY)

NOVEMBER, 1953

I want to thank you on behalf of all of us who listened, learned and were inspired by you last night. . . . As you talked—and as your thoughts and spirit have been percolating in me I know now I've . . . heard one of the most Christian talks I've ever heard. Why? Because the dignity and worth of every individual was assumed by you—and you implemented (or showed how *we* could implement) that belief—which I conceive of as the basic contribution of Christ.

Thank you. You have performed for Children's Court and the community a wonderful service. (Syracuse, NY)

JANUARY, 1954

It was indeed a pleasure to listen to your talk on client-centered therapy broadcast over Station WGBH Boston, on December 21, 1953. I had read another article on this subject in the *Scientific American* and I had become deeply interested not only professionally but also as an approach to living.

The feeling that humanity is able to move spiritually forward and is able to meet its hardships is most reassuring. (Walpole, MA)

UNDATED, FROM A STUDENT

I had an instructor for 140-141 whom I shall never forget. The man possesses such a quiet wisdom and such an inner calm as to be almost unbelievable. He is as understanding, as tolerant, as open minded as you could want anyone to be. Some of the statements that he has made in class I shall carry with me in all my dealings not only with students, but with the world around me. He has given me a fuller understanding of people—shall I say he gave me a good start. (No known address.)

UNDATED REACTION REPORT, *from a student (EDF 641)*

The first few meetings you spoke about "unearned" and "earned" authority. As I look back over the semester, I have come more and more to appreciate just what these words mean. When I enrolled in your class, I had been told, "You will like this man, Combs—everyone should have the opportunity to have a class from him."

The first few meetings when you explained your method of procedure, I could hardly believe anyone could have so much faith in and understanding of people—and never deviate from this behavior. In the many class meetings I have had with you—I have never seen you fail in either of these—and the opportunity to display other kinds of behavior has surely presented itself several times throughout the semester.

The class meeting that is—and I believe will always be—the most vivid to me was the night you explained what client-centered therapy meant to you—and the [effect] you believed understanding others' perceptions will come to have in the world at large. I am not an ardent attendant at any church—however, I have never seen "religion in day-to-day living" as clearly as I perceived it this night you were explaining what I believe must be your philosophy of life. I saw very clearly how completely you accept yourself and others as I had never before felt so deeply. . . . as I perceive it, you have "earned" authority. I will always consider having known you as one of life's rare privileges.

(No known address.)

References

Hunt, J. McV. (1961). *Intelligence and experience*. New York: Ronald.
Kelley, E. (1947). *Education for what is real*. New York: Harper & Row.

Lecky P. (1961). *Self-consistency. A theory of personality.* (F. C. Thorne, Ed.). Hamden, CT: Shoe String. (Original work published 1945)

Murphy, G. (1947). *Personality: A biosocial approach to origin and structure.* New York: Harper.

Rogers, C. R. (1947). Some observations on the organization of personality. *American Psychologist, 2*(9), 358-368.

Snygg, D. (1941). The need for a phenomenological system of psychology. *Psychological Review, 48*(5), 404-424.

Arthur W. Combs in Florida (circa 1955)

CHAPTER SIX

Changing Goals and Directions

During the latter years of my time at Syracuse a series of events occurred that were destined to change the course of my personal life and my professional career as well. Personally, I began to discover facets of myself I had never dreamed existed. Professionally, I began to drift from psychology to education. Both shifts in direction were stimulated by traumatic events that demanded reexamination of prevailing goals and the search for new roads to fulfillment.

How Can This Be?

My experience at Goddard College resulted in the discovery that there were other possibilities for a self more extensive than I had imagined. That realization was now producing vague feelings of dissatisfaction with my current life and an urge to explore my personal potential more broadly. Though it shocked me to think it during these years, I was beginning to feel there was something missing from my marriage. Millie and I performed our expected roles as a married couple. We were able to communicate feelings, however only so long as they were positive. We could express our love for each other fairly openly. Feelings of anger, stress, or personal longings were quite another matter. Millie was markedly dependent upon me, acquiescing in almost anything I asked. She asked very little of me. Her troubles were borne stoically, rarely shared. (Or, perhaps I was too blind to perceive them).

For my part, I could not freely express my longings for love or for greater sexual involvement for fear they might be rejected. Thus, I did not express whatever anger, fear, or frustration I felt from time to time. I was still too firmly in the grip of my childhood lessons that anger is something you do not express. Though I sometimes found myself annoyed or angry at Millie, such feelings were carefully suppressed. Nor could I ask for whatever it was I wanted or needed. Instead, I set aside or suppressed my personal yearnings, tried harder to serve the needs of those about me, and focused attention on dealing with the reality I encountered.

Just before leaving for the 1948 APA meetings, something happened between Millie and me which left me feeling particularly angry and frustrated. I do not remember what brought it on and I am sure Millie was unaware of my mood. Whatever the case, I left for the convention seething. At the conference, I sought out a woman I had known at Ohio State and ended the evening in bed with her. Afterward, I was consumed with guilt and remorse. What I had done shocked me into examining my assumptions about myself and my marriage. I was forced to confront the fact that I was not so happily married as I supposed, that I had frustrated longings like millions of men before me. I was also capable of immorality, infidelity, and excesses of anger. I remember living through the convention in a kind of daze and making a shambles of an address I had to give. In the weeks following, I continued to agonize over the unpleasant thoughts I had to face up to. I finally resolved to redouble my efforts to live up to the standards of marital existence I had grown up with. Counseling with Ted Landsman helped me to begin accepting myself as I was. I was discovering, now, in my late thirties, that there were aspects of myself I had never been aware of before.

Feelings of Identification

During this period, I had the first of a number of unforgettable feelings of wordless identification with others that I have come to cherish and wonder about during my lifetime. As I mentioned in Chapter 4, behind the house in which the university temporarily located us was the studio of Ivan Meštrović, a renowned Croatian sculptor the university had invited to campus as a resident artist. One snowy night at Christmas time, Millie and I were returning to Syracuse by train and Meštrović and his wife were in our car. Students on the train were rowdy and rudely jostled the little man in a skull cap as he made his way through the aisle.

I was deeply distressed at their treatment of him. When the train reached Syracuse we offered the Meštrović s a lift in our car. The two women sat on the back seat chatting about children and grandchildren. Though Meštrović said not a word as we drove through the softly falling snow, I had a powerful feeling of communication with him. When we reached his home, he said, "Thank you" and I replied, "I am deeply honored, Maestro." With that, he patted my knee and left the car, leaving me with a feeling of having been communicated with on the deepest of levels—a beautiful experience I have never forgotten.

A second episode of similar wordless communication occurred with a neighbor in Fayetteville. Because Sandy and George had children the ages of ours, our two families became fairly well acquainted. Sandy had been in and out of hospitals several times with a diagnosis of schizophrenia. She had been getting along fairly well for several years when, suddenly, she had another relapse and took to her bed. Her family was distraught and unable to rouse her out of her lethargy and coma-like state. I felt very badly that she was ill. About a week after the onset, I asked her husband if I might speak to her. He agreed and I went upstairs to her bedroom where she lay with eyes closed, responding to no one. I said to her, "Sandy, it's Art. I just want you to know that I care." No response. So I sat on the edge of the bed and held her hand for perhaps twenty minutes.

As I was leaving, I met her husband at the foot of the stairs and was surprised to hear myself saying, "Sandy will be getting up this afternoon, George!" I had a feeling of absolute certainty when I said it but, simultaneously, a feeling of wonder, since there had been no verbal communication between Sandy and me. As I had sat holding Sandy's hand, I had felt a warm feeling of identification with her. Certainly nothing concrete in our interaction warranted such a prediction. Nevertheless, Sandy did get up that afternoon and to this day I am still puzzled at how I knew that she would.

Changing Interests

By 1951, our clinical program had grown as far as I could carry it. We had 45 graduate students at various stages of progress toward the doctorate and a faculty of five professors teaching clinically related courses. We were only accepting 15 students each year from several hundred applicants, so the quality of our students was extremely high. Employers readily employed our graduates, and the program was in process of being accredited by the American Psychological Association. Despite this success, however, I was beginning to feel a sense of disenchantment with clinical psychology.

Most programs and practitioners seemed hopelessly embedded in traditional behavioristic thinking and practice. Clinicians were trained to be researchers first and practitioners after that. My experiences in therapy and perceptual-experiential thinking were causing me to raise serious questions about the very assumptions on which much of clinical psychology at that time was based. It seemed to me that the current preoccupation with statistics, research, diagnosis, and abnormal psychology and exclusive immersion in behavioristic thinking was thwarting the growth of an exciting new profession. I felt increasingly hemmed in.

At the same time, my experiments with therapy, education, industry, administration, and the military were opening my eyes to vast new fields for psychological study and application. I began to see clinical psychology as essentially rehabilitative, whereas the far greater social need lay in prevention, helping people to avoid getting sick. In addition, I was becoming more intrigued with the concept of self-actualization that Don and I had proposed in *Individual Behavior* and its implications for health and fulfillment.

The more I thought about transcending rehabilitation and the status quo, the more I was drawn to education. Our public schools are the only place in our society where we have an opportunity to make important inroads upon the next generation. Parents are important, but they are not organized. The church does not reach everyone and its influence is far less significant than formerly. The only agency through which we can reach the next generation in any organized fashion is through our public schools, especially through teachers. Few psychologists showed much interest in perceptual-experiential thinking in those years, but counselors and educators responded eagerly to its concepts. Accordingly, I began spending more and more time with teachers, supervisors, and administrators while relying on the other members of our clinical faculty to carry the clinical psychology program.

Organizing Psychologists

In 1949, I was elected president of the New York State Psychological Association (NYSPA) and began the first of many trips to New York City for meetings associated with that office. I enjoyed chairing these meetings. My counseling skills, perceptual approach to questions, careful listening, and penetration to basic assumptions were highly effective in group deliberations and decision-making. At this time, psychologists in private practice were beginning to seek legislation to license the profession. Many of our discussions at NYSPA meetings revolved around that problem. When I completed my term as president, I was approached by a steering committee with the request that I head an organization representing all the psychologists in the state to write a

Arthur W. Combs (circa 1950)

licensing bill and lobby it through the legislature. After much thought and some trepidation, I agreed to the request. It seemed to me that here was a challenging opportunity to find out whether the ways of dealing with human problems that I was learning from perceptual theory, the practice of therapy, and the application of such thinking to educational problems would work in such a hard-headed practical situation. I decided to pursue the test. We began the campaign by establishing the Joint Council of New York State Psychologists with me as its chairman.

I requested a sabbatical leave from the university and set about the task. The problem was a huge one. There were 23 separate and sometimes antagonistic psychological groups in the state. Before getting started on legislation, it was necessary to get these diverse interests together in an umbrella organization with authority to speak for all psychologists in the state. After that, I focused on composing a bill satisfactory to all these varied factions, introducing it to the legislature, and getting it passed. The Joint Council began by inviting representatives from each of the psychological organizations in the state to join the project. Getting everyone aboard required travel throughout the state and countless hours of consultation. Simultaneously, I chaired the task force, which began the process of trying to write a bill everyone could live with.

Writing a satisfactory bill proved a monumental task. The psychologists of the state were widely disparate. There were academic and research psychologists in the colleges, psychoanalysts of a dozen descriptions, various gurus and their disciples, clinicians, child psychologists, industrial psychologists, and more. Some were deeply anxious to secure legal recognition; some couldn't care less. There were even some who opposed the idea entirely. In addition, we had to cope with opposition of the medical profession and its enormous political clout. Many in that profession felt psychologists in private practice were invading the sacrosanct domain of medical practice.

As part of the effort to write this bill, we invited groups of psychologists to a series of work sessions to debate the proposal. One of these was with a group of psychoanalysts held at the Harriman Estate in the Adirondacks. This lovely home was now being used for conferences by many agencies in the state and nation. For a time, Eisenhower had used it as a retreat. On arrival there, I found we had been assigned to the Eisenhower suite, a beautiful set of rooms complete with a library. Louis Long and I joked about which of us would be sleeping in Mamie's bed. After the day's discussion, fifteen or more psychoanalysts gathered around the conference table in the library of our suite for drinks and conversation. The conversation soon turned from licensing to the sharing of shocking, amusing, or titillating experiences these psychoanalysts had had over the years with some of their patients. I found it amusing when one of these psychoanalysts made a Freudian slip as he was holding forth. His reaction was astounding to me. "Oh, my God," he cried. "Another two years of analysis!" Then, overwhelmed, he covered his head with his arms and collapsed on the table!

It soon became clear that licensing for helping professions like psychology or counseling is quite different from licensure in other professions. Licensing in medicine, for example, can be tied to a concrete, clearly definable act or procedure that can then be made the legal prerogative of the medical profession. Psychology and counseling have no such clearly defined functions. Psychologists carry on their profession by talking, a procedure in daily use by everyone, even children. The only alternative to defining the profession legally is to restrict the title "psychologist" to persons with prescribed levels of training, supervision, and experience. Such certification grants the privilege of a title but does not bar persons from practice who otherwise engage in counseling or therapy so long as they do not call themselves psychologists. This distinction between licensure and certification was very difficult for many psychologists to understand and accept. It still is in many places. For months, I chaired meeting after meeting, producing draft after draft before we finally settled upon a certification bill.

I become a lobbyist. The next step was to find a legislative sponsor to introduce the bill, organize a public information effort, raise money to pay for our dissemination of information, and lobby the bill to passage. We found a sympathetic sponsor in the House and I began to work closely with the people in his office. Some of our New York City colleagues who worked on Madison Avenue took on the public information task. Several psychologists in Madison Avenue advertising firms took charge of the financial functions involved. Others assumed responsibility for letter-writing chores in their local organizations. I shifted energies full-time to the lobbying effort. Each day I was joined in Albany by volunteers from the various psychological organizations in the state to help make contacts in the legislature.

The first week at the legislature, I was asked by a downstate representative to come see him in his home district. When I found my way to his "office" in the back room of a Manhattan bar, this sleazy character assured me our bill would never pass without his help—available for a sizable contribution to a dummy organization. I was shocked and repulsed by his proposal. In no position to make an enemy, however, I swallowed my disgust and said I would talk it over with our Joint Council. I left the bar feeling unclean. My ideas about democratic government hit a low ebb.

Two weeks later, a legislator took me in hand to explain that I was making a major mistake. "Legislators are not leaders, Art," he said. "They are *representatives* of the people. They are mostly average Joes with a few brilliant ones and a few stinkers among the lot—just like the rest of the population. A legislature made up of leaders would be a disaster. They would keep us all in turmoil!" Once I understood these assertions, I began to have an enormous respect for our representatives. Most are hard-working, conscientious human beings, honestly trying to represent their constituents. The real genius of the democratic system is that these mostly average folks manage, year after year, to do an extraordinarily good, albeit conservative, job. Witness the fact that very few laws need to be rescinded.

I later wrote a report of what I learned about legislatures entitled, "A Lobbyist's Report," published in the last issue of *Progressive Education* (Combs, 1957). In it, I pointed out that we do a great disservice to young people by failing to help them understand the true character of their elected officials. Teaching young people that legislators are leaders can only result in disillusion with government and failure to grasp the true meaning of democracy. The common opinion that politics is a dirty, untrustworthy business is a threat to our way of life. The article also dealt with common misconceptions about party politics, the lobbyist's role, and the ways in which legislators serve their constituents.

While the legislature was in session, I was joined throughout the week by psychologists coming to help lobby our licensing bill. Hotel reservations were limited in Albany, so I frequently shared my room with another male psychologist. One night I was awakened as a widely known psychologist (my then roommate) climbed into bed with me. Startled awake, I exclaimed, "Hey! What's going on here!?"

"Oh," he replied, "I thought you were my wife!" A likely story!

"Well, believe me, I'm not!" I remonstrated. This was a lobbying hazard not mentioned in the instruction books.

As the final days of the legislative session wound down, my lobbying efforts redoubled. My anxiety was not helped when, one day, the lobbyist for the medical profession assured me our bill did not have a chance with the power of the medical profession firmly arrayed against it. Nor did it help to compare our piddling budget with those of a dozen other organizations having millions at their disposal. On the final day of the session, I rallied our troops. Our sponsor suggested I rush to the entrance hall when our bill was called in case he needed me. In the meantime, I took a seat in the balcony to watch the proceedings. After a long wait, I heard our bill called and raced downstairs to be available. As I entered the area, I heard the clerk call:

"Albro, Mailler, Steingut, Younglove: Ayes a hundred and forty, no's none, bill's passed" and I collapsed on a handy couch. The bill had passed without objection! That night I took our sponsor and his staff to dinner in celebration. When I turned in the bill to our Madison Avenue treasurer with an apology for its size, he called me to say, "My God, Art. Did you really entertain them? I spend that much to take someone to lunch!"

Getting Governor Dewey's signature on the bill was the next step. Unfortunately, the Kefauver Committee in Washington was investigating a series of government scandals and was making noises about subpoenaing the governor to testify. Dewey became conveniently ill. No one could reach him for days, except for his personal physician. We tried desperately to contact him, to no avail. Eventually we learned the governor had vetoed our bill.

I returned to Syracuse bowed but unbroken. Though disappointed at the outcome, I was proud of the success of the Joint Council effort. Personally, I came away affirmed by the proof, provided by this experience, that the things I believed and advocated really worked in the practical world. After I left the state, a second effort was mounted, resulting in passage of one of the first bills in the nation to recognize psychology as a profession. Here is how I heard about it from Florence Halpern, one of my co-workers on the Joint Council:

"This is a sentimental gesture, but I would like to be one of the first to tell you that on Wednesday, April 28th the Governor signed the bill certifying psychologists in New York State. All this winter. . . , I kept thinking of the terrific spadework you had done back in 1951. I am sure that if it had not been for your wisdom and patience in welding together the many conflicting interests of New York State psychologists as well as introducing us so favorably to the powers in Albany, we would not be celebrating today" [Letter dated April 23, 1956].

The Demise of Our Clinical Program

Following the legislative battle in the fall of 1951, I plunged again into my accustomed life style: teaching, supervising our program, consulting, and writing, totally oblivious to any warning signs that things might change. Returning home after Christmas in Ithaca, I found a message to see Harry Ganders, Dean of the College of Education, "before December thirty-first." Concerned about the urgency of his message, I went to see Dean Ganders on the twenty-ninth. Without beating around the bush, he informed me that the university was forced to make drastic cuts in faculty and that he had just mailed notification to three of my clinical staff that they were not to be rehired.

I was staggered. I could not believe what I was hearing. I presented every argument I could think of, to no avail. I was especially appalled at what to do about our commitment to the 45 graduate students who would be left high and dry by this action. When I asked about them, the dean said, "Art, you don't have that many students." Again, I was astounded. I reminded him that we did, indeed, have that many. I had given him the list only a week before. All my arguments and pleas got nowhere and I left his office in a daze, wondering how I could face our staff and students, who would be returning from the holidays with no hint of the tragedy they were about to experience.

In the face of declining numbers of veterans, the university found itself confronted with rapidly dropping enrollments and an overextended faculty. To meet this emergency, the university was instituting drastic cuts across the board. University regulations required that when staff members were to be released, they had to be notified by January first of the year in which they were being cut, hence Ganders's call before New Year's Eve. All three of the clinical staff being discharged were not yet on tenure. They were also vulnerable for other reasons. In the dean's eyes, the clinical program was an appendage of the primary thrust of the College of Education, the training of professional educators. Cutting the clinical program made it possible to save more of the teacher education faculty. These explanations did little to assuage my pain in the process I now embarked upon.

As students and faculty returned to the campus I had to inform them of the dreadful news. These were some of the most agonizing days I have ever known. At first there was panic, rage, and despair. Then, gradually, we began to confront the reality of our circumstances and search for solutions. That was not easy. Clinical programs everywhere had long waiting lists so the possibilities of transfers for our students were slim. Here is what I wrote to several friends at the time:

> You may be interested in knowing something of what has transpired with me these last few months. The University has been for some time in serious financial difficulties and these have recently become much worse. The place is as panic-struck an institution as I have ever seen. When I returned from my Xmas vacation I was called in by the administration and informed that my three staff members had been notified of their dismissal as of June 1 and that my program of graduate training was also being discontinued as of that date. What a shock! Nine years of work down the drain overnight!

For the past several weeks I have done nothing but tear around from place to place trying to pick up the pieces and repair the damage. All this with my staff and our 45 graduate students looking to me as Moses to lead them out of the wilderness. Never having had a self-concept as a prophet, this has been a great strain. Little by little, though, we are getting things under control. I have been searching for new places for my staff. They came here largely to work in this particular program in spite of fine offers elsewhere and I have become very fond of them over the past few years we have worked together. As a result I am deeply concerned to find them good jobs elsewhere. Anything you can do to spread the word that there are some good experienced clinicians on the loose at Syracuse will be deeply appreciated.

The most serious aspect of this problem is the situation of our graduate students. I am canceling my trip to Colorado this summer to stay here and see what we can do to get them as far along in the program as we possibly can. Those who are well along we can probably squeeze through to their degrees. Those who are not so far along are another problem. We are all appalled at the callous disregard of human values in the way this shut down was accomplished and hope that, somehow, the students not so far along may be absorbed into other programs. Many are very fine people who have made great personal sacrifices and we just must find a way of helping them make this adjustment. Can you help? I would deeply appreciate any information or assistance you can offer in sounding out other programs as to their willingness to accept a student or two.

The administration has not fired me. In fact, they are raising my salary and want me to continue expanding my work in the field of human relations. I do not see, however, how I can continue to work in this atmosphere for any length of time. Right now, however, the major problem is in finding places for my staff and students. We have had one wild time around here these past few weeks. I am exhausted from sheer listening and running about trying to pick up the remains. Little by little, though, things are settling and now we have to prepare for the great exodus.

From Frying Pan to the Fire

Some students simply gave up. A few were able to gain admission to other programs. Others decided to stay and argue with the administration. Indignant parents came to the campus. The student newspaper got involved. Members of the faculty protested and numerous expressions of shock and dismay began to confront the administration. After some weeks, in an effort to find some solution to the problem, the chancellor agreed to keep one of our staff, Ernst Beier, for an additional year while we worked to get our students through. He also decided that our program did not belong in the College of Education and, over my strenuous objections, moved the whole program into the Psychology Department in the College of Arts and Science.

In those days, Syracuse had two departments of psychology; one in Education and one in Arts and Science. The Psychology Department in liberal arts was responsible for general and theoretical psychology and research. The Educational Psychology department was housed in the College of Education and specialized in educational and applied psychology, developmental studies, counseling, and our clinical program. The traditional psychologists in the Psychology Department were antagonistic to the humanistic orientation of our clinical program. They believed that counseling and psychotherapy were unfortunate diversions from the "pure science" they advocated. They were particularly critical of me and of perceptual-experiential thinking.

Transferring the clinical program from education to the Psychology Department thus took us "out of the frying pan into the fire." Students now had to prepare to meet the requirements of a very different faculty, many of whom were antagonistic to the clinical program or strict behaviorists unsympathetic to the humanistic assumptions of clinical practice. I found this abhorrent. I decided to stay only long enough to see as many of our students through to their degrees as possible. As director of the program, however, I caught the full force of both overt and covert antagonism.

In the College of Education we were a self-contained enclave. Many on that faculty were intrigued by perceptual thinking and found it made good sense applied to problems of education. To most of the Psychology Department, however, such ideas were anathema, unscientific, and a threat to the prevailing behavioral orientation of traditional psychology. In that department I was ostracized by my colleagues, openly or subtly shunned. In faculty meetings I was ignored, and my projects were obstructed. I was told that *Individual Behavior* was a fraud and I was a charlatan. I was passed over for promotion in the most cursory fashion.

Only one person in the Psychology Department seemed to have any understanding of what I was about: Roland Waters, a physiological psychologist. One day, Roland said, "Art, I've read your stuff and puzzled over it a lot and I can't find any serious holes in it. But look, I'm about a year from retirement, so don't ask me to change." I could understand that and I deeply appreciated his honesty. For a professor who has spent his life immersed in a particular frame of reference, it must be a difficult thing to have someone come along and say you were wrong or on the wrong track. The rest of the department, however, treated me like an outcast.

Living in such an environment took a terrible toll on me. Though I maintained a brave front, inside I was deeply wounded. My migraine attacks became much worse. At first they occurred weeks apart, but during the last two years they were happening almost every week. Sometimes, attacks would begin with a loss of peripheral vision. The first time this happened, I was in a department store. As my vision closed in more and more, I became frightened that I was going blind. It never occurred to me then that the cause of my affliction lay in my life style.

I came closer to landing in a mental hospital during this period than at any time in my life before or since. The gains I had made to recover from early feelings of rejection were surely being put to the test. Had it not been for the positive strokes I was receiving off campus from the psychologists of the state and from workshops I was conducting, and the positive responses to my speaking and writing, I am sure I would have suffered far more damage than I did.

The Pain Continues

The second year was no better. In fact, the harassment grew worse. When I was passed over a second time for promotion, I decided to appeal to the college faculty and stated my case, in part, to the dean as follows:

> Last year when I was passed over by the committee of full professors, I went to see each one to discuss the reasons for this action. I was told I had been by passed because:
>
> 1. The scholarliness of my writing was questionable.
> 2. My contribution to psychology was negligible.
> 3. I was "different" from the rest of the department.
>
> The first two of these reasons are utterly without foundation. My publications have been highly praised throughout the field of psychology and are quoted repeatedly. I have been asked to develop these ideas time after time in conferences and symposia all over the country. Though my contribution to psychology seems to appear negligible to the four or five full professors in this department, it does not seem so to the 2000 psychologists in New York State who have elected me to positions of leadership year after year for the past six years.
>
> The third of the above reasons thus seems to become the real issue. As one of the committee expressed it to me, "Art, you're a real nice fellow, but why don't you be like the rest of us?" Such an attitude seems to me to be highly dangerous. Even if it were possible for a man to change his attitudes, beliefs, and life work to conform to tradition, I believe it would be a tragedy of the first order. Actually, my background and training were as traditional as those of my colleagues on this committee. For the past seven years, however, I have been increasingly attracted to a new and more dynamic approach to psychology. This is by no means a radical shift and is a point of

view shared by hundreds of outstanding psychologists from coast to coast. It is even shared by other younger men in this department.

I am proud of my record as a psychologist and as a professor at Syracuse University and I am entirely willing to stand on that record. I do not believe, however, that it has been fairly evaluated by the Committee on Promotions in this department. I believe that more is at stake in this matter than the problem of an injustice to a member of the faculty. There is also the question of whether there shall be room in a particular faculty for difference of opinion. I believe a faculty which does not value or encourage new ideas is embarked upon a road destructive to itself and to the university of which it is part. I do not think it is fair to me or good for the University that this decision should become final.

Arthur W. Combs (circa 1952)

A review panel was appointed and I laid my case before them. After an extensive investigation they concluded that: whereas I was a popular instructor, past president of the New York State Psychological Association, Chairman of the Joint Council, had more graduate students and publications than anyone in the department, and was held in high esteem by teachers and administrators off campus, nevertheless, they did not believe a review committee from outside a professor's discipline should overturn the decision of a professor's peers. This decision gave my colleagues in the department much pleasure but convinced me that things were unlikely to change and it was time to leave. I redoubled my efforts to get our remaining students along and put out the word that I was available.

Early Attitudes toward the Humanistic Movement in Psychology

The humanistic movement today has advanced so far that it is hard for younger psychologists to believe the intensity of the opposition it incurred in its early days. American psychology desperately sought acceptance as a science, prompting early psychologists to look for ways to make their discipline as neat and respectable as the physical science model. Like that model, behaviorism relied upon external observation for its data. Preoccupation with stimulus-response made possible the building of an elaborate theory based upon direct observation and subject to experimental manipulation. Unfortunately, this also restricted the profession to external observation, providing the illusion of objectivity but keeping the profession from addressing significant problems of human experience.

The revolt of early humanistic psychologists against the mechanistic approaches of behaviorism and their insistence upon the critical importance of exploring people's experience was seen by many behaviorists as a threatening prospect that could only lead to the bastardization of psychology. It was, therefore, strongly opposed. Because experience lies inside people and cannot be directly observed and manipulated, humanistic psychology was initially labeled unscientific and suspect. Perceptual psychology, of course, played directly into this fear and was consequently derided and attacked by many traditional psychologists when it first appeared. What was happening to me at Syracuse was not an isolated incident. Carl Rogers was met with hostility at Ohio State and again at Wisconsin. When William Snyder followed Rogers at Ohio State, he met a similar fate, as did Ted Landsman at the University of Maryland in later years.

The antagonism of traditional psychologists toward the humanistic movement in psychology also had its unhappy effects upon students. Many of our students at Syracuse were attracted to our program because of its humanistic orientation. Typically, in the first years of their study they became enthusiastic about perceptual psychology and its implications for counseling, psychotherapy, and education. This enthusiasm often disappeared by the time they prepared for their comprehensive examinations or dissertations and had to meet the requirements of behaviorally oriented psychologists on their examining committees. The pressure to be "scientific" was more than many could resist. I recall my shock some years after leaving Syracuse when a psychologist, whom I had regarded as one of the most sensitive and understanding of our students in his graduate days, invited me to visit his campus and see the wonderful things he was doing. Imagine my dismay when I discovered he was teaching beginning courses in psychology by programmed instruction from his book on the topic. Or, when he led me to his laboratory—complete with scores of rats!

There is an unhappy arrogance about many academic psychologists that shows itself in the bland assumption that their science is vastly superior to the accumulated experience of people in the helping professions like teaching, social work, counseling, pastoral care, and the like. One of my distinguished colleagues at Syracuse once chided me for expressing concern about the effect of a faculty action upon students. "Oh, come off it, Art," he said, "Everyone knows the only reason we have students is to make it possible to do research!" Another, a well known child psychologist, saw nothing amusing in my joking remark on the birth of his first child that "now you can talk like an expert." Instead, he drew himself up to full height and, in withering tones, remarked, "I don't think that will make any difference." It did, though.

Further Experiments in Teaching

With the phasing-out of our clinical program underway, I turned attention during the next two years to experimenting further with the implications of perceptual thinking for education. I began a series of classes for graduate teachers and administrators at Drumlins, a public golf and country club a few miles from the campus. In the relaxed atmosphere of this setting we explored perceptual ideas and what they meant for professional education.

Our classes usually met for an hour and a half in late afternoon, broke for dinner, and resumed for several hours in the evening. Again, I applied the atmosphere and techniques of therapy, maintaining my own role primarily as helper or facilitator. Everyone was on a first-name basis. In a very short time the groups developed an extraordinary rapport. Discussions were spirited, barriers were overcome, and personal learning proceeded by leaps and bounds. I was delighted at the extent and depth of the learning that was occurring. I was also discovering new and more meaningful personal relationships with students. In place of the stuffy reserve of traditional faculty-student relationships, I found myself involved in exceptionally caring human interactions in which the instructor was learning as much or more than the students. Here are some excerpts from the term-end reaction report of one of the participants:

> I felt very uncomfortable at the first group meeting. Silences were not only frequent but seemed tense and embarrassing. The leader took little part. I wondered how I could possibly stand fifteen such sessions lasting from 5 til 9.
>
> What a different feeling we had in the very next session, and from then til the end of the course. We couldn't any of us bear to miss a meeting. (I mean "we" literally—not just myself). We had a good talk to begin with in the lecture period; and we had started on the readings. We were all working in some branch of education; and we had a leader who proved to be both sensitive and on the ball. When 9 o'clock came, we still didn't want to break up;

> but went on talking and arguing for another half hour or so. In that second session we seemed to feel we were one group, not just separate individuals. Different points of view—yes, but trying hard to communicate and express ideas that were important to us and to understand those expressed by others. We seemed to have a bond; to be acceptant or at least tolerant—and to attend closely to whatever someone else was saying.
>
> This has been one of the most rewarding experiences of my life. Not just because I have devoted much time to the readings, though they have been intensely interesting and thought provoking. I've always been conscientious about assignments; but I honestly think I put more than usual on the work simply because no one was forcing me to do any of it. I could choose my own books and knew I was responsible only to my self. If I wanted to learn something—not just for an examination or term paper but because it was a subject close to my heart—here was my opportunity.
>
> This was part of the reason it was rewarding. But [so too was] the fellowship of the group, just being part of a group that was not merely intellectual or theoretical but intensely interested in children, in people, in education, in not just studying about human relationships—but in putting into effect *better* human relations.

A year after I left Syracuse, one of these classes held a reunion and each participant commented briefly in a note they sent to me.* From these comments one can catch something of the flavor:

"You would be amazed at the turn-out tonight!"

"This has been a most enjoyable reunion with only a few missing members."

"What fun to see so many here from last spring's course. Still all those good feelings abound."

"We're missing you but your good work still goes on in our hearts and lives. . . ."

"What magic that people with such varied backgrounds meet so congenially! It was a kind fate that brought me to your course."

"Here we are again! I wonder if your ears are burning because we are rehashing our good times of a year ago and wishing you were here with us."

Working with Administrators

Just before leaving Syracuse in the fall of 1951, Robert Fisk, a professor of school administration, and I ran a workshop for chief school administrators.

* Editor's note: For more on this group's response, see Heart-Warmers section at the end of this chapter.

Together we taught a "Seminar in Human Relations for School Administrators" at Drumlins. Each session met for 2 hours in the late afternoon, adjourned for dinner together, and resumed for another 2-hour session. At the start, one session dealt with administrative problems and the other with human relations questions. Sessions were designed to aid members of the group to explore their own experience in the light of human relations principles derived from perceptual psychology. Group members were helped to explore their personal beliefs, attitudes, and convictions, were supplied information relevant to their concerns, and were helped to formulate new meanings and to translate these into personal action.

Three weeks into the program, the group requested that we drop the sessions on technical administrative matters and operate entirely in the freer human relations mode. Accordingly, we worked for the remainder of the semester as a free discussion group with the two instructors acting as facilitators and resource persons. Checking my notes at the end of the semester, I found the group had covered about eighty percent of the material I had originally planned to present. They also covered twenty percent that they wanted to know about that I never thought to include. It is that twenty percent that keeps an instructor on his or her toes.

In an accompanying program of research, data were obtained prior to, during, and after these sessions from the administrators involved and from the personnel they supervised. From these data, important changes in these administrators could be observed, resulting in conclusions like the following, among others:

Individuals behave in an increasingly warm and democratic manner.

Positive changes occur in attitudes towards self, other adults, and children.

Individuals become more democratic with less need to demand respect and greater concern about understanding, respecting and aiding others.

Results of this study were published in a special issue of the *Journal of Social Issues* (Combs & Fisk, 1954).

The results of these experiments were not only important support for perceptual thinking. They were also very moving and self-fulfilling experiences for me. I found myself increasingly able to share who and what I was in ways I had never done before. Such personal involvement was also experienced by many of the participants, many of whom reported important changes in their own attitudes and personalities. Several of these classes also instituted annual reunions and I heard heart-warming reports from many participants, even years afterward.

Recapitulation

Refining a Belief System

The primary thrust of the Syracuse years to my search for fulfillment was the development of a well-organized, comprehensive, and internally consistent belief system. The discovery, with Don Snygg, of perceptual psychology laid the foundation for a cohesive set of beliefs that has affected every phase of my professional existence as psychologist, teacher, counselor, administrator, program builder, and speaker. Writing *Individual Behavior* with Don set the process in motion, but the experiences of program building, counseling, training clinicians, speaking, lobbying, writing, and experimenting with the broader implications of perceptual theory during the Syracuse days expanded and refined the theory, on one hand, and provided support and affirmation on the other. It confirmed what Don and I said about the theory in the introduction to *Individual Behavior*, "that it is, if not the truth, then something very like it."

I had a growing feeling that I was privileged to be in on the ground floor of a veritable revolution in psychological thought and action. Perceptual psychology was no flash in the pan, but a fundamental contribution with wide-ranging consequences. This realization gave an enormous boost to my feelings of security as a professional psychologist. Even the attacks upon me and upon perceptual psychology that I experienced during the last two years at Syracuse, devastating as they were, added to the strength of my convictions. The fact that my belief system could weather such storms was, itself, indicative of its basic strength. That strength, in turn, gave support and encouragement to my sense of self.

A Growing Sense of Self

Professionally, I grew by leaps and bounds. A growing list of publications suggested that I was becoming a psychologist with something solid to contribute. Increasing requests for consultation and election to leadership roles by my professional peers gave evidence of the esteem accorded me by my profession. The destruction of the clinical program and the dreadful years that followed, while poignant and painful, also forced a time of testing, reassessment, and redirection of my professional energies. A major requirement for self-actualization is possession of an integrated belief system, and perceptual psychology laid the foundations for the growth of a personal as well as a professional frame of reference. Increasingly, I was beginning to utilize a perceptual orientation in my personal life. I was becoming better able to understand myself and my relationships to people around me. I was seeing personal events in larger perspective. I was beginning to accept myself more fully, discovering new and hitherto unknown parts to my personality and possibilities.

The warmth and caring of my students in the Drumlins context, the depth of their learning and the obvious enthusiasm of their response to me and our classes, were unquestionably fulfilling to my personal desires for love and acceptance and my professional longings for respect and affirmation. They did much to help counterbalance the repudiation and stress I experienced during the two years I spent phasing out the clinical program. Needless to say, such affirmations were deeply meaningful to my damaged psyche as I sought to deal with the destruction of our clinical program and the rejection of my colleagues in the Psychology Department.

I was still not sure of my acceptability in most everyday human interactions, though. I still expected rejection. But all this was slowly changing. Painful as the experience at Syracuse was, living through it provided proof that I could survive, that there was basic strength in my being. There was also significant evidence from my experiences at the APA convention, at Goddard College, and the response of students to my teaching experiments that there were positive and attractive aspects of my personality. I was beginning to give myself more fully to others, even if I could not accept their gifts in return. Compliments or praise were still embarrassing, though secretly cherished. The belief that no one could possibly care for me if he or she ever "discovered what I was really like" was still with me but beginning to abate somewhat.

Despite the progress I was making in self-development, my fundamental feelings of rejection were still alive and well. I was learning to give myself fully in situations where I felt sure I was needed, as in counseling, teaching, or speaking. Without that assurance, I hung back or avoided contacts. I often felt "like a sore thumb" at social events. Social affairs like cocktail parties or receptions where it was necessary to make small talk were dreadful to me and to be avoided. I felt awkward and out of place. As one of my students once explained me to another student, "The trouble with Art is, he never talks unless he has something to say." People who did not know me well often expressed surprise at seeing a very different person when I was lecturing, consulting, or counseling. Unfortunately, many others interpreted my shyness as aloofness or, worse still, as uncaring.

Openness and Acceptance

My decision to shift my energies from the rehabilitative (reactive) mode of clinical psychology to the preventive (proactive) potentialities of education

Millie, Carol, Peter, and Arthur (1953)

opened a whole new area for deeply enriching, broadening experience. The enthusiasm of teachers and administrators for perceptual-experiential thinking was professionally exciting. The warmth and acceptance students exhibited toward me was personally supporting and fulfilling. All this encouraged explorations of teaching and administration and so opened new and promising vistas for further exploration.

I feel sure the sense of security provided by these events made possible the expansions of self and openness to new experience that occurred during this period. First, there was the counseling experience with Ted, in which I discovered it was all right to be me. One of the requirements for effective therapy is the counselor's firm belief that "there but for the grace of God, go I," that there is no behavior anyone would not be capable of, given the right circumstances. The experience of infidelity at APA gave new meaning to that principle applied to my own personality, a painful but necessary experience. The weekend at Goddard expanded my sense of "This, too, is me" and so led to the further question, "What else is there to discover?" I was finding a healthy base for personal growth and opening doors for still more insights to come.

Feelings of Identification

Although I certainly did not realize it at the time, the personal growth and change I was experiencing were beginning to have their effects upon my family life. I continued to be a confirmed workaholic. Indeed, the problems of the last two years at Syracuse made it more necessary than ever. I was so involved with my professional problems that time for family matters was blatantly lacking. Our family looked like a stable one on the surface. I am sure I felt it was, too. As I look back on it now, however, there was little real communication going on. I lived in two worlds: the vital and fulfilling world of my professional life and the comfortable but static world of my marriage. Often, the time I had at home was taken up with migraines on weekends or long hours spent in writing. When caught up in a writing project, I could spend countless hours completely engrossed in the project. I could concentrate so completely on a project that I would often work many hours at a stretch, then suddenly become aware that I was tired, hungry, or aching. It was only years later that I came to realize how much I had lost during this period of time in opportunities to be closer to my children.

I had strong yearnings to explore myself and the world while Millie was primarily preoccupied with safety and maintenance of things as they were. Sooner or later these fundamental differences in life style were bound to collide and demand adjustment. Among the many families I have counseled over the years, I have seen many such instances of couples growing apart. Indeed, the experience of therapy can speed the process if the growth of one party outdistances the other or starts one partner off in directions unacceptable to the other. This happens so frequently that I have come to regard it as an ethical requirement of my practice to forewarn couples of the possibility.

Outside my family, I was beginning to make some firm friends. Don Snygg and I developed an especially caring, sharing relationship that went far beyond professional concerns. Likewise, Earl Kelley and I hit it off on his visit to Syracuse. Our friendship continued until his death years later. Among my graduate students, I came to value, especially, the friendship of Ted Landsman and Dan Soper. Ted, of course, was my counselor at the time of my discovery that it was all right to be me. Our friendship continued for years after, one of those relationships that simply picks up as though the persons involved had never been interrupted whenever they get together, no matter how long the separation. This was true for Dan Soper as well. I had absolute trust in Dan, placing him in charge of all students working in our clinic. He became a spokesperson for our graduate students and a warm and understanding friend.

Heart-Warmers

Excerpts from cards, letters, and notes that Art preserved in a file bearing this title.

MAY, 1954

I have wanted to take a course with you for a long time. I first heard about you from other students, "Take a course from Dr. Combs if you can, he's wonderful! But matriculate early, his classes are soon filled." Next, I heard you speak one afternoon during the summer session in '49. I remember you saying that people are resilient, that they can take adverse experiences and snap back. You were talking about adolescents, especially. I heard you talk again one evening in 1950 at Park Center church. This time you told about a little second grade boy who had a new raincoat and spent the day walking in the rain instead of going to school. I was thrilled when I received through the school the letter telling about this course. At last, I would take a course from Dr. Combs. . . .I don't see how you could make the course better. . . .I wish that I could come to Florida and earn my doctor's degree working with you. (Syracuse, NY)

UNDATED, STUDENT EVALUATION (ED PSY 251-Seminar in Human Relations) CIRCA SPRING, 1954

To me, the study of the phenomenological point of view has been exciting, for it seems so logical and workable as a way of studying behavior and helping people. . . . It is no exaggeration when I say that [this] has been the most helpful graduate course I have ever taken—helpful to me in my personal adjustment, and helpful in gaining new insight in my work. . . .It should be a *must* for all school personnel. . . .It is a certainty that, first of all, a course of this type should be required in every teacher's college. . . .

The news of your resignation from Syracuse University came as a great shock, for I thought that the "powers" would eventually realize that they had an outstanding person on their faculty. I wish you success in your new position and hope that you will have the opportunity to develop some of your ideas which seem too progressive here. . . .We shall miss you! (Syracuse, NY)

DECEMBER, 1954

. . . I appreciate your help more deeply than I can say. I am glad you were in Syracuse when I needed that help. (Endicott, NY)

APRIL, 1955

Here we are again! I wonder if your ears are burning, because we are rehashing our good times of a year ago and wishing you were here with us. . . .

You would be amazed at the turn-out tonight. . . .

We're missing you but your good work still goes on in our hearts and lives. . . .

What magic that people with such varied backgrounds meet so congenially! It was a kind fate that brought me to your course. . . .

There is only one thing wrong with this get-together—the knowledge that we are no longer a class anticipating the arrival of our "Prof." . . . (Syracuse, NY)

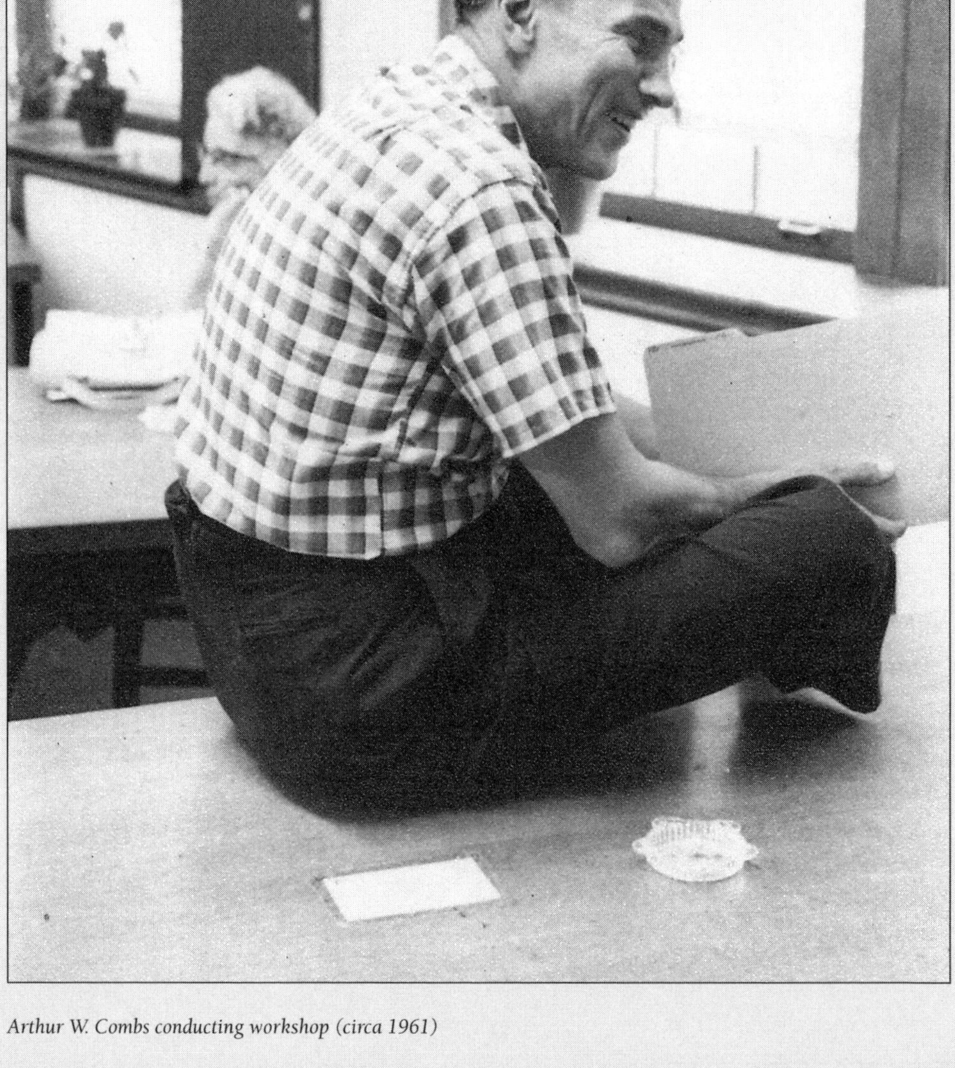

Arthur W. Combs conducting workshop (circa 1961)

CHAPTER SEVEN

New Beginnings

The hostility and rejection I experienced at Syracuse left deep scars. For years after, I avoided traditional psychologists, dropped out of psychological organizations, and chose my psychological colleagues with great care. I also began to think about other areas in which I might make acceptable contributions. Shortly after the Syracuse debacle, I wrote to Earl Kelley:

> Let me see if I can outline my thinking to this point a little more clearly. I think I have talents as a teacher. I think, too, I have abilities in the way of getting people to work together smoothly and happily toward a common goal. As for my interests—they lie in the field of personality theory and its implications for social action. It has always seemed to me that the important question for the psychologist was to discover the best possible ideas one could about the nature of man and his behavior. Once having that, one should be able to discover new and better ways of dealing with human problems in many realms of human action. Thus, I am interested in consistent personality theory and its implications for education, psychotherapy, group action, labor relations, etc., etc.
>
> I started out as a teacher, shifted to clinical psychology because I felt a need to help individuals more effectively (myself too, probably) but as time has gone on, I have become less and less satisfied with clinical psychology as dealing primarily with the rehabilitative aspects of things. In the meantime my interests have broadened and deepened and I now find myself back in education, seeing it as the ultimate hope of producing social change and more effective living. I think I return to education bringing something that I have learned from my "period in the wilderness." So, I guess I find myself primarily as an educator with a deep and abiding feeling that this is the most important occupation in the world.

When Dan Soper completed his doctorate at Syracuse, he accepted a position at the University of Florida. When he heard of our problems at Syracuse, he suggested my name to J. B. White, Dean of the College of Education there. Shortly after, Dean White invited me to come to Florida for a visit and to explore the possibilities of a move to Gainesville.

The experience was almost unbelievable. People there warmed to my thinking and expressed their delight and interest in perceptual ideas without restraint. I felt wanted and appreciated everywhere I went. It seemed too good to be true. When J. B. told me, "Come on down, Art, and do whatever you want," I accepted immediately and flew back to Syracuse to resign and prepare for the move. My years of travail at Syracuse were at an end.

Starting Over

On my return from Florida in March of 1954, we put our house on the market and began preparations for the move to Gainesville. It gave me much pleasure to turn in my resignation effective after my last class in June. I also enjoyed letting people know that I was leaving with a promotion and a substantial raise in salary. It was good to know that I was appreciated, sought after, and so well regarded in Florida. I felt an enormous sense of relief that my difficult days at Syracuse were at last coming to an end. For the remainder of the year I redoubled my efforts to get as many as possible of our remaining students through to their degrees.

During the next few months, I was recurrently moved by the outpouring of good wishes in response to the announcement of my leaving. This left no doubt that my teaching efforts were truly significant in the lives of many students, teachers, and administrators. During my years at Syracuse, I had learned to give myself to my students wholeheartedly. Their letters and comments made clear that they appreciated the person as well as the ideas of their teacher. Needless to say, their expressions of thanks and good will were fervently cherished, even if they also caused me embarrassment and a feeling of wonder that people cared so much.

Dean White found a cottage on a lake near Gainesville where we could spend the summer while looking for a permanent place to live. This was a marvelous time for the family. The location was charming and none of us was under pressure. For once, I had an opportunity to spend some quality time with our children. Everyone was involved in the search for a new home in Gainesville. When we were not house-hunting, we spent our time swimming, loafing, or exploring the surrounding country. In August, we moved into a brand new house not far from the university and began to get ready for the opening of school.

The Florida Environment

My appointment [as professor of education] at the University of Florida was a dual one in the Department of Personnel Services and the Educational Foundations Department. When I arrived to take up my duties, however, I found that the Psychology Department in the College of Liberal Arts was insisting that I be assigned there also. Still smarting from my experience at Syracuse, I was not happy with this troika arrangement but agreed to it, providing I was not responsible to the chairman of the Psychology Department and was totally budgeted in the College of Education. When Dean White and I went to meet the Dean of the Graduate School to settle upon these arrangements, Dean Grinter asked, "How is it, Dr. Combs, that a psychologist of your talents and distinction wants to work in the College of Education instead of the Psychology Department?" In later years, Dean White was fond of telling about this interview and of his astonishment and glee when I replied to the graduate dean, "I guess it's because I've grown up." I do not remember the interchange, but it may have occurred as J. B. reported it, for I was still hurting so from my Syracuse experience.

The Department of Personnel Services at the University of Florida was just in the process of being established and I happily joined in formulating its design. From my work at Syracuse, I was convinced that the various helping professions attached to the public schools (like counseling, school social work, psychology, and nursing) should be seen as more alike than different since all must be based upon fundamental conceptions of the nature of persons and how they grow and learn. My colleagues liked this notion. Together we proposed that students seeking training in any of the helping professions would begin their programs together in a series of basic courses in the Personnel Services Department. After that they would specialize increasingly in their chosen areas as their experience progressed. The idea attracted a good deal of attention off campus and helped to bring a whole series of government-subsidized students to our department over the next few years.

Interdisciplinary foundations of education departments were a common feature of most colleges of education in the fifties. Over the years since, they have largely been eliminated as colleges of education have been increasingly restricted to instruction in the how-to aspects of teaching. Exposure to the underlying disciplines of psychology, sociology, philosophy, and research is now provided on most campuses in separate departments housed in other colleges. This tends to compartmentalize learning so that many students make their way through these required courses with little or no integration of ideas from the basic disciplines into their development as truly professional educators. Universities generally describe themselves as "communities of scholars." Actually, they are more like collections of prima donnas, groups of specialists each doing his or her own thing.

Our Foundations of Education Department was a remarkable and scholarly group. The department included professors representative of the

Arthur W. Combs (circa 1962)

basic disciplines upon which education is based: psychology, sociology, philosophy, statistics, and research. Many of its faculty were persons of high-level competence and distinction. The department was completely egalitarian, elected its own chairperson, and sought to operate in truly democratic fashion. The mutual respect and acceptance among the faculty was outstanding. These qualities facilitated a fruitful cross-disciplinary interchange of ideas. While differences of opinion and philosophy existed among the faculty, these differences were tolerated and accepted to an extraordinary degree. Many faculty members made friends outside their own disciplines, enjoying each other's company socially as well as academically. It was a perfect atmosphere for me. I enjoyed the widespread acceptance and stimulation of my confreres. It was just what I needed to begin the healing process after the trauma of Syracuse.

The Psychology Department was another matter. It was a carbon copy of the one at Syracuse. Its faculty was, almost exclusively, behaviorally oriented. It was also chaired by an autocrat who decided everything, even to the extent of personally approving every graduate student's program every quarter. To fill my commitment to teach one-third time, the chairman assigned me two courses, each open only to doctoral students about to complete their programs. He then permitted only two or three students to enroll. This was a strange situation. The Psychology Department apparently felt they had to have me attached to the department but also felt embarrassed by my influence and sought to keep me at arm's length. In the meantime, my undergraduate classes in the College of Education grew rapidly to forty or fifty enrollees and it became necessary to restrict my graduate classes to fifteen or twenty each quarter. After several years I pointed out this discrepancy to J. B. White. We agreed it was a poor use of my time to be assigned teaching responsibilities in psychology and I resigned from that department.

Even after I left the Psychology Department, however, this nodding acquaintance continued. After I had been at the University of Florida for four years, much to my surprise, I was invited to talk to a meeting of Psi Chi, the honorary society in psychology. As the date approached, several of my graduate students warned me that I was being set up, that a plan was afoot to confront me with questions designed to "destroy" perceptual psychology. Sure enough, as I completed my talk, I was bombarded with hostile questions that I managed to field with ease. During the talk I made the point that behavior was not a function of the stimulus but of its meaning. To illustrate, I pointed out that a handful of jelly beans offered to a child three weeks before Easter had a very different meaning than the same offer on Easter morning when the child was overloaded with candy. On the way out of the meeting, the new chairman of the department said, "My God, Combs, that illustration devastates behaviorism." I was never invited to speak again.

My office at this time was in Norman Hall, which housed both the College of Education and the P. K. Yonge Laboratory School. As a consequence, the halls were full of youngsters at all levels of schooling from kindergarteners to high school seniors. Education faculties can become isolated all too quickly from the front lines of public education. This arrangement, however, kept us intimately in touch with the population we were concerned about.

I thoroughly enjoyed these early years at the U of F. It was a sustaining and fulfilling experience to be regarded as a person of distinction and respect. People listened to my ideas, sought my assistance, and treated the perceptual thinking that I was advocating with an attitude of "of course." A statistician in the Foundations Department even came to sit in on one of my classes for an entire semester, the only time in my entire career that a colleague ever did that. My courses were popular and I began to attract a few graduate students who found perceptual thinking provocative. Educational Foundations did not have the kind of employment opportunities that exist in clinical psychology, however, and I never again had so large a group of graduate students as in my Syracuse days.

Making New Friends

Slowly I began to make friends with some of my colleagues. I renewed acquaintance with Dan Soper in the Personnel Services Department and, together, we gave shape to its developing program. We became fast friends. In the years after, I frequently turned to him for counseling and guidance. It was nice to have someone I could walk in on with the request, "I need to talk, Dan. Have you got some time for me?" It was a rare privilege to share my concerns and explore my questions, whether personal or professional, with this skillful counselor and warm human being.

Dan Soper with his daughter Vicki (circa 1960s) P. K. Yonge Laboratory School, Gainesville, FL

I also became acquainted with Justin Harlow, head of the Student Counseling Center. He, Dan, and I made a practice of meeting weekly to talk about anything that moved us, personal or professional. Another friend I came to value was Kimball Wiles, a professor in the Department of Curriculum and Instruction who urged me in 1956 to attend a convention of the Association for Supervision and Curriculum Development, an organization that was to become an important part of my life for the next thirty years.

In the Foundations Department, I especially appreciated the friendship of Hal Lewis, an educational philosopher, and Vince Hines, in social foundations. After years of being a loner, I was beginning to reach out to folks around me.

Some Significant Publications

With Dan Soper, I renewed my interest in research. Together we wrote two papers: "The Self, Its Derivate Terms and Research" and "Planning Future Research in Education" (Combs & Soper, 1957; Soper & Combs, 1957). The first was an attempt to bring some order to the confused terminology in the literature about the self and its functions. The latter was a plea for educational research from a perceptual orientation.

In the late 1950s and early 1960s, Dan Soper and I began arranging for yearly conferences on Personality Theory and Counseling Practice. These sessions were well attended by counselors and educators in the area. We were able to bring people like Carl Rogers, Earl Kelley, Gordon Allport, and Abe Maslow to make presentations. Sidney M. Jourard and Ted Landsman also participated in these conferences. Out of my preparations for these conferences came two papers. One, "Adjustment . . . Through Guidance and Special Services" [Combs, 1958], was an early result of an attempt to expand the application of perceptual thinking begun in 1947. It focused on some of the implications of perceptual thinking for the practice of counseling. A second paper, "A Perceptual View of The Nature of 'Helpers'" [Combs, 1961], was an attempt to examine the belief system of the therapist. It addressed the behavior of the counselor as a function of the counselor's perceptual orientation.

The second most frequently quoted article of my career was also published about this time, namely: "The Myth of Competition" [Combs, 1957]. In this article I suggested that competition is a highly overrated means for motivating people. I claimed that, contrary to general belief, we live in the most cooperative, interdependent society the world has ever known. I pointed to three basic facts about competition that make it undesirable as a technique for motivation. These are: (a) the only persons motivated by competition are those who believe they have a chance of winning, (b) when people are forced to compete and do not believe they can succeed, they are not motivated—instead, they are discouraged and disillusioned, and (c) when competition becomes too important, morality breaks down and any means becomes justified to achieve one's ends. These ideas were met either with celebration or castigation. No one, it seemed, was indifferent to this message.

Revising Individual Behavior

At the request of the publisher, Don Snygg and I began to think about a revision of *Individual Behavior* in 1955. We agreed through correspondence that each of us would tackle half the chapters, submit our chapters to each other for criticism as each was completed, and meet in the summer of 1956 to work on it together. I threw myself into the project with my usual intensity, sending off each chapter as I completed it. I also arranged for Don to teach several classes on our campus in the following summer so that we could work together on the manuscript. Although I dutifully contributed my chapters as we had agreed, I heard nothing from Don in reply. By the time summer came, I had completed first drafts on seven of the ten chapters in my allotment.

When Don arrived on campus for the summer quarter, we met for our first session together. I was astounded to find he had not written a word. Worse still, he had not even read what I had sent him! I was devastated and deeply hurt. I could not conceive that our long and intimate friendship appeared to mean so little to him. His only explanation was that he simply could not bring himself to write because he was certain that the revision would never live up to what we had done in the original version. He was clearly in pain and apologized frequently for letting me down. As the summer progressed we met three or four more times but he was still reluctant to tackle the task. In the autumn, we parted with his promise to go to work on his portion of the text as rapidly as possible. I had little hope that matters would really change. Accordingly, I turned, sick at heart and feeling betrayed by my friend, to the task of finishing my chapters.

As the weeks went by I continued to send my chapters to Oswego with no response. In desperation, I finally wrote him to say:

- That I was deeply hurt but trying to understand his problem.
- That I had too much invested in *Individual Behavior* at this point to drop the project.
- That I therefore proposed to continue writing my part.
- That when I finished my part, I would start writing his portion until the job was completed.
- That the book would be published with my name first according to our original agreement.
- That we would divide the royalties proportionally according to our chapter contributions.

Don agreed to this proposal and I set about the task of completing the book.

Of all the writing I have done, this was the most difficult. Don never contributed a line for the second edition, so I was left to complete the task entirely by myself. I had plunged into my share with a great deal of anticipation. Doing Don's half was sheer drudgery. In time, I came to understand that he really was unable to keep his part of our bargain and my feelings of hurt were replaced by sympathy for his plight. I could only regret that we missed opportunities to once again enjoy our former camaraderie. I wrote in the foreword of the second edition: " . . . I have written this volume alone. Dr. Snygg's influence, however, will still be discerned in this volume in much of the material carried over from the first book. His influence may be observed too, in many of my own contributions, I am sure, for the stimulation and growth afforded by the intensive collaboration with such a man, I find, is a continuous, developing thing. I count that period of our former partnership as one of the most truly creative experiences of my life."

The first edition of *Individual Behavior* set forth an outline for a systematic, comprehensive theory of psychology from a phenomenological orientation. Because the word "phenomenological" is a considerable mouthful and rare in most vocabularies, I substituted the term "perceptual" in the second edition to describe the experiential field and as synonymous for personal meaning. The revision title thus read, *Individual Behavior: A Perceptual Approach to Behavior*. The book was almost doubled in size. It also included more than six hundred references supporting its basic tenets. My unremitting interest in the applications of theory was also manifest in greatly expanded sections entitled The Individual and Society, Some General Implications for Human Relationships, How People Can Help Themselves, The Goals and Purposes of Education, The Teaching Relationship, The Personal Approach to Treatment, and a final chapter suggesting ways for carrying out research in a perceptual framework entitled "The Exploration of Meaning." The book was well received and sold more than fifty thousand copies by 1975.

I Discover ASCD

Many of the faculty in the College of Education at UF were members of the Association for Supervision and Curriculum Development (ASCD) and two of our faculty had been national presidents in prior years. ASCD in the fifties was primarily composed of principals, supervisors, teachers, and "idea people" from higher education. The organization represented the liberal wing of American education, eschewing concern with political and housekeeping matters to concentrate on the implications of ideas for education, curriculum, and human relationships. Its conferences were stimulating events designed so that everyone attending had opportunities to get personally involved. At Kim Wiles's suggestion, I began in 1956 to attend its annual conferences and found myself thoroughly enjoying its people and its programs. Attendance at ASCD conferences also provided renewed opportunities to see my friend Earl Kelley on a fairly regular basis.

In 1957 I was asked to make a keynote presentation at the next annual meeting in Seattle. I put together a talk, entitled "Seeing Is Behaving" [Combs, 1958], in which I discussed some of the implications of perceptual thinking for education. This was one of the largest audiences I had ever addressed and, despite my qualms, the speech was enthusiastically received. As I came down from the stage, Kim Wiles told me, "Art, that speech will make you ten thousand dollars." I thought he was joking but he turned out to be right. The speech launched me as an educational consultant. I began to receive requests for speaking and consulting engagements from schools and colleges all across the nation. Forty years later, at a gathering of former presidents of ASCD at the national convention, the master of ceremonies suggested that each person "tell who he or she is and say a few words about the most effective speech they ever heard." I was astounded to hear four people in the group nominate my "Seeing Is Behaving" address in 1958. I have no idea today what I said on that occasion. I spoke from notes and the notes are long since gone, but I would surely like to know precisely what I said.

It was good to find that others appreciated perceptual thinking and its spokesperson. Consulting trips expanded my understanding of American education. They were also great fun. I had priceless opportunities to observe American education in action, from preschool to graduate school, with students, teachers, counselors, supervisors, and administrators at every level. The humanistic movement in psychology and education was also making itself felt and I had a satisfying feeling of being both a part of the movement and a contributor to its advancement. Even working on the revision of *Individual Behavior* was contributing to my growth. As I plowed my way through the revision, I was forced to think through its tenets principle by principle. Simultaneously, the process of exploring its implications served to broaden the scope of the theory and provided important tests of its potential in relation to the demands of practical application.

Some Peak Experiences

In 1954, Maslow wrote *Motivation and Personality*, in which he described experiences of a transformative and transcendent nature that he later labeled "peak experiences" [Maslow, 1962, 1970]. One of the consulting trips I made in 1958 was to the ASCD chapter in Puerto Rico, where I had a peak experience that made a lasting impression upon me. I was staying at the guest house on the campus of the University of Puerto Rico. After several days and evenings of speaking or socializing, I declined the invitation of my hosts for still another round of entertainment and asked for an evening alone. About nine o'clock, while wandering idly about the campus, I came to the auditorium. A light was on in the lobby, so I walked in and sat down in the unilluminated theater. A group of musicians was coming onto the stage for some sort of rehearsal. Soon an entire orchestra had assembled and sat waiting for its leader. Sure enough, he soon appeared. It was Pablo Casals!

For several hours I sat enthralled in that cloistered space watching that marvelous old man rehearse his orchestra for the Casals Festival coming up several days later. He was so warm and human and was obviously loved and respected by the musicians. His young wife was sitting down front with the new bride of one of the musicians. At one point the orchestra surprised the bridegroom by launching into the Wedding March instead of the piece he expected. Everyone cracked up at his confusion. Casals invited the young bride up on the stage to be introduced to everyone in the orchestra. I was indelibly touched by the scene, especially by Casals's sensitivity, gentleness, and surprising shyness. I felt a profound sense of oneness with this remarkable human being. It was, indeed, a rare privilege to have had such a priceless experience. Years later, I would have another reason for my feeling of identification. Like Casals, I, too, married a much younger woman.

I had two more peak experiences during this period. One occurred on a trip to Washington with Justin Harlow, my friend at the University of Florida. As we were standing in the aisle, waiting to deplane in Washington, a young woman holding a baby was seated next to a window. We looked at each other and in an instant were communicating without a word between us. As we got off the plane, Justin asked, "Do you know that woman?" "Never saw her in my life," I replied. "Well, she sure talked to you," said Justin. "Yes, and I talked to her!" I replied. As we passed where she was sitting, the young woman was running her nose through the baby's hair. She was obviously enjoying the smell of her baby's head. I, too, have loved such a tender, intimate moment, and for an instant we shared a common bond.

The third incident occurred in [November of 1963] when I was speaking on St. Simon's Island off Georgia, the day John Kennedy was shot. There had been a storm and electricity to the island was cut off. Accordingly, the news did not reach me until just before I was to leave for home, when I overheard it on a car radio. When the black cab driver arrived to take me to the airport, we listened together to the news on his radio. He was crying and so was I. Sad as it was for me, it was infinitely more so for my driver. For him, Kennedy was a symbol of hope that the evils of racial intolerance might come to an end. All the way to the airport we shared our feelings of grief at this terrible event, becoming one for awhile in our anguish. At the airport we hugged each other and then went our separate ways. The incident remains for me an instant of beauty, sadness, and unity shared to the fullest with a fellow human being.

Research on Children's Self-Concepts

When the College of Education built a new Laboratory School, Dan Soper and I designed its counseling center, complete with play therapy room. When the school opened, Dan left the Student Counseling Center and became the Lab School psychologist. Shortly after, we applied for a federal grant to trace the development of the self-concept in the 50 children entering the Lab School kindergarten in the autumn. Our plan was to follow these children throughout their school years to map the growth of their self-concepts from year to year. Our proposal was accepted with the stipulation that the study deal with the data statistically, including presentation of its findings by means of factor analysis. This converted the study from an exciting clinical analysis of developmental growth to a bland study of general trends. Reluctantly, we accepted the stipulation because we believed we might still achieve our goals in spite of the restrictions. Accordingly, we set up an office in the school, hired several assistants, and began to make regular observations on 50 children.

The original plan for this research was to follow each child individually, mapping the growth of self-concept from the time the child entered kindergarten for as long afterwards as he or she remained in the school. The literature abounds with information about the development and behavior of children both in school and out. We know very little, however, about their internal life, the perceptual worlds from which behavior arises. It was our hope in this study to shed some light on how children see the world about them and how their perceptions of self change in the course of their school experience. Unfortunately, the restrictions laid upon us changed the focus of our efforts from insight into the nature of children's experience to a statistical study in which individual experience was obscured or washed out. We worked hard at the research but found the task we were required to carry out increasingly onerous and foreign to our real interests. Accordingly, after two years we decided to terminate the study and turn to other things.

The results of our study were published in a United States Office of Education Monograph in 1963 with the title, "The Relationship of Child Perceptions to Achievement and Behavior In the Early School Years" [Combs & Soper, 1963]. The research is of interest in three respects:

1. It represents a pioneer effort to explore the perceptual experience of children. Doing research in a perceptual frame of reference is complicated, for experience lies inside the child and is not open to direct observation. That fact has been a serious roadblock to experiential

research. Our study suggested a way to surmount that obstacle through the use of inference and demonstrated some fruitful procedures for making such observations.

2. The research lent corroboration to the enormous importance of the self-concept in behavior. Indeed, the child's feeling of being adequate or enough seems so central to personality as to outweigh all other perceptions of self.
3. The study suggested the importance for teachers and school personnel of including perceptual-experiential data in determining goals for children, establishing curricula, and developing educational strategies.

These are substantial contributions to be sure, but far less significant than we might have found if we had been given a freer hand to operate from a more solidly perceptual-experiential approach. A splendid opportunity to investigate the nature of self-concept development in the course of schooling was thus aborted by the requirement to utilize research techniques inappropriate to the problem. I still think it a great pity that we were unable to carry out the project we originally proposed.

Some Perils of Consulting

Unappreciated Messages

Not everyone I contacted in the course of consulting with school districts about the country was affected positively by my humanistic message. Some found it downright threatening. For example, I made a speech in California, entitled "The Myth of Competition," in which I made the same points articulated in my paper of the same title [Combs, 1957]: that we do not live in a competitive society but in the most cooperative, interdependent society the world has ever known. A young teacher who was impressed by this argument repeated my remarks in his home community. This action precipitated a public demand from parents and the press that he be fired. They were sure he must be a communist intent upon undermining the patriotism of American youth. Fortunately, he had a tape recording of his talk and was able to satisfy the appeals committee appointed by the school board that he was merely a young man carried away by youthful enthusiasm, not a communist seeking to undermine the well-being of American youth.

On another occasion, after a speech in Orange County, California, I received a poison pen letter. It contained the threat that "You will never go home alive if you ever set foot in this county again." Stubborn man that I am,

I made arrangements to return the following month. Those who are humanistically inclined in education have always been the objects of attack from some quarters. We have been reviled as ungodly, communists, corrupters of youth, and practitioners of "secular humanism," considered by some to be a highly dangerous religion. The shrill cries of these critics have done an enormous disservice to American youth and to the nature of education by throwing unwarranted roadblocks in the path of the most promising innovations American education has experienced in a hundred years.

I recall an occasion when Earl Kelley and I were scheduled to give a major address at the ASCD Annual Convention. We agreed that each of us would speak for only 20 minutes, making several crucial points, then leave the audience to chew on the ideas. We each made our talks and expected the meeting to close on those notes. But the then-president of ASCD, noting he had 20 unscheduled minutes, began to remind the audience that they ought to go see the exhibits, and went on and on about the value of the exhibitors' fees in helping to pay for the convention facilities. As the president droned on, Earl was having a fit. "Look at that S.O.B.," he said to me in a whisper. "Will he never shut up? He's ruining what we were trying to do." He fumed and fussed in my ear with more choice profanity than I ever heard from him until the meeting was over. I felt pretty outraged myself, but had hardly an instant to get a word in.

Other Problems on the Road

Before speaking in California on one occasion, I had all my correspondence with the assistant superintendent. I first met the superintendent at the foot of the stairs to the stage where the assistant superintendent handed him a sheet of paper. The superintendent then said to me, "Let's go," and we walked up on the stage. He stepped to the podium, made a few announcements, and launched into a long and flowery introduction. "Our speaker today comes to us from the University of Florida. He is widely known for his expertise in . . . , he has degrees in . . . , he has been honored for . . . , he has written . . . , etc., etc." Finally, he said: "It gives me great pleasure to introduce . . ." and at this point he looked at the paper the assistant superintendent had handed him, studied it, turned it over several times, then turned to me and asked, "By the way, what's your name?" The audience loved it!

Then there was the time a superintendent told me on the way from the airport, "I am so disgusted with my teachers. I've tried everything to get them to fill the seats down front but they always sit as far back as possible. But this time, I've foiled them. I've scheduled you to speak in an auditorium that won't hold them!" Sure enough, when we arrived, every seat was filled and the overflow was standing around the sides of the room!

Once, in Nashville, I was unpacking my suitcase. I tossed my pajamas onto the bed and, as I turned around, was surprised to see a black bikini undergarment on the floor. "Hey," I said to myself, "where did that come from? I know it wasn't there a moment ago." Then, I thought, "It must be Pam's (my daughter-in-law). They do their laundry at our house and I'll bet her panties got stuck with static electricity to my pajamas. Hey, that will be a good joke when I get back home." Then it dawned on me: "Suppose it's not hers, what then?" So I changed my mind and dropped them in the wastebasket.

After a little while, I thought, "What will the maid think? Heck! They have to be Pam's" and I stuck them in the toe of one of a pair of shoes in my suitcase, determining to myself that I would think about all this later. Finishing my assignment in Nashville, the next day I flew on to Seattle, where I was picked up by the hospitality committee. They took me to my hotel and sat while I changed clothes. When I opened my suitcase to take out my shoes, the panties dropped to the floor at their feet. They were clearly titillated and glanced at each other with knowing expressions. What could I say? I could not tell them they were my daughter-in-law's panties. Who would have believed that? So, feeling embarrassed, I quickly tucked them back in the suitcase and said not a word. Back home, I decided to play it safe. I mentioned the incident to no one and surreptitiously added the panties to the next load of laundry the young couple brought over.

Making a point about deciding what is really important on the job, I once told an audience about observing in a teacher's classroom at the end of a difficult day. She was having a hard time and needed an observer in her room like a hole in the head. Hoping to let her know I understood and to apologize for adding to her troubles, I walked up to her desk when the bell rang. Before I could deliver my speech, a small boy came in with a note. She read the note, threw it on the table and exploded before my eyes.

"How stupid!" she exclaimed. "How can he be so absolutely picayune? Doesn't he have anything better to do? As if teachers don't have enough to worry about," etc., etc.

Not knowing what this explosion was all about, I continued to listen, then picked up the note from the desk. It read: "At the end of the day all window shades must be adjusted to the half way position." The note was signed, J. J. Smith, Superintendent. At this point my audience erupted into gales of laughter and I stood there wondering what was so funny. Later, someone explained. That very day they had all received exactly such a note from the gentleman who introduced me!

On another occasion, after swimming in a motel pool in Andrews, Texas, I returned to my room to dress. I rinsed out my bathing suit and turned to hang it on a rack behind me while turning off the sink faucet at the same time. My gold signet ring (worn by my father in the first World War) caught on the faucet, split, and caught a good-sized piece of skin. It was very painful and I was stark naked. I struggled desperately to release the pinched skin. It proved to be impossible with only one hand. So I went to the door and tried to get the attention of several male colleagues still at the pool, a hard thing to do while keeping your body out of sight! After some time I managed to catch their attention. When they came into the room, they howled with laughter as I hopped about pleading for help. When they had had a good laugh, they rescued me from my predicament.

Discovering My Physical Self

On a more personal level, the security I found in my professional life was opening my horizons and freeing me to further progress as a human being. I began to pay attention to my physical being. During my childhood years, listening to one's body was a sin. No one in our family was allowed to complain of aches and pains. Only serious illness excused taking care of oneself. To be ill was a sign of unacceptable weakness. As a consequence, I grew up ignoring my body to such an extreme that, when I was ill, I would often know of it first from the comments of persons around me. But little by little now, as I increasingly came to accept myself, I began to take better care of what Kelley called "the meat house you live in." After several failed attempts, I gave up smoking. I also began to value regular exercise and took up jogging, walking upstairs, and the like, a pattern that continues today.

Opening Cracks in the Family

While all these events were occurring in my professional life, my home life was changing as well. My expanding, changing sense of self was beginning to have its effects upon my marriage. Like the relationships of millions of couples before me, our relationship had settled into a comparatively rigid structure. Millie carried out her roles of mother, housekeeper, and wife and she did it very well. I brought home the money to keep the family running and filled my roles as father and husband acceptably, if not notably. My way of loving then was to give myself in service, provide for my wife and children, do what seemed called for in given circumstances. Outside observers would have described our family as exemplifying a "happy marriage." Each of us, including the children, I feel certain, felt loved and wanted. Our family met the accepted criteria. We filled each other's basic needs. If we failed each other, it was not for lack of caring but for lack of knowing what else was possible.

Though we fulfilled our roles with love and respect, we were unable to communicate fully from heart to heart. Neither Millie nor I knew how to deal with anger. It frightened us so that whatever anger we felt went unexpressed. I was surely not the easiest person in the world to live with. Nevertheless, in all the years of our marriage, until the very last days, I cannot recall an outburst of anger by Millie. For my part, I had learned to repress anger so thoroughly in childhood that its appearance in our relationship was unconsciously muted, repressed, or diverted elsewhere.

We dealt with events and family matters but we rarely spoke of our deeper feelings. For example, when we got word that Millie's mother was near death in Connecticut, I sprang into action in the approved fashion of males raised in our things-oriented culture and my usual approach to crises. I made arrangements to cover my classes at the University, raised the money for the long trip North, and readied the car before we set out for New England driving non-stop.

Mother Mitchell died before we got there. She was taken to Ithaca, New York for the funeral. So, on arrival in Connecticut, we immediately headed for Ithaca despite the presence of a heavy snow storm. Through it all I kept a "stiff upper lip," taking care of what I thought was required of me and the situation and dealing with matters in business-like fashion. Years later, Millie told me that I had been totally heartless, with no sense of what she was going through. I remember being shocked at her comment and hurt that she questioned my concern. Though I found it possible to respond to my clients with complete understanding, I was unable to do so with my wife. She, in her turn, was equally unable to convey her love or anger to me. We got along smoothly enough on the surface while deepening cracks were developing beneath.

I was becoming aware that there were other, more satisfying and fulfilling ways in which men and women could relate to each other. As I felt more secure in myself and my professional life, I began to long for something more in my personal existence. Unfortunately, the patterns set in place over twenty-five years of marriage would not have been easily changed even had we been aware that change was necessary. I felt restive and restrained and groped about for some sort of change. Though I did not recognize the signs at the time, it is a common experience for people in therapy to discover that the growth they achieve individually as persons may have the effect of

Mrs. and Mr. Arthur W. Combs (Art's parents—circa 1960)

widening communication gaps between husband and wife. This happens so often that I make it a practice to warn clients of the possibility and to suggest whenever possible that both partners seek therapy at the same time. At the time I was struggling in my own marriage, I was not aware of what is now commonly accepted in marriage and family counseling.

Mother and Dad were living in Greensboro, North Carolina now. I began to make visits to see them whenever I had consulting trips in the vicinity, which happened quite frequently. These trips gave me opportunities to reopen communication with my parents. Little by little we developed a new relationship. I began to recognize that my mother had truly loved and cared for me in my childhood, that she was the unhappy victim of her own childhood and unresolved conflicts. Such insights opened the door to a new relationship. I felt sympathy for her struggles and was struck by a poignant sense of her courage in dealing with them. As my need for their approval gradually disappeared and as I began to understand them more compassionately, my anger gradually dissolved and I started to feel a love for my mother and father that I had not known before.

Perceiving, Behaving, Becoming

In 1958, I was asked to chair the 1962 yearbook committee of the Association for Supervision and Curriculum Development. At the time, most yearbooks were prepared in a fashion guaranteed to produce mediocrity: the project was assigned to a committee composed of people from every walk of the profession, widely scattered to assure geographic distribution, and provided with a budget so small that members could not get together at any time except at the annual conference and at their own expense. Yearbooks produced in this manner usually turned out to be pallid "least common denominators" of the committee's deliberations.

I felt passionately about the aims and purposes of ASCD and wanted the 1962 yearbook to reflect these in a more substantive way. I also knew that whatever we define as the nature of health must, of necessity, be a major goal for education. Beginning from that assumption, I proposed to invite four eminent persons from psychology and education each to write a paper on the nature of the truly healthy, self-actualizing person. Following that, I proposed that we ask a committee of educators to explore the implications of those ideas for educational thought and practice. The editorial board agreed and I began by inviting papers from Carl Rogers, Abraham Maslow, and Earl Kelley, and I contributed one myself.

Over the next three years, our yearbook committee studied these papers, discussed them thoroughly, and explored what such ideas might mean for the educational process. We met each year at the annual conference to share and critique ideas, then assigned various members of the committee to write portions of the text. I acted as editor and did a large part of the writing myself. As was typical at the time, we had a very small budget and our committee only met in person at the national conference. The committee was also highly diverse, drawn from a wide variety of educational practitioners, from kindergarten to national administration.

Those serving on the committee were asked to set aside their usual assumptions about education, to digest a whole set of new concepts, and to show how those might be implemented in the public schools. I thoroughly enjoyed the experience of working with these fine people. I acquired a profound respect for their capacity to confront issues and formulate promising innovations. The methods and relationships I had learned in my lobbying days and in my experiments in teaching proved to be valuable once again in bringing order and agreement among a widely diverse group of persons. Throughout my career, I have found that when intelligent people are given support and the freedom to explore, they arrive at excellent solutions to human problems—a fact our forebears established in the basic democratic principle that, when people are free, they can find their own best ways.

After three intensive years in this process, we were ready to send our creation to press. There only remained the necessity for a title. After a hilarious brainstorming session, including such tongue-in-cheek suggestions as "Freeing Freddy to Function Fully," we settled on *Perceiving, Behaving Becoming: A New Focus For Education*. The book appeared on schedule in the spring of 1962. Producing the yearbook confirmed my belief in the importance of exploring fundamental assumptions in the search for innovation and change. It proved to be a stupendous success and continued to outsell more current yearbooks even twenty-five years later. It has had an effect upon education far more extensive than any of us on the committee could have imagined during the time we were engaged in producing it. For practitioners already drifting toward more humanistic approaches to teaching, it provided a theoretical basis for many of their experiments and the support of knowing what others were thinking and trying. For others, the book was an introduction to humanistic thought and practice and a source of ideas to try in their local settings. Even now, some thirty years later, I am told by educators of many persuasions how much the book contributed to their own professional growth.

A Seminar on Helping Relationships

During this same period, Dan Soper and I were engaged in a series of explorations into the nature of the helping process. The significance of empathy applied to students and clients was becoming increasingly accepted in education and counseling. Soper and I now began to apply this understanding to teachers and counselors as well. In support of our explorations, we instituted a seminar open to faculty and graduate students interested in examining helping relationships. The seminar met regularly for consideration of the helping relationship and how it might be researched from a perceptual orientation.

Out of this group came my conviction that proper understanding of helping relationships requires a perceptual orientation. I felt sure the dynamics of helping had to be understood as a perceptual problem in the interplay of the perceptions of helper and helpee, especially in terms of the helper's ways of perceiving self, others, and the nature of the helping task. This was the germ that gave form to a whole series of researches over the following twenty-year period.

Dan Soper (circa 1960), Gainesville, FL

At first, we attempted to find out if good teachers could be distinguished from poor ones on the basis of their knowledge about how they ought to behave. This study revealed that *both* good and bad teachers know how they *ought* to act. Furthermore, looking at the methods helpers employ proved no more a means of discriminating between good and poor practitioners than did looking at knowledge. Despite hundreds of studies on the topic, research is unable to distinguish any method that can be clearly shown to be characteristic of either good helpers or poor ones. Accordingly, we turned our attention to exploring the matter from a perceptual orientation. Our seminar began by formulating a list of hypotheses to be examined. These were expressed in dichotomies such as: good helpers are perceptually oriented versus objectively oriented, see themselves positively rather than negatively, are person- rather than things-oriented, have open rather than closed purposes, and the like.

These explorations resulted in several papers and researches. Dan Soper and I carried out a study entitled "The Perceptual Organization of Effective Counselors" [Combs & Soper, 1963], in which we examined the perceptions of counselors on 15 of the hypotheses proposed by the Helping Relations Seminar. We were astounded to discover that 14 of the 15 hypotheses clearly distinguished between good and poor counselors. To find that many significant differences in a set of 15 hypotheses is extremely rare in psychological research. We sensed that we were on to something big, and others apparently thought so too. This study was awarded an "Outstanding Research" commendation from the American Personnel and Guidance Association in 1963.

Recapitulation

A Recovering Self

These early days in Gainesville were a healing period. My developing self, so deeply wounded by the experiences at Syracuse, regained its balance and resumed its groping toward fulfillment. The traumatic events at Syracuse raised some serious questions. Was I a fraud? Was perceptual thinking not really the firm foundation I believed it was? Was falling in love only an attempt to relive my adolescence? Though I hadn't stated those questions to myself overtly at the time, my psyche was probing the world for answers to them. After Syracuse, I was again addressing the question: "Is it all right to be me?"

The introduction to ASCD opened a whole new world of experience with American education. The relationships and encounters I had within the organization and the consulting, writing, and speaking engagements that ASCD made possible provided priceless opportunities to learn about education at every level. In turn, my approach to education from a perceptual orientation brought a new perspective to its problems and processes.

Having made the transition from a concentration on education to one on psychology and therapy, and then back again, I returned to education enriched by having been away. Perceptual thinking spoke to teachers and supervisors in ways to which they could readily respond. As a consequence, I was in increasing demand as a speaker, consultant, and workshop leader. This acceptance by the profession provided important stimuli for my professional growth. It also contributed to a feeling of confidence in my abilities to perform effectively as a spokesperson for the humanistic movement in education.

Affirming Beliefs

It was a marvelous, confirming experience to discover that despite the rude battering it received at Syracuse, perceptual thinking was alive and well and growing stronger than ever during the early days at Florida. Painful as it was dealing with Don's withdrawal from the task, revising *Individual Behavior* drew me back to a careful review of the theory. It provided yet another opportunity to re-examine its principles, research its support, and extend its application in ways that buttressed its foundations and broadened its scope. Producing the 1962 yearbook afforded further opportunities to test and explore the soundness of perceptual thinking applied to education. The response to its message reaffirmed the position. My belief system had evolved into a firm set of guidelines or personal theory constituting a supportable basis for thinking and living, both professionally and personally.

Out of the perceptual approach came two important additions to my basic system of beliefs. One was an understanding of the crucial character of assumptions in human thinking. Theory construction teaches the importance of basic assumptions to the solution of problems. That lesson has ramifications for problem-solving no matter what the area of exploration. The discipline of beginning from basic assumptions frequently gives those engaged in it a valuable head start.

The second major contribution was recognition of the importance of the helper's perceptual organization to the helping process. We are an objectively oriented society. Everyone is focused on the behavior of students, clients and patients. In the early sixties, few were concerned about the perceptual or experiential world of helpees. And almost no one approached the helping task with an eye to the perceptual organization of the helper. Dan Soper and I were pioneers in that effort.

Personal Acceptance

The acceptance I experienced professionally contributed also to my growing strength as a person. Because I was successful professionally, I was more able to confront myself as a person and so to explore aspects of my personality in greater breadth and depth. I was freed to begin exploring such questions as "What else is me?" and "What else can I be?" These questions were unsettling but enticing. In addition to the feeling "It's all right to be me" born in my counseling experience with Ted Landsman, and the feeling "I can make it" discovered in the course of my survival at Syracuse, I was now experiencing feelings of "I am enough" in my professional life.

My personal life was another matter. Here, I did not feel enough. Instead, I had feelings of dissatisfaction with the status quo and was struggling with the growing awareness that there were other, more fulfilling, ways of being with myself and those about me. The more firmly my professional life was established, the more I was set loose to fathom the farther reaches of personal being and becoming. This does not always occur with professional success. Indeed, job success in many walks of life only has the effect of locking the person into a never-ending search for higher and higher levels of achievement in the workplace, to the detriment of broader, more personal growth. This often happens to "captains of industry" and to eminent psychologists as well. It could have happened to me.

I am not quite sure how I escaped that restricted and over-specialized path. Perhaps it was the strength of my personal longing for love and acceptance that kept me exploring personal relationships beyond their contributions to external achievement. Perhaps it was the beauty and excitement I found in the human relationships I developed in the personal interactions associated with my teaching or counseling. Or, perhaps I was very lucky in some of the warm human relationships I began to experience in these times. Whatever the reasons, I am deeply grateful that I did not bog down in a cul-de-sac of professional success but kept on exploring more internal potentialities.

Identification

The success of my professional efforts in the early years at Florida led to a deep and abiding feeling of oneness with the project of American education. I felt then, as I do now, a deep sense of empathy with teachers everywhere. We understand each other. I have total confidence in the capacity of teachers to confront and solve the knottiest of problems if they are given the freedom and trust to do so. I feel myself to be an integral part of American education. I respect its significance and appreciate its enormous potential for human welfare. I feel, too, that I am a contributing factor in the humanistic movement—not only in education but universally. My identification with education contributed to my success as a speaker and consultant on educational questions. Counselors know that deep empathy not only facilitates communication with clients, it is therapeutic in its own right. The same can be said for empathy as related to education and educators.

Widening Horizons

On a more personal level, these years were marked by a closer relationship with my mother and father. I began to love and appreciate them in fresh and more mature ways. In similar fashion, I was reaching out to form important long-time friendships with a number of males that would continue for many years. Among these were Dan Soper, Justin Harlow, Kimball Wiles, Hal Lewis, and J. B. White. Relationships with these fine people were helping me discover unparalleled depths of human experience.

Heart-Warmers

Excerpts from cards, letters, and notes that Art preserved in a file bearing this title.

JANUARY, 1956

I thought you would like to know that after the workshop for Vocational Rehabilitation counselors last spring, you were unofficially selected as not only the best on the panel but also you ran a close race for the best instructor for the whole three weeks. (Gainesville, FL)

UNDATED

The conference is over and all of you have gone your separate ways to serve another group in other or the same ways. . . . In today's paper a George Eliot poem said what I'd like you to feel about your impact on us. It is from "The Choir Invisible"—and says in part, "Oh, may I join the choir invisible of those . . . who live . . . in minds made better by their presence; live in pulses stirred to generosity, . . . in thoughts . . . that pierce the night like stars, and with their mild persistence urge men's [search] to vaster issues." (Louisville, KY)

JUNE, 1958

This is just a little note to read on the plane.

Your class was stimulating and invigorating mentally.

You charmed us with your know-how, shocked us out of our lethargy and impressed us with your innate kindliness toward us and toward your fellow teachers as shown by your comments on their auditorium appearances. (No known address)

UNDATED, FROM A STUDENT REACTION REPORT IN PSY 729

I feel that I have gained more from the two courses that I have taken from you than from any other two courses that I have ever taken in college. It has been a real privilege to have had the opportunity to be a member of your classes. I have gained a great deal of respect and admiration for you as a teacher, scholar and most of all as a "real" person who is making a tremendous contribution to psychology, education and to the many students who have had the opportunity to have known you. I think my feelings are well summed up in a remark I heard a student make to a good friend of his the other day, "You just must have at least one course under Dr. Combs before you leave the University of Florida." (Gainesville, FL)

MARCH, 1959

You were a tremendous success. Even the most critical of our workshop participants (among these are our men administrators) had the highest praise for the content of your message, as well as for your delivery of that message. "Can't we bring him back to Hamilton County?" was often asked on the evaluation sheet. (Cincinnati, OH)

NOVEMBER, 1959

My vocabulary is not extensive enough to describe your contributions to our A.S.C.D. Institute. I dislike the word very much, but I guess your talks can best be classified as "inspirations" to the group. Never have we had such a large audience remain for 2 days to listen to the same speaker. (St. Louis Park, MN)

FEBRUARY, 1960

Belatedly I want to express my personal thanks for your excellent presentation which made our Winter Conference a success. (The flu finally caught up with me.) . . . The request for tapes of your speeches has overwhelmed us. Never before have we had such a response. Over a hundred requests have been made for these tapes. (California ASCD, Southern Section)

UNDATED, FROM PRINCIPAL OF ELEMENTARY SCHOOL

Friends Like You
Friends like you mean a look and a smile
That lift the load from each weary mile;
Friends like you mean a hand's warm touch
When the task I face seems a bit too much;
Friends like you mean a day's glad start
With a brighter mind and a lighter heart;

Sunshine, flowers, skies of blue;
That's what it means to have friends like you! (No known address.)

OCTOBER, 1961

You have captivated our teachers, and they have nothing but praise for the excellent presentation which you gave at our joint in-service conference. The evaluation sheets are so complimentary of you and your work, and I am sure each of us has received a tremendous challenge and renewed inspiration to work more diligently toward improving education in Kentucky. . . . Thank you again for a superb job. (Owensboro, KY)

OCTOBER, 1961

As I have indicated to you before, I cannot begin to express my appreciation fully for the great contribution you made to the improvement of attitudes toward teaching among our teachers. Everyone has been very complimentary of the program and considered it the best that we have ever planned. (Owensboro, KY)

OCTOBER, 1961

We all respect you as a school person and know that your wisdom and good judgment will be a steady influence upon our teachers for years to come. We have conducted in-service programs for several years, and according to the evaluation sheets from the teachers, this was by far the best one we have had. (Owensboro, KY)

OCTOBER, 1961

Thank you for the very excellent contribution which you made to our In-Service Education Conference. . . . You probably wouldn't be able to wear your hat if you could hear and read all of the favorable comments concerning a certain professor from the University of Florida. One suggestion read like this, "Please, please let's have Art Combs again." Another, "Everything Art Combs said went straight to my soul and I felt clean and proud of being—just being, and I felt so humble that I was a teacher of children." (Owensboro, KY)

JANUARY, 1962, *from a letter to ASCD headquarters, a copy of which was forwarded to Art*

You must be receiving hundreds of letters praising the new Yearbook. Here is another one to add to the pile. Our people are unanimous in their expressions of appreciation that this work was made available. . . . "Perceiving, Behaving, Becoming" is a new high-water mark of achievement which is certain to bring added acclaim your way. (Tucson, AZ)

JANUARY, 1962, *from a letter to ASCD headquarters, a copy of which was forwarded to Art*

I've just browsed through your new yearbook. It's make-up has a real "come-hither" quality about it and the content seems fresh and inviting. Looks like you've hit a home run with the bases loaded. . . . I'm anxious to get deeper into it. The thirty-eight basic propositions claimed my attention at once. (Washington, DC)

JANUARY, 1962, *from a letter to ASCD headquarters, a copy of which was forwarded to Art*

Please accept my most hearty congratulations on the publication of the new Year Book. This is a beautiful job and one of the most provocative pieces of professional literature I have seen in a long time. (Nashville, TN)

FEBRUARY, 1962

I was one of several who listened to your presentation on the topic, "Psychology and Learning" yesterday, January 31st at Redlands.

I don't know when I have heard a more stimulating and thought-provoking presentation. . . . (Barstow, CA)

FEBRUARY, 1962

It was really wonderful to spend that evening with you in . . . such an informal atmosphere.

There is something about you that made me like you very much. Even when I was a student and you a professor I was never scared of you and I had always a deep admiration for you. . . . I just wanted you to know that I enjoyed very much your visit to New Paltz, . . . (New Paltz, NY)

FEBRUARY, 1962

Now the time has come when perhaps I can settle down long enough to get written to you this long overdue letter; the Uruguayans have made their tearful farewells (just after Col. Glenn was launched into outer space) and life at the College is getting back to normal. You deserved to be told long before this what an impact your visit at New Paltz really made—not only on the Uruguayans but on all of us who were privileged to spend some time with you. Undoubtedly many other people in your lifetime, to whom you have given so much of yourself, have told you what a "great guy" you really are and my feeling that way is just another recognition of your sincere contribution to people.

Lest you think I am exaggerating the reactions of the Uruguayans, I can give you a bit of objective evidence. I asked them to respond anonymously to a short, written questionnaire, which I have had translated from Spanish into English. I had stressed the fact that the answers of each one should be in terms of what the seminar had meant to that person personally, and I have reason to believe that their reactions were given spontaneously and reflect the way individuals felt. On the two questions relating (1) to the identification of the five or six experiences and/or resource persons which had meant the most to the person during the entire period of the New Paltz stay; and (2) if the period of the seminar had been longer, what activities or time with which resource persons would they have liked to have had extended, all twenty-one named *you*. Further, you were the only person named by all of them in answers to these two questions. Sixteen of them included the camp week-end among their most significant experiences; and fifteen of them named Esther (more credit to you). The visit with Mrs. Roosevelt, which I thought was a "highlight" for all of them, their school being named Escuela Franklin Delano Roosevelt, was named by only eleven as being among their five or six most significant experiences; ten of them named the visit with the Governor (he was charming with them, laughing and chatting with them in Spanish). But you were the only one named by all of them. When I told these results to some of the people at the College who had a chance to be with you (including my daughter . . .), their comments were: "Well, does that surprise you?" or "I'm glad they realize what an opportunity they had to be with him." (New Paltz, NY)

MARCH, 1962

We have received many excellent comments on our recent Guidance Conference held at Winthrop College. You are responsible for this conference being so successful, and we appreciate very much the assistance you gave to us. (Columbia, SC)

References

Maslow, A. H. (1962). *Toward a psychology of being*. Princeton, NJ: Van Nostrand.
Maslow, A. H. (1970). *Motivation and personality* (2nd ed.). New York: Harper & Row.

Arthur W. Combs with unidentified individual at meeting of the American Society of Personnel Administration (ASPA), forerunner to the Society for Human Resource Management (SHRM). Photo taken circa late 1960s.

CHAPTER EIGHT

Growth and Change in the Sixties

Much has been written of the sixties as a time of national turmoil. It was a time of turmoil for me as well, both personally and professionally. These years included the high water mark of my professional career, including a burst of productivity that resulted in 60 publications and speaking/consulting engagements in all 50 states. They also saw the beginning of profound changes in my personal life as the focus of my reach for fulfillment shifted from external to internal sources of satisfaction.

My Children Leave Home

Throughout the fifties I was so deeply involved in the problems and excitement of my professional career that I spent little quality time with my two growing children. I did not neglect or abuse them. Neither did I purposefully seek closer relationships with them. Like thousands of workaholic parents before me, I was there when needed but left most of the nurturance and care to my wife. In consequence, though I loved them and cared for them, I really did not know my children. Nor did they really know me. I was not aware of this lack in my life until the early sixties, when both children left home. Carol graduated from high school in 1957 and enrolled at the University of Florida. Two years later, Peter graduated and was off to Stetson University, a smaller institution near Daytona Beach. Then, in 1961, Peter joined the Army and Carol left home to be with her boyfriend, Jerry, who was starting graduate work at Emory University in Atlanta.

I remember vividly the day Carol left. I had been in the hospital for four days for a hemorrhoidectomy. As I walked in the front door, my daughter was just leaving for Atlanta. We embraced, said good-bye, and she was gone. I was suddenly overcome with a crazy mixture of grief and relief: grief at the realization that Carol was probably leaving for good, and relief at escape from the indignities of my hospital experience. I remember throwing myself on the bedroom floor and sobbing uncontrollably.

Peter, Millie, and Art (1961)

Now that it was too late, I began to regret not having closer relationships with my son and daughter. As a psychologist I was aware that children normally break away from their parents in adolescence and, too often, never find happier relationships afterwards. I was saddened at the realization of my inadequacy and promised myself that I would take advantage of whatever opportunities they offered me down the road to share myself more fully with them. Shortly after, two such opportunities were especially meaningful for me.

The first was a heart-to-heart conversation with Carol close to the time of her wedding. Afterward she wrote me, in part, "What I want to say is mostly that I love you. When you were talking to me in the car I loved you so much I thought I couldn't bear it. The relationship between a father and daughter is so close to the center of being—that it is hard to talk about. But I do love you.

"It is a process of endless amazement getting to know you as a person (not that fathers aren't people—but you know what I mean). There is so much about you that I don't know—I know you have been trying to talk to me lately and I am so glad.

"And now I am getting married. But you are really gaining a daughter instead of losing one because we are getting to know each other. And I am

Art with Carol on her wedding day (December 27, 1959)

even getting to know me! I feel that in spite of setbacks and hindrances, I am moving steadily toward the beginning of some synthesis—things are falling into place and I think some great and permanent ideas are emerging. The first idea of all is that the most important thing in the world is love. The love that people have for each other is so very precious and important; people don't tell each other about it enough. They don't let down their masks and become human, they don't give when they feel like it or let others give to them. People are so shy, so afraid of being hurt. But love is so joyful, even if it does hurt because it is so deep a thing.

"But, (I just realized) this was part of what you were telling me in the car!"

The second was a very moving experience with my son. Peter was in training at Fort Knox before his assignment to Europe. When a consulting engagement took me to the vicinity, I suggested he see if he could get a day off so that we would spend some time together. He was granted a pass and I picked him up at the fort in a rental car. This was a special time for each of us. We loafed around, went out to dinner, and then to the movie *West Side Story*. After a late-night snack we turned in and quietly talked from one bed to the other until we fell asleep. Next morning, I dropped him off at the fort and left to keep my consulting engagement. Our few hours of togetherness were memorable for each of us and we have often reminded each other since of that very special time. To this day, I get a warm and tender rush when I hear Bernstein's music from *West Side Story*.

I Fall in Love

Once my children were gone from home, I became more aware that my interactions with Millie were becoming increasingly strained. Our communication was clumsy and inhibited. I was beginning to question our way of life. I began to realize that I had long accepted the familiar comfort of our home and its relationships because I was unaware that there was anything more to expect. Now professional success was making it possible to turn more attention to the personal side of life. I was finding heretofore unrealized satisfactions in interpersonal relationships and discovering wider, more fulfilling ways of being and becoming. In the midst of these shifts in awareness, for the first time in my adult life, I fell in love.

Kathy and I met at an educational conference in Washington. She was a highly intelligent and innovative teacher in an alternative school, a strong, sensitive, and attractive woman eight years younger than I. Kathy had been married before our meeting and had a young son in his teens. The humanistic thinking that I promoted found a ready response in her. Indeed, she had been putting such principles to work in her classroom long before our meeting. Professionally and personally, we were kindred spirits. Soon we were seeing each other regularly, becoming more and more deeply involved.

After a year, our relationship had become so intense as to seriously interfere with my marriage. Accordingly, Millie and I entered counseling with a friend in the clergy to see if our union could be salvaged. The experience was a disaster. Far from the empathic person-centered relationship that my view of counseling required, this counselor felt it necessary to listen, then show us the way. Since Millie wanted to keep the relationship and I was threatening to break it off, I was cast in the role of perpetrator with Millie as the victim. Our counselor treated my dilemma as the consequence of an immature urge to relive my adolescence. "Surely, a man of your intelligence and training can see how silly that is," he chided. He even presented me with a book inscribed, "To Arthur Combs on his 21st birthday"! However well-meaning, his ministrations only compounded my distress and increased my feelings of guilt. Distressed at his inadequacy as a therapist and frustrated by lack of resolution, after several months I suggested a marital separation for the summer. Millie agreed.

I was scheduled to teach in the summer quarter at the university in Bellingham, Washington. Accordingly, when school was out, Peter and I crossed the country by car. Peter had just graduated from high school and I welcomed his company. I tentatively shared some of my dilemma during the trip. On the advice of our counselor, and despite my protestations, Millie shortly followed by train and we spent a strained and unhappy summer.

On our return to Florida, I ceased counseling and turned to my friend Earl Kelley for advice. He was sympathetic and understanding but advised me, "Never get a divorce. Do what you need to, but never hurt Millie." Earl meant well but he, too, responded with tragic advice. What he proposed reduced my relationship with Kathy to "an affair," called into question my personal integrity and the sincerity of my love for Kathy, and enormously increased my feelings of guilt and despair.

Finally, the pain was so great that I sought out a lawyer to file for divorce. To my utter dismay, I discovered there were only two grounds upon which it could be granted: Millie's infidelity or her abusive behavior. I was devastated. Neither of these were grounds that applied in my case. They could not be claimed without insulting and demeaning my wife or living a lie myself. The pain of this reality was unbearable. With a heavy heart, I turned to breaking off my relationship with Kathy. It was not until ten years later that I fully realized the error of my decision.

To help assuage the anguish of my plight at the time, I threw myself once again into one activity and another. Hoping that immersion in some common projects might improve our relationship, and despite Millie's reluctance, I planned a trip to Europe the next summer. We bought a car in Europe and spent the summer touring the continent. Peter was in the Army, stationed in Germany, so we picked him up and he went along with us for a couple of weeks through Switzerland and Italy. Instead of the improvement in our relationship that I had hoped for, however, we returned home exhausted and took up where we last left off. Next, I threw myself into the joys and frustrations of building a new home. I also took on an increased load of consulting engagements and buried myself in research and writing projects. For her part, Millie updated her teaching credentials and went to work as an elementary school teacher.

Some Effects of the Sixties

The early sixties were an exciting time at the University of Florida. The College of Education was rapidly gaining national stature: it was looked to as a place where good things were happening. Kim Wiles was elected president of ASCD, becoming the second member of our faculty to serve in that position of leadership. The entire campus was experiencing the winds of change as students, like those at many other colleges across the country, rose in revolt against the university administration and demonstrated against the Vietnam War. At the same time, the university was beginning to respond to growing demands for desegregation and admitted its first black students.

Events of the sixties had an enormous impact upon my growth and self-understanding. The breakdown of many of our institutions, the civil rights

Art Combs, Millie Combs (1963)

struggle, the tragedy of Vietnam, the revolt of young people, and the reaffirmation of human values characteristic of those tumultuous, disturbing, and stimulating days had at least three major influences upon my life:

1. They corroborated my feeling of oneness with the human condition.
2. They reaffirmed the significance of the humanistic movement and the importance of perceptual thinking.
3. They gave new impetus and urgency to my growing need for personal fulfillment.

Here are some excerpts from a tape-recording of a conversation I had with several former students in the mid-sixties:

"One of the things I'm deeply impressed by these days is the movement of young people of this generation and their demands for a counterculture. I'm convinced that many of the concerns of these young people are going to have great significance and I have a terrible need to feel, somehow, that I am involved in that process because I think it will mean so very much, not only for me as an individual but for our society as well.

"It seems to me that the times we are living in represent a shift in human energy expenditure from . . . original problems of finding food, clothing, shelter and conquering of the environment. . . . We are now able to control our environment and to produce food, clothing and shelter as never before in the course of history. Today our problems are human problems, rather than problems of things. I think that fact is basic to the development of the whole humanist philosophy. As Tom Hanna* puts it, we have shifted from a third person conception of dealing with human problems to a first person conception. That is to say, from dealing with humans as objects to man as experiential person. As I look at the trend in world events, the history of humankind has been increasingly toward greater and greater recognition and expression of the fundamental dignity and integrity of persons. Though we have gone through terrible periods in which human beings have been degraded, as for example in Nazi Germany and in our own country with the American Indians and the Blacks, we have also been climbing, little by little and bit by bit, toward increasingly greater recognition of human dignity and integrity. It finds its expression in such things as the development of the United Nations, the World Court, women's liberation and the right to vote, elimination of child labor, the rise of labor unions, even several wars fought to oppose dehumanizing influences. We also see it in the civil rights movement, concern for the elderly and the instrumentation of Social Security, the march toward socialized medicine. I have a feeling there is a trend in the world toward increasingly humanizing concerns.

"I find myself confronting the question, 'What do you do with the remaining years of your life?' I don't feel at this point like an old man and I have no intention of retiring until I absolutely have to. However, the question arises, 'having done the things that you have done, come this far, where do you go from here?' Especially, how does one go about achieving real self actualization in the maximum degree possible?"

The Roots of Prejudice

Johnnie Ruth Clarke was the first black doctoral student at the university. I was not on Johnnie Ruth's committee but served as her counselor and friend as she pioneered her way through the labyrinth of graduate bureaucracy, the notoriety of her position, and the personal problems all this entailed. I have never forgotten the day she passed her final orals. It was a moment of joy and

---

* Editor's note: Tom Hanna, then chair of the Department of Philosophy at the University of Florida, went on to found the Novato Institute for Somatic Research and Training in Novato, CA and become editor of *Somatics Magazine-Journal of the Bodily Arts & Sciences*. Among the best known of the seven books he authored are Hanna (1970) and Hanna (1989).

shame for me, an object lesson in the depths of prejudice. I was standing in the hall outside my office when Johnnie Ruth emerged from her exam at the far end of the hall. As she left the room, she caught sight of me and came flying down the hall crying, "Art, Art, I passed. I passed." She flung her arms around me and we hugged each other with joy at her accomplishment. But, in the midst of our hug, an ugly thought hit me: "I wonder who saw this." There it was, the detestable remnants of the culture I grew up in.

It passed in a flick of an eyelash and I returned to sharing a moment of triumph with this truly remarkable woman, but this fleeting experience had a poignant effect upon me. I saw myself as a liberal in those days, unshakably opposed to segregation, committed to the concept of the equality of human beings. I shared my beliefs openly, actively seeking to change the system wherever and whenever I could. Nevertheless, the message from my depths in responding to Johnnie Ruth's hug revealed the fact that I still had unreconciled and unacceptable parts of myself to confront and come to terms with. The incident forced me to further examine my belief system for other inconsistencies.

I had told myself that not everyone can march on Selma; some of us must advance the cause through teaching and acting on the home turf. Now I began to ask myself if that was only a cop-out, a product of the fear of violent confrontation I learned in childhood. In time I was able to forgive myself and to appreciate the value of my less dramatic but nonetheless significant contributions made through teaching, smoothing the way for minority students, and taking a stand for human rights. To this day, however, I cannot see clips of that fateful march on Selma without feelings of regret that I was not among those participating in this heroic statement.

My personal involvement in the Civil Rights movement was far less dramatic. In the early fifties it was necessary one day to take my daughter Carol to the emergency room at the hospital in Gainesville. I was fascinated to notice on the doctor's table three beakers of alcohol, containers for thermometers labeled White Oral, Colored Oral, and Anal! Apparently there were some levels at which desegregation did not matter!

While consulting at Southern University in Texas during the desegregation days, I was invited to lunch with the all-black faculty and we went to a downtown cafeteria-like restaurant. As I pushed my tray along the serving line, I was aware that the servers were placing my choices on the plate with unusual firmness but paid scant attention to the matter. Our group sat in the middle of the seating area. As I chatted with those around me, I was only slightly aware that we were the object of almost everyone's eyes. I understood, however, when we left the restaurant and one of my hosts said, "Thank you, Dr. Combs. You just helped us integrate that place!"

Graduate Work at Florida

During the sixties, a number of top-flight graduate students came to the College of Education. Some worked with me using hypotheses developed in our Seminar on the Helping Relationship for their doctoral dissertations. Most have gone on to make important contributions in colleges of education elsewhere. One of these students became a lifelong friend. On a consulting trip to Kentucky in the mid-sixties, I met a young teacher, Richard Usher, who was so highly recommended by everyone who knew him that I encouraged him to come to Florida and arranged an assistantship for him. Of all the graduate students I have sponsored, Dick probably understands me and perceptual thinking best. I value his friendship and his magnificent capacity to interpret perceptual thinking for teachers and administrators in the field.

It saddens me to think of the opportunities I missed to be closer to many of my students in these years. A number of factors prevented the development of deeper relationships. For one thing, my basic shyness and hesitation to reach out to people around me was easily interpreted as aloofness or lack of caring. I hesitated to impose upon people. Unless I felt especially needed, I was unlikely to be warmly responsive. Because I had strong feelings that graduate students were capable persons, I saw my role as facilitator and helper rather than as director or mentor while responding to student needs. Students have told me since that they reacted to me in quite different terms. Unhappily, they interpreted my behavior as lack of concern or even rejection in some cases.

I was also preoccupied then with my professional life. My workaholic attitudes and schedule must surely have created the impression that I was too busy or that I expected similar behavior in those around me. For my part, I sometimes felt that people were putting me on a pedestal and were fearful of approaching me. It's pretty lonesome on a pedestal and there were many times when I would have given a great deal for warmer, more personal relationships.

I'm reminded of Earl Kelley's story of how he met John Dewey. He went to a convention and just on the spur of the moment when he had a couple of drinks he called John Dewey and said he was interested in speaking to him. Dewey invited him up to his hotel room and later told him, "You know, I've been here all by myself and I've been so terribly lonesome." I know that feeling. I have done a great deal of work as a consultant and I have spent many a lonely hour in hotel rooms in various parts of this country. It has just never been easy for me to make the outgoing attempt to seek out human interaction. It has to do with the fundamental problem of rejection. If one is rejected and has asked for nothing, that is pretty much something one is able to take in stride. When you hold out your hand to someone, however, and then you are rejected, the rejection is increased manifold. And I guess maybe it's something like that that has been characteristic of me. I have a great capacity to communicate from heart to heart with people when I *know* that they need me. It is not so easy for me to do when this is not the case.

It seems to me that graduate work in most American universities is currently pretty discouraging and disillusioning. We are still living with demands and procedures held over from medieval times and thinking. Work for the doctorate in most institutions is often a stressful, threatening, and demeaning experience. In addition, many graduate programs have been reduced to a series of hurdles, small steps to be completed in fixed sequence. This tends to keep students concentrating upon details rather than the basic thinking and broad considerations that foster the development of a truly significant practitioner. I think it an anathema that graduate programs in too many institutions prescribe the student's every course or experience. Doctoral programs without a single elective are all too common.

I believe graduate programs should be highly selective in the admission of students, then give them greatest possible leeway to construct their own program of learning experiences with the help and guidance of a committee tailored to their needs. Such committees ought to be the student's friends and advisors, rather than his or her examiners and executioners. Somewhere along the way, each student should confront some "moment of truth" at which he or she has opportunity to demonstrate competence in a scholarly fashion. In place of the trauma of examinations, I would substitute the building of a portfolio to which student and faculty would contribute evidence of competence and developing expertise. The student's mentor ought not be a part of the evaluation process, except, perhaps, as the student's advocate. This would remove the advisor from the role of judge and make possible the kind of helper-facilitator relationship a doctoral program ought to involve. In such a setting the dissertation defense would be not an examination, but a celebration.

I fought long and hard to institute changes along these lines in graduate programs at the University of Florida, but managed to effect only minor modifications in the hoary traditions of academe. I served several terms on the university's graduate committee and battled regularly for more humane policies. Every year, for example, I made a pitch for a substitute for the Graduate

Record Exam (GRE) required for entrance to graduate work. The GRE had to be given at a set time for all students and grades were not available for at least a month later, leaving students in considerable anxiety. I proposed giving our own exam, which could be scored in twenty minutes and was equally as selective. But after the ensuing discussion, the matter was laid to rest as the dean of the graduate school said disparagingly, "Dr. Combs, the GRE is used by Harvard, Princeton, and the universities of Missouri, Indiana, and Illinois. Surely, you would not want us to leave that distinguished company, would you?"

The Humanistic Movement and the Human Condition

For several generations, American education has been slowly but surely moving toward a more humanistic orientation. For most of its existence, public education has been dominated by an autocratic, controlling philosophy that comes about as a consequence of preoccupation with changing behavior into someone's conception of what is right and proper. Behavioral psychology confirmed such thinking. Stimulus-response concepts and behavior modification strategies led directly to management philosophies inhibiting the ability of education to adapt to the realities of modern society. Little by little, the enormous educational colossus is moving in more appropriate directions. Teachers everywhere are discovering more effective ways of carrying out their tasks by employing more humane and person-centered philosophies. I believe the humanistic movement is absolutely essential for our times, an inevitable destiny for education. If it did not exist, we would have to invent it. My two papers, "Humanistic Education: Too Tender for a Tough World?" [Combs, 1981] and "What the Future Demands of Education" [Combs, 1981] are attempts to express that conviction.

Once before, education experienced a humanistic tendency in the "Progressive Education" philosophy of the thirties and forties. That movement came to an unhappy end primarily because it had too narrow a foundation. It was based, almost exclusively, in the philosophy of John Dewey. Dewey recognized the human quality of learning, advocated "learning by doing," and called attention to the importance of involving the need or interest of the learner. Teachers here and there were intrigued with these ideas and a few schools, like the laboratory school at Ohio State, experimented with implementation of Dewey's thinking. Unfortunately, there was little confirmation of Dewey's concepts from the social sciences of the day or in hard research data. The excesses of some of progressive education's advocates also made it the object of public ridicule. A cartoon, for example, showed a little boy plaintively asking, "Do I have to express myself today?" Jokes were made about children doing anything they pleased. It was finally done in with the nation's preoccupation with the Second World War.

Today's humanistic movement is a very different animal. It is part of a much larger humanist movement occurring in all of the social and political sciences. It also finds firm support in modern psychological research. Perceptual psychology, for example, provides a comprehensive, systematic, internally consistent underpinning for the humanistic movement, as do several other psychological schools of thought, e.g., the work of Carl Rogers, Abraham Maslow, and other Third Force psychologists. The movement gives me a sense of being involved in a phenomenon much larger than myself and all of education and psychology. I believe it has significance for all human endeavors for as far ahead as we can discern. It gives me a corroborating feeling of fulfillment and privilege to be able to make a significant contribution to its advancement.

This sense of oneness, of being in the stream, does not apply only to the humanistic movement. I have such a feeling about the human condition in its entirety, about the universe itself. It seems to me that each of us is a series of organizations. Smaller and smaller ones within our bodies constitute various systems, organs, tissues, cells, atoms, etc., etc. We are also part of larger and larger systems: families, neighborhoods, countries, the United Nations, the earth, the solar system, galaxies, and the universe itself. Moreover, we are both products of such systems on the one hand and determiners of them on the other. This makes each of us both product and producer of the universe itself. For me, that requires living and being in ways that harmonize with the whole.

This experience of oneness with the human condition and the responsibility it entails has a fundamentally spiritual quality for me. I do not belong to any religious sect or denomination. In fact, I have never felt the need of a formal church. I recognize and understand that others find one dogma or another a source of satisfaction and I will defend their right to do so. A Methodist minister friend once told me, "Christ gave us a beautiful philosophy and a way of being with each other. Paul gave us a church and we have been in trouble ever since." I feel one with and in touch with the essence of religion, but feel no need for its formal structure.

President of ASCD

In 1965, I was asked to permit my name to be placed in nomination for national president of the Association for Supervision and Curriculum Development. I agreed, never expecting the membership would elect a psychologist instead of a well-known educator. To my surprise, I was elected. That plunged me into a three-year whirlwind of involvement with American education. ASCD's presidents spent a year as president-elect, followed by a year as president and a year as vice president, serving all this time on the Executive Committee as well. As a consequence, I launched into a three-year period of speeches, policy-making, program planning, and coordinating the operations of a five-thousand-member organization made up of teachers, supervisors, administrators, and college personnel. The College of Education was pleased at my election and lightened my teaching load so that I could spend more time in these new responsibilities.

A major task of the president-elect was to aid in planning the annual conference for the year he or she was president. I chose as my theme for the 1967 meetings in Dallas "Humanizing Education: The Person in the Process." Humanistic approaches to education were just beginning to gain a measure of acceptance and I was pleased to be able to give the concept a boost. Keynote addresses were made by Carl Rogers, Harlan Shores, William Van Til, Sidney Jourard, and Galen Saylor. My presidential address [Combs, 1967] was titled with the theme of the conference, "Humanizing Education: The Person in the Process." The Texas chapter of the association surprised me with a trip to a western outfitter, where I was decked out in cowboy togs from ten-gallon hat to boots and spurs. They arranged a program of lavish hospitality including a giant chuck wagon dinner and square dance.

For five days I found myself surrounded by the warmth, acceptance, and appreciation of the membership. I had a clear sense of being valued, loved, respected, and caught up in a great and important movement. The culmination came in a standing ovation from three or four thousand participants at the close of my presidential address. I have experienced many such ovations since. They always affect me deeply. This one, however, was very special. In all my relationships with ASCD, then and now, I feel wanted and appreciated.

At that time ASCD was primarily made up of people who were supervisors and curriculum directors, humanistically oriented school administrators, or educators from the universities and colleges. Members were interested in ideas and people. Innovative ideas and practices were welcomed, debated, and put to the test of action. A deep concern for persons pervaded the thinking, activities, and publications of those associated with this group. I felt thoroughly at home with the organization and its people. In addition to the 1962 yearbook, *Perceiving, Behaving, Becoming*, I wrote, edited, co-authored, or contributed to such monographs in ASCD's publications program as *Educational Accountability: Beyond Behavioral Objectives* [Combs,

1972], *Humanistic Education: Objectives and Assessment* [Combs, Aspy, Brown, Clute, & Hicks, 1978] and *Humanizing Education: The Person in the Process* [Combs, 1967] as well as numerous shorter articles for the organization's journal, *Educational Leadership*. I was also a frequent speaker and participant at ASCD's annual conferences or its many state and local chapters around the country. This warm and sustaining relationship continued for more than thirty years.

During my three years in office, I made appearances in 30 states, chaired dozens of meetings, and participated in innumerable committee sessions, workshops, and planning meetings at the Washington headquarters, the annual conference, or membership meetings in the various states. It was a priceless opportunity to observe American education firsthand everywhere in the nation. I was thrilled to be involved in the process and grateful for the opportunity to broaden and deepen my perceptions. I found, once again, that the skills I had acquired in applying perceptual thinking to group operations came in handy.

More Perils of Consulting

In 1967, while I was president of ASCD, the association, for one of its Executive Committee meetings, rented a seven-room suite at the Sheraton that had just been vacated by a senator. This was a weird experience for me. Since all the other members of the Executive Committee and staff lived in Washington or its environs, I was left to wander about that huge suite in lonesome splendor! I was not accustomed to such opulence. I felt as though I were lost in a museum. I also had a taste of power in the course of our meetings. The agenda called for deciding upon the location of our annual conference three years hence. The conference committee recommended two cities: Las Vegas and San Francisco. In the course of the conference, our delegates would probably spend in the neighborhood of a million dollars. When it came time to vote, the Executive Committee vote was tied. It was up to me to break the deadlock! Never in my life, before or since, have I had to determine where such sums would be spent. My financial life has been spent at much humbler levels. Knowing that many public school boards would take a very dim view of providing stipends and expenses to send their teachers to Las Vegas, I cast my vote for San Francisco.

Once I was scheduled to make an address to a conference in Frisco, Colorado, a town about 10,000 feet in altitude. From Gainesville I took a plane to Tampa, Florida, where I spent the night in a motel a foot or two above sea level. The next morning, I boarded the plane for Colorado. When

I reached my destination, I was met at the airport by the program chair and whisked up the mountain. Arriving at the hotel, I was told, "You are on in twenty minutes," just time enough to change clothes and glance at my notes. Once I was introduced, I launched into my address. After only a minute or so, however, I became so dizzy from altitude sickness I had to talk to the audience while sitting down. I had come from sea level to 10,000 feet in a little more than four hours.

On another occasion I arrived in Los Angeles for a week of twice-a-day speeches at school districts in the L.A. area. When I reached my hotel, the taxi driver unloaded my bag. I laid my briefcase on the roof of the cab while I dug the fare from my wallet, and paid the driver. Then I turned to pick up my suitcase and reached for my briefcase—but it was gone on top of the cab, which raced away into the traffic! There I was, scheduled for 10 appearances in the next five days with all my notes, references, correspondence, and plans somewhere in Los Angeles. After I got over my initial panic, I found I got along quite well, as I discovered I did not really need the materials I had lost and perhaps even managed better than usual because I was speaking extemporaneously. I gained new confidence in these circumstances and have not spoken with more than a bare outline ever since. Two weeks after I returned home to Florida, some kind soul in L.A. sent me my briefcase with an unsigned note: "Thought you might need this!"

I also recall a time I was scheduled to speak in Cobo Hall in Detroit, Michigan. In preparation, I planned my usual informal chat with the audience of school administrators. When I arrived, I found that Cobo Hall seats thirty or forty thousand and my audience of perhaps three hundred was scattered here and there among the thousands of seats. I stood at the podium, a tiny dot on the main floor of the amphitheater with thousands of empty seats rising far above me, with a few people in small groups lost in space here and there. So much for an intimate chat!

One summer in the early sixties I agreed to teach at Western Washington University in Bellingham, Washington. The books and references I ordered for my class were not there when I arrived. Day after day, my students and I suffered in frustration without the materials we needed. At the end of the first week, I arranged for a movie. The audio-visual assistants wheeled in the equipment, discovered they needed a new lamp for the projector, scurried about to find and install one, then started the movie, only to realize it was the wrong one. After more scurrying about, they found the right one. Nearing the end of my patience, I asked a student at the back of the room, "Please, Bill, will you pull down that shade for us?" Bill did and the whole unit came crashing down, flooding the room with bright sunshine. That day at the Faculty Club, someone asked how things were going.

"I think I'm jinxed," I said, "Evil spirits are after me."

At this, one of the faculty leaned across the table and very seriously said that I was lucky, because he was an accomplished exorciser of ghosts, goblins, and evil spirits. I was not much amused.

On Monday, our materials had still not arrived and I was doing the best I could with a short lecture. Suddenly, the door opened and three faculty members marched in. The first had a clothes tree carried like a lance. The second carried a mirror and the third carried a large flashlight. They stood in a row across the front of the room and unrolled a scroll, declaring with a great flourish that "On this day of our Lord " they had come to exorcise the demons in Professor Combs's classroom. Following this, the man with the clothes tree waved it about, all the while declaiming that he carried the lance of virtue against which no demon could survive. The second individual, a woman, asserted that it is a well-known fact that witches cannot bear to see themselves in a mirror. With that, she flashed the mirror about the room with a solemn face, shouting, "Begone, you evil spirits!" Next, the gentleman with the flashlight announced that he carried the light of knowledge, before which no evil thing could survive. This done, they presented me with an official scroll as a guarantee of their services and solemnly marched from the room. Needless to say, I enjoyed every moment of the farce and forgot my frustrations. But even at the end of the semester, some of my students were still asking: "Dr. Combs, that day those other profs came into our room, what were we supposed to learn that day?!!!"

New Relationships with Parents

One of the fringe benefits of being president of ASCD in the year after leaving office was the privilege of representing the organization at an international conference of educators. That year the meetings were held in Dublin. I invited my mother to join Millie and me for a couple of weeks touring England and France after the conference. I was coming to terms with my past and my trips to Greensboro were helping to bring a more mature acceptance and love for my mother. Charlotte was in her eighties now and would be making her first transoceanic flight to join us in Dublin. Her flight was delayed in New York for five hours and she missed her connection at Shannon airport for the trip to Dublin. When I inquired about the delay, airline officials informed me they were sending her from Shannon to Dublin by taxi—across the whole country! I was quite worried about how she would hold up under all this and anxiously awaited the arrival of her cab. When it came, she popped out of the car, introduced me to all the other passengers, and asked, "Can I have a drink?" After which, I helped this remarkable elderly lady upstairs for a nap! She proved a delightful companion during our travels and I enjoyed the opportunity to share so much with her. I came to see her in a new light as a feisty and lovable human being.

A Trip to Germany

One of the consulting trips I accepted during the sixties was an appearance in Berchtesgaden, Germany, at a workshop for supervisors and administrators employed by the Overseas Schools program of the Department of Defense. Two events on this trip were especially notable: one amusing, the other horrific. Arriving at the airport in Frankfurt, I was ushered to a VIP lounge and asked to wait in order to join the party of the Assistant Secretary of Defense, who was also on his way to the conference. When he arrived, he was accompanied by a colonel acting as his aide. I was astounded to find that I, too, was assigned an aide for the occasion, a major no less. The four of us took off together in a small plane.

After a beautiful low-level flight across the country, we landed at an airfield near Berchtesgaden. Here the troops were lined up to honor the secretary and I discovered that I was expected to inspect the troops along with the secretary. So, with my major trotting along at my heels, I solemnly marched down the line. At Berchtesgaden I was put up in a VIP suite and provided with every convenience, all at government expense. I was also invited to go along with the secretary and his party for a boat trip on a beautiful lake in the region. This, however, was not included in my contract. Weeks later, I received a bill from the Defense Department for $4.35, the cost of my ticket for the boat ride. Such are the wonders of government bureaucracy!

Completing my stint at Berchtesgaden, I drove back to Frankfurt with a supervisor friend, stopping overnight in Munich on the way. It was fall and the Oktoberfest was in full swing. We spent the evening drinking and singing with hundreds of other happy celebrants in the Hofbrau Haus. The next morning, we drove to Dachau. What a shock! As I walked about this former concentration camp visiting the "showers" and the crematorium, I was overcome with horror at the enormity and the bestiality of the Holocaust. How could it be that the same people I enjoyed so much last night were capable of this? What did this mean about the fundamental nature of human beings? The visit had an enormous impact upon me. It extended my feeling of oneness with the human condition and reaffirmed my belief in the significance of the humanistic movement and the basic concepts it sought to advance.

In and Out of Administration

Ted Landsman came to the campus one summer and stayed to join the faculty of the Department of Personnel Services. About the same time [1968-1969], I was elected to chair the Department of Foundations in Education. Accordingly, I resigned from the Personnel Services Department to devote full attention to my increased responsibilities. I was pleased at this vote of confidence from my colleagues in the Foundations Department. After a year, however, my duties began to pall and I asked the dean for permission to resign from the chairmanship. I have been in and out of administrative positions a number of times in my career. I appreciate the power to get things done that an administrative position carries but, at heart, I am fundamentally a counselor and teacher. Whenever I am away from these latter roles for very long, I begin to yearn for the more personal relationships they afford. I enjoy having the means to advance the programs of immediate concern to me. But I find it distasteful to be responsible for matters not directly related to those ends. Despite many offers of higher administrative roles, I have never regretted my decision to remain a teacher and counselor.

I Lose Good Friends

In the late sixties I suffered two very personal losses. The first was a result of Dan Soper's decision to leave the University of Florida for a position at Southern Illinois University at Edwardsville. Dan had been growing increasingly restive with his position as psychologist at the Lab School. He wanted to return to a university faculty. I sympathized with his desire but saw him leave with great regret. Dan and I had become close friends and counselors for each other. His departure from the U of F left a big hole in my life. No one could quite replace the intimate relationship we had during his stay. Though we remained good friends until his death, we never again had opportunity to resume our former relationship.

The second loss I experienced was that of Don Snygg. Don wrote me in the mid-sixties suggesting a third revision for *Individual Behavior*. After doing the second revision alone, I had no stomach for a repeat performance. Accordingly, he set out to do it himself. I spent a happy few hours with him in New York City talking about the new edition. He was about to remarry and shared his happiness with me. Six months later, he died of a heart attack. I felt a deep sense of loss at his passing. In spite of our authorship difficulties, I loved him very much. He made an immense contribution to my growth and fulfillment. I am forever grateful for the years of our friendship and partnership.

Good and Poor Helper Researches

As mentioned in Chapter 7, in the early seventies several of my graduate students completed doctoral dissertations on good and poor helpers using hypotheses formulated by our faculty-student seminar on helping relationships. In time, these studies grew to 15 dissertations on the topic of the helping role, exploring more hypotheses and extending the range of helping roles covered to include teachers, nurses, elected leaders, dormitory counselors, administrators, and Episcopal priests. The results proved to be so exciting that I sought an opportunity to test some of the hypotheses on a much larger population. Subsequently, I designed a project to explore the perceptions of good and poor teachers and found a school district with several hundred teachers willing to cooperate. The opportunity seemed just too good to miss.

To fund the study, I applied for a research grant from the U.S. Office of Education and received what must be one of the most remarkable research rejections ever. The project was rejected because, said one of its evaluators, "If the findings of the proposed study should be in the directions anticipated by the principal investigator, the results would be at best useless and at worst, most dangerous"! This, for a study designed to find out how good teachers differ from poor ones! The loss of this priceless opportunity was a bitter pill. Over the next fifteen years, however, a series of doctoral dissertations at the University of Florida and elsewhere amply confirmed our original perceptual hypotheses.

Despite hundreds of researches on teachers, counselors, social workers, supervisors, administrators, public servants, and the clergy, clearly distinguishable differences between good practitioners and poor ones have still not been found on the basis of either knowledge or methods. Approaching the problem perceptually, however, our researches demonstrated that good helpers can be clearly discriminated from poor ones on the basis of the belief systems of the helper. These studies, for example, showed good helpers could be distinguished from poor ones with respect to five major areas: the helper's basic frame of reference, the helper's beliefs about what people are like, the helper's self-concept (beliefs about self), the helper's purposes, and the helper's fundamental authenticity.

These are significant findings about helper belief systems, but many more remain to be uncovered. Even more important contributions of these researches are (a) their corroboration of the significance of seeking understanding of helper performance in the experiential world of practitioners rather than in their objective performance and (b) their demonstration of the feasibility of perceptual research through the systematic use of inference.

The first publication of these results appeared in a monograph from the University of Florida Press, entitled *Florida Studies in the Helping Professions* [Combs with Soper, Gooding, Benton, Dickman, & Usher, 1969]. In it, I discussed the rationale for our position and reported on four of the studies completed to that date. There have been many more since, on teachers, counselors, administrators, public officials, and pastoral counselors, all with results confirming our original hypothesis. Unfortunately, none of these individual efforts ever got published. Accordingly, I summarized them in a paper for *The Person-Centered Review* in 1986 under the title, "What Makes a Good Helper? A Person-Centered Approach." The findings of these studies have far-reaching implications for both theory and practice in all of the helping professions. I regard them as among the most important researches with which I have been associated and the most significant contributions I have been able to make to my professions.

Rogers began the person-centered approach with nondirective counseling, a method of therapy. Later, he decided the important factor in therapy was not the method but the relationship of counselor and client, which he described in essentially objective terms as characterized by the communication of empathy, congruence, and positive regard. Our researches on good and poor helpers went one step further to seek the dynamics of helping processes in the perceptions or belief systems of helper and helpee. This in no way detracts from the magnificent contributions Carl made. Our studies could not have happened without his prior work. That we could see a step further than he was only because we were standing on his shoulders.

The shift from behavioral thinking to an experiential frame of reference is a slow and painful process. At the time these studies were being conducted, education on the national scene was being subjected to widespread demands for greater accountability. To meet these demands, people everywhere were requiring teachers and administrators to adopt the Behavioral Objectives model that was currently in vogue in industry. The Florida State Department of Education was pushing these ideas on all schools in the state. My strong objections to this mandate resulted in an invitation to Tallahassee to discuss the matter with its advocates in the department. I spent a frustrating day there arguing with intransigent bureaucrats and statistically minded "research experts." I returned to Gainesville in a fury. In the next two days I completed a rebuttal manuscript entitled *Educational Accountability: Beyond Behavioral Objectives* [Combs, 1972]. The piece was published as a monograph by ASCD. I still regard it as one of the better things I have done.

Recapitulation

Positive Views of Self

These years at the University of Florida were peak ones for my professional career. I became a prominent educator. By the end of the sixties, I had made appearances in every state and in six foreign countries. I had published 12 books or monographs and more than a hundred articles. I was the recipient of the John Dewey Society Award for Outstanding Contributions to Contemporary Education, an award for outstanding research from the American Personnel and Guidance Association, and two awards at the U of F for teaching and scholarship. I was national president of ASCD. I had pioneered a new theory for teacher education and was prime mover for its implementation in practice. I saw myself as part of a vast and important worldwide humanistic movement and a significant contributor to its advancement. My professional cup was running over. My days were full of challenge and excitement. I was happy, with more than enough feedback from the world of education to counteract my earlier doubts about my worth and acceptance. Whatever else might be in doubt, I had proof aplenty that I had not lived in vain.

All these successes contributed enormously to positive views of self. That, in turn, provided a reservoir of personal security from which to confront and cope with the world. The inner security provided by my professional accomplishments had yet another effect. It made possible turning greater attention to matters of personal fulfillment. I began a more active search for personal growth. As this process advanced, personal integrity and authenticity became more and more central in my personal value system. I did not know it then, but these values were destined to change my entire life style. With my professional self established and secure, I was freed to explore the further potentialities of what Art Combs, the person, might be or become.

As my children left home, I was also confronted with my inadequacies as a parent and the realization of what I had missed by way of warmer, more intimate relationships with the people I dearly loved. These insights, too, contributed to my growing awareness of the price I was paying for preoccupation with the professional side of my existence.

Openness and Acceptance

The social and political events going on in the sixties had a profound effect. My sense of identification with the times opened my world of perceptions to unfamiliar, broader, and more humane areas for involvement. I began to ponder my values and to raise the question, what is worth working for? At the same time, my involvement with ASCD and widespread consulting engagements expanded my horizons to national and international arenas. I came to accept education as the field in which I could best use my talents and energies. I valued my role as teacher and educator while my experience as psychotherapist and theorist brought vital perspectives to education at every level. It intrigues me that the term "educational psychologist" slips so easily off the tongue while "psychological educationist" seems a strained expression. Yet, that is what I was becoming, an educator using psychology as a tool to advance his chosen profession.

Identification

The universal warmth and acceptance I experienced in ASCD and the enthusiasm accorded my consulting and speaking engagements enhanced my feeling of oneness with those working in education everywhere. They also strengthened my identification with the humanistic movement and the sense of being one with something much bigger and more significant than self.

On a more personal level, I felt a keen sense of loss in the untimely death of Don Snygg and the departure of Dan Soper from the U of F. I continued to miss opportunities for closer relationships with students. My love life, after Kathy, was on hold. On the other hand, I was finding new ways of relating to Carol and Peter. I also began a lifelong friendship with Dick Usher during this period. I found it easy to give myself to persons who needed me (students or clients), but found it embarrassing to accept love in return.

Belief System

This period at U of F was a time for clarification, expansion, and testing of my basic system of beliefs. Through writing, I can confront ideas, test them against each other internally, refine their expression, and explore their application to the practical world of events. I was at a productive high during this period at U of F, publishing more books and articles than at any other time in my career. The early sixties were an exciting time at the University of Florida. The College of Education was rapidly gaining national stature; it was looked to as a place where good things were happening. Kim Wiles was elected president of ASCD, becoming the third member of our faculty to serve in that position of leadership.

The experience of falling in love with Kathy opened a whole new world for me. I discovered well-springs of caring and capacities for intimacy that I had never known were possible even though the experience plunged me into severe conflict. I had to choose between fulfilling a larger, better self (others called it self-indulgence) or continuing to live for others in accord with my childhood heritage. Coming to terms with the relationship with Kathy gave me a glimpse of what might be, then shut the door on its achievement. Painful as that was, it left behind an image of what could be, and that, in itself, was a growth experience destined to have its repercussions later on.

Heart-Warmers

Excerpts from cards, letters, and notes that Art preserved in a file bearing this title.

JANUARY, 1963, *from a student*

This is something I feel I owe you—or perhaps myself—because your course seems so unfinished to me. If I edit this, I'll never write it, or else I'll rip the meaning out, so this is just my thoughts, mistakes, and inconsistencies given in an effort to better express what your course has meant to me. You seem to me to be one of the most genuine persons I have ever met. When you say something, I believe it. . . . If this were not so, I would not be able to believe a word of your theory, because it truly hinges upon the hypothesis that man freed from crippling inhibitions and fears WILL be a better person—that man can and needs to be genuine, congruent within himself. With this you have flung open the door to a new way of life for me, one I had but very tenuously sensed before and was very fearful of trusting myself to. . . . I still don't know where I am going but I don't fear it any more, for I have experienced what a person can be like as himself and am content that it is good.

Thank you from the bottom of my heart for sharing with us your personal experiences. To have a grasp of what went into the formulation of your theory helped me understand it so much better. . . . [My husband] is impressed by the amount of personal therapy I received from your course. It was painful to face aspects about myself that I did not like, that I feared, but somehow, even in a class situation, you managed to make real to me that you did care, that you did believe in me, that you could accept me. This gave me the courage to pour out some of these feelings to you in letters, other things I would talk over to myself as if to you, and there was a difference to me. Never before in my whole life have I grieved so much over classes ending. . . . In a way I felt as if something very wonderful were ending for good, but this isn't exactly so. I have come out of this experience far better able to find meaningful experiences in other courses, with other groups of people. You have to experience something like this to know it is possible, and this knowledge, attitude, openess [sic] toward experience makes the chance of it happining [sic] again in other situations much better.

. . . You showed me what Fromm was speaking about, what Bowen was talking about—that one could love with integrity, without dependence. That it could be simply an expression of what is there, neither controlling the other nor being controlled by the other. I saw you as warm, spontaneous, accepting, enthusiastic, and very real—and I discovered that I loved you. This wasn't falling in love, by any means, but more discovering some fairly undercover feelings I had been sitting on for years. I have never loved my husband so freely, been able to express it so spontaneously, been less fearful of feeling warmly toward others. He wants to thank you himself for this, even though he does feel a little envious that he was not able to help me to this himself. He has had a hard time with my changing and his not being sure where I was going and having to readjust to new relationships with me.

Yes, I would like to have you as a therapist because for me the relationship is such that there would be very little resistance within me to this relationship. But knowing you has made it possible for me to trust others enough to accept another as a therapist, and this is no small change. For years I have been progressively more dissatisfied within myself, wanting help desperately but even more afraid of therapy. That sounds funny coming from the wife of a psychiatrist, and I couldn't understand these feelings on my part until recently. I seem to resent directiveness where I am personally involved very much; I wasn't sure what psychotherapy had to offer me, but I felt I would have to give up my hard-won independence, my integrity before it would help me and these I was ready to hang onto 'till I completely gave up. How was it going to give ME self-confidence to turn to some expert and have him subtly direct me in the way he thinks I should go. That's putting it rather strong, but I sure felt strong about it. Also, I want to see how this works for the expert before I try it for myself—like child psychologists with impossible children and marriage counselors who chase pretty girls, I can't believe anything they say. I know too much about psychiatrists to be fooled by the magic cloak deal. If it's so good, why doesn't it work for them? How can someone help me become more comfortable with my feelings when he is working so hard to keep his under control? How can he help me with hostility when his breaks out when he's had enough to drink? [My husband] says I expect too much of therapists, and I guess I do, but is it worth it for me to have to spend the first couple of months working through my attitudes toward him?

You showed us your values, your feelings, your beliefs in a way I had never experienced before. I felt I knew you better than I had really known anyone, except perhaps my husband, and in some ways I am surer of you than I am of him. But this feeling about you didn't simply turn me into an idolizing fan of one Art Combs—strangely enough it helped me see these same elements in others much better than I ever had before. In fact, I think it would be more meaningful to me to have another person as therapist because the more experiences you have with different persons being accepting and trustworthy, the easier it is to believe this about yourself and others. . . . Sure I have a long way to go, but life is so much richer and more meaningful right now that the way does not seem hard and tedious. The candles I made for you . . . seemed to express my very deep gratitude for the light you have given me better than any brief card. The only way in which I can repay you is to pass this light along in the same spirit and way it was given to me. (Gainesville, FL)

MARCH, 1963

I wish to thank you on behalf of the Guidance Conference Committee for your time and effort in making the Twelfth Annual Guidance Conference such a success. . . .

I express the will of the entire Committee when I say that your participation helped to make our meeting the kind of high level conference which should be expected of counselors. (Orangeburg, SC)

MARCH, 1963

There are just no words quite adequate enough to tell you how much it meant to all of us your being with us last week. (Columbia, SC)

FEBRUARY, 1964

I was among those fortunate enough to hear your address at the MCA Annual Conference yesterday. I consider it one of the truly great talks I have been privileged to hear. Not only did it clearly express a philosophical point of view which provides much to stimulate one's thinking but it also provided much which can be practically applied to my work today. Many of your points hit too close to home even to be comfortable to listen to. All through the address I kept thinking, "I saw a kid like that yesterday" or "X is like this." . . . I heard many say that speaker wise this was the best conference yet. (St. Paul, MN)

FEBRUARY, 1964

Re: MCA Conference. . . . Each time I have had the privilege of hearing you, Dr. Combs, you have given me something I feel I can really make use of to improve my work. I find I am definitely not alone in feeling this way. . . . We broke all previous records in counselor attendance. (St. Paul, MN)

FEBRUARY, 1964

On behalf of the Division of Education & Psychology, I should like to thank you for the increased interest you aroused by your two addresses last Thursday.

I knew that your visit would be of great interest to our faculty; but, frankly, I did not expect your impact on our student body to be so appreciable. I was criticized just yesterday by a student who declared that I "was doing just what Dr. Combs said not to!" The class and I went on to a profitable discussion of just what you had to say. (Duluth, MN)

UNDATED

I have just [sic] your masterpiece "The Myth of Competition."

There is one thing worse than a half truth. That is an *educated fool*. "The Myth of Competition" is obviously the work of an educated fool. Please spare us any more of such rambling, pointless ballyho!! [Signed—Not an admirer.] (Excelsior Springs, MO)

JULY 28, 1964, *from a student enrolled in EDF 641*

Dr. Combs, I wish to express my gratitude to you for a rich and full learning experience this summer. It is impossible to describe my feelings about what the course has meant to me personally and what it will mean to my professional teaching, but I can tell you that it has been an experience in personal and professional growth.

I have been exposed to teaching in five institutions of higher learning and you are doing the best job of teaching of any of the professors I have known. Your students *know* what you believe about teaching, they know you teach in accordance with these beliefs and they know you work hard. I hope you know that the nights, afternoons, and weekends you spend reading student papers and preparing for classes are deeply appreciated. It is obvious that you believe that what you are doing is important, and it *is*.

The kind of professional teaching you are sharing and the writing you are producing is essential if we are ever to achieve our goal in education.

It should be gratifying and exciting to you to know that your students are paying tribute to you and your work in the only possible way they can, by making your ideas come alive in their classrooms and in their interpersonal relationships with *their* students. (Gainesville, FL)

JULY, 1964, *from a student reaction paper*

Students (and this goes especially for those students who are teachers) resent a teacher (supervisor or administrator) who directs their activities too closely, but they also are very likely to be anxious when given too much independence by their teacher (supervisor or administrator). I believe your unique structuring of the class takes care of both needs. Not, of course, complete freedom, but yet not completely structured; challenging but not threatening; practicing what you preach; teaching by *percept*, not by *precept*, at the same time goal directed not anarchy. (Gainesville, FL)

OCTOBER, 1965

[Regarding the] European Branch—A.P.G.A. workshop that we had here in Wiesbaden last Saturday, I want to thank you for your participation which really made the whole day a big success. Many individuals have expressed to me their gratefulness and appreciation. One counselor told me that the most helpful thing she could imagine would be to play a tape of your talk every week for herself to hear.

Personally, the reiteration and reinforcement of my own basic beliefs was something I have long been needing. One meets over here so many people that have little faith in the individual's capacity for self-direction, or that don't really believe in it even when they profess to. And I had begun to question whether my reliance on the simple relationship between the client and myself was not sheer laziness to dig out other tools and use them. Anyway, such guilt feelings have slipped away and I feel strong and effective. (APO New York, NY)

OCTOBER, 1965

May you continue to inspire and encourage teachers and all you come in contact with for years to come. The world is a better place because of people like you with messages like yours. (Ferdinand, IN)

AUGUST, 1966

I thought you might like to know that in the opinion of the enrollees, you made THE outstanding contribution to the Institute. For this, my personal thanks and appreciation. Many of the ideas and concepts which you presented were well remembered and referred to by the enrollees throughout the entire program. . . . (College, Alaska)

SEPTEMBER, 1966

Our deepest thanks and appreciation go out to you for your visit to our 1966 Workshop. Your talk has set a precedent which will be a challenge for us to follow.

. . . our Superintendent, made the following report to the Board of Education and I believe it reflects the views of all our staff members:

> Probably the highlight of the entire program was the address on Tuesday afternoon to the entire staff by Dr. Arthur Combs, National President of ASCD and Professor of Education at the University of Florida. The writer has never seen a speaker "tuned in" to the audience any better than he was. Considering the heat and humidity, the attention and applause he received was real testimonial of his effectiveness. (Bellevue, NE)

OCTOBER, 1966

I was present when you delivered the address, "What Can Man Become," at the Northeast Division of the Indiana State Teachers Association annual convention at Fort Wayne, Indiana. This is the finest address that I have ever heard. Its importance to teachers is tremendous.

Since I can not trust my memory to recall all of the essential content, please send to me a copy of the address. I realize that this might be quite difficult for you to do, but my possession of your ideas would be priceless in working with students, teachers and parents. (Grabill, IN)

NOVEMBER, 1966

It was a great privilege to have you as a main speaker at the Southeast Division Conference on Instruction of ISTA. I cannot summarize my feelings, and those of the audience, any better than the superintendent I overheard saying, "Dr. Combs had a real message; here was a speech that every teacher should hear." I might add "several times" in order that they receive the full impact of everything that you said. (Bloomington, IN)

DECEMBER. 1966

Art, your work with us was the most meaningful short workshop we have ever had the opportunity to participate in, and I only hope that we can capitalize on the excitement it has engendered for the improvement of program for our students [sic]. (Burlington, WA)

FEBRUARY, 1967, *unsigned note*

Death is no stranger to us. Daily its existence and inevitability confronts us. And yet, we are never truly prepared to accept its reality . . . nor the pain which overwhelms us when its presence comes into our immediate world.

One of your students deeply shares the sorrow and sense of loss you are experiencing from the death of your friend and colleague, Dr. Snygg. (Gainesville, FL)

MARCH, 1967

Our teachers were very pleased to have heard you. They were inspired. Many of them resented my making it a "command attendance," but afterward they were aglow and profuse with their compliments for your stimulating discussion. (Centralia, WA)

MARCH, 1967

It is difficult for me to express my gratitude and appreciation for the leadership, help and support that you have provided this year. You were a stalwart out among the troops, you gave a significant message and lift to the many groups who heard you, you helped the office with tremendous understanding and backing at very critical times. Your modesty and frankness made it easy and a pleasure to work with you. A very significant element has been the fact that you have a point of view, but you also have something important to say. (Washington, DC—office of the ASCD)

MAY, 1967

It would be difficult to measure the tremendous contribution your thoughts and presence made at our workshop on May 26th. All participants agreed that it was a most enlightening experience as well as an increased understanding of the potential of a self-concept program in our school system. (Orlando, FL)

OCTOBER, 1967, *from a note sent by fourth-grade teacher to her superintendent*

I have taught school for 25 years. In all those years of "Institutes" Friday's was the *best* ever.

Dr. Combs, the speaker, was the *best* I have ever heard in education.

It was the *best* planned meeting I have ever attended.

Thanks! (Portland, OR)

OCTOBER, 1967

I am a teacher in the Springfield, Missouri school system and heard your address at our district teachers' meeting last Thursday morning. I just wanted you to know that I deeply appreciate what you had to say. I felt very inspired and challenged to put into practice some of your ideas. I can't wait until Monday to try them out!

Since it is so easy for teachers (and everyone else) to get into a fixed routine which eventually turns into a rut, I am glad to have the opportunity to be motivated once in awhile to change my goals and direction. (Springfield, MO)

NOVEMBER, 1967

I have had you "on my mind" and on my correspondence list since TPGA [Texas Personnel and Guidance Association] Conference in Houston. You have been discussed, quoted, and deeply appreciated all over the State of Texas—and particularly in Houston. . . . My wish is that you may enjoy good health to continue your vital contribution to humanity. (Houston, TX)

DECEMBER, 1967

This is to attempt to find adequate words to express my gratitude to you for all you have done to help me these past years, and in particular the one just past. . . . Please know, though, that you have been the significant person in whatever growth I may have enjoyed since leaving Orlando in 1958. (Tampa, FL)

JANUARY, 1968

Wednesday, January 17, will always stand out for me as a red letter day. Your appearance in Grand Rapids at our dinner for supervising teachers was an outstanding service to this community.

After reading your works over the years and listening via tape recordings to your speeches, the opportunity to talk with you and listen to you personally was a great thrill. I am sure both the people of Grand Rapids and those students and faculty who heard you on the campus of Western Michigan University will recall with delight your intellectual approach to humanness in education. Very striking to me was your response to people who might question your views. The same soft people-oriented delivery you used in your address you applied to those who might differ in philosophy. The proof of any belief is in its being lived. (Grand Rapids, MI)

MAY, 1968

How do you do, sir? First of all, I want to introduce myself to you. . . . I came from Seoul, Korea. . . . I was a high school teacher before I came this country. [sic]

I happen to read the book *The Professional Education of Teachers.* It is a wonderful book that I have ever read. [sic]. I think you are the very educator whom I have been looking for. I support your idea from the bottom of my heart. . . . If you don't mind, I would like to correspond with you. . . . under your guidance, I would like to find something within myself. (Charleston, SC)

MAY, 1968

. . . The inspiration and enthusiasm which your address [to the Doctoral Society of the United States International University] generated could possibly be measured one way by the response from those who were regrettably unable to attend. As you know, we used a tape-recorder for your address, particularly for those who were not present. But because of the excited response which spread across campus, our Executive Board decided to type your speech from the tape for the many people who wished to capture your simulating words. . . .

Speaking only for myself and for those with whom I have had an opportunity to exchange views . . . the impact of your presence here has been profound. . . . We especially appreciated your informal manner, candor and dialogue with the audience. (San Diego, CA)

JULY, 1968

I am happy to report to you that we have used your book *The Professional Education of Teachers* as one of the basic texts for [courses I have taught at Michigan State University and Utah State University]. Frequently at the last class meeting I have asked for an evaluation of the texts. Happily, I can tell you that your book was rated best in all cases. (Port Huron, MI)

OCTOBER, 1968

Last year I was a student in Dr. Ray Kuiper's class of Introduction to Audio-Visual Materials at Indiana State University at Terre Haute, IN. At the end of the term one of the questions asked by Dr. Kuipers in our evaluation of the class was "What was your most profitable experience as a result of this class? Why?" After reading my answer to the question, he suggested that I send a copy of it to you. I quote from my paper:

> Although my projects provided much that I believe will be of value, it may surprise you to learn that I believe the introduction to the work of Dr. Arthur W. Combs was my most profitable experience as a result of this class. While I may never be in a position to have much or any influence toward the professional education of teachers, I do expect to be a teacher in an elementary classroom. And I expect the theories of Dr. Combs to be instrumental in the way I teach in that classroom. I was particularly impressed with his theory that a student's self-concept affects his behavior and his behavior affects his self-concept. If I can keep even this theory alone uppermost in my mind as I teach, I believe that both my students and I will have gained much of value from this introduction to Dr. Combs' tape and book. I thank you for making this experience available to me.

The name of your tape that Dr. Kuipers used in our class was "Seeing Is Behaving." He also made available to us your book entitled *The Professional Education of Teachers*. Dr. Combs, I am forty years old and have had some previous teaching experience; I believe that some of my respect for your theories is expressed in my above quote. (Hampstead, MD)

FEBRUARY, 1969

During the last few days I have been reflecting [on] my life. What an influence, inspiration and guide you have been! You have opened more "doors and windows" for me than any other person.

Thanks for sharing yourself with me and others! (Laie, HI)

APRIL, 1969

Fifteen years ago—in Schenectady, NY—you counseled me very wisely. At the time I was wrestling with the career-motherhood dilemma. You suggested that I consider my life as analogous to a pitcher of water—full, for a period, of the joys of a homemaker and motherhood. Little by little, as the children needed me less, I could re-enter my career. I cannot tell how often that sage advice has consoled me! (Syracuse, NY)

SEPTEMBER, 1969

The Reading Workshop was an outstanding success. It seemed that each speaker rose to new heights. We were so fortunate to have you make the Reading Workshop the success that it was. What you have done for the teachers in [this] area will keep them always in your debt.

"Thank you" is such a small word and cannot begin to express how much your coming meant to all of us; but on behalf of all of those of us who planned this workshop, thank you from the bottom of our collective hearts. (Turlock, CA)

DECEMBER, 1969 *[from professional colleague whose well-written and highly anticipated book was regrettably withdrawn from the market by the publisher after it was discovered post-publication that no one connected with the project had secured permissions for the use of extensive quotations in the text]*

It is difficult to put into words what your letter means to me. For years I have admired and respected you as a person and as a colleague in my fields of interest. To know that you care and are concerned helps me to bear some of the pain. Thanks so much for caring and expressing your empathy so sincerely and meaningfully. Frankl tells us that deep meaning comes from suffering. If this be true, my life—both personal and professional—should take on much greater depth of meaning.

A note of confidence from you is precious. (Muncie, IN)

UNDATED, FROM A STUDENT, CIRCA 1969*

It would be difficult for me to express my feelings in a conference, so I decided to write you this note instead. I came to the university four years ago and was placed in the University College's honor's program. During my two years at the U.C., I made about twenty friends. Today four of the twenty are students; the other sixteen have quit or flunked! I have to ask myself, what kind of school flunks or discourages 75% of its brightest students? What process choked sixteen of my friends? It is true that all lacked "direction" and that all lacked "motivation," but none lacked intelligence, curiosity or energy. School for them had become an amusement. Discussions were about the latest mess various scheduling or educational bureaucratic measures had caused. It became a status symbol to miss the most classes and still pass (three classes was the record). The only "academic" discussions were about professors' personalities. Occasionally a book from English or a science problem would be tossed about, but all other interests were external to the "academic" community.

Now, I have to ask, what prompted the four to stay in? Two are medical students and want to make money. One is brilliant, can pass any test impressively and has no reason to leave. And the fourth stumbled across a flexible undergraduate program in psychology.

As [for myself], I stumbled across a flexible program in education. Much of the bureaucratic crap has been avoided. Without the concern for grades and passing tests, I have been able to spend the energy doing things that were important to me. I have felt secure enough to grow and mature in ways that were impossible my first two years at the university. I have been able to

* Editor's note: See chapter 9 for discussion of the development of the Childhood Education Program (CEP) that this student so much appreciated.

relax and retain some semblance of human existence. It astounds me to realize how many students scratch an existence from one exam to the next with leisure only through drugs or alcohol. (I seem to remember making those scratches my first two years here.) I do not feel I have attained any academic excellence, but I am as prepared to teach in public schools as any other graduate from here. In brief, I think the program you set up has eliminated those obstacles common to all sixteen drop-outs. It has provided a relaxed, secure environment conducive to self-exploration and personal growth.

I don't want any feedback from this note. I simply want you, Dr. Combs, to know that your program is a vast improvement over my first two years and probably was the most instrumental factor in keeping me number five instead of number seventeen. I appreciate your efforts, want you to know it and hope to emulate some of your practices in my own classroom. (Gainesville, FL)

References

Hanna, T. (1970). *Bodies in revolt: A primer in somatic thinking*. New York: Holt, Rinehart & Winston.

Hanna, T. (1989). *Somatics: Reawakening the mind's control of movement, flexibility, and health*. Cambridge, MA: DaCapo Books.

Arthur W. Combs (1972)

CHAPTER NINE

Art's Odyssey

Growing Personal Problems

By the late sixties, my professional life was in top form. My personal life, from all outward appearances, had settled into the generally assumed and/or expected life of an upper-middle-class college professor approaching retirement. But in many ways it was on hold. Millie and I participated in the social life of our college. We attended football games with the husbands and wives of the faculty, entertained and were entertained by colleagues and friends. We were involved with other senior members of the college in a dinner group that met once a month at one or another's home. In spite of this apparently settled and comfortable life style, I was restive and uneasy. I was becoming increasingly disenchanted with the way of life I had slowly drifted into. Life seemed too habituated, too smug and self-satisfied. As I looked around at the members of our dinner group, I found myself able to predict what they would say or do before it happened. My colleagues at the university and our friends in the dinner club seemed to be wrapping themselves in soft cocoons, protecting themselves from risk, change, and further growth.

By this time, Peter was working on a degree in architecture at the University of Florida. Carol had married Jerry Hole, lived in Boston while Jerry finished seminary, and then moved to the Virgin Islands, where Jerry was a high school teacher at a church-run school and a part-time minister at a small church in Fredrickstadt. Relationships with my mother and father were improving. Whenever I had a consulting engagement within shooting distance of Greensboro, North Carolina, where they lived, I took the opportunity to drop in for a day or two. They never quite understood what a psychologist was or what I did but they were impressed that people seemed to find me significant. These times together were warm and pleasant occasions over good food and conversation. I developed an unaccustomed appreciation for my parents. I learned to accept and understand them as warm, loving, and lonely human beings. I was also deeply touched by their love for each other.

At home, however, my personal life was in trouble. Ten years had passed since the breakup with Kathy. I tried very hard to reconstruct my marriage. I sought opportunities that would involve Millie and me in activities that I hoped might bring us closer together: a trip to Europe, building a new home, buying a condominium at Crescent Beach, spending a summer in the Virgin Islands. All this was a typical workaholic and external approach—*DO* something about your problems. Unfortunately, the fundamental problems in our marriage were not matters to be solved by changing "things." They were problems of incompatible attitudes, values, and long-established habits brought about by one party's changing self and the other party's focus on stability and avoidance of risk. As our relationship shuffled along with little change, I began to feel that my breakup with Kathy was a serious mistake. I had only postponed an inevitable day of reckoning.

The security provided by perceptual theory and the success I experienced in giving myself completely as therapist and as teacher resulted in unambiguous feelings of satisfaction so far as my professional life was concerned. The disparity between my professional and personal life, however, was becoming increasingly incongruous. It seemed to me that I was only playing a role in my personal life. I yearned for the unity of thinking, feeling, and acting that I found so freeing and delightful professionally. I was growing to value personal authenticity with ever-greater certainty. To be who I was, what I was, wherever I was seemed a highly desirable way of living and being.

In the course of my travels as lecturer and consultant, I had many opportunities to form relationships with strong, independent professional women. I was far too shy and fearful of rejection to take the initiative in seeking relationships with them on my own. Now and then, however, I found it possible to accept an invitation for an uncommitted liaison in the safety and obscurity of distant places. In these fleeting relationships I discovered new facets of myself and new capacities for truly intimate communication. For five or six years after the breakup with Kathy, I gave up these relationships. In the late sixties, however, I began once more to engage in occasional affairs, only now with a longing for greater permanence. This resulted in several deeply meaningful encounters that only increased my sense of frustration that I could not be freely and openly what I was and could be. I was ripe for drastic change.

Helping Relationships

During my first ten years at the University of Florida, I taught a course in "Helping Relationships" based upon the perceptual principles of *Individual*

Behavior. Many of my experiments in teaching and my efforts to apply counseling techniques to educational practice were carried on in these classes. It was a natural, then, to think about putting the subject matters of those classes into book form. Two new faculty members, Donald Avila and William Purkey, had joined the Foundations Department and showed great interest in the perceptual approach. They also taught sections of the Helping Relationships course as part of their instructional load. As newcomers to academe, they were under pressure to write as well as teach. Accordingly, I invited them to join me in writing two books: *Helping Relationships: Basic Concepts for the Helping Professions*, a textbook, and *The Helping Relationship Sourcebook*, a book of readings. We agreed that I would be primarily responsible for the text, with criticism and contributions from Don and Bill, while they would compile the sourcebook. Out of this partnership grew a friendship with Don and Bill that I valued highly during the remainder of my years at the university.

To start the project, I took a summer off. Millie and I rented an apartment overlooking the Caribbean on the island of St. Croix, where Carol was then living. This was an idyllic arrangement. I spent the mornings writing in our apartment on a hillside only fifty yards or so from the beach. Here I could look out over the blue waters of the Caribbean while I worked. Afternoons were spent snorkeling on the reef just off shore or sightseeing among the islands. Evenings were spent with Carol and Jerry, relaxing at local bistros or attending local functions. By fall, the manuscript was nearly finished. I returned to Gainesville to subject it to the criticism of Don and Bill. In 1971, *Helping Relationships: Basic Concepts for the Helping Professions* [by Combs, Avila, & Purkey] and *The Helping Relationship Sourcebook* [by Avila, Combs, & Purkey] appeared. They were adopted enthusiastically in many places.

I Lose More Friends

After Dan Soper left the University of Florida, Justin Harlow and I continued to meet regularly, as we had when Dan was there. We shared a great deal, often acting as informal counselors for each other. One afternoon, shortly after we had lunch together, Justin died of a heart attack. I found myself without still another close friend and companion. This loss had a macabre, yet poignant twist. Months after his death, I answered the door bell and was handed a Christmas package—a yule log cake made of French pastry from Justin! During the summer he had visited a favorite French pastry shop in St.

Augustine, where he ordered the yule log confection to be delivered to me at Christmastime. Though taken aback, I was also touched by this unexpected reminder of my dear friend.

Months later I was awakened in the night by a phone call from a minister who informed me that Kimball Wiles had been killed in an auto accident. I was stunned. Before I could recover, the caller went on to say that Kim's wife, Hilda, wanted me to speak at the funeral. Kim was such a vibrant, outgoing person. He was a vital force in education, especially in the field of supervision. He had succeeded J. B. White as dean of our college. I had followed Kim as president of ASCD. We taught workshops together, thought in similar channels, were passionately involved in ASCD affairs, and were warm personal friends. His eulogy was, probably, the most difficult talk I have ever made. I had all I could do to complete the eulogy without breaking into tears. His death left me even more alone.

I suffered a third loss the following year when Earl Kelley died. Earl and I had become fast friends, beginning with our acquaintance at Syracuse. He contributed one of the four basic papers for the 1962 ASCD yearbook and we often appeared together on the platforms of one or another educational conference. Our thinking ran in the same channels. I was deeply influenced by his book, *Education for What Is Real* [Kelley, 1947], his statement of the implications Adelbert Ames's work and demonstrations on perception for educational thought and practice. He was in much demand as a speaker and consultant. Often when either of us was making a consulting trip, we would pull out "our friendship ruler," apply it to the map and discover that, lo and behold, Detroit (where he lived) or Gainesville (where I lived) was on a straight line from our homes to New York, Seattle, or whatever city we were headed for. What a shame not to stop and see "old Earl" or Art. So, of course, we often followed our ruler's mandate. It was painful to watch the decline of this maverick thinker, "the Will Rogers of education," and much-loved friend during his last years.

My reactions to these losses were the usual. I threw myself even more into my work. I wrote books, dozens of articles, and consulted in schools and colleges all over the country. I poured myself into teaching and counseling with such absorption that there was little time or opportunity for more personal matters. I was a one-sided human being, deeply fulfilled in my professional life but sadly lacking personally. Sadder still, I was not even fully aware of my empty existence. I know now that there were many who held out their hands in offers of love and friendship, but I did not recognize them or, perhaps, I was fearful of opening old wounds. In any event, my personal life was motionless while my professional life soared.

Millie and Art in Hawaii, 1967

Some Foreign Travel

During this period I made a consulting trip to Paraguay, still under the tight control of its long-time dictator. The opportunity to spend several days in Peru and at Machu Picchu was the highlight of this trip but the sight of young soldiers on every corner with machine guns slung on their shoulders made a lasting and repugnant impression. Being treated by the dictator's personal physician for a monumental attack of Montezuma's revenge did little to assuage my revulsion.

I had a second visit to autocracy on the occasion of a trip to Berlin for a conference on teacher education. Three of us delegates crossed the Berlin Wall through Check Point Charlie for a day in East Berlin. I have never forgotten the contrast between the smiles of carefree shoppers thronging the streets of West Berlin and the pall of stolidity, hopelessness, and nearly empty streets on the other side of the wall. Nor have I forgotten the consternation I created in a shop when I asked to buy a map of East Berlin, a strictly "verboten" article.

I made happier excursions to teach workshops at the University of Alaska and in Hawaii. I have especially fond memories of our cosmopolitan workshop in Hawaii.* A hundred students from countries all around the

* Editor's note: See Heart-Warmers section in this chapter for poem presented to Art on this occasion.

Pacific rim and from its island cultures were involved in our workshop, in which everyone was minority. The last day of our group experience was a luau on the beach to which students brought their native dishes to share with each other. This was a delightful, heart-warming experience I shall never forget.

Some Significant Publications

Most significant of my published shorter pieces during the latter part of the sixties were:

"The Perceptual Approach to the Helping Professions," a paper presented to the National Association for the Study of Perception [Combs, 1970].

"The Human Aspect of Administration," published in the *Colorado Journal of Educational Research* [Combs, 1970].

The "Foreword" that Victor Raimy asked me to write for the long-overdue publication of his 1944 original and definitive theory of the self-concept [Combs, 1971]. The Ohio State University library was arranging for the publication of Vic's dissertation because it was so frequently called for. I was touched by Vic's request and honored to sponsor such an important document.

Already mentioned in Chapter 8 was *Florida Studies in the Helping Professions* [Combs et al, 1969], a monograph published by the University Press at U of F. I edited and wrote much of this monograph, pulling together some of the helping relationship researches completed by our graduate students at the University of Florida.

"Two Views of Motivation," which was slated for publication in a *Handbook of Research on Human Motivation.* *

Coming to Terms

After returning from St. Croix, I had a dream one night that my daughter was crying inconsolably for me. It was very vivid. It woke me up and I lay, half awake and half asleep, talking to her. I found myself saying, "Don't cry for

* Editor's note: This was a paper Art wrote for inclusion in a book edited by Jack Frymier. After a long and futile search for this publication, I learned from Jack Frymier that the publisher initially committed to publishing this book subsequently decided not to go ahead with it, and the book was never published (personal communication, June 17, 2003). A copy of the paper, which Art also gave as a speech in June, 1970, is available from the Field Psych Trust.

me, Carol. You don't need to cry for me. My life to this point has been so good that nothing can ever take that away from me. I know I have not lived in vain." I went back to sleep and awoke in the morning with a feeling of inner peace that lasted for months. I think the loss of my friends over the years before forced me to consider the possibility of my own demise at some lower level of awareness. In the course of those confrontations, I apparently came to terms with my own mortality. Whatever the cause, the experience left me with the conviction that some vital turning point had been reached and some vital reorganization was occurring in my psyche.

I began turning greater attention to a more active search for personal growth. As this process advanced, integrity and authenticity became more and more central in my overall value system. I did not know it then, but these values were destined to change my entire life style.

The Childhood Education Program

As a consequence of the work Dan Soper and I were doing on the nature of helping relationships, I began to think in the mid-sixties about the implications of these ideas for teacher education. I started a paper setting forth my ideas in a kind of theory for teacher preparation. As I worked on it, the paper got longer and longer. Soon it was too long for an article and too short for a book. Having no idea where to send it for publication, I put it in a desk drawer, where it lay for several years. Then, one day, I mentioned it during a conversation with J. B. White. He asked to read the manuscript. He felt it contained important new insights for teacher education and he urged me to get it published. Accordingly, I went back to work on the manuscript and produced *The Professional Education of Teachers: A Perceptual View of Teacher Preparation* [Combs, 1965]. When the book appeared I began to receive requests to "tell us where we can find teachers who were trained that way," or "Can we come see your program?" Alas, I had to reply that we did not have such a program, nor did I know of one anywhere employing such theory.

Three or four years later, while talking shop with several members of the Elementary Education Department, they asked, "Art, can't we try putting the ideas in your *Professional Education of Teachers* into practice?" The notion, at first, seemed too good to be true. As a result of that discussion, however, a group of about twelve of us from the Foundations Department and the Elementary Education Department began a series of meetings in which we explored the concepts I had proposed. Thus came into being one of the most exciting and productive experiences of my professional career.

For several generations, most programs in teacher education assumed that proper training of teachers required exposing candidates to:

1. opportunities for acquisition of a body of knowledge in some subject or subjects,

2. understanding of the foundations of education: philosophy, educational psychology and the function of the school in our society,

3. acquisition of effective methods of teaching, capped by
4. a period of supervised practice teaching.

This is essentially a mechanistic approach that treats teaching as a skill to be taught, learned, and applied. Traditional programs teach newcomers to the profession *about* teaching rather than helping them *become* teachers. Looking at the problem from a perceptual-experiential viewpoint and applying what we had learned from our researches on the helping professions, it seemed to me the more appropriate goal of teacher education was the production of true professionals. Teachers must be more than delivery systems. Education requires teachers who are creative problem-solvers, persons who can confront the complexity of teaching responsibilities intelligently, calling upon their knowledge and experience to find or create appropriate solutions.

We do not say of students in medicine or law that they are learning how to law or doctor. Rather, we say they are becoming lawyers or physicians. Just so, instead of teacher "training" programs where students learn "how to" teach, I proposed tackling teacher preparation as a matter of personal becoming. That simple shift in goal requires many changes in thinking and practice. It calls for helping aspiring teachers to develop personal belief systems that are accurate, comprehensive, internally congruent, and appropriate for the teaching task. Such an approach differs considerably from teaching facts and methods. Beyond this basic shift in the goals of teacher education, I proposed a new set of assumptions for teacher education drawn from perceptual-experiential learning theory.

With minor changes, the gifted group of faculty from the Foundations Department and the Elementary Education Department set about formulating how such ideas might be implemented in practice. We spent nearly a year exploring possibilities and making plans for a new Childhood Education Program that was put in operation with 50 randomly selected students entering the College of Education in the spring of 1969. The program began with the basic assumption that the education of a teacher must give priority to facilitating the development of a comprehensive, internally consistent belief system in the person becoming a teacher.

To implement this hypothesis, our program established a whole series of pertinent innovations. Among these were participation in field experience throughout the program, elimination of grades in favor of systematic personal evaluations, creation of a need to know before providing information, involvement of students in all aspects of planning and administration, close and continuous interaction of students and faculty, individualized approaches to student learning, elimination of "courses" in favor of "learning projects," and more. After the first semester, we increased the number of students to 100 and then to 120 by the end of the second year.

In addition to being chairperson for this project, I served as a seminar leader for a group of 30 undergraduate majors. Upon enrollment, students were assigned to these seminars for the two-year period of their participation in the program. As a consequence, seminars included students at all levels of preparation, from beginners to students about to graduate. The seminars operated as therapy-learning experiences covering all sorts of matters: professional, personal, informational, experiential. Working with these delightful young people over a two-year period was at the same time a source of professional inspiration and extraordinarily satisfying personal interactions. For most of my career in university work, my contacts were, for the most part, with graduate students. This was the first time I worked extensively with undergraduates and the first time I had an opportunity to be closely involved with students and faculty over so long a period. I owe the program much for its contributions to my personal and professional growth. The same can be said of my experience with my colleagues in this remarkable faculty, who designed and operated this innovative contribution to teacher education. I cherish, especially, the lasting friendships I formed with Hannelore Wass, Walter Busby, and Robert Blume in the development and advancement of this program.

Traditionally, university programs grow over a period of time by accretion. Beginning from some original logic, bits and pieces are added over the years, but rarely does anyone question the fundamental assumptions on which the program is built. We broke new ground in the CEP by starting from a carefully selected set of novel assumptions, then building the program to implement those assumptions wherever they led. The program operated side-by-side with the existing, more traditional one. This gave us opportunity to make comparisons between the two programs and to mount some research efforts aimed at pin-pointing significant differences.

Unfortunately, we never acquired the funds to carry out the kind of research program we felt was truly adequate. Nonetheless, from what little research we completed, and from our own observations and those of supervising teachers in the field and from the students themselves, it was clear we were into matters of much significance. Our students scored about the same as those in the original program on traditional tests of knowledge. They were superior, however, in understanding themselves, their students, and the purposes of education, on one hand, and in coping with the realities of classroom experience, on the other. They had the makings of true professionals.

We published two books and a number of articles on the CEP program. The first book was *Humanistic Teacher Education: An Experiment in Systematic Curriculum Innovation* [Wass, Blume, Combs, & Hedges, 1974]. Unfortunately, the book had a short life because the publisher went into bankruptcy soon after it appeared. The second was more successful. It was titled *The Professional Education of Teachers: A Humanistic Approach to Teacher Preparation* (2nd ed.) [Combs, Blume, Newman, & Wass, 1974]. It sold more than 13,000 copies.

Professional Burnout

Although I continued to be thrilled with the CEP program and with my experience with its undergraduate students, I was finding the graduate classes I had taught for 25 years and the ponderous bureaucracy of graduate education more and more burdensome. As a three-term member of the university's Graduate Council, I tried year after year to break the iron grip of hoary tradition, with no success. My enthusiasm was waning for some of the things I was engaged in. Travel was becoming a chore instead of a challenge. Though I still resonated to audiences and relished the highs of speaking and consulting, the tedious, repetitive anonymity of what went with it was becoming increasingly onerous. Every airport, hotel room, banquet, or reception line felt like every other one. In addition, universities were moving from the expanding and stimulating years of growth following the war to the plodding, conservative, "play it safe" patterns of a static or contracting economy. University work was losing its glamour and excitement.

About this time I received a request, instigated by Dick Usher, from the University of Northern Colorado to consider the possibility of a distinguished professorship there. I was intrigued by the idea and spoke to our vice-president for academic affairs about the prospect. He told me, "Art, why would you want to do that? We can do the same for you here. Just let me go to work on it." I accepted his offer and declined the invitation from Colorado.

In the fall, the university announced the appointment of a colleague in the Foundations Department to the chair of Distinguished Research Professor. When I inquired about my own appointment, the VP was most embarrassed. "I'm terribly sorry," he said, "but we simply can't appoint two distinguished professors from the same department in the same year. Next year. . . ." The following year, a Distinguished Professorship was awarded to another member of our college who was, in my opinion, of limited academic but high political talent. Insulted and angry at this continued breach of promise, I began to think I had been too long at the University of Florida.

After 17 years at UF, I was ready for a change. Millie, however, was customarily fearful of risk-taking. When I broached the question of leaving the university, she became perturbed at the very thought. "Why can't you be like our friends?" she asked, pointing out examples from our dinner club. This only increased my concern. Looking at our friends, I was appalled. I did not want to be safe. I wanted to face fresh challenges, explore new aspects of life and personal growth. I began more openly to seek greater fulfillment of my personal needs and entered an uncharted phase of my life.

I Meet Susan

On a consulting trip to a graduate workshop at Bowling Green University in Ohio, I met a remarkable young woman, Susan Kannel, who was to change the course of my life. Susan was an outspoken 23-year-old graduate student. She met life with a no-nonsense acceptance of reality and a heartwarming zest for new experience. In later years she would regale our guests with the story of our meeting, beginning with her dismay at the very "straight," 59-year-old "expert" she was sent to pick up at the airport. Later, at a workshop party, she was amused by my shy and fumbling advances. For whatever reasons, she brazenly cut through the amenities and invited an intimate encounter. I was startled and intrigued by her straightforward, unabashed openness and threw myself into the relationship with joy and abandon. Two days later, when the workshop ended and we parted company, we agreed to meet again in Washington at the Personnel and Guidance Association conference.

In Washington, we renewed our relationship, a deeply satisfying encounter for each of us. We were being and communicating with each other in a fashion I had never before experienced. Months later, Susan decided to come to Gainesville to find a job and establish residence so that later she could enroll for graduate work as a Florida resident. When she and a friend arrived in town and rented a trailer outside the city, I was delighted. With

Susan close by, however, the necessity of resolving my personal dilemmas became more pressing than ever. I knew it was time to confront the unhappiness in my personal life and make some crucial decisions.

Accordingly, I mapped out a plan of action: I would enter therapy for four months until the end of the school year. I would make no decisions during that time. Instead, I would use the therapy sessions to explore every aspect of myself and my life situation. I would buy a camper after that, spend the summer alone exploring the West, giving myself time to think things out and determine what to do with my life. Millie was deeply distressed by all this. She tried to dissuade me from this seeming madness, but I felt a desperate need to get away from all the connections of my usual life in order to sort things out. I looked forward to the summer with great anticipation.

In the next few months I explored myself and my life from every angle, with the help of a local therapist. I reviewed my professional career, my feelings of burnout, and what I might do next. More personally, I examined my relationship with Millie and our friends at the U of F. I reviewed my breakup with Kathy and my relationships with other women over the years. I retraced turning points in my personal growth, from my first experience in counseling with Carl Rogers through the stages since to my current unrest. I came to no conclusions, simply confronting and clarifying who and what I was and the questions calling for resolution.

In June, I bought a camper and equipped it with what I would need for three months on the road. I began to call my plan "Art's Odyssey," though some of my friends labeled it "Art's Idiocy." Peter was planning to hitchhike through the West, so I invited his company as far as Salt Lake City, where I had a consulting engagement. When school was out we took off. I thoroughly enjoyed the opportunity to get reacquainted with my son. Along the way, I shared with him some of my struggles. I was deeply moved to find him understanding and sympathetic. In Salt Lake City, Peter's girlfriend flew in to join him in his travels. I took them to the edge of town, watched them begin to hitchhike for parts West, then turned to set out on my own quest for self-understanding.

On the Road

For the next two and a half months I never saw a soul I had known before. I drove from camp site to camp site throughout the West, hiking, fishing, loafing, sightseeing as the mood struck me. I did my housekeeping chores, talked with people I met in campgrounds or on the trails, read from the books I had brought along, or simply did nothing at all. I enjoyed the driving and made up ribald limericks* about everyone I knew as I rolled along from one location to another.

I had brought my typewriter along, expecting to do a lot of writing, but only got to it for two short intervals. Mostly, I vegetated, enjoying the release from responsibility and the opportunity to follow, unhassled, my moment-to-moment whims. I simply flowed with life and lived in harmony with my environment for two and a half months.

Then, one night in Glacier National Park, everything came to a head. I had spent an especially beautiful day hiking a park trail with a young couple carrying backpacks who were heading up the mountain to spend the night. As the afternoon faded, we parted, they to continue up the mountain and I to return to my camper. After cleaning up my supper things, I turned in early. Several hours later I awoke with an overwhelming feeling of loneliness and despair. I cried. I screamed. I threw myself about in the camper. I have no idea how long this continued. I only remember the desolate feeling of being utterly alone and the feeling of desperation. I think I was lost in a psychotic episode. Sometime during the night, exhaustion overtook me and I fell asleep in my bunk.

I awoke in the morning to the sound of birds singing in the woods and with an oceanic feeling of calm, certainty, and oneness with the world. I knew exactly what I had to do. I packed up my things, turned my camper around, and headed back for Gainesville. Sometime in the night, I had come to terms with myself in a kind of conversion experience I have sometimes seen in my clients in psychotherapy. After months of frustration, weeks of therapy, and more months for reflection, the solutions to my conflicts fell into place. My days of torment, doubt, and confusion were over. I would be my authentic self. I would give up living the life others wanted of me. I

---

* Editor's note: One such limerick, shared with Fred Richards and subsequently published in a book Fred wrote in 1977 (Richards, 1977), went as follows:

> SHEEPSKIN
> (Limerick written for Fred Richards by a famous psychologist
> and a beautiful person the day Fred completed his Ph.D.)
> "There once was a man named Fred
> who said as he climbed into bed,
> if you don't want to lay
> I'm willing to stay
> while you sit on my face instead."

Art actually recited this limerick following the formal portion of Fred's doctoral orals, held in Gainesville, FL (1972), much to the surprise of those present. He not only offered the limerick as a toast but removed his tie, and autographed it. The tie still hangs in Fred's home.

would be who I was, what I was, wherever I was. I would trust my value system to provide the guidelines for action. I would return to Gainesville, terminate my marriage, divest myself of my administrative responsibilities, be as honest and genuine as I knew how to be, then live with whatever happened next.

On the way back to Florida, I realized there was no hurry. I had a consulting engagement in Reno a week later, and I did not have to be back in Gainesville until time for classes in early September. Why not stay on the road? During a call to Florida, I discovered that Susan was visiting friends in Bowling Green, Ohio, so I drove there, invited her to join me, and we headed West for Reno. For the next two weeks we toured the National Parks, then made our way back to Florida.

A New Way of Life

With a heavy heart, I faced the necessity to act on my hard-won decisions. I was sad for the hurt I would bring to Millie. I loved and cared for her, but I was strong in my conviction that separation was the thing I must do. Parting from Millie after 38 years was painful beyond words, so much so that I cannot recall the conversations that brought it about. Each of us was deeply wounded by this abrupt uprooting of our accustomed way of life. Somehow, however, in the midst of our sadness and regret, we managed to cope with our separation without hurtful recriminations to haunt us in the future.

A few days later I began the process of stripping my life of non-essentials. I found a small apartment and moved in. From my former home I took only my clothes, the furniture in my study, and a few books and art objects with special meaning for me. I have always hated wearing ties. One of my first acts was to get rid of several racks full that had accumulated over the years. I saved only two for emergencies, like funerals or weddings. One does not have to be a psychologist to recognize the symbolism in that act.

I had lots to learn in my apartment. For years, I had depended upon a wife to run the house. Now it was my turn to do the cooking, cleaning, laundry, and housekeeping that someone else had done for me for so long. It was good for me. I found it surprisingly satisfying. Among other things, it helped me become aware of the chauvinism I had insidiously absorbed from the culture I grew up in. Susan is an outspoken champion of women's issues and took much delight in calling attention to the remnants of my macho upbringing. After years of lavish family Christmases, I spent the holiday that year watching a movie with a Jewish friend in a nearly empty theater.

Friends and acquaintances, observing the breakup of a seemingly happy marriage of 38 years, were deeply puzzled. They came up with numerous hypotheses to explain the matter to their own satisfaction. My behavior was irrational, shameful, possessed. I was seduced, crazy, or anti-social. Some people looked at Susan and me and said to themselves or others, "Look at that dirty old man taking advantage of that nice young woman." Or, if they took my side, they said "Look at that unprincipled young woman taking advantage of Art." Then, of course, those who considered themselves more psychologically hip said, "It's clearly a case of a man who is afraid of growing old, involved with a woman who needs a father figure." Despite their conjectures, the dissolution of a marriage is a singularly private affair that can only be comprehended from the perceptions of the persons directly involved. Here are some excerpts from a letter I wrote to my mother and father at the time attempting to explain what was happening with me:

> I feel happier and more content than I have in a very long time. I feel as though I am being fundamentally honest with myself and the world. I am not dissembling. Instead, I am trying to live openly and honestly with everyone. Some people, I know, do not feel one ought to be like that and do not approve of me, but that worries me not at all. I feel good and right and it is me that I have to live with—not other people.
>
> All my life I have been doing what other people wanted me to do—building programs, teaching, counseling, whatever. In recent years we have seen a great many people, especially the young ones, turning away from some of the established values and seeking new kinds of satisfactions in life. I guess I have felt that too. Anyhow, over the past few years I have had a terrible feeling that I just wanted to get everybody and everything off my back and find out just who and what I am and what I want to do with the rest of my life.
>
> Some people have assumed that all this was because there was another woman involved. That is not true. I have known several women over the past five years but I have no intention of ever marrying again. Currently, I have a very dear friend and we have spent a lot of time together these past few months, but neither of us is under any illusions that this is a permanent commitment and that is the way we want it.

Cutting Loose

At the university, I resigned from all of my administrative and committee chair posts. Some people reacted to these activities with reproach. They asked, "But, Art, how can you do this to us?" I replied, "Look, I've been living all my life serving people. For once, I'm going to do what I want." Even as I said that,

Art Combs teaching (1972)

I had sharp twinges of guilt. It is not easy to give up lifelong patterns of behavior. Besides, deciding to follow one's own guidelines sounds selfish and ego-centered. Yet in the years that followed, I made a fascinating discovery. When I behaved in ways that truly expressed myself and fulfilled my own need, I was, invariably, better for those around me too. I was reminded of Maslow's [1954] discussion of coping and expressive behavior [previously described here in Chapter 1, pages 14–15]. Coping behaviors are means to an end, the things we do to get things done as we deal with life. Expressive behaviors have no aim or goal but are simply natural expressions of what we think and feel (pp. 180–181). He also pointed out that among self-actualizing (supremely healthy) persons, by simply expressing themselves, they behave in ways that are good both for themselves and their societies (synergy).

I was learning a new way of life. Until now, the major focus of my energies had lain in serving others, doing what was good for them. It was no accident that my choice of professions landed me in clinical psychology, education, and counseling. These were areas in which I could carry out my efforts to be a caretaker and be applauded for doing so. Working in such areas made possible a feeling that I had made a significant contribution to society while simultaneously bolstering a sense of personal satisfaction. Service to others in the professions I have chosen is no sacrifice. For me, it is a fundamentally gratifying, self-nourishing experience. What I was now giving up was being *driven* by the desire to serve, even at the cost of meeting my own need.

Learning to Care for Self

The focus on serving others extended to my personal life as well. I was a good husband and father, seeking to support and sustain the welfare of my wife and family. My self-effacement, however, extended to the smallest matters. Cocktail parties and teas were painfully uncomfortable because I was a dud at small talk. I could do very well chatting with people when I knew they wanted to hear what I thought. Talk for talk's sake left me tongue-tied or mute. Faced with the question of where to go for dinner, I almost always avoided making a decision. "Where would *you* like to go?" was my standard reply.

Professionally, my concepts of self expanded over the years from self-doubts to "It's all right to be me," even to "It's good to be me." I was only now edging toward such beliefs in my personal life. I was starting to be as authentic there as I had learned to be as counselor or teacher. In a professional role, I could accept compliments and expressions of love and caring with appreciation rather than embarrassment and distress. In my personal life, such expressions would leave me embarrassed and confused. Now, however, I was starting to take them in stride. I could accept them graciously with a simple "Thank you" or "It was nice of you to tell me." My personal self was catching up with my professional one. My life was becoming less cluttered, less complicated, more straightforward, expressive, and authentic.

Living alone was good for me, a continuation of my odyssey in the camper. I had time to think, read, write, or simply loaf as the spirit moved me. My relationship with Susan was like a refreshing breeze. I learned a great deal from her honesty and assertiveness. There was no room for dissembling. Once I reported to her, "The president asked me to serve on a select committee to . . ." That was as far as I got. "Select committee, Art?" she replied, "Oh, shit!" I had to laugh as she cut through to the heart of pomposity. I was, indeed, seeking to impress her with my importance. Our relationship became more honest and straightforward. We spoke what we felt, holding nothing back. I learned while growing up to refrain from communicating my feelings if they might distress another and to avoid confrontation if at all possible. Now I was experiencing a more open way of relating, and enjoying it immensely.

Neither Susan nor I had any intention of marriage. We were content to maintain our separate apartments, free to come and go as we pleased. No matter the past, we lived and communicated in the here and now and found life to be very good. Who I was professionally was of no concern to Susan. I don't believe she ever read one of my books. Quite the contrary. She often joked with our guests, "I use his books to help me fall asleep!" I was having a grand and priceless experience with a strong, independent, assertive human being who met me on equal footing. I loved every moment of it and still do.

The Perceptual Psychology Revision

Before Don Snygg's untimely death in 1967, he had agreed at the request of the publisher to do a third edition of *Individual Behavior*. After his death, Harper and Row asked me to take it on. In view of my experience with the first revision, I simply could not face the thought of doing another. They were insistent, however, and I was loath to see the book go totally out of circulation. Accordingly, I enlisted the aid of Anne and Fred Richards, who had studied with me at the U of F, to take on the prime responsibility for a rewrite. Anne had come as a student to our doctoral program with a bachelor's degree from Brandeis University, where she had worked with Abraham Maslow. She was a top-flight student with a keen mind. She was fascinated with the perceptual approach, had an extraordinary grasp of the literature, and her doctoral dissertation was a collection and critique of devices for presenting and illustrating perceptual concepts. Her husband, Fred, was not one of my advisees at the time, but was also intrigued with perceptual thinking. Subsequently, when Fred pursued the doctorate through Union Graduate School, I served on his doctoral committee, and I had a deep appreciation for his intelligence and sensitivity. I felt very good about leaving the primary task of revision to this talented couple while I would act as consultant and occasional contributor.

The first edition had been subtitled, *A New Frame of Reference for Psychology*. The second was subtitled *A Perceptual Approach to Behavior*. We decided that the third edition should drop the behavioral connotations entirely and offer itself boldly as a distinct psychology in the humanistic frame of reference. We named it, *Perceptual Psychology: A Humanistic Approach to the Study of Persons*. Anne and Fred did a superb job with the revision. It appeared in 1976. It has since been reissued by the University Press of America [Combs, Richards, & Richards, 1988].

Recapitulation

A Positive Self

The late sixties and early seventies saw the beginning of a major change in my growth process. For years I had poured most of my energies into my profession. The period 1969-1975 was a most productive one. I completed eight books or monographs and 40 articles or chapters in books. Many of my publications were reprinted in books of readings, some were translated into other languages. At the same time I began to feel burned out professionally. I yearned for greater fulfillment in my personal life and during this period I began to seek it.

During the forties I had experienced an intellectual conversion, set off by Donald Snygg's [1941] paper on "The Need for a Phenomenological System of Psychology." That experience channeled my talents into 25 years of professional growth. Now, in the late sixties, I experienced a new conversion experience, this time focused on the growth of my personal self. It was to have ramifications for years to come. The events of my childhood left me with feelings of not being enough, with doubts about my acceptability and lovableness. I became a caretaker/helper, seeking love, acceptance, and recognition through the helping professions of teaching, counseling, consulting, and their implementation through program building. There was certainly nothing wrong with that. Although my striving for adequacy took the form of trying to compensate for something missing in my life, the results were good for me, the people I worked with, and the professions themselves. I found much pleasure in my work and made some important contributions as well.

To this point I was a workaholic, driven to achieve in the helping professions what I lacked personally—an acceptance of self as a valuable and lovable person just for who and what I was. But now that imbalance started to right itself as my personal self began to catch up with my professional one. My two selves began to come together as I sought greater personal fulfillment. The authenticity I had come to value in my roles as teacher, counselor, speaker, and consultant became equally important in my personal life. I began to feel it was good to be me, that I was a unique and valuable human being. I was more spontaneous more frequently in my approach to events.

Meeting Susan, the experience in therapy, and the catalytic nature of my summer "odyssey" opened a vast area for growth. I began to confront myself with greater openness and candor. In my relationship with Susan, I caught a glimpse of a more authentic way of being. In the course of therapy I explored its ramifications, and in the solitude of my travels I found the courage to make the break to a new and more fulfilling way of being and becoming. The confrontation with death played a part in advancing my becoming as it forced me to rethink what life is all about and what values are truly worthwhile as the bases for making choices.

The process continued as I learned to live alone. There I discovered additional facets and personal capacities. The preoccupation with serving others that I inherited from my childhood began to give way to an appreciation for privacy and self awareness. It was not always pleasant to become aware of the baggage I carried from my upbringing, like the suppression of feeling and the chauvinism our society imposes upon its male citizens. But even such insights contributed to growth for me. One cannot do much about events one is unaware of or refuses to confront.

Acceptance and Openness

The critical changes in self-perception during these years were accompanied by increasing acceptance of self and others on one hand, and greater openness to experience on the other. After half a century of submerging self in service to others, I was beginning to accept what I needed as legitimate too. I could listen to my internal stirrings, wants, and desires as well. I could even seek their fulfillment, on occasion, despite the fact that others might not understand or approve. I was discovering that my worthiness was not something that had to be purchased through contributions and service. I was a worthwhile, even lovable, human being just because I was the unique and valuable person known as Art Combs. Earl Kelley once wrote to me, "Art, do take care of yourself. There is only one of you and we can't afford to lose you." Earl made much of the idea that every human being is precious because there never has been and never will be another like him or her. I was beginning to appreciate that idea.

At the same time I was becoming more open to experience, in closer touch with reality. It sounds like a fundamental contradiction that I was becoming more open by turning inward rather than outward for my satisfactions. Nevertheless, it was true. I was becoming more open to the realities of Art Combs, the person. Previously inhibiting perceptions of self, openness to experience, and brand new ways of seeing self were integrated into a broader, more human, personality. I was becoming a freer, more autonomous human being. This made it possible to confront more problems of living straightforwardly and honestly, untrammeled by the pressure of custom or social approval. With greater personal security, I could be more open to alternatives, less bound by custom and tradition and freer to find my own best ways of being and becoming. I learned to look at self and the world through new eyes and so achieved a qualitatively different appreciation of events. I was weeding out negative and inhibiting concepts and replacing them with more positive and congruent views of self and the world.

Identification

In the relationship with Susan I discovered a level of communication, openness, and trust I had not experienced previously. As our relationship grew, I felt increasingly free to express every thought and emotion without restriction, secure in the knowledge that these would be accepted and valued. I was entering an unprecedented and healthier relationship between a man and a woman. In place of the male-female stereotypes instilled from my childhood and the culture, I found myself in a relationship marked by honesty, equality, affectionate generosity, and spontaneity. Even our hurts and disagreements could often be aired, shared, and resolved in angry or tearful communion that somehow strengthened rather than weakened our bond. Our relationship was not governed by oughts, shoulds, or role expectations. Rather, it was characterized by mutual acceptance and adaptation, shifting and changing as necessary to meet our own and each other's need. Indeed, it went far beyond anything I had previously known was possible. I was ushered into a liberating appreciation of the meaning of love and identification, not only between a man and a woman, but with the larger human condition as well. Forgiveness and understanding came more easily, as did tolerance and acceptance of human foibles and a more profound connectedness with both the joys and the tragedies of human existence.

Belief System

During this time I began to apply perceptual thinking to the dynamics of the helping professions and the perceptual organization of helpers. Applying perceptual thinking to the problems of teacher education and the opportunity to put those ideas into operation in the CEP program was a powerfully affirming experience. It provided another arena for testing perceptual-experiential assumptions and expanding their applications. The success of these explorations added further corroboration for the soundness of the theory. The CEP program allowed me to refine concepts and provided continual evidence of the usefulness of perceptual thinking. These concepts were further affirmed by the findings of numerous research studies on good and poor practitioners in the helping professions.

The development of my belief system was entering a new phase. For years, my thinking and explorations had concentrated on the development of perceptual theory and its implications for counseling and teaching. I worked very hard in that effort: writing, experimenting, innovating. Now, I was finding that preoccupation less satisfying and compelling. In its place, I turned to explore the more personal sources of fulfillment mentioned in the paragraphs above and spent less time and effort on professional matters. It felt good to discover that my personal and professional systems were mutually consistent. My belief system was proving to be not only a trustworthy professional theory but also a hopeful and optimistic way to confront advancing age, accumulated experience, and the world at large.

From time to time in the years since, I experienced twinges of guilt for not being a more ardent advocate of the theory Don Snygg and I formulated. When I moved from Syracuse to Florida, I shifted energies from the development and dissemination of theory to the applications of perceptual thinking for education. This was partly due to the rejection from psychologists that I experienced in the destruction of our program at Syracuse. It was also a function of the warm reception accorded perceptual-experiential thinking throughout education, which assuaged my sense of injury on one hand and encouraged my work in education on the other. I was more concerned with its contributions to the understanding of human beings than with selling the concepts to the psychological profession. This left no one to champion perceptual-experiential thinking among psychologists. I have some regrets about that, but we human beings are fallible and our energies are limited. Given the values that guide my life, I would make the same choice today.

Heart-Warmers

Excerpts from cards, letters, and notes that Art preserved in a file bearing this title.

FEBRUARY, 1968

The eulogy you gave for Kim [Kimball Wiles] was exactly right. It was a comforting, moving, tribute to a great man by a great man. (Boca Raton, FL)

APRIL, 1970

Everyone with whom I spoke was enthusiastic and responsive to your keynote address. You can always be depended upon to focus on the human quality and characteristics that are basic and relevant as we attempt to consistently improve and refine our programs. (Roslyn, NY)

NOVEMBER, 1970

Our Fall Seminar was a most exciting and rewarding experience for me. . . . I enjoyed every minute of it thoroughly, but I think the most heart warming experience was the moment I first realized that the man who wrote of humanistic teaching and humanistic education was indeed a very humanistic person—a most warm, understanding, and caring person. I could spend this letter thanking you for the message you gave us, the questions you made us ask ourselves, the subtle challenge you left planted in each of us, but instead I am going to say thank you for your "Arthurness," for the sheer pleasure of meeting a man who does not talk or act from the head alone, but who has a great deal of heart in all that he does. Your students are very lucky indeed. . . . may you continue to turn on people for a long, long time. (Minneapolis, MN)

APRIL, 1971

It is a pleasure for me to indicate to you that you have been clearly the highlight of our 1970-71 seminar series [in Illinois]. Far too frequently, a seminar speaker stimulates some immediate interests but his presence and ideas appear often to have very tentative and short range impact. The frequency with which I hear your concepts being discussed even at this date leads me to believe that you have made a lasting impact upon our thinking. (Macomb, IL)

MAY, 1971

Your note today was joyously received and your touching letter of July 69 was a life-saver. I seriously thought at the time that I was out of it for good. I lived for a long time on feelings expressed in your letter. (Odessa, FL)

MAY, 1972

On behalf of the [Ontario Educational Association] may I extend our thanks for your magnificant [sic] address at our opening session. The reaction to your talk was amazing and we have not had a speaker who has stimulated our delegates as you were able to. . . . (Toronto, Ontario, Canada)

UNDATED

Helping Relationships—Hawaiian Style
Tune—Pearly Shells
1. Doc-tor Combs—
Come Ha-wai-I—
Tell-ing us to love—,
Ur-ging us to care—.
What he's teach- ing—
Is the spir-it of a-lo-ha
That we say—to all "Aloha Dere!"
2. As to pro-cess—
In the class-room—
'Easy goin' style—.
How to make it swing—?
Just re-mem-ber—
When the go-ing gets too rough
That the answer is this:
"Cool head main ting!"
3. An-gry notes—
In the da-ta—.
Feel-ings in the raw—,
Tem-per ris-ing too—.
How to reach him—;

How to help him find his way?
"Easy Bruddah, Mo bettah no huhu!"
4. When self-image—
Takes a beat-ing—
You help to get the facts—
Square-ly in their place—.
Then you ac-cent—
All the best things that he is.
"Eh! Try smile! It no can broke your face."
5. Repeat verse one. (Honolulu, HI)

NOVEMBER, 1972

The area is still buzzing from comments about your talk at both the district and Phi Delta Kappa meetings. . . . One of my friends commented that they had never seen me quite so contented as when you were speaking to the Phi Delta Kappa group and I sat listening to you. The comment went something like this, "You looked as if you had just finished a tremendous gourmet meal, and now you were sitting back relishing its [after effects]." Thanks so much for being with us! . . . . You're a breath of freshness that enters a lifetime too, too seldom. If only there were more Arthur Combs to carry forward the cause of humanistic psychology. (Bethlehem, PA)

AUGUST, 1973

. . . Now to my plan. First of all I intend to remain aware of what is really important to me and not incorporate what "everybody" else is doing. By the end of last year, with one class, at least, I had lost touch. I was concerned for control and covering what other, more experienced teachers were teaching. I needed Summer School to rediscover my ideas for a renewal of my energy, to become committed again to a sense of humanity. . . .

I do want to tell you again how important your workshop was for me. The book, *Helping Relationships*, was the most significant reading I did all summer. The concepts of the creation of intelligence, the circular effect of the self-concept and the growth principle are very meaningful for me. I find now I have more faith, not only in my own instincts but also in people generally. I can go into any "helping relationship" believing in myself and the "powerful" ally I am working to help. (Corvallis, OR)

JUNE, 1974

Dr. Combs, dictating that little note to me at the end of this tape was just the nicest thing to do! I felt like weeping a little tear or two on listening to it. It was very thoughtful and kind of you to think of it. . . . I will miss you and miss doing your tapes, which have always been so clear and easy to type from. It seems so strange to think of this Department without you. . . . I wish you all the good luck and happiness in the world in your new life in Colorado. (Gainesville, FL)

References

Kelley, E. (1947). *Education for what is real*. New York: Harper.

Maslow, A. H. (1954). *Motivation and personality*. New York: Harper & Row.

Raimy, V. C. (1971). *The self-concept as a factor in counseling and personality organization* (Doctoral dissertation, Ohio State University, 1943). Columbus, OH: Ohio State University Libraries.

Richards, F. (1977). *Never wrestle with pygmies: Notes for a novel and assordid poems.* Carrollton, GA: R Mark Press.

Snygg, D. (1941). The need for a phenomenological system of psychology. *Psychological Review, 48*(5), 404–424.

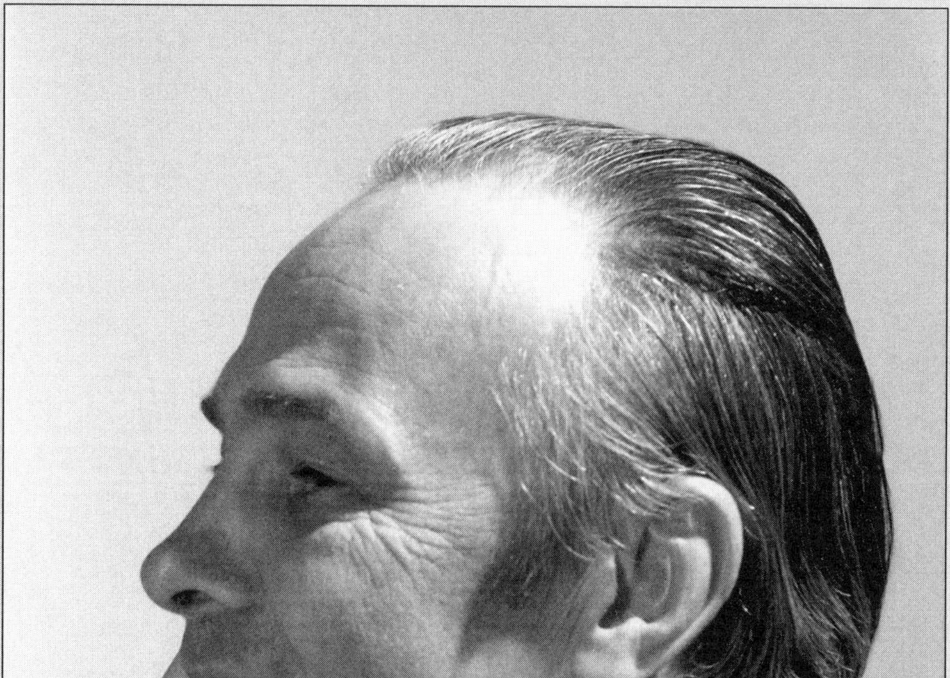

Arthur W. Combs in Greeley, CO (circa 1977) Photo by Monte Clute

CHAPTER TEN

A New Way of Life

In the spring of 1973 I received a rude shock, coming face to face with my own mortality. As part of my annual check-up, routine X-rays of my lungs showed a spot the size of a golf ball in a place that could not be reached by bronchoscopy. My physician suspected cancer. Consultation with an oncologist confirmed the possibility. I would need an exploratory operation at once. I was desolate. Just as I was embarking upon a buoyant and exciting phase of my life, I was threatened with the possibility that it would all come to a crashing halt. "How long can I wait?" I asked. Five days at most was the answer. I knew that opening the chest meant a long recovery, even if no sign of cancer was found, so I set about getting my affairs in order. I updated my will, turned in my camper for a smaller car, canceled consulting engagements for the next three months, arranged for substitutes to teach my summer classes, spent a number of tearful sessions with Susan, and reported to the hospital.

Next morning I was shaved and prepped for the operation. My surgeon dropped in to review the procedure he was about to follow and ordered one more set of X-rays. I waited in my room, ready to be wheeled to the operating room. Instead, my surgeon came in to say, "Professor, go home. The spot is entirely gone. I have no idea what it was but it was certainly not cancer." What a relief! I hardly knew what to do with myself. I had accepted the inevitable, made all those preparations. What now? In a daze at this sudden turn of events, I called Susan, who came to take me home. Next day we had a celebration party at my apartment.

Needless to say, this experience had a profound effect upon me. One does not look death in the eye and come away unaffected. I had much to digest and think about. Several years before, I had invested in a condominium being built on Crescent Beach and it was now available to occupy. Given that all of my professional obligations were canceled for the next three months, I moved in and settled down to think and write. Weekdays I kept house, walked the beach, swam and fished in the surf, caught up with my reading, and spent several hours each day working on a book or article. I had a clearer sense of the importance of living in the present and resolved, henceforth, to savor the day-to-day experiences of life with a keener appreciation. For some years I had been actively following a program of jogging three or four times a week. With an awakened respect for health and personal growth, I now added to my regimen daily sessions of meditation or self-hypnosis. I had lots of time to confront the state of my life and relationships. Weekends, Susan joined me at the beach and we had many happy hours together. Among other things, we talked often about our relationship, including the discrepancy between our ages. We agreed that my death was an eventuality we would have to face one day. Meantime, we would follow the dictates of our hearts.

Living Together

In the fall we decided to move in together. We rented half a duplex and began life as partners. Neither of us had any thought or desire for marriage. We valued being together solely because we wanted to be, feeling no need for official sanction from any quarter. I learned to cook and bake bread. We began to take tennis lessons. Weekdays we worked at our respective jobs. Many weekends were spent at the condominium. We went surf fishing, or fished off the docks at Cedar Key; we explored Florida's rivers by canoe, and made trips to Sanibel Island, St. Petersburg, Miami, and the Everglades.

At Christmas, we visited Susan's folks in Massillon, Ohio. This was a scary prospect for me. I was apprehensive about how they would regard me. It could not be easy for them to accept the fact that their daughter was involved with a man four years older than her father. I need not have worried. The Kannels were warm and accepting beyond belief and have remained so over the years since. Never once have they made me feel uncomfortable. I have become truly fond of them and I am deeply grateful for their open-hearted acceptance of me.

As our relationship matured, Susan and I decided to buy a house. This added yet another dimension to our lives. We enjoyed furnishing the house and making improvements to the property. We made new friends and took special pleasure in entertaining them in our more spacious surroundings. I frequently invited my classes from the university for sessions in our living room. Life with Susan was delightful. I was deeply in love with her and could hardly believe the constancy and depth of her feelings for me. It seemed too good to be true. I was not at all sure it would last, so I resolved all the more to live each day to the fullest.

After a year shared in this home, our relationship was feeling very solid. We began to toy with the idea of having a child. Soon we were discussing the question seriously, examining the matter from every angle. We had no doubt that we could be good parents. The sticky questions revolved around the problem of my age. Would it be fair to the child? Would it be fair to Susan if she were left alone to raise the child? One of our friends recoiled in horror at the idea, pronouncing it irresponsible. For my part, I was intrigued by the thought. It seemed to me a further expression of our loving relationship. It would also provide a second chance to be a better father. I felt real regret that my workaholic compulsions during Carol and Peter's childhood prevented more intimate relationships with them and resolved that, if Susan and I had a child, I would be a more available parent. Besides, being a parent already, I felt that Susan ought not to be denied this important and fulfilling experience if she wanted it. We faced the possibility that I might not make it to see a child to maturity. We finally agreed that no child ever has a guarantee that both parents will be there throughout its growing years and decided that we were willing to run that risk. So began a five-year roller coaster of hope and despair in the effort to get pregnant.

Death of a Good Man

That year (1974), my father died after a short illness. I spent some warm, meaningful, and thought-provoking times with him in his last days and was present at the end. In all my life, he had never kissed me, but he did so three times in those last days. Among the matters we talked about, three things especially have remained with me long since. Once, exasperated at his weakened condition, he said, "Arthur, I'm not afraid to die. I want to die. But my God-damned medulla won't let me." Another time he reminisced, "Basically, I have been a good man. I have lived a life that has been helpful and useful to other people. One thing I can say, Son, is, in all my life, I have never done a mean thing to anyone on purpose." I was struck by this reflection. What a beautiful thing to be able to say! How many of us will be able to say as much?

The third comment completely changed my understanding of him. He said, "Arthur, one thing I can say with great satisfaction: I have spent my entire life serving people. I've kept a host of people from getting sick or dying." As I mentioned earlier, my father was a veterinarian in the federal meat inspection service. In childhood memories of him at work, I see him standing in a noisy, steaming slaughterhouse with pans of pig entrails moving by in front of him synchronized with the pig's carcass moving on a rail behind him. Quickly he would make a small incision here or there in guts or carcass and decide its fate: passed, passed for cooking, or condemned. As I grew up and joined the work force myself, I remember feeling sorry for him. I wished he did not have to work in such dreadful and demeaning conditions. Now, as he was dying, he spoke of fulfillment, of a lifetime of service contributing to the welfare of millions. How different things look when seen from another's perspective. This kindly, gentle man, whom I hardly knew as I was growing up, turned out to be a person of dignity and integrity, possessed of a nobility I had not heretofore appreciated or suspected. He had not lived in vain.

My father belonged to no religious sect. Instead, he believed there is a great Spirit in the world, a God who provides the universe with order and function. He had a deep reverence for that Spirit but little or no patience with established religions in any form. Accordingly, we held no service at the time of his death. Instead, some time after his cremation, those of us in the family who survived him spent a quiet evening together reminiscing about our experience of him as husband and dad.

Like my father, I have no belief in life after death. Rather, I believe that whatever immortality we may have is the consequence of the life we have lived. To illustrate that belief, I have sometimes told the following anecdote: Once I was fishing with a friend. We weren't catching anything and we began to talk philosophy. When the topic turned to life after death, my friend said, "I believe there are three kinds of immortality, Art. There is the kind you get through your children, but you can't count on that. If they don't live to reproduce, that is the end of the line for you. Then, there is the immortality the clergy offers us. But it, too, is not certain. We have only their word for it. The priests could be wrong. The third kind is the only one you can be sure of. That is the immortality we achieve through the impact we make on other people throughout our lives. That impact goes on forever." Even the concrete works or writing that we leave behind can never have that kind of permanence. The third kind is the one that makes most sense to me.

Decline of the Childhood Education Program

While the above-mentioned changes were occurring in my personal life, things were shifting at the university as well, but not in a direction that was pleasing to me. I grew more and more distressed and began to consider the possibility of resigning. The fourth year of the CEP's operation, at a meeting of the Elementary Education Department faculty, it was decided that the CEP program should become the official one for all students and that the old program would be phased out. This seemingly corroborative action unfortunately opened the gates to a flood of problems that finally resulted in the demise of a glorious and badly needed innovation in teacher education. Faculty members who had voted themselves into the program soon found that they did not understand or agree with some of the philosophy and practices developed by the original planners. Locked into a program with which they found themselves "out of sync," they became anxious and threatened. As a result, they sought, either consciously or unwittingly, to return to more familiar concepts and practices. Their anxiety and confusion was transmitted to the student body, who, in turn, began to doubt the value of their educational experiences.

The dean of the college was upset by the confusion, became embarrassed by the program, and felt it necessary to apologize for it. Eventually, he was reluctant to provide it support. This despite the fact that it was becoming widely heralded outside the campus. Visitors were coming to see it in action from all over the country as well as from foreign lands. "Art, the State Department of Education will be upset," the Dean told me. I pointed out to him that our college ought not be taking its cues from second-rate administrators who typically make up such departments. Instead, the University of Florida, as the state's great university with a faculty of distinguished educators, ought to be leading the way to educational innovation and telling the State Department what needed to be done. He was shocked at my presumptuousness.

Added to these difficulties, Florida's Board of Regents realized they had overbuilt the university system after the war and they imposed a series of severe cutbacks in the financing of the state's colleges of education. We began to lose key figures in the program. The combination of all these events produced a rapid decline in the program, contributing further to the sense of frustration I was beginning to feel about university work.

Some Significant Publications

During this period, I completed two important articles. The first grew out of an address to the Association for the Study of Perception: "Why the Humanistic Movement Needs a Perceptual Psychology" [Combs, 1974]. While the humanistic movement in psychology was slowly making headway, it was seriously handicapped by lack of a basic theory to provide order and direction for its myriad expressions. Third Force psychology needed a comprehensive theory of meaning and I proposed that the perceptual frame of reference first introduced by Snygg and myself might contribute to filling that bill.

Arthur W. Combs lecturing in class (circa 1975)

Sidney Jourard, a prominent psychologist of the humanistic persuasion, was on the faculty at the University of Florida and he and I had appeared together on several occasions. In 1974, he died in a tragic accident while working on his sports car. At the memorial conference held to honor him, I took the occasion to make a second pitch for more fully utilizing the insights of open systems, discovery-oriented, experiential thinking in the humanistic movement in an address entitled "A Choice of Futures" [Combs, 1977]. The psychology profession was slowly shifting across the spectrum from a behavioristic frame of reference to a more humanistic orientation. The progress, however, was very slow. Most humanistic psychologists were more certain about what they were against than how their concerns and efforts were associated with any particular theoretical base. Indeed, many humanistic psychologists eschewed any hint of association with a theoretical framework. They turned away from behaviorism with such determination as to reject any suggestion of becoming reinvolved with anything that smacked of a theoretical system or school of thought.

I believed then, and still do, that perceptual-experiential theory can make an important contribution to a more humane psychology. As Don and I phrased it in the introduction to *Individual Behavior* in 1949, "As an outline of a theory we expect that like everything else in science, this frame of reference we propose may undergo shifts and changes as it is subjected to wider consideration. As fallible human beings we can only hope that this is, 'if not the truth, then very like the truth.'" Abe Maslow predicted in the late forties that humanistic psychology would be *the* psychology in thirty years. The profession was running late on that schedule and my papers were designed to prod it along.

I was also involved as editor and contributor in a series of articles reporting on our teacher education experiments with Walter Busby, Robert Blume, Art Newman, and Hannelore Wass (discussed in Chapter 9). The sec-

Charles Horn, Art, Susan, Ted Landsman, Mary B. Landsman, Mary Horn (Micanopy, FL. Photo taken by tripod circa 1975)

ond edition of the book about our CEP program, *The Professional Education of Teachers: A Humanistic Approach to Teacher Education*, was published in 1974.

Time to Move On

Soon after Susan and I moved into our new home, Millie filed for divorce. Millie and I split everything we owned, with Millie keeping the house we had built in Gainesville and I retaining the beach condominium. I was surprised that the consummation of the divorce had so little effect upon me. Through the four years of our separation, I had adjusted so completely to my partnership with Susan that when the divorce occurred, it seemed only anticlimactic. The matter of my previous marriage to Millie was behind me and I was well into a different way of life.

In 1975, I began to think seriously of leaving the university to make a living as a writer and consultant. The thought of cutting off my roots in academia was simultaneously scary and challenging. Yet it seemed a grand opportunity to demonstrate to myself that I could, indeed, make it on my own. On several occasions, Susan and I had stayed at Dick and Mary Usher's cabin in Allenspark, Colorado. Discovering that some adjacent lots were for sale, we bought them with an eye to building a cabin of our own one day. Now we began to think about the possibilities of taking up residence in Colorado. We were tired of Florida's heat, humidity, and bugs. We longed for a place with change of seasons and a drier climate.

Early in 1976 we took a week to explore Colorado's front range in search of a congenial place to live. After visiting towns for 200 miles along the Rockies from Pueblo to Fort Collins, we settled on Greeley and I set about severing ties with the University of Florida. During spring break that year, we flew to Greeley and bought a house. Back in Gainesville, we began the process of selling our home and packing for the move to Colorado. I applied for early retirement and closed out all my campus commitments. A friend at Grambling University told us the university was in need of books for its library. Accordingly, I packed two and a half tons of books and shipped them as a donation. Soon after the last class of the spring quarter, we saw our collection of goods loaded on a van and said goodbye to our friends. Then we set out for Colorado with a car full of plants and two sedated cats.

Settling in Greeley

Setting up housekeeping in our Colorado home was a real adventure. Susan has a marvelous flair for color and home decoration. Our house very quickly became a comfortable, attractive place to be. The lot included a rose garden for Susan and a vegetable garden for me. It was almost thirty years since I last had such a garden and I thoroughly enjoyed working the soil and growing some of our own food. Colorado was in the midst of its centennial celebration of statehood. We attended events like the Fourth of July parade and the Greeley Stampede (Greeley's cowboy celebration, complete with rodeo and country singers). Life was casual and pleasant. We explored mountain trails, planted trees on our mountain acres, and played tennis almost daily. Shortly after arriving in Greeley, we learned of an obstetrician/gynecologist in Denver who was making a name for himself as a fertility specialist. We began to make frequent trips to Denver for consultations, which we combined with shopping expeditions and visits to a sampling of Denver's restaurants.

Arthur W. Combs in Allenspark, CO (circa 1975)

Susan and I made fun trips to the Oregon Coast during these times.

Arthur W. Combs (circa 1977). Photo by Monte Clute

We turned consulting trips for me into vacations for both of us. We attended the Shakespeare Festival in Ashland, Oregon and went salmon fishing out of Depot Bay. Several times we explored the delights of San Francisco and San Diego. On one occasion we spent several hours with Carl and Helen Rogers at their home in La Jolla, California. My concentration on education while at the University of Florida took me away from intensive involvement with psychology. As a consequence, Carl and I had little or no contact for many years. This was the first time in thirty years that I had an opportunity to chat with Carl beyond a few words in passing. It was good to see him again. I especially enjoyed having Susan become acquainted with these special people from my early days.

Changing Professional Commitments

I continued making consulting trips around the country during these early days in Greeley but not so frequently as before. Some of this was due to the fact that I no longer had a university connection. People did not know where to find me and assumed I was retired and out of circulation. I have never been comfortable with the label "retired." I do not feel I retired from the University of Florida, for example. Rather, it seems to me that I resigned for good reason. I was disenchanted with academia and wanted to try my wings in a different arena. Even after 15 years, I look upon my retirement income as delayed payment for services rendered. "Being retired," like writing an autobiography, puts emphasis on the past, whereas I am far more interested in being in the present and becoming in the future. I have not retired from life, only changed my goals and life style.

While enjoying life in Greeley, I was also engaged in the revision of *Helping Relationships* and published an important paper on "Self-actualization and the Teaching Function of Counselors" [Combs, 1976]. In it, I set forth my beliefs that (a) the proper goal of therapy is self-actualization and (b) therapy is fundamentally a learning process, so counselors are teachers whether they wish to be or not. The paper made the point that whatever counselors believe is the nature of self-actualization must automatically become the goal of counseling and the factors determining self-actualization must provide the guidelines for counseling practice. Likewise, since counseling is a learning process, what counselors do must be guided by their theory of learning. Many counselors have a hard time being labeled as teachers. They tend to see teachers as autocrats and themselves as facilitators or helpers. Modern conceptions of good teaching, however, value facilitation rather than autocracy just as conceptions of good counseling do.

The second editions of *Helping Relationships* [Combs, Avila, & Purkey, 1978] and *The Helping Relationship Sourcebook* [Avila, Combs, & Purkey, 1977] appeared in this time period, and I turned to writing *Myths in Education: Beliefs that Hinder Progress and Their Alternatives* [Combs, 1979]. The latter book grew out of a speech I had made many times about some of the inaccurate assumptions on which much of educational practice is based, like the myths of competition, right methods, fixed intelligence, the value of failure, or if it's hard it's good for you. My publishers were intrigued with the ideas and arranged to have the book illustrated. It is the only illustrated book I have done.

As chairman of ASCD's Commission on Humanistic Education, I edited and did much of the writing for the Commission's monograph on *Humanistic Education: Objectives and Assessment* [Combs, Aspy, Brown, Clute, & Hicks, 1978]. A major problem for humanistic educators was the difficulty of satisfying parents, administrators, and the public that humanistic approaches were, indeed, improvements over the status quo. This monograph was an attempt to help address that issue by defining what humanistic education was all about and proposing ways by which its values could be demonstrated.

I had no regrets about leaving Florida. I was happy and excited by the changes in my personal life. Sometimes I missed teaching, however. It troubled me that our innovative Childhood Education Program was beginning to unravel before we left Florida and continued to do so after our departure. Years afterwards, only a few of its innovations remained. Like the clinical program at Syracuse, this was the second time in my life that I had thrown myself full tilt into the building of a major program only to see it disintegrate before my eyes. The sadness and loss over the Florida program affected me less than the debacle at Syracuse, however.

Some years after leaving Syracuse, I was bemoaning what had happened there when one of the people who had been through the program chided me, "Don't feel bad, Art," she said. "Sure, the program is gone but the people who were in it are out there. What they experienced is still part of them and the influence goes on even if the program is dead." Of course, she was right.

It is the impact upon people that really counts and I had evidence aplenty that students from both programs were making a difference in the far-flung places in which they had settled.

The Pain of a Miscarriage

In 1977, after three years of alternating anticipation and disappointment bordering on despair, Susan finally became pregnant and we were eagerly looking forward to our "blessed event." But it was not to be. Susan had a miscarriage and we were back to square one. The experience was devastating. As a counselor, I had known that miscarriages were often as stressful for parents as the death of a child, but now I experienced full force what I had only known second-hand before. Susan was overcome with grief and depression while I felt futile and inadequate to find some way to help. Our lives felt rudely shaken. Our grief was made worse by such well-meaning comments as, "It's just nature's way of assuring that you are not left with a hopelessly handicapped child" and by contrast with the happiness of some of our friends whose children were born at about that time.

Following months of healing and trying again, we decided to seek an adoption. We soon discovered, however, that the difference in our ages did not make us prime candidates for parenthood in the eyes of adoption agencies. They took an even dimmer view of the fact that we were not married. To improve our chances, we decided to get married. Two days after Christmas, we combined a secret wedding with our monthly trip to our fertility specialist. Leaving the doctor's office, we stopped off in a judge's chambers for a short ceremony with his clerks as witnesses. The formalities over, we crossed the street to a cocktail lounge for a toast before driving back to Greeley. We enjoyed our unmarried way of life and believed so strongly that official recognition would do nothing positive for our relationship that getting married seemed almost like a cop-out. Aside from Susan's folks, we never told anyone but the adoption agencies about our change in marital status until several years later.

A Trip to Mexico

In 1978, a group of Mexican educators came to visit with me and some of the education faculty at the University of Northern Colorado in Greeley. In view of the opposition that humanistic education encountered in the states, I was astounded to find that the leader of the group was interested in these ideas because "humanistic education is simpático with our revolution!" The following year I was invited to conduct workshops on humanistic education in four Mexican cities. Susan accompanied me on this trip. We had a delightful three weeks exploring four quite different parts of the country and enjoying the hospitality of our Mexican hosts.

In preparation for the trip, Susan and I decided to enroll in a conversational Spanish class at our local community college. At the end of the quarter, we felt we needed more instruction but discovered there was no follow-up course available. Instead, there was only a section open to fifth-quarter students. The instructor assured us not to worry, that we would get along very nicely, so we enrolled despite my misgivings. As the class progressed I experienced an object lesson about self-concept that has stuck with me ever since. Night after night I sat in that class while all around me fellow students, including Susan, were jabbering away in Spanish and I had not the slightest idea of what they were talking about. I felt embarrassed and humiliated and, for the first time in my life, found myself at the very bottom of the class.

Then, one night, our instructor asked me a basic question in Spanish: "Arturo, cómo se llama?" (What's your name?). I was thoroughly traumatized. I could not remember my name! Not even in English! I sat there immobilized, while wave after wave of shame and confusion swept over me and tears of frustration came to my eyes. In the midst of this experience, the thought came to me, "My God! This is what millions of school children experience every day of their lives!" I have talked and written much about the significance of the self-concept and the importance of helping children develop positive views of self. This experience brought the lesson home to me as nothing else has. It is now seared into my soul.

Our Baby Is Born

Soon after returning from Mexico, Susan became pregnant again. We were overjoyed. For the last three months of gestation, our physician restricted her to bed or the living room couch while we waited anxiously, hoping for a normal birth. We enrolled in Lamaze classes and prepared together for labor and delivery. The baby was born in August. Delivery was difficult because the umbilical cord was wrapped around the baby's shoulder. After agonizing hours watching a fetal monitor as our baby struggled for breath, the baby emerged. The doctor announced, "You have a baby girl" and handed her to me for a few precious moments. We named her Lynn Ann.

This experience and the birth of Erin Elizabeth, two years later, had a profound effect upon me. In the days when my two earlier children were born, fathers were told to "get lost" or "go boil some water." With Lynn and Erin, I was a partner at the delivery and shared the joy, the anxiety, and the relief of childbirth. I cherish the memories of holding each of our children while the nurses tended to Susan. The memory of cradling each child in my arms, the feel of rubbing cheek to cheek, and the smell of a tiny head under my nose is imprinted forever. I was bonding with my children in a fashion not permitted in earlier years. What a beautiful experience! What a shame that so many fathers were denied this precious opportunity for so many years.

Lynn's arrival brought enormous changes in our way of life, as every new parent discovers. We were enthralled with her presence but we were no longer so footloose and fancy free as we were before her arrival. Babies are exhausting as well as charming. I learned to enjoy the feeling of warmth and closeness while rocking our babies to sleep in the dark and quiet after midnight. Later on, I relished equally much the care and tenderness I experienced tucking them in after a wee-hours trip to the bathroom or comforting them after a nightmare, precious moments for a loving father. Our two girls have been a never-ending source of wonder and fulfillment beyond my fondest expectations.

My Mother Comes to Greeley

When Lynn was a year old, my mother came to live in Greeley. It was a wrenching experience for her to leave her friends in Greensboro but it was becoming increasingly difficult for her to manage an apartment by herself. In Greeley she had a pleasant apartment in a retirement complex and I began seeing her every day or so. It was a relief to me to know that she was closer by, where I could be available in case of emergencies. She was enraptured by her new grandchild and lived just long enough to see a second one. She had cancer of the lungs, probably a consequence of many years spent in a small apartment with a heavy smoker. She finally succumbed at 91. I had long since resolved my early feelings about her. I had come to understand and appreciate her as a lady of charm and good humor who met the problems of life with strength and dignity.

One night I was awakened by the phone ringing. It was my sister, calling to ask, "What is going on?" She had a call from our mother but was unable to make out what mother was saying. I explained that mother sometimes had trouble speaking clearly. Half an hour later I was awakened again, this time by my brother, Chuck. He had had the same experience. I gave him the same explanation and decided to check things out in the

Chuck Combs (left) and Art (right) with their mother (circa 1980)

morning. A few hours later I was again awakened to learn that mother had died.

At the nursing home, the young attendant told me that mother, with a great deal of urgency, had wanted to call her children. The attendant helped her find the proper phone numbers for Chuck and Dot but could not make out who my mother was asking for after that. Apparently, mother knew she was dying and was making last calls to her children.

I was distraught that I had not been available when she was trying to make her farewells. The young attendant was in anguish, also. My first feeling was anger at her incompetence. This was followed by the realization that it was not her fault; she tried to help but mother could not make herself understood. I regret that I was not at mother's bedside at the end. I was sad to learn of her death, but I was at peace with the love and warmth of our relationship in her last years.

Distinguished Professor

In 1980 I was invited to accept a distinguished professorship at the University of Northern Colorado in Greeley. Because I was enjoying an unhassled way of

Arthur W. Combs (circa 1986)

life too much to return to full-time university work, I only agreed to join the faculty on a limited basis (one-quarter time). I was hired primarily to do in-service work with the faculty and was expected to confine any teaching to guest appearances in various classes. For a year, this program worked very well and I enjoyed the experience. Unfortunately, the university was confronting serious fiscal problems. To bring matters under control, the regents brought a new president aboard and gave him orders to cut faculty and curriculum. This he proceeded to do by lopping off individuals and whole departments in what I considered to be ruthless fashion.

Since the faculty had no organization to engage in effective negotiations with the administration, I suggested at a faculty meeting called to address the crisis that they elect a steering committee to represent them. They did and I was promptly elected to the committee. This threw me into the middle of the fracas and left me little time for other activities. Yet, as an untenured part-time member of the faculty, my role could be little more than advisory. After three years, I decided that I had better things to do with my life. In addition, I had long ago paid my dues in university politics. Fed up with the politics of the university and the in-fighting it fostered, I resigned the professorship to turn attention to other activities.

During the four years I was on the UNC faculty, a group of elementary professors and I began to design a new training program for elementary teachers. Like the program at Florida, we began with a series of fundamental assumptions about learning and behavior. With this as a basis, we started to implement the assumptions with a group of 50 education majors. We called our program the Teacher Education Experimental Group (TEEG) and operated it successfully for two years despite the turmoil going on in the university generally. I have warm feelings for the faculty and students who were involved. It was a fun time and we were on the way to developing a fine program. Unfortunately, the climate on campus worked at cross-purposes to our continued success. Several key figures left the university for other jobs, and the administration was more concerned with trying to maintain the status quo than committing itself to innovations. Soon after, I resigned. There were but two or three left to lead the program and it began a rapid disintegration. Sadly, this provided me with a third experience of seeing a promising innovation dissolve.

Aside from my work at the university, I organized my time to spend about three hours a day at writing, correspondence, or preparations for consulting engagements. The remainder of my days was devoted to enjoying the family and sharing household responsibilities. The *Myths in Education* book appeared to a satisfying reception. I also produced two notable papers, published in the *Phi Delta Kappan*. The first, "What The Future Demands of Education" [Combs, 1981], was an attempt to advance the cause of educational reform. I saw our schools and colleges as woefully out of sync with the demands of the world into which we were moving. Trying to change the American education colossus is a slow and frustrating affair. In the paper I sought to point out several of the scenarios futurists assure us are before us and what these require of us if education is to carry out its responsibility for contributing to the preparation of youth for the world they will inherit.

The second paper, "Humanistic Education: Too Tender for a Tough World?" [Combs, 1981], was an attempt to meet the prevailing criticism that humanistic education was an effete and even dangerous philosophy. I explained that it is, in reality, an absolute necessity for the world we are moving into. Furthermore, far from being a vague idea, it is solidly grounded in a veritable mountain of research that can only be ignored at the price of falling hopelessly behind.*

Early in the eighties I began work on *A Personal Approach to Teaching: Beliefs that Make a Difference*. In this volume I tried to point out the importance of theory in the practice of teaching. The book is highly personal as well, for in writing it I took the opportunity to set forth my own personal theory or belief system about the teaching process. This publication appeared in 1982 and received only modest acceptance.

---

* Editor's note. In these articles Art explained how our world has become more interdependent and technologically advanced, with the result that "the power of each individual for good or evil has been enormously increased. The more interdependent the society, the greater the possibilities for individuals to disrupt the system. Today, anyone can buy a gun in a mail-order house. Poisons are available in any seed store. Each of us travels our highways encased in a ton of steel capable at any moment of becoming an engine of death and destruction for dozens of other people. It is this utter interdependence that has made it possible for terrorists to threaten multitudes" (Combs, 1981, p. 446).

A Growing Family

While I was on a consulting trip in Brazil, Susan phoned to let me know that she was again pregnant. We were delighted. In March of 1981, our second daughter, Erin Elizabeth, was born. Again we went through the partnership of pregnancy with anticipation and joy and I had a second cherished opportunity to bond with a newborn daughter at the time of childbirth. We were happy to be a two-child family and decided that was fulfillment enough. Some months later, I had a vasectomy. My surgeon was much amused at performing the operation on a 69-year-old man. We joked about whether the operation would be covered by Medicare.

The family took a number of vacation trips to Florida during these years. Sometimes we stayed in the condominium apartment we had formerly owned where Susan and I had spent so many blissful times in the early days of our relationship. It was good to return to Florida and its beaches. It also gave us opportunities to visit with Carol and Peter, my grown children, and their families, and to renew acquaintances with old Florida friends. After a week or ten days, however, we were happy to return to Greeley and our Colorado home. People are often surprised that we left Florida to live in Colorado "of our own accord." We have never doubted or reconsidered our decision. Besides the friends we knew there, with whom we keep in contact, the only things I really miss from my Florida days are the beaches and seafood fresh from the ocean.

Susan became actively involved in community affairs in Greeley, especially with women's issues. She was a member of the founding committee for A Woman's Place, a shelter for battered women, and a long-time member of its board of directors. She was in frequent demand as a speaker and assertiveness trainer. An outgoing, friendly person, she has been very good for me. Her enthusiasm for whatever projects she tackles is uplifting. One cannot help but be caught up in her effervescence and zest for life. We think alike about many issues but respect each other's differences, too. Where she is high-strung and excitable, I tend to be laid back. Where I am shy and reticent, she enters relationships with ease. Susan is a non-screener, aware of and responsive to everything around her down to the least detail. I, on the other hand, am a screener, with a tendency to zero in on some events to such an extent as sometimes to be oblivious to more important matters. This lack of attention sometimes makes me forgetful, while Susan is likely to remember everything. It is fascinating to us that our two girls are one of each, both physically and temperamentally. Lynn is a carbon copy of Susan, while Erin has personality characteristics very much like those of her father.

Lynn, Arthur, Erin, Susan (1985) Photo by Tony Wu, Contemporary Studios, Greeley, CO

When Carol was very young and I was a struggling graduate student, I frequently took her for walks to places like the state fair grounds or the university farms; sometimes we would take a bus trip downtown, or simply walk about the neighborhood. These trips became the topics of stories at bedtime, when I would review in great detail what we had done. Later, with Lynn and then Erin, I told similar stories about the children's adventures starring a heroine named Emily, who was actually the child I was entertaining. Emily was the star of stories about the day she saved the ducklings, rescued her cat, went to see the helicopter, had to go to the hospital, went to grandma's house, and many more. Sometimes these also involved Abigail, Emily's sister. I thoroughly enjoyed these times with my tiny girls and, even in adolescence, they would remind me of an Emily story they fondly remembered. When Lynn and Erin were four and six, we bought a female Labrador setter, a lovely dog that, of course, we named Emily.

Our Autumn-Spring Relationship

Sometimes the age difference between Susan and myself produced amusing situations. Once while shopping for a coat, Susan took me along for my opinion. When we arrived at the store, the saleslady gushed, "Oh, good, dearie, you've brought your Daddy to see it." Answering the phone, I was often addressed, "Mr. Kannel?" I always said "Yes." After all, women have been answering to their husbands' names for generations. When I am out somewhere with the children, people often say to them, "Having a nice time with your grandpop, girls?" or to me, "It's nice to have an outing with your grandkids, isn't it?" Mostly, I take these remarks in stride without explanation or comment. But sometimes, I get a mischievous kick out of telling a too-intrusive individual, "I beg your pardon. These are not my grandchildren. They are all mine," and enjoying the confusion such statements generate. More recently, I thought it hilarious to watch Susan's reaction when my grandson from my first marriage called her "Grandma." Although our relationship seemed puzzling to others, from our point of view it wasn't difficult to understand. We were together because we loved each other, enabled each other to feel more adequate, and liked the way we lived as a couple.

Back to Work

For five or six years after arriving in Greeley, I was totally content to savor my family-focused way of being. The relationship with Susan was almost idyllic. We had lots of time for each other and the children. I worked at writing, occasional consulting, and the garden. We played tennis, shared household duties, and lived a thoroughly contented existence. As I told people who inquired about what I was doing, "I do everything I want to do and nothing I don't. You can't beat it!" I was happier than I have ever been before or since. (Lucky, too!) As the girls grew from toddlers to pre-schoolers, however, I began to feel a growing urge to get back to work professionally.

After leaving Florida, most of my professional work was confined to consulting trips and writing. These were activities that could be done at my leisure, leaving plenty of time to give myself over to my blossoming personal life. I had no desire to return to the kind of immersion in professional affairs characteristic of my life before coming to Greeley. My workaholic days were over. I no longer felt compelled to be in the midst of my former professions. Yet I did not want to drop them completely. I still felt that I had important contributions to make. Thus, I sought ways to return to my professions, but on my terms this time: as a scholar/practitioner rather than an indentured servant.

At first, I explored the possibilities of doing some occasional teaching at the University of Colorado or Aims Community College in Greeley. Unhappily, I quickly discovered the truth that "a prophet is without honor in his home country." My offers were kindly acknowledged but nothing ever came of them. This was a bitter pill, for I love to teach and I am also very good at it. Rebuffed at teaching, I turned my attention to counseling and community service. One of the nice things about being a therapist is that one can continue to practice this profession as long as one pleases, accepting only as many clients as one feels comfortable serving.

In 1984, I accepted the invitation of David Welch, George Tate, Barbara Porter, and Daniel Bruns to join them as a partner in Community Counseling Associates, a private counseling practice. This was an ideal arrangement, for I could do as much or as little as I pleased while keeping in close touch with a group of splendid associates. I also accepted a post on the board of directors of the Weld Mental Health Center, an organization serving all of Weld

Daniel Bruns, Barbara Porter, George Tate, Art Combs, and David Welch Community Counseling Associates, 1987

County. For a couple of years, I led monthly support groups for hospice personnel and similar weekly sessions for administrators of a family practice residency program. To provide greater communication among local psychologists in private practice, I organized a monthly dinner and conversation group. On a broader scale, I accepted the post of associate editor for a new journal, *The Person-Centered Review*, devoted to the advancement of person-centered thinking and practice. All these activities put me back into more active professional contacts.

Some Writing Projects

During this period, I wrote "What Makes a Good Helper?" published in the *Person-Centered Review* [Combs, 1986]. This was an attempt to summarize the findings of numerous studies on good and poor helpers with which I have been involved. The results of these studies were not generally known, probably because almost all existed only as doctoral dissertations gathering dust on library shelves. As I explained in Chapter 8, I regard these researches as among the most significant contributions I have stimulated or produced. They demonstrate that, whereas we have been unable to distinguish good and bad practitioners on the basis of knowledge or methods, we can find clear differences in the belief systems of helpers. This is, at once, an affirmation of perceptual-experiential thinking and a major shift in focus for exploration of the helping professions. If success in the helping relationships is a function of the helper's belief system, the dynamics of these professions must be sought in the perceptual organization of the helper, rather than the methods employed. That fact has widespread implications for the theory and practice of helping as well as for the design of professional training programs.

The second notable paper was a follow-up on my earlier piece, entitled, "The Myth of Competition—Twenty Years After" [Combs, 1979]. The gist of the article is that we have made little progress in the ensuing years. The myth is still with us, only slightly diminished with time. In a similar reflective mode, I spoke at the ASCD national conference on "Perceiving, Behaving, Becoming—Twenty-Five Years Later." This assessment of the 1962 yearbook was more hopeful. I was able to report that the yearbook was alive and well and still selling more copies than any yearbook in history.

Yet another book I wrote, *A Theory of Therapy: Guidelines for Counseling Practice*, appeared in 1989. I had an unprecedented experience with this book. Until 1988, I had never had a manuscript for a book rejected. The manuscript of this book was rejected 30 times, however! The situation has taught me humility. The original draft was written in the first person, in a "this I have learned" style that publishers seemed to feel made it unlikely of acceptance as a college textbook. After converting the book to more traditional format, it was immediately accepted for publication by two publishers. I still believe the original format was better.

A Heart Attack?

In the spring of 1988 I had a second confrontation with my own mortality. Experiencing severe chest pains, I sought medical advice and was promptly ordered into the hospital for observation and cardiographs. Once again, Susan and I underwent some frightening times. After several days, I was given a heart catheter examination. It is a unique experience to lie on a table and watch a catheter bouncing around inside your heart. When it was over, my cardiologist told me, "One thing you can be sure of: you will never die of a heart attack. In fact, your cholesterol count is at third-world levels." Good news, indeed. Apparently my chest pains were caused by a hiatal hernia (a protrusion of the stomach up through the diaphragm into the chest cavity); this was unpleasant but far less serious than a heart problem.

A Reunion and a Parting

Just before Carl Rogers died in February of 1991, I wrote a review of his *Freedom to Learn for the 80's.** I sent him a copy along with a letter telling him about our CEP program at Florida, an innovation much like some of those he reported in his book. I also took the opportunity to tell him some of the things I had been involved with since I last saw him and to express my regret that we had seen so little of each other over the past 35 years. He wrote back, "I appreciate knowing more about your life and work. I, too, have felt it very strange that our paths have crossed so seldom when our hearts and minds were running along such similar tracks. . . . Let's try to change the past and keep in closer touch with each other. . . . I'm delighted to have renewed our contact and I send you my warmest love and greetings." I was deeply touched by his letter, but before I could reply, his death cut short any possibility of renewing our relationship.

I loved and admired Carl both personally and professionally. I am grateful that he introduced me to the profession and stimulated the development of some of my early thinking. His influence upon psychology was enormous and is still not fully realized. I am glad, however, that I chose to go my own way. I purposely avoided being labeled a "Rogerian." I want, rather, to be identified with perceptual-experiential psychology and its applications to therapy and education. I believe my decision has been a wise one. Yet I still harbor regrets about opportunities for further collaborative work that were lost along the way as a result. A few months before his death, Carl and I shared confidences with one another during an hour-long talk at a conference in Chicago and parted with mutual expressions of love and respect. I wish we might have had many such occasions in our careers, but it was not to be.

I Make New Friends

One of the more delightful aspects of life in Greeley has been the acquisition of a number of male friends. In addition to Dave Gonzalez, Rene Oya, and David Welch from our Community Counseling staff, I have frequent contacts with Larry Kerrigan from Weld Mental Health and Jerry Christensen, director of the UNC Lab School. I especially value my relationships with the members of a men's group, operating for a year and a half at this writing. This group was started following a conversation with Marc Ringel about "A Gathering of Men," a television program in which Bill Moyers interviewed

* Editor's note: I have been unable to locate a copy of this review.

poet Robert Bly about Bly's presentations and group discussions on men's issues. After both of us saw this program, we pondered the question, "What does it mean to be a man in the nineties?" We decided to get a group of men together to explore the topic and each of us invited others we thought might be interested. Its members, besides me, include, Jim Fittz, master cellist from UNC; Dave Gonzalez, a colleague in Community Counseling Associates; Roy Wardell, a rancher; and two physicians, Marc Ringel and Tom Flower. All are sensitive human beings with whom I have been able to share experiences on a far deeper level than is generally true for most men in our society.*

Working with Alternative Schools

Our daughters, Lynn and Erin, attended the University of Northern Colorado Laboratory School and I have been frequently involved in its parent programs as the girls have progressed from kindergarten to fifth grade. For several years the school has been seeking to redefine itself and to take a more significant role in Colorado education. It has been good to be a part of this process. I am intrigued with the promise and potential alternative schools represent, having served as consultant to five or six and as external auditor of several more. I am convinced we shall not make much progress in the reform of American education through the tired old approaches that attempt to bring about change from the top down. Instead, I believe we must recognize that no great progress is likely without fundamental changes in teachers and widespread involvement of teachers and community residents in the planning and implementation of change. Our thirty-year movement toward larger and larger schools and the attempt to apply industrial techniques to the education process is a serious error. I am more and more convinced that real reform in American education can only come about through the cumulative effects of innovative solutions to local problems. Thus, I would like to see many more alternative schools organized around groups of teachers with common ideas

* Editor's note: As a letter from Marc Ringel clarified, the group got together in the basement office Art used for his part-time therapy practice. He shared it with several other therapists. Persons in the group told something of their personal stories, and decided to meet every other week in the morning at 7 a.m. for 1½ hours to discuss their lives as men. Art would supply the place and the coffee and the rest in the group would take turns bringing breakfast. "It took us MDs and PhDs years to figure out a rotation list that mostly avoided the missed or double meals that frequently came from confusion over whose turn it was to bring the food," Marc wrote. Early on, those in the group agreed to try to make more "I feel" than "I think" statements and, "of course, got . . . better at doing that over the years. We've probably missed fewer than five meetings ever since our first one eleven years ago," Marc wrote in 1999. The group remained intact for three years after Art's death, at which time Marc Ringel left the group (personal communications, 1999, 2005).

Susan and Art (1983) Photo by Nancy Campbell

they would like to try. There are faint signs in the eighties that this notion may finally be coming to fruition here and there in the charter schools being promoted in half a dozen states. I have tried to make this case in a paper entitled, "New Assumptions for Educational Reform" [Combs, 1988].

Recapitulation

Growth of Self

The years in Greeley have been a time of continued personal discovery. I have grown as a person but less dramatically than was the case in the recent past. Growth now is more in the nature of a consolidation of previous gains, of fuller exploration of the meaning of prior changes. I have discovered more about myself as person, lover, husband, father, and friend. I can even think of myself as an essentially good man without embarrassment. I am no longer at war with myself. I feel a sense of contentment with what I have become. I am all of a piece, an authentic, valuable human being. I am loved and fulfilled as never before in my life, secure within myself, content to be who and what I am. My personal and professional selves are no longer disparate. There is a deep "trust in my organism." I am a truly happy man in every respect.

With the achievement of this sense of personal peace and integrity, I have turned once again to professional matters, but on a new plane. I no longer contribute from a compulsion to serve or to achieve in one part of my life what I lack in another. Rather, I have found increasingly that what I do for myself turns out to be good for others as well, while what I do for others is somehow good for me too. The more fully I am free to be me, the more positive the outcomes of whatever I do as father, husband, friend, citizen, or as teacher, counselor, writer, or consultant. Having had the privilege of experiencing all this, I would not trade what I have become with anyone on earth.

Acceptance and Openness

With expanded perceptions of personal integrity and fulfillment has come a new acceptance of self and the world. I could acknowledge the dissolution of a third innovative program, the latter at UNC, with equanimity. I could likewise accept the death of my mother and the possibility of my own demise as facts of life. I have become more philosophical, able to abide the inevitable forces of human change and so more capable of seeing events in longer perspective. It is easier to accept my own mistakes and to treat those made by others with understanding and patience. I have been acquiring a new humility and a readiness to laugh at myself.

These attitudes, in turn, make it possible to be more open to events, to see them more clearly. I am less tempted to see things as I would like them to be, more able to perceive "the bitter with the better," as the saying goes. I have a new appreciation for the difficulty of effecting major changes in human beings and a concurrent acceptance of the inevitably slow pace of change. These achievements in personal growth have made me more perceptive of the world around me and more tolerant of ambiguity.

Identification

The most transforming event of this period has been the discovery of new capacities for love and loving. My love for Susan has grown ever deeper and more fulfilling. I continue to be astounded at the richness of her love for me. Even our hurts and disagreements can often be aired, shared, and resolved in angry or tearful communion that, somehow, strengthens our feelings of love and togetherness. This new and deeper relationship is so fulfilling that I am finally able to close the book on my childhood inheritance of rejection. I can never again feel totally alienated or unwanted. Nor

Erin, Art, and Lynn (1988) Photo by Susan Kannel

does it stop there. I have also become a more appreciative and compassionate human being. Similarly, I feel deeply bonded to our children and constantly enthralled to watch their growth from beautiful babies to charming toddlers and school girls, learning to cope with the joys and pains of confronting the world. We are a loving family brought even closer for having experienced the pain of miscarriage and confrontation with death along the way.

Feelings of identification and oneness have extended beyond the family to friendships established with a number of sensitive males. These relationships have come about and are sustained by my own increased openness. They have contributed at the same time to personal feelings of security that I am a lovable human being. In turn, the experience of loving and being loved in these relationships extends outward to increased feelings of oneness, not only with humanity, but with the universe itself.

Belief System

The most important changes in my belief system during this period have been the expansion and integration of beliefs about self and about my relationships with the persons close to me. A greater acceptance of self has become an important part of my belief system. I feel more whole, more loved and loving. I value authenticity in all that I do. I have a firm belief that I am basically a good and valuable human being. It is good to be who and what I am. It is also all right to stumble and make mistakes. People and what happens to them are important above all.

It is good to be tender and loving and to let people know who you are. The macho image imposed upon males in our society is a sad and crippling phenomenon. I feel more than ever a sense of togetherness, of being integrated, that the professional and personal portions of my beliefs are cut from the same cloth. The distinctions between coping and expressing, work and play, become increasingly fuzzy and unimportant. Warm, uninhibited relationships have assumed a new value in the economy of my field of awareness.

I continued to publish during this period but less frequently than before. It was time for my professional life to slow down while my personal life caught up. It was good to go back to work, albeit less driven and with a greater sense of relaxation. The perspective of perceptual-experiential thinking applied to the problem of educational reform brought new and more fruitful approaches to light. The same thinking, applied to the nature of helpers, opened yet another area for exploration in the helping professions. In similar fashion, participation in private practice provided fresh opportunities to experience firsthand the dynamics of human personality and the opportunity to refine perceptual thinking through the test of practice. The experience of a second chance at parenthood is also providing an arena for testing basic assumptions that is by turns challenging, tragic, delightful, ecstatic, hilarious, and heart-warming, but never dull.

ADDENDUM: This chapter was written in the spring of 1990. I had no warning then of what would befall me the following year. The idyllic existence described above was about to change drastically. I am currently in the midst of those changes. When sufficient time has passed to provide some perspective, I will return to the tale.

Heart-Warmers

Excerpts from cards, letters, and notes that Art preserved in a file bearing this title.

MAY, 1978

This last week we conducted an in-service workshop on the Implications of Brain Growth Development to Curriculum and Educational Methods. . . . The three guest lecturers participating in this workshop were:

Dr. Herman T. Epstein, Professor of Biology, Brandeis University

Dr. Conrad F. Topfer, Jr., Professor of Curriculum and Instruction, State University of New York at Buffalo

Dr. Arthur Combs, Distinguished Professor, University of Northern Colorado.

Approximately 250 UNC staff, students, public school personnel, and faculty from neighboring universities attended the two-day workshop which was jointly sponsored by the College of Arts and Sciences and the College of Education.

My primary purpose in writing to you is to note the outstanding contribution made by our distinguished professor, Dr. Arthur Combs. Although I knew he would contribute significantly to the workshop, I did not know the full impact he would bring to the success of the workshop with his tremendous experience, sophistication, and high intellectual ability. His humanistic approach brought all facets of the workshop to a focus of understanding that is rarely achieved in such activities. I applaud you and those who are responsible for making available such academic quality as demonstrated by our distinguished professor, Dr. Arthur Combs. (Greeley, CO)

OCTOBER, 1980

I think it's very difficult to say goodbye to you because you are a great man to us.

But as I have to tell you good bye, I hope that you continue to be a person with the power of transmitting good things clearly and with ease the way you do.

You are leaving but your ideas will stay and will be developed here, with success, I hope. (Belo Horizonte, Brazil)

SEPTEMBER, 1984

Art, I have thought often about the long relationship we have had. . . . and of course it started long before you ever met me. Your writings had a profound impact on me and you were one of two "strangers" who helped shape the direction of my early life. (No known address)

JUNE, 1988

I would like to thank you for your superb contribution to our recent conference on Issues in Teacher Education. Your presentation on "New Assumptions for Change" was, for all of us, the highlight of the two-day program. I have rarely witnessed such a powerful and thought-provoking presentation, rarely seen such a reaction produced in a group of foreign language educators. Eyes and minds were opened. My only regret is that I was not able to capture and keep every word to hear and hear again. My notes are a very poor substitute.

We were truly honored by your visit, enlightened and inspired by your message. Thank you for giving so generously of your time and wisdom. (Hastings-on-Hudson, NY)

References

Rogers, C. R. (1983). *Freedom to learn for the 80's.* Columbus, OH: Charles E. Merrill Publishing Co.

Arthur W. Combs (1994) Photo by Katherine Ward

CHAPTER ELEVEN

A Time of Testing

To this point, my autobiography has been written from the long perspective of looking back at my life. From here on, I will write my story closer up, more in the form of a journal. I will attempt to up-date my journey and my thinking from time to time as the spirit moves me.

In the early nineties, the idyllic life I had been living came to a screeching halt. It was almost, as I described it later, as though the fates had decided I was getting too smug and it was time to teach me a hard lesson in humility. The trauma began for me in August of 1990. Susan and I went to a favorite restaurant. While we were eating, two women passed us and sat at another table close by. They were obviously intimately associated and Susan could hardly keep from watching them. Several weeks later she confided that she thought she needed therapy and began to see a lesbian therapist in town. So began a long struggle over her sexual identity that lasted for a year and a half. Meanwhile, I acted as a kind of unofficial co-therapist, trying to help her resolve her dilemma on the one hand and trying to cope with my own feelings of increasing desolation on the other.

Little by little I could feel her slipping away from me. She suffered great pain as she wrestled with the matter of her authentic identity. So did I. We spent many a tearful hour together as I sought to be helpful to her and cope with my own despair simultaneously. About nine months into this maelstrom, I wrote Susan a letter that illustrates the pain we were both experiencing:

> Dearest Susan:
>
> This letter is in reply to your request to know where I am. I will answer that but first I want to set down as best I can how I see the struggle you are currently involved in because I need to know if I am truly understanding you or not.
>
> What I understand about where you are:
>
> You have come to the conclusion that you are essentially a lesbian and have been for some time. Now you are struggling to discover the full meaning of this realization and what you need to do to implement it. You feel very deeply your need to find a place in the lesbian culture and you expect

to spend the rest of your life living out your new identity. Without me, you would move at once to realize that way of life.

You also love me deeply and, like me, appreciate and marvel at the special relationship we have had for the past twenty years. You are torn, as I am, at the thought of terminating that relationship and by your awareness of the suffering that is causing me.

Currently, you are wrestling with a further problem; namely, you have become aware that most of your life you have been living and caring for other people all the while "stuffing" your own needs. You are asking, what do you owe to others and what do you owe to yourself. You are asking what do you need to truly be your own person. I understand that struggle for I have dealt with it in my own growth over the years and counseled a hundred others as they explored the problem and discovered their personal solutions.

I understand the pain of your struggle. It tears me up to see how much you suffer. I also admire your courage and determination to see it through. And, even though the solutions you finally come to could spell disaster and heartbreak for me, nevertheless I applaud what you are doing, support it in every way I can and wish you happy and satisfying conclusions.

Where am I? As best I can say it—like this:

First, above all, I love you more than words can express. There is no other love in my life that remotely approaches the depth, the power and the exquisite beauty of my feeling for you. Our life together has been the most beautiful, honest, fulfilling and precious experience of my life. The thought that I could lose that is the source of my sadness and pain.

I accept your conclusion that you are lesbian. I recognize the pain of your struggle and I am deeply moved at the depth of your love and concern for me. I would not have you turn back on the path you are on. I have resolved many of my own issues in the way you are doing now and I could not ask for you less than the peace I experienced in my own growth.

I feel sad that this has happened to us. I feel helpless, living in limbo, waiting for you to complete your journey. From time to time it overwhelms me and I feel a need to scream out in pain.

As the letter suggests, this was a terrible time for me. I spent my days caring for the house and children while Susan worked at her job in Denver. I sought help for myself in counseling with Dave Gonzalez. I deeply appreciated the support of our men's group. I did not give up hope that Susan would return to our family until October of 1991 when I wrote another letter:

Dearest Susan:

I am writing this letter because I do not think I can say it without breaking down completely.

For years and years you have lighted up my life. When you came home from work my whole life lit up. Just seeing you made me feel alive and full of love and caring. Even running into you in the hall or as you came out of a room my heart would go out to you. I would want to greet you, tell you I loved you, share some small information or feeling. I felt a sense of trust and understanding and acceptance so that I could and wanted to reach out to you, to communicate on some level if only to pat you in passing. I was secure in our relationship and able to share anything and everything that came to my mind.

For the last few months this has begun to change and since you have come back from South Dakota has completely disintegrated. I do not know how to talk to you or relate to you because I am no longer sure that I am either wanted or needed. When I come on you suddenly I no longer feel joy but anxiety. I do not know if you even want to acknowledge my presence. I get tongue tied, not knowing what to say or how it will be heard or even if it is wanted.

I don't know what to do about this or if it can be alleviated in any way. But this much is certain—I can't stand living this way much longer. It is just too devastating.

The End of a Marriage

Shortly after, we decided to separate and Susan found an apartment. Telling the girls their home was breaking up was one of the hardest things I have ever had to do. They now began to live in two homes with their own bedrooms in both places, spending days with me as well as evenings and weekends, determined each week in family meetings. Christmas that year we had yule trees in each home and separate celebrations. The day after Christmas, the girls left with their mother for a week in Massillon with their grandparents. I could not wait to get the Christmas tree out of the house. Three years later, I still could not remember what I did for the twenty days following their departure. The time is still a total blank.

Now began a year of grieving and depression. Early in January of 1992, we filed for divorce, split our assets, and placed our home on the market. The divorce was final in March. We sold the house. I bought a condominium and began to settle into another way of life. I still had major responsibility for the girls during the day and we all met Sundays to schedule who was where in the following week. I was chronically concerned about the children, continually fearful of the adjustments they had to make. Actually, they did surprisingly well. Much better than I did.

It was no easy task overcoming my sense of loss and grief over twenty of the most marvelous years of my life ending this way. Though I managed to carry on from day to day, I was in severe pain for a long time. I began to worry about my age and my body reacted with a series of medical problems complicated by a whiplash injury from an auto accident and the physical

Arthur W. Combs, Mary Hart, Anne Richards (sitting) Katherine Ward, Fred Richards (standing) Carrollton, GA (1994)

therapy it entailed. I sought solace in a trip to see my friends, the Clutes; to vacation in Florida; to visit my son, Peter, in Atlanta, and my friends Anne and Fred Richards in Carrollton, Georgia. David Gonzalez made himself available at any time for counseling sessions and I am immeasurably appreciative of his friendship and professional skill. I found support as well from the members of our men's group and a woman friend, who not only helped to restore my sense of personal adequacy, but introduced me to the world of music as well. A major contribution to my healing came from my relationship with my daughters, Lynn and Erin. The daily tasks of caring for them kept me grounded in reality and I was immensely grateful for their empathy in response to my pain and for their frequent assurances of their love for me.

With all this help and support, little by little, I regained my equilibrium and once again picked up the threads of my life. I started to take better care of myself physically. I began a program of regular exercise and walking. I indulged myself with massage, engaged in daily meditation, and paid more attention to healthy nutritional habits. Professionally, I taught several classes at UNC and increased the number of clients I was seeing at Community Counseling Associates. Engaging in the practice of psychotherapy has always been a creative experience for me. At this time, it was also a diversion from thinking about self as I devoted my attention to helping someone else.

Writing Projects

In the late eighties, I started to write a book on the need for new assumptions in education. The nation was in the midst of a widespread demand for long-overdue educational reform but most efforts approached the problem from the same manipulation-of-forces assumptions that worked for industry. It seemed to me that model was totally wrong for education. In industry, workers are part of the machinery to produce a product; in education, *the worker IS the product*. If industry were organized for the benefit of the worker, it would surely not be organized the way it is. I wanted to call attention to the importance of operating from new assumptions. Writing has always been a task in which I could get totally lost for hours at a time so, despite my personal problems, I was able to complete the manuscript for *The Schools We Need: New Assumptions For Educational Reform* and the book appeared in 1991.

During this period, Dave Gonzalez and I finished the manuscript for the fourth edition of *Helping Relationships*, which appeared in 1993. I must admit, however, that Dave did the lion's share of the work. I wrote four articles in the early nineties about issues I felt very concerned about, but none made it into print. One called attention to differences Carol Gilligan and her associates [Gilligan, 1981, 1982] had discovered about the goals and values that govern thinking in men and women. According to these researches, men tend to think in terms of logic, power, law, rights, and rules whereas women focus more on relationships, caring, and the impact of events on human experience. I also made the case for a "get with it" approach to governance that was characterized by the people-oriented style of thinking considered characteristic of females. In another paper, I sought to make the case for returning government to the people by changing the role of congresspersons to debaters instead of informants for their constituents, who would then vote in person by computer. In yet another, I proposed a Commission on the Public Interest that would study legislation and executive branch policy and report their value to the larger public interest. I thought that such a group might strengthen the backbones of legislators so they could act more like statesmen or stateswomen instead of advocates for special interests.

In another piece, I dealt with the hazards of current diagnostic practice in the counseling field. In it, I called attention to the inadequacy for an increasingly person-centered profession of an objective, symptomatic classification system based on symptoms or behavioral expressions of what is going on inside the individual. I also proposed the establishment under American Psychological Association (APA) auspices of a task force or commission to design a diagnostic approach more adequate for person-centered practitioners. I still think these were good ideas, but I did not work very hard to get them into print. They were fun to write, but once I had them on paper the mechanics of getting them published were sheer drudgery.

A Holistic View of the Universe—My Religion

Early in the nineties, I saw a Bill Moyers TV program exploring "Healing and The Mind" [see Moyers, 1993]. I was fascinated with his review and found that many of the things he reported fitted nicely with perceptual-experiential psychology and with what I had learned from firsthand experience about the theory and practice of psychotherapy. I was particularly impressed with the evidence that people's perceptions have profound effects upon bodily condition and health. This program presented in dramatic fashion one more line of evidence in support of perceptual approaches to human experience.

In the second edition of *Individual Behavior* I had suggested the continuity of the organism with the universe, expanding on the idea in years following, but now I began to find it increasingly part of my thinking. I came upon a similar and even more profound corroboration of the notion of continuity with the universe and for perceptual thinking in the works of Deepak Chopra [1990, 1993] and in the findings reported in quantum physics [Capra, 1991, 1996]. Quantum physicists were telling us that all things, material or not, including human beings, were rooted in a common cosmic unified field, and that matter was but temporary field organizations interrelated with all other fields. This provided a scientific foundation for my long-held belief in the unity of all things and the relationship of humanity to the universe.

I had expressed a similar concept in the second edition of *Individual Behavior* [Combs & Snygg, 1959] and it was good to find it confirmed in physical science. In that publication, I made the point that the universe is made up of organizations and that organizations maintain themselves as best they can until something causes them finally to disintegrate. I also spoke of the person as an organization made up of ever-smaller ones looking inward: digestive, reproductive, excretory, etc. These in turn were made up of still smaller ones: tissues, cells, atoms, protons, electrons, etc. I thus had the feeling that a person is one with the universe from which he or she came. On the other hand, the person exists as part of other organizations stretching out from self—family, relatives, neighborhood, town, state, country, Earth, the solar system, the universe itself. Thus I see myself as continuous with the universe and whatever produced and motivated it (pp. 38–40).

Small wonder that I have been intrigued with the concepts of quantum physics and the idea that matter and organization arise out of a great space field. Deepak Chopra [1993] called this field "a field of intelligence," which makes much sense to me and fits my beliefs about organization. Like everything else in the universe, I am a product of that great field, call it God if you wish. Likewise, my self is a part of larger and larger organizations as far as these extend. What I am and what I do, even what I think, feel, and express, are part of the great intelligence from which all things have arisen. I am not only part; my very being changes the nature of that intelligence. So, I am not only a product of the great field of intelligence; my very existence modifies it. This gives me a profound feeling of being an expression of an infinite field (God?). It also means that how I live my life, who I am, what I think, feel, love, hate, whatever, is significant in its contribution to this great universal field.

My task in life, like that of any other organization, is to maintain and enhance self. So I seek, therefore, my own self-actualization. I am also a social animal, aware that personal fulfillment is more likely if human beings can work together to boost each other's fulfillment. I, therefore, seek the maintenance and enhancement of my fellows as well as my self. I feel one with them (identification), which I experience as love, caring, or compassion towards others. When entropy catches up with me, my matter will return to the great intelligent field from which I came and which, by my very existence, has been in some small measure modified—enriched, if I have lived my life well; wounded if I have not.

I do not believe I will be reincarnated in some other body. Instead, I believe I will simply return to the field, blend with it, and maybe in some later time part of what was me may become part of another organization. This is my religion. It gives me great peace and a sense of oneness with something much greater and more exquisite than I am. At the same time it gives me a sense of purpose and a way of being in the world and with my fellows. I have felt no need to join a formal sect or church or established religion, although I revere many of their teachings and am profoundly moved by the art and music they have produced. I have often been described as a "deeply religious man" and I think I am, though not in the usual sense.

The Silent Revolution

For many years, I was primarily concerned with the importance of perceptual-experiential thinking for understanding individual behavior. As the validity of the perceptual approach became more and more corroborated, however, I began to be aware of its implications and applicability in areas beyond the understanding of individuals. I became aware of its relevance to much wider areas of collective human endeavor, for example, government, education, medicine, and international affairs. I began to see how our culture is rooted in materialism, a things-orientation, and how that orientation is responsible for many of the ills of our society. The methods of this things-centered approach involve manipulation of the forces of the environment.

These methods have led, especially through scientific discovery and the industrial revolution, to the most productive society ever. Indeed, we have reached a point wherein humanity's age-old problem of wresting from the environment the food, clothing, and shelter fundamental to survival is essentially solved for vast numbers of citizens. We now have the know-how to feed, clothe, and house the entire world—IF we had the will to do so. We have moved from the era of physical science to the era of social science, where we find ourselves faced with the human problems of how to find personal fulfillment in an ever-more-crowded world and how to live successfully with each other.

We have tried to solve these human problems by treating people in the ways that worked so well for things: manipulation of the forces acting upon them. But people are not things. They think and feel and decide, for example, whether or not to cooperate. It became increasingly apparent to me that our culture has been undergoing a silent revolution as we shift from the previous materialistic world to a person-centered one, from things to people. Accordingly, I began to work on a trade book for the general public and invited Dave Gonzalez to co-author it. We wanted to do two things: (a) to call widespread attention to the revolution and the problems it posed in hopes our book might speed the transition, and (b) to suggest ways in which a perceptual-experiential understanding might facilitate adaptations to the people problems confronting our changing culture.

I sent inquiries or the manuscript for *The Silent Revolution* to probably fifty publishers or agents, with no luck. I have therefore laid it aside. Perhaps one day I will get back to it. I still think it is a very timely book and conveys a vital message—but obviously others do not currently see it so. Right now, I have more important things to do than seek a publisher. Why is that so hard for me?

A New Sense of Peace and Fulfillment

In the throes of the intense anguish I experienced before and after the divorce, I often wondered whether I would ever again experience the sense of peace and fulfillment I had achieved during the years with Susan. Those times seemed so idyllic that I couldn't imagine it likely I would experience anything similar to them again. Early in 1994, however, I began to experience a resurgence in personal growth. As often happens in human lives, the experience of trauma, painful though it may be, can also trigger important internal transformations. And so it was with me.

About a year after the divorce I began to reach the end of my grieving process. My health and vigor were returning and daily life was becoming more comfortable for me. One morning as I came down the stairs to my living room, the sun was shining through the glass doors to the patio and I surprised myself thinking, "I like this place. This is my home and it feels good." For months I had one kind of concern or another to explore in our men's group meetings. Now, I found I had less and less of a pressing nature to talk about. I was enjoying the company of my daughters, Lynn and Erin, more. We were having fewer arguments and more happy and comfortable times with each other. I was increasingly fascinated watching them grow into beautiful young women. Lynn grew to be 6' 1" while I discovered I had shrunk two inches and was now 5' 5½." My weekly meetings with Susan were no longer strained or painful. I became aware that important changes were going on in the very core of my being.

For sixty years I had never been without a woman in my life and in the year following the divorce I longed to replace my loss. I thought about how I might arrange to meet someone and asked my friends to keep me in mind when they encountered eligible "possibilities." Now I found the urgency of that yearning had disappeared and I was quite content with my single life. I felt as though inside me I had moved to a different stage of being, a kind of step-up in my sense of personal fulfillment. I had a new burst of energy: physical, intellectual, professional, and spiritual. I found renewed interest in keeping fit and real enjoyment in carrying out my exercise program. Walking and working out were more fun. Intellectually, I had a series of insights that enlarged my understanding of counseling, psychology, education, and governmental affairs. Every now and then, I would wake in the night, lie quietly musing, and find some innovative way of looking at old problems.

These changes in my belief system produced changes in my behavior that I noted with pleasure and astonishment. I found myself more able to say "no" when friends or acquaintances made a suggestion or request that didn't appeal to me. For most of my life, when someone asked where we ought to dine or would I like to do this or that, I would find myself unable to choose or would insist on doing what others wanted. I now found it possible to

Anne Richards, Lynn Combs, Art Combs, Erin Combs Greeley, CO, July, 1993

assert myself openly and straightforwardly. Most notably, however, my current state of being was bringing about changes in my relationships in therapy.

I had long experienced a deep connection with my clients during counseling, but now I became aware that it was more solid than ever. It was also producing greater effectiveness. Three clients in one week experienced "conversion experiences" or sudden dramatic insights destined to make major changes in their being and becoming. One of these clients thanked me for helping her make such a change. I replied that she need not thank me, that she did it herself, that I was only the midwife. She would not have it so and insisted, "No. I could not have done it without you. It is your authenticity, your realness that made it possible for me to look at my own." As she said that, I had the feeling, "That's it, Art. That's how you've changed. You've gone to another level of being who you are."

A New Set of Trials

One evening in June of '93, I promised Erin I would play a game with her after I had gone to the kitchen for a glass of water. As I returned to the living room, I suddenly lost all sight in the left half of my field of vision. By next morning, it had improved so that I could see all but the upper left-hand quadrant of my visual field. My physician sent me to the hospital for a CAT scan. My physician, an ophthalmologist, and a neurologist concluded I had suffered a mild stroke. This was pretty scary, but I was assured it "happens all the time." Then in February of 1994, while paying for gasoline for my car, my right arm lost all feeling, a condition that lasted for half a day. This sent me back to the hospital for further tests and my physicians concluded I had had another stroke. I am so sick of people and physicians who tell me, "Well, Art, at your age (this is to be expected)!"

About this same period, I had fallen in love with a beautiful woman in her fifties whom my daughters described as "just right for you, Dad!" Indeed, she was, even to the extent of being in the same profession. The same afternoon that my physician informed me that I continued to be at risk of stroke, and would need to guard against that for the rest of my life, I was dealt another blow. Shortly after the call from my doctor, my new woman friend broke off our relationship because the difference in our ages was just too great a handicap to her. The simultaneous effect of the rejection by my friend and the reports on my physical health were traumatic. I sought out my friend Roy Wardell and we talked and drank manhattans till late that night. For several weeks afterwards, I wandered about in a mild depression as I struggled to redefine my existence. I was forced to confront the realities of my aging in no uncertain terms, both physically and with respect to the likelihood that I might never again find a loving relationship with a woman. Of the two, I believe the latter was hardest.

As if these reverses were not enough, following installation of a new dental bridge I developed a "temperomandibular" joint dysfunction that made chewing and swallowing very painful. A week later, while helping clean up the condominium area where I lived, I slipped on the creek bank and broke my leg in five places. That required a steel plate in my leg and immobilized me for nearly three months. Two months to the day after breaking my leg, I suffered a freak auto accident. Here is a letter to Carol and Peter designed to inform them of these events:

> Dear Carol and Peter:
>
> This is going to be a long newsy letter bringing you up to date with what has been happening to me. Hang on!
>
> Seems like the gods looked down at me and concluded—this guy is getting too damned arrogant for his own good. Let's cut him down to size! And they sure have till I am yelling back at them—Enuf already!
>
> After the divorce came the whiplash accident which did not lay me up but was painful and involved a long series of Physical Therapy sessions. All clear now.
>
> Last fall, one night I discovered I had lost vision in the upper left hand quadrant of my field of vision. Checking it out, they could find nothing

wrong with my eyes and concluded I must have had a small stroke. That was confirmed by a CAT scan and other tests. The condition has not changed since.

Next I fell madly in love with a beautiful woman who decided the difference in our ages was just too much of a handicap for a successful relationship. Alas!

Shortly after, I had a new bridge installed in my mouth followed in a few days by an inability to open my mouth wide enough to bite on a hamburger without considerable pain. I can now open my jaw wide but after twenty chews or so my jaw muscles and tongue become so sore I have difficulty chewing and swallowing. They are still trying to figure out what is going on here. Meantime, it curbs my eating which helps me keep my weight in reasonable limits.

Next, about a month ago, my right arm went numb and stayed so for seven or eight hours. So another session with the CAT scan which shows another small lesion in my brain and confirms the diagnosis that I am at risk for stroke. For that I am on a drug called Coumadin for the rest of my life to thin my blood. Coumadin, by the way, is rat poison!

A week later I broke my leg. After the divorce I said to myself, "Hey! I have been taking care of lawns and property clean-up for more than sixty years. I've paid my dues and will move into a condo where all that will be taken care of hereafter. Well, this spring the condo association said, "Let's all get out on Saturday and clean up the flotsam and jetsam left over from winter." So, I donned an old (and slippery) pair of sneakers and went off to help. Starting down the creek bank to snag a paper bag in the creek, my left foot slipped and I crashed down on my right leg, breaking it in five places. I heard the sickening snap and knew I was in trouble. The fire department and ambulances came rushing to the 911 call and whisked me away to the hospital. Erin was quite incensed that the ambulance did not take me with lights flashing and siren screaming. She feels I was badly cheated!

At the hospital I was given a choice—a cast to my hip for four months or an operation to install a steel plate, in which case I would be getting around at least in two months. I chose the latter. After five days I came home and have had the help of a nurse aide four hours a day until yesterday. I have a huge Bledsoe boot on my leg and have begun to put weight on it. It will not go through my pant legs. Lucky it is summer time so I can wear baggy shorts like modern adolescents! Real cool, man! After a month I graduated from wheel chair to walker. Thanks Carol for the water bottles and especially the bucket to fasten on the walker. Using a walker takes two hands so only way to carry stuff is like a dog—in your teeth!

Wait! Can you stand some more? A week ago I was going out to dinner with a friend and as we rode to the restaurant I noticed I could not see out of the center of my right eye. Another series of tests and the docs are trying to find out what is going on. There is nothing wrong with my eyes so they conclude the problem is in the optic nerve. If I look at your face with my left eye closed I can't see anything but a black spot but I can see all around you quite OK. Speculation now has it that the trouble lies in an inflamed temporal artery and tomorrow, after seeing my surgeon, I'll go for an outpatient biopsy of the temporal artery. The suggestion is that the artery inflammation is cutting off oxygen to the optic nerve and may also be causing the sore jaw problems too. So now I am on heavy doses of Prednisone—a steroid which makes me uneasy. Who knows! I may turn out to be one great hunk of muscles!

It's been quite a siege. For about three weeks after the break, I went through a period of depression. I have always taken my body for granted and been in good health. Suddenly it seemed like everything was falling apart at once. I have also never given much thought to my age and all of a sudden I found myself facing the possibility of failing faculties, etc. That's all behind me now and I am back to being in good spirits. I'm back to writing, have made several speeches from a wheel chair, I have some truly fine men friends in a men's group I started four years ago. We got together then to explore what it means to be a male in the nineties. We're still meeting bi-weekly for some truly wonderful sessions together. Yesterday, for the first time in two months, I scootched upstairs on my bottom, took a bath—heavenly after two months of sponging! Last night slept in my own bed and room. Today I had some help to put my living area back in order after two months of living solely on the first floor with only a half bath. I haven't yet gotten up the nerve to go downstairs to the family room. You have no idea what two beautiful young teenage females can do to a room in fifteen minutes, much less two months!

Tomorrow I go back to see my surgeon and he promises me I can then graduate to a cane. Hooray! I make progress.

Well, that's the story. I'm taking it one day at a time and I feel surprisingly well and happy. I am deeply involved in a new foundation—SAVE AMERICA—EDUCATE OUR CHILDREN—We hope to make an impact on educational reform. The foundation has reprinted my book, *The Schools We Need*, and is giving it away with memberships. I enclose a copy for you. I am also deeply enjoying my two girls who recently have discovered that their old man has some interesting ideas and knows something about adolescent problems. We've had some delightful talks and have grown closer. I love it!

Time to quit. I won't mail this letter till after I hear what my surgeon has to say about my leg.

Seems like I have wasted two beautiful months of summer. The girls and I are hoping to spend a week at the beach in latter August and I hope we will get to see you both then.

Love—Dad

What? Again?

Next day, after seeing the surgeon and getting his okay to start being more mobile, Erin and I visited a frozen yogurt shop and started home. After stopping at a stop street, as I accelerated to turn the corner, the right wheel of my

Lynn, Carol, Peter, and Erin (1995) in Greeley, CO

car dropped into a culvert with such a shock as to set off the airbags. Fortunately, Erin was unhurt, but my airbag ripped my hands from the steering wheel with such force as to break both wrists, six or seven hand bones and six fingers, and caused a compound fracture of my right arm. After five and a half hours of surgery I woke in the hospital—a tri-plegic with casts on both arms and a boot on my leg! What a feeling of helplessness and indignity! To be unable to wipe oneself or feed oneself was a very hard lesson in humility. I was deeply comforted by the tenderness and concern expressed by Lynn and Erin and the help they provided to feed me at meal times.

After ten days in the hospital and the rehab unit, I returned home for another two months of confinement. I was stunned by all that had happened to me, bored at my forced inactivity, and frustrated by my helplessness. For a couple of weeks I slipped into a period of depression and was grateful for week-long visits from Peter and Carol. These visits were sustaining interludes for me and awakened in all three of us a very satisfying sense of reconnection after a long period of separation.

By September I was slowly recovering from my wounds. My spirits were much better. Sharing my problems at our men's group, I came to the following conclusion: My current struggle is what to do with myself after all that has happened to me. Susan and the girls tell me I should not be driving. But living in this town without transportation is like being in prison. I do not

Art with Walter Busby in Greeley, CO (July, 1993)

want to be a danger to others, however. Next day I talked to my surgeon, Tom Flower, (my family physician), and Jeff Weeks (ophthalmologist) about my dilemma. Each said to avoid night driving whenever possible and use extra caution in daytime. I decided to give up night driving altogether and use extreme caution in daytime.

It bothered me that the attitudes of some around me would suggest that I resign myself to a restricted set of activities expected of a very old man. I wrestled with finding a proper stance at this time and found myself saying: "I have to admit that I am 82. That does not mean I have to be resigned to being old. I do not want to fight being old. Neither do I want to be resigned to old age. There is an alternative: To accept my age and my handicaps. That is, to accept the reality of the limitations they impose and to live as fully as possible with them. In other words, to meet the realities of old age gracefully."

The Schools We Need

Early in 1994, I became acquainted with another remarkable human being, Donald Busby, brother of Walter Busby, one of my friends at the University of Florida. Don had become a very wealthy entrepreneur, owning and operating his multiple companies from Denver. Having suffered at the hands of inadequate schools as a child, he decided to see what he could do to further

Arthur W. Combs talking with his daughter Erin during a visit to Carrollton, GA, 1994

the cause of educational reform. Don's idea was to develop a nationwide grass-roots organization of parents and teachers who would create a force to return public schools to local control by the teachers, parents, and students directly involved. I helped to put him in touch with a group of reform-minded educators and in May of 1994 *Save America—Educate Our Children* was launched with a professional money raiser to provide the capital and a board of directors to determine its mission and strategy.

Don had 5000 copies of my 1991 book, *The Schools We Need: New Assumptions for Educational Reform,* reprinted with the intention of giving them out to contributors to the foundation. Unhappily, the project failed. A year later, our men's group made an outing of retrieving the copies of my book and bringing them to Greeley. I then faced the problem of how to get them into the hands of people in positions to affect educational reform. I decided that for every copy I could sell at $15, I would mail ten free copies to persons in position to affect educational policy. Five thousand books is a lot!

In September of 1994, our Community Counseling Associates corporation folded as three of our members withdrew. I then began renting an office by the hour as needed to work with my self-imposed limit of five clients a week.

Back on Track

In March of 1995 I attended a concert with Marc Ringel. Somewhere in the middle of the concert, I was suddenly struck with the thought, "I'm a happy man again!" It was such a warm and pleasant feeling and it lasted for weeks. I think it represented the end of my grieving over the divorce and all my subsequent physical problems. People around me confirmed that I looked like I was back to the "Art Combs we knew before the divorce"—a wonderful feeling for me.

Dick and Mary Usher (1999)

Notes from the summer of '95: What a shock! Getting my driver's license renewed. It is good till 2002! The turn of the century is upon us!

I have particularly enjoyed renewing acquaintance with Dick and Mary Usher, who spent a couple of days with me and I visited them in the mountains, once with the girls and once alone. These are very special people for me. Dick understands perceptual thinking better than anyone I know. Better still, he understands me! Mary is one of the most loving, caring women I have ever met, forever generous and outgoing and with an inimitable spiritual quality that touches and heartens me deeply. They are wonderful friends whom I love very much. I wish they were closer by for longer periods.

A new experience—being sued. After the accident at Thanksgiving in 1992, my passenger and I each suffered whiplash injuries. Mine cleared up after several months but my friend's hung on for a long time. After a year or so, my insurance company refused to pay her any longer, so she found a lawyer who would take the case on a contingency basis and brought suit against me. What a hassle! My first brush with the law. I thought at first it would not bother me—but it did! For some time I had been feeling uneasy about the relationship and had a sense that it was going nowhere. The litigation provided a good excuse to end the relationship.

A Book on Leadership

I began a new book with Kathy Whitaker and Ann Miser, looking at educational leadership from a person-centered perspective. Kathy is on the faculty at UNC in the Educational Leadership Department and Ann is a former director of the Lab School. The project is just underway, but looks like it could produce an important contribution. The book is based upon the "what makes a good helper" researches and person-centered thinking, which I summarize, and Kathy and Ann explore the implications for the leadership field. We stimulate each other well.

About this time the Professional Psychology Department at UNC invited me to teach one course a semester and made an office available for me, where I began to spend two hours three days a week.

Absence of a Theory of Meaning in Psychology

I feel more confident than ever about the significance of a perceptual approach to psychology. It is fascinating to see how modern brain and immune system research arrive at conclusions similar to those I espoused years ago. The brain is now understood as a marvelous organ for making meaning of experience [Caine & Caine, 1994] and the function of the immune system is described as "maintenance and enhancement of the self"—right out of perceptual theory!* Sooner or later, psychology must establish itself as a psychology of meaning, but oh, how slowly it moves toward that obvious goal. Here and there are tentative movements in that direction, but mostly applied to some small function of human behavior. The idea of finding a comprehensive, systematic, generally accepted theory is even shunned in many quarters. It's as if somehow one is sullying oneself to seek for such universal explanations. I keep asking myself if my certainty that we must move to a perceptual psychology is arrogant or naive. But every way I look, I feel more certain of the urgent necessity of establishing a psychology of meaning and aware of the value of perceptual field thinking in contributing to that end.

I am also surprised in a way at how my conviction regarding the value of a psychology of meaning grows ever more certain while at the same time I feel no great need to become embroiled in campaigns for its achievement. I have recently learned of three instances in which authors in education and psychotherapy have totally ignored my contributions. I have no pressing need to demand recognition, however. Recently, I was invited to apply for fellowship status in the Division of Humanistic Psychology, a distinguished company. I declined the invitation, because I felt no enthusiasm for the idea and the paperwork involved seemed not worth the effort. Indeed, I am not "working at" anything these days. I write, I talk, I counsel because it pleases and fulfills me. Though I see the social distress caused by failures to deal effectively with human problems, etc., I feel no need to carry a torch or ride

---

* Editor's note: Despite an extensive search of publications in Art's personal library and elsewhere, I have not been able to locate the source of this quote.

into battle. I feel a sense of certainty that my professional contributions have been positive but I feel no need to parade them, fight for them, or spend great energy on them. I am content to be who I am, to enjoy my friends, my work, and my two magnificent daughters from day to day. A nice sense of peace.

Some New Insights

In the course of a conversation with Dick Usher, I spoke of an incident in the early fifties. I had made an enthusiastic presentation on therapy and perception at a psychological meeting. On completion of my talk, Nevitt Sanford, then an important figure in psychology, rose to comment: "Listening to Dr. Combs's presentation reminds me of the man who discovered so much because he had read so little." (!!!) At the time I was stunned by the remark and afterward wondered if perhaps Sanford might be right. Since the conversation with Dick, I have come to see the matter in a different way. I believe one reason I have been able to take some innovative steps in psychology and education is because I have not been a traditional scholar in either domain. I have been able to make contributions in psychology and education precisely because I left each of those fields for a time. When I returned, it was possible for me to approach each from different perspectives and to see things from a new angle.

I think it is quite possible for someone to be so immersed in the literature of the field as to be blinded to perceptions outside the establishment. I recall a review Carl Rogers did many years ago of a book on personality theories. It went something like this: "Reading this book reminds me of being taken on a tour of the battlefields. The author points out the scene of one battlefield after another, telling us what happened and who was involved, but nowhere in the book do I find the author!" I think that happens in much scientific writing. Promising minds are lost in the pursuit of the literature. They spend so much time discovering what others have said that they have little, if any, time to consolidate their own experience or venture into realms of innovation of their own making. Such a way of life is frequently forced upon graduate students in the course of their graduate work. They are customarily taught to study the works of others carefully and intensely, to write in the prescribed "scientific style," and are evaluated on how well they "know the literature." I never got caught up in that. I was always in search of more personally satisfying explanations of events. I was bored with the weighty tomes one had to peruse in the library but found myself intrigued with ideas and alternative suggestions.

In short, I believe we can become so inbred from too much reading of what others have done that our own offspring cannot break out of the mold.

I am not uninformed, but neither am I a scholar in the usual sense. I believe the contributions I have been able to make are in no small measure products of my movement back and forth between psychology and education and my fascination with the personal exploration and refinement of my own thinking. I have come to believe that Sanford's castigation (above) was in fact a compliment, though neither I nor the audience believed it then.

Recapitulation

Self under Siege

This short period in my life was indeed a time of testing. The various troubles to which I was subjected provided a series of tests for my degree of growth and capacity to cope with adversity. My sense of self came painfully under siege. This caused me immense suffering, both physical and mental, but somehow I survived, and the experience produced both new insights for my self-concept, new directions for my professional life, and a new respect for my abilities to cope with the exigencies of existence.

The shift in self-concept from happily married to divorced and alone did not come easily. In addition, the clear indications of aging and limitations on my physical being made it necessary to redefine the ways in which I regarded my physical self. I was forced, once again, to confront my own mortality and come to terms with that inevitability. But out of it all, I seem to have emerged with a stronger sense of self, a clearer awareness of who I am, and a satisfaction of having survived the tests with personal dignity and integrity intact.

A New Sense of Acceptance

Looking back as a psychologist at the experiences of this period, I am struck by the degree of acceptance I was able to muster in dealing with the formidable circumstances confronting me. Though I suffered anguish, loss, and abandonment in my divorce along with excruciating pain, curtailment of my physical abilities, and clear warnings of my possible demise, I did not fight or deny reality but met each traumatic event head on. Friends in our men's group have commented upon how quickly (it did not seem so to me) I adjusted to the divorce and got on with my life. My surgeon commended me for the spirit with which I engaged in the healing programs I needed and the toleration for pain I showed from time to time.

Observing matters from this perspective, what I did and how I behaved do not seem to me either heroic or courageous. They seem only a consequence of accepting the reality of what was happening and getting on with whatever made it possible to cope with these occurrences. I feel a bit embarrassed at others' understandings of my resilience. How I dealt with my problems was no macho demonstration of manhood or pride in accomplishment. Believe me, I welcomed the skill of my surgeon, accepted gratefully the TLC of my nurses, treasured the rally-round of my children and the support and love of my friends like anyone else would have done. Looking back on my life, I am surprised to recognize that this capacity to accept myself and the world has always been there to some degree and has been growing during the years. My recognition of it here is like the "Aha moments" occasionally experienced by my clients when they become aware of an insight that has been sensed at some level all along but that only now has risen into consciousness.

Learning to Live Alone

The breakup of my marriage was a terrible shock. I was desolate for a time by the collapse of the most beautiful twenty years of my life. Now (March of 1997), I still see Susan frequently to talk about Lynn and Erin's welfare, plans, or finances, or when attending a volleyball game, tennis match, or high school event. I have long since accepted the dissolution of our relationship, however, and recognize the unavoidability of its occurrence.

I am sometimes asked by some brave soul if I would ever want to get married again. Immediately after the divorce I wanted very much to find someone else, but no longer have a feeling of urgency about this. I would like a new relationship. If it happened, I would surely enjoy that, but I do not feel a great pressure to make it happen. I am not seriously looking for another love and I am content if I never find another. I enjoy the life I live, the friends I have, especially the men's group begun in 1988, Larry Kerrigan, Dave Welch, and the students and clients with whom I am in touch.

Professional Matters

As uprooting and earth-shaking as this period has been, I am fascinated by the stimulation it has afforded to my thinking and beliefs. I feel instinctively that the perceptual field perspective for approaching psychology is inevitable. Despite the uproar in my personal life, I continue to find my beliefs about human personality, society, and the meaning of life (especially the relationship of persons to the universe) to be remarkably sound and corroborated in all kinds of ways in contemporary spheres. The concepts Don Snygg and I set down in the earliest editions of *Individual Behavior* are currently being expanded and confirmed in the thinking of workers in many disciplines. Little by little, psychology seems to be moving toward a perceptual way of thinking, although most psychologists are still unaware of such movement. I am much excited by this trend and begin to think that, at long last, the profession may be ready for conceptualizations Don and I proposed nearly fifty years ago!

Heart-Warmers

Excerpts from cards, letters, and notes that Art preserved in a file bearing this title.

NOVEMBER, 1993

A voice from your long ago past finally taking the time to say thanks! It all began back in 1970 when I came to UF and entered in the NEP with you as my seminar leader. Unknown to me at that time, my life would never be the same. . . . You helped transform this pig-farmer's daughter with poor self-esteem to someone who has been blessed with immeasurable success. I learned so much from you . . .

- the most difficult child to love needs it the most
- empower children to take control of their learning
- practice the teachable moment
- meet them where they are
- make it meaningful
- make them feel important
- make friends with the janitor
- and so much more . . .

As I travel the country, giving speeches and touting my philosophy, I know that my roots go back to your preaching, cajoling and nudging me to be different; telling me that it didn't make any difference where I came from or what the college counselors said I couldn't do; and your belief in me that I could do anything I decided to do. . . .

My heartfelt thanks to you for being the kind of person who cared enough to make a difference in so many lives. (Gainesville, FL)

APRIL, 1995

I have just ordered and received a copy of your article, "What Makes a Good Helper?" (which appeared in the *Person-Centered Review* in 1986). The article inspired me to attempt to locate your address and to write you to express my thanks. I have admired you and your work for many years, beginning in 1976 when I was a master's level student in Counseling at Oregon State University. I was fortunate at that time to hear (via audio tape) a talk you had given at the ASCD conference in 1974. I was greatly impressed with what you said about good helpers.

Much time has passed since that first encounter. I have been an elementary school counselor since 1977. In 1988, I returned to Oregon State and received my Ph.D. in Counseling four years later. Since then I have been asked to teach various classes at OSU, i.e., Working with Parents (for teachers and counselors), Fundamentals of Counseling (for master's level preservice teachers). As I first prepared to teach, I remembered your talk and was able to obtain a copy of the tape. I have, since then, played the tape for students in my classes. They continue to be impressed with your message. It is as relevant today as it was in 1974, and perhaps, even more so.

Education has gone through many "changes" throughout the years (I've experienced many myself in the 30 plus years I've been involved). One thing, however, never changes and that is the importance of the *person* giving the service. You were so right when you emphasized the teacher as a person over "methods" and "knowledge." One teacher in the school in which I work said that no one ever discussed her belief system or stressed taking better take care of herself, being authentic and trusting her best answers as important things she could do for herself and her students. What innovative thinking you had over 20 years ago!

I have attempted to incorporate your ideas in my life and in my interactions with others. I work with first-grade children and parents to teach them how to communicate better with one another and how to be more responsible for self. It is delightful to see how easily children can learn this. Parents seem to take a bit longer!!

So often in life we don't take time for the meaningful things in life, such as, expressing appreciation, celebrating "the good," being kind, accepting, and caring with our fellow beings, whoever they may be. This letter is my attempt to do that now.

My deepest thanks for all you have written. You've made an important contribution to our world. I hope this letter finds you in good health and fine spirits.

In appreciation and celebration of your being, . . . (Corvallis, OR)

JULY, 1995

Thank you for speaking to my Understanding Self class. Your presence affirms your writings. Many students wrote in their reflections papers that you gave them renewed hope and affirmed their own beliefs. I particularly appreciate your willingness to give of your personal time.

You exemplify an effective educator who has been and is person-centered. Thank you for sharing life with us. (Greeley, CO)

References

Caine, R. N., & Caine, G. (1994). *Making connections: Teaching and the human brain.* Menlo Park, CA: Addison-Wesley

Caine, R. N., & Caine, G. (1997). *Unleashing the power of perceptual change: The potential of brain-based teaching.* Alexandria, VA: Association for Supervision and Curriculum Development.

Capra, F. (1991). *The tao of physics* (3rd. ed.). Boston: Shambhala.

Capra, F. (1996). *The web of life: A new scientific understanding of living systems.* New York: Doubleday.

Chopra, D. (1990). *Quantum healing: Exploring the frontiers of mind/body medicine.* New York: Bantam.

Chopra, D. (1993). *Ageless body, timeless mind: The quantum alternative to growing old.* New York: Harmony Books.

Gilligan, C. (1981). Moral development. In A. W. Chickering and Associates, *The modern American college: Responding to the new realities of diverse students and a changing society* (pp. 139-157). San Francisco: Jossey-Bass.

Gilligan, C. (1982). *In a different voice.* Cambridge, MA: Harvard University Press.

Moyers, B. (1993). *Healing and the mind* (B. S. Flowers, Ed.). New York: Doubleday.

Arthur W. Combs hugging a dinosaur at Swetsville Metal Sculpture Garden 1997—the occasion of Arthur's 85th birthday (near Fort Collins, CO) Photo by Alan Wilkes

CHAPTER TWELVE

Confronting New Limits—My World Closes In

NOTE: With this chapter I have decided to stop writing a Recapitulation section at the end of each chapter. In previous chapters, I have tried to show how my life was affecting my reach for self-actualization and health. From this point on, I will leave that consideration to others who have known me to be added after my death.

3/21/96

On a trip to Boston with Lynn to look at a college possibility, we took off one afternoon to visit the JFK Library. On the subway, Lynn and I stood holding on to an upright. A woman and a child were sitting in front of me. Soon, the woman got up and motioned to me to take her seat. Instead, I gave it to Lynn. Several nights later while lying awake in bed it hit me: "My God! That lady was giving her seat to an old man!" What a jolt! Another stark indicator of my age and another squeeze on the parameters of my world!

In February I had a cataract operation on my remaining good eye. A few hours after the operation, I developed great pain in the eye. I was home alone and unable to read the phone book and had a moment of panic at my feeling of helplessness. Erin soon came home from school and a neighbor took me back to my surgeon, who managed to reduce the fluid pressure. Next day he told me, "If you had not come back to see me, you would have lost sight in that eye!"

I become more aware of the closing in of my world. I can no longer run up or down stairs. I find my gait lurching at times and I tire more quickly. The combination of aging and limitations of sight also makes my coordination sloppy, especially when dealing with fine motor motions. I'm apparently handling it well, however. One of my students at UNC stopped to tell me yesterday, "Art, you know I work in geriatrics, and I have to say you are amazing." I wasn't quite sure whether that was a compliment or an insult but thanked her anyhow.

Earlier this month I went to New Orleans for the first ASCD meeting I have attended in fifteen or sixteen years. I was nervous about my speech, but as the room filled to overflowing, it all came back to me and I was once again my old self on the platform. A good feeling. I also attended the luncheon for past presidents and was greeted with much enthusiasm. Each past president was asked to tell when he or she was in office and to share the most effective speech he or she recalled. I was astounded that six of my colleagues mentioned how moved or struck they were by speeches I had made. A reaffirmation for me!

One aspect of my awareness of the world closing in on me has been a kind of keeping a wary eye on myself to catch any signs of mental deterioration. So far, so good. In fact, I am rather astounded at my productivity of late.

The Silent Revolution is in the hands of an agent, and I have just completed my part of the book on leadership with Ann Miser and Kathy Whitaker.

5/23/96

Several months ago I woke one morning with a very strong premonition that I had not long to live. The feeling was so strong that I made a lunch date with Tom Flower and shared the experience with him. In particular, I spoke of my fear of being one day in a hospital with tubes running out of me in all directions. I asked if he could help me acquire the means to suicide—not that I had any thought of using it just now, but I felt some urgency to have the means in my hands in order to be sure I had final control. Tom, of course, was sympathetic but unable to honor my query. I also spoke of my premonition to our men's group and was deeply touched by their understanding and support. I have finally decided what I can do about suicide and have worked out the details. Unfortunately, my idea requires that I be able to get around. That leaves me without control if I am disabled or in hospital.

Several weeks after the above, someone in our men's group spoke of his fear of committing suicide. In the ensuing discussion I found myself saying I have no fear of it nor of doing it, that I believe this is a *right* of anyone. I have had many clients who considered the idea of suicide. I have never had one who did it. I believe one reason is that I thoroughly respect their right to do so. I believe my lack of fear about it makes it possible for them to examine the matter fully—in the process of which they find new reasons for living. Actually, I welcome the thought that this is my right and I would have no trepidation or hesitation to take that means—when the time seems right. I do not see the matter as an escape or a relief. Neither do I think it matters what others may think or feel. One must do what seems personally right and I have discovered in recent years that when I do that, it turns out to be best for others as well.

Two books have been exceedingly meaningful to me of late. Deborah Meier's [1995] book *The Power of Their Ideas* is absolutely fascinating. She describes how for twenty years!!! (how have I missed her?) she has been running schools in central New York City and Harlem with 95% graduation rates and subsequent success in college. So many of the ideas she has put in operation support my own thinking and beliefs. How I wish I had known about her years ago.

I have also been deeply moved and stimulated by Meg Wheatley's work. I read her *Leadership and the New Science* [Wheatley, 1994] and was so excited that I wrote to her and sent her a bunch of my stuff. She graciously replied and sent a copy of the manuscript for a new book to come out this summer, *A Simpler Way* [Wheatley & Kellner-Rogers, 1996]. What a book. It reads like poetry! It echoes and expands my thinking about the nature of humanity, our relationship to the universe—the works! It has helped me to refine a number of aspects of perceptual thinking and underlines the vital importance of a psychology of meaning based upon a field approach. It also stimulated me to invite Anne [Richards] and Dave [Welch] to a redo of *Individual Behavior*.

Anne came to Greeley for a conference with Dave and me and we have started a revision, to be called *Being and Becoming: A Field Approach to the Study of Persons*. It looks like a good thing. I am surprised, however, at my feelings about it. I took no notes during our discussions and feel a sense of pleasure at the idea of working on it, but it's not a priority for me. I think psychology needs it and it may help to spread the perceptual field idea. I am glad to be working on it but I will be content that it be largely Dave's and Anne's project.

I expressed my excitement and satisfaction that I am having so many good ideas of late. Anne (bless her heart!) pointed out that I probably do not have many more years to contribute and asked if I am writing them down like Maslow did near the end of his life. I found myself telling her no, that Abe had a feeling that what he had to say was terribly important and thus he made a concerted effort to get it all down. He spent a lot of time dictating what later was published as his journals. Much of that is kind of stream-of-consciousness stuff. I feel quite content with what I have been able to contribute. I have a feeling that it is mostly good. I am also thankful and excited at my continuing capacity to spawn new concepts and see new relationships, but I have no pressing need to make sure these are out there in the public eye. Nor do I have any feeling of urgency that my ideas be recognized. I feel, rather, a sense of contentment at still being in the stream, a part of something much bigger than myself, that it doesn't matter whether I try to push events forward or not, that they will come in due time and that I am not necessary. It is enough that I have been and contributed. The universe is in process of seeking fulfillment with or without me. It is good to know I have been able to be a facilitator of the process, but I have no exaggerated sense of my importance. If my impact has been good, others will find it so and build upon it in the same fashion that I took off from the contributions of my predecessors.

7/19/96

Thinking about the relationship of human beings to the universe of late, I have been intrigued with the idea of a universe (and all other organizations) perpetually seeking order. All things are forever in process of being and becoming—being who or what they are and becoming what they can. This is a benevolent view of the universe, a hopeful concept that is concordant with the fundamental need of human beings to maintain and enhance the self. I have also become increasingly aware of how our things-oriented culture continually screws up this process. Getting control of things and our world has released us from much drudgery and made it possible for us to spend more time and energy on matters beyond sheer survival. We have pursued control of the world so far and so successfully, however, that like having too much of any good thing, it is turning on us and creating more and more problems for individuals and for society.

Our worship of things and their control and manipulation twists and distorts the growing-up process. Being and becoming have been reduced to be Something and become Something with a capital S. This is producing millions of citizens convinced that they are not enough, that they should be something other than who they are. Almost all my clients are like that, suffering from feelings of not being what they should or ought. What a relief for them when they reach the point of saying, "It's all right to be me. I don't have to be what others think I should."

I lay awake the other night thinking about being and becoming as the nature of organization and the universe. This means that the goal of the universe is not to achieve some end, but simply to be freely in the process. What the universe asks of us is that we be who we are and become what we can. It's the process, stupid, not the end or goal! As I applied this thinking to my own life, I became keenly aware that that has increasingly become my way of being. Being in process has become far more important than what I do or what I produce. Not only that, it has made it possible for me to act and produce in generally positive ways, not only for me, but for those I influence as well.

Looking back, I believe the reason for my divorce from Millie was that I found myself surrounded by forces valuing goals (acquiring things, titles, honors; conformity, various oughts and shoulds) that strangled my being in the process. In the midst of all this I experienced the personal importance of being in the process. As a student, I never worked for grades or felt they were very important. Even my doctorate is not a matter of much moment for me now, although it's something I consciously set out to acquire at one time. I am often embarrassed by other people's use of it. I have rarely used the title "doctor" (except, on occasion, when making a reservation, I am chagrined to admit). My success as a speaker has never been because I was trying to get an audience to respond or behave in a way I desired. I enjoy the experience for its own sake as a dialogue with a group. The question-and-answer period is always more fun than the talk itself. Repeatedly, across the span of my life, I have enjoyed just being in the process, content to let the outcome be what it will.

The same is true for my therapy sessions; I have no goals for my clients beyond the hope that this experience will prove helpful to them. I simply engage myself fully in the process and go where it will with confidence that doing that is all that is necessary. After a while, my clients and I come to a place where we know it is time to stop—so we do. And as I think of it now, it is seldom that my clients terminate with a plan of action or even mention what they are going to do. Instead, they leave with a feeling of confidence in themselves, certain they can handle matters successfully—a feeling that I also share but which neither of us even feels prompted to discuss.

I have never advertised or bragged about the innovations I have produced. Mostly they were achieved by filling a need, creating another, then filling that. Both programs I built and saw destroyed were developed in this fashion. Step by step, without an overall plan or clear objective, I brought the clinical program at Syracuse in the College of Education into a full-scale operation without asking permission or mapping out a plan. No wonder Dean Ganders was incredulous when he fired my staff and found 45 doctoral students left high and dry and screaming betrayal. Until that moment, he never knew the program had become such an integral part of his college.

The importance of the process is true for my writing as well. I find writing an exhilarating experience, a real high. I hate searching for a publisher and have often been content not to seek publication for something I have written. Though I appreciate commendation, I do not seek it, nor do I feel devastated if I don't get it. The process is infinitely more important to me. What people may think of me or my work is an artifact of the work itself, never a pre-meditated goal. I am increasingly aware that I am not a goal-oriented but a process-oriented person and I am fascinated with that discovery about me. It explains so much for me about my life and behavior. It explains my deep-seated yearning for authenticity. It also explains why things and appearances are of little concern, why cars are simply a means of transportation for me and I don't know one from another, why I don't really care where we eat, hate to go shopping, rarely remember a movie or a book when it's over despite enjoying it in process (a quality that mystifies others who have seen me enjoying it but come to realize that later on I am quite unable to report who was in it, or even what it was about on many an occasion). I get unhappy when I am not in process. I ask myself, am I a workaholic? I don't think so. Workaholics are consumed with goals. These days I don't feel I HAVE to work and I am not unhappy at having to stop.

9/24/96

As part of my new "Be Kind To Art" kick, the girls and I went to see Peter and Nancy in Atlanta and attended three of the events at the Olympics: a lovely trip that gave me opportunity to be close to three of my children and get to visit the Olympics too!

At lunch with Marc Ringel last week, I was intrigued when Marc told me, "Art, you've changed in the last year or so. Your horizons have widened and you are more spiritually oriented." I had to admit that was true. I am absorbed in larger issues, like my relationship to the universe. Such are the problems that interest me now. I am not unhappy at not doing therapy despite its long-time meaning for me. I am more excited by farther reaches phenomena, e.g., problems of prevention, the nature and effects of our culture, field theory, etc., etc.

Marc further observed that he thought this surge in creativity and interest in other fields was a consequence of my divorce and the physical trauma I have experienced. He's right about that, too. Events like that shake us out of our ruts, opening the way for creativity, innovation, and new areas for exploration. I feel very good these days. I am vigorous, active, feel strong for a man my age and, best of all, my brain and field of meaning is constantly in motion and producing fresh and exciting insights. Life is fun! Not ha ha fun, but exhilarating, grounded in a solid feeling of being in process and finding fulfillment.

Betty Siegel, a former colleague at U of F, is now president of Kennesaw College [an institution that became Kennesaw State University in 1994] in Georgia. Last spring she conceived the idea of an Art Combs Get-Together with former faculty and students I have known. The event is scheduled for next week and I am looking forward to seeing old friends once more at Betty's mountain home. I plan to attend a seminar in Denver put on by Meg Wheatley, then fly on to Atlanta. Afterwards, I will drive home to Murray, Kentucky with Dick and Mary Usher to stay for a few days, then fly home. I will also get to spend a day with Peter and Nancy, and Dave Welch and Anne Richards and I will spend some time working on *Being and Becoming*. Quite a busy, happy week! Full of exciting, lovely people!

I have started teaching a graduate seminar on Changing Schools with Gary Galuzzo, Dean of Education at UNC. The class is invigorating and I seem to have lost the anxiety I had some time back about whether I could still deliver when I had to. Another sense of fulfillment and renewal, and I love every minute of it. My cup runneth over! Lynn asked if she could enroll in the class. I was somewhat hesitant to okay a high school student into a graduate class and was not sure how Gary would react. Lynn went to see Gary and he said, "Sure, we need a voice of the student in the class." Since we were talking about educational reform, it would be helpful to have "a consumer" in the group. Well, she has done extraordinarily well. Not intimidated but a fully with-it member of the class who made important contributions, she has been remarkable and I have thoroughly enjoyed having her on board. Now she knows a little about what her Dad does. What a girl! Though the experienced educators in the group acknowledged the value of reform and explored the questions in great detail, little in the way of action followed. I was surprised that this did not upset me. Instead, it was another indication of the difficulties inherent in producing change in a bureaucracy. These were good people, sincerely interested in reform, but finding it tough to know where to begin and confronted with obstructions of a hundred varieties.

10/11/96

Just back from a wonderful nine days full of love and caring and reaffirmation.

Last Tuesday I drove to Denver for a seminar with Meg Wheatley and Myron Kellner-Rogers about their new book *A Simpler Way*. Had dinner with them before the seminar. Delightful people on the trail of very important ideas that have generated in me some fascinating new insights that tie perceptual psychology to foundations in the universe itself. A professional affirmation. When others come to the same conclusions you have, that confirms the likelihood that you are on the right track.

Next day I flew to Atlanta and had a couple of days with Peter and Nancy. What marvelous people my son and his wife have become—and they seem always truly glad to see the old man.

On Thursday, Dave and Marie Welch arrived. I met them at the airport and we drove to Carrollton to stay with Anne and Fred Richards. That evening Dave, Anne, and I went to work on the book. It was awful. Dave had obviously done nothing in preparation for our work together and indicated he was involved in two other projects that would have to come first. Anne, on the other hand, had done a great deal of work on an article for publication, with an enormous compilation of references from the literature. She knows the literature backward and forward and I so admire her skill at that. It quickly became evident we were each approaching the task from widely different perspectives.

As we struggled with trying to come to some sort of agreement on the first chapters, it became increasingly clear to me that we would never be able to pull off writing together with two thousand miles between us. Accordingly, next morning I shared my feelings with Anne and Dave. Dave was relieved. Anne was distressed at first, but soon realized we would all be better off each doing our own thing without trying to produce a common project.* Accordingly, we dropped the collaborative project and in the afternoon we took off for the "Art Combs Get-Together" at Betty Siegel's place in the Georgia mountains.

What an amazing weekend! Twenty or so folks from Florida—faculty and students. I spoke for an hour off the cuff about what had happened to me since 1976 and where I seemed to be today. I felt very good—relaxed, comfortable, and at home with all these old friends. Next day, the discussions continued as we talked, reminisced, and shared what everyone else was into, breaking up after brunch at Betty's mountain home. What a warm, renewing, reaffirming experience with an exceptional group of people in cel-

* Editor's note: Subsequently, as an outgrowth of these discussions, Anne produced the article "Metapsychology: Revisiting the Past, Confronting the Present, Serving the Future" (Richards, 1997); David Welch collaborated with graduate student Chris Breier in producing a series of videotaped interviews highlighting Art's professional legacy [Theory (Parts I and II), Contributions to Education (Parts I and II)]; and Art wrote the book *Being and Becoming: A Field Approach to Psychology,* which was published in 1999.

Art Combs Get-Together, October 4–6, 1996, Big Canoe, GA From left to right: Front row: Katherine Ward, Will Neville, Mary Usher, Shirley Avila, Marie Welch; Second row: Terry Jennings, Walter Busby, Betty Siegel, Art Combs, David Welch, Dick Usher, Joel Siegel, Fred Richards; Back row: Gerald Jennings, LaVerne Glover, Anne Richards, Dee Blume, Bob Blume. [Others present but not pictured included Scott and Mary Busby.]

ebration of a wonderful time when we felt so excited by new ideas and a shared sense of being involved in something much bigger than all of us!

Around noon I took off with Dick and Mary Usher for the drive to their home in Benton, Kentucky for three more days. All three of us felt privileged to have shared the weekend with each other. Mary and I spent an afternoon sight-seeing and watching the boats go through the locks at Kentucky dam. I spent the next day with Dick at the University and attended several of Dick's classes and talked about "What Makes a Good Teacher" in his graduate class. These are two extraordinary people, generously caring of each other and of everyone with whom they come in contact. My friendship with them has certainly been one of the most rewarding, loving relationships I have ever known. Yesterday I came home suffused with a sense of fulfillment, affirmation, and warm feelings of appreciation at a truly beautiful mingling of kindred souls. A sense of having touched and been touched by a group of very special human beings.

12/2/96

In men's group, Marc asked what was the nub of your being that made you take a more positive direction than your siblings? As I thought about that, it seemed to me a combination of things: (a) Experiencing myself as a rejected child created a sense that I had to make it on my own, a dependence upon self, and a commitment to hard work; (b) Becoming a rebel early as per the Maypole story [see Chapter 2, pp. 28–30] fostered a developing sense of integrity and encouraged greater independence in thinking; (c) Being accustomed to working within the system taught me to be innovative but without direct confrontation. With my mother, I realized early that direct confrontation brought disaster and feelings of guilt. So, I learned to avoid confrontation and find ways of achieving my goals without it. I don't think I have understood this before, but this was the way of dealing with things that my father employed—to quietly do your thing, compromising when necessary to reach objectives in peaceful ways (his way of dealing with Charlotte and with his work).

3/20/97

After returning from Atlanta, I began to grow a beard. Lynn and Erin did not like it much at first but almost everyone else told me they liked it—thought it made me look distinguished. A few days ago I shaved it off, much to Lynn's distress; she complained it made me look like a kid! I only grew my beard because it had been many years since I last had one and it seemed a fun thing to do once again. I shaved it off because it did not seem like me. The beard made me look more distinguished but I have never really been concerned with how I look. Rather, it seemed like a pretension, so I did it in.

I am currently being interviewed on videotape by two different groups. Graduate students in professional psychology have asked me to discuss a bunch of topics and I am doing so once a week. The other occasion is under a grant that Dave Welch has. In this one I am being interviewed in a professional setting by Dave and Chris Breier, a delightful grad student.* I am enjoying the taping session because it gives me an opportunity to hold forth on my professional beliefs and also respond to personal questions about my career. I feel honored at these efforts to capture some of who I am and have been and am flattered by the attention. But it also feels suspiciously like this is a "last-rites" project to get me on tape before something happens to me

* Editor's Note: These tapes are available from the University of Northern Colorado, Greeley, CO.

David Welch, Chris Breier, and Art Combs (Greeley, CO, 1996)

and this makes me a little uneasy. Have enjoyed the sessions much, though, and look forward to seeing the final products.

In men's group a week ago we realized we are coming up on our ninth year together in the fall. We commented at length at the unusualness of such a group lasting for so long a time and each of us talked a bit about the significance of this association for us personally. What a wonderful group of men! How deeply they have affected me and how deeply connected I feel with them! What a privilege! How rare to feel so deep and abiding a love!

5/18/97

I'm surprised to see I have not written anything here since March—three months ago! Actually, the time has been quiet and inspiriting in almost every way. Lynn is about to graduate and will be off for three weeks in France. Erin is just back from two weeks in Germany and is now driving—wonderful young women! And I delight in their company every other week.

I have been concentrating on the rewrite of the 1959 edition of *Individual Behavior*. It goes very well and I have a solid feeling of satisfaction with the manuscript. I think it will be an important contribution. I am also struck by how little needs to be modified from the '59 edition. I have cut a good deal out to make a shorter, tighter presentation but nearly all that I review is

The Men's Group (1997) Taken at Swetsville Metal Sculpture Garden by Alan Wilkes From left to right: Marc Ringel, David Gonzalez, Roy Wardell, Tom Flower, Art Combs, Jim Fittz

as good today as it was when I originally wrote it. Primarily the changes revolve around making it a straightforward field theory, tying it to the nature of the universe, highlighting humankind as product of the need of organizations for identity, and underscoring the discovery of meaning as a function of self perception. I am removing much in the applied sections and adding to the effect of the culture, the nature of good helpers research, modern thinking about organizations, and a historical perspective on field theory. I meditate, exercise, walk, and write in a daily pattern that suits me well. I am calling the new book *Being and Becoming: A Field Approach to Psychology.*

I have withdrawn the *Silent Revolution* manuscript from the agent I was involved with. I think the book needs a new orientation in line with what I now believe about this culture—namely, that we are into the decline that Arnold Toynbee [1957] predicted and are due for increasing chaos as we collapse. As Toynbee also suggested, in the midst of decline the seeds for a new culture are already on the scene. I believe those seeds may be seen in the shift from the era of physical science to the era of social science, and especially the emergence of a more person-centered world. These developments call for a set of person-centered assumptions about the nature and functions of human beings from which to begin. If one looks at our present culture from a person-centered orientation, it becomes clear how we lost our way, why we are in the fix we are in, and the directions we need to move to find a more fulfilling way of living and being.

I have really come to value the friendship and wisdom of Gary Galuzzo, dean of the college with whom I taught a seminar in the fall. Unfortunately for me, lucky for him, he is leaving here to go to James Mason College in Virginia. I shall miss him greatly.

I started reading Ernest Becker's [1973] Pulitzer Prize-winning book, *The Denial of Death,* in which he shows how Adler, Freud, and many others have based so much of their thinking on our "inherent " denial of death and points to much in the current world as being motivated by that "universal" fear. I believe all these people miss the point. Sure, many of us are afraid of death, but by no means is that universal. Fear of dying is not a motivational force inherent in life itself. Instead, the universal need of the organism, I believe, is maintenance of organization or identity. That is the prime motivation and it is grounded in our link to the organization of the universe itself.

To be sure, death marks the end of a person's physical organization and the end of his or her conscious self. To build a psychology or explain a culture on the fear of that event misses the point and provides a negative approach to human affairs. People develop themselves and their societies in relation to the need for identity and fulfillment, a proactive effort. Being fearful of the end, and attempting to deny it, is a reactive mode. The important message for me is that I and the universe I inhabit are both seeking fulfillment of identity. We are both on the same side in what we seek. I do not have to fight that tendency. I need to learn to live with it, to be and become the best I can. Errors like Becker's and those he so admires are what comes of looking at things from an outsider's perspective and seeking trends in statistics. Individuals do not spend the majority of their lives trying to avoid death; they seek instead for personal fulfillment and build lives they believe may help them to achieve that end.

Reading some of the above leaves me with a feeling that some of it sounds pretty arrogant—as though I had solved the problems of psychology and the world in general. And I wonder if, like theorists before me, I am stuck somehow while the world passes me by, if maybe there is already extant a better, more accurate frame of reference that I am not aware of or am defending myself against. I keep trying to be awake enough to see that if and when the inevitable occurs, but to date most of what I see only tends to corroborate the field view I have come to believe in. Is my vision so clouded that I cannot appreciate a better alternative? I hope not. But I also recognize that that could happen. I guess the only solution is to emulate Patrick Henry, stand up for what I think and exclaim: "If this be treason, make the most of it!"

6/25/97

Gary Galuzzo is leaving the university and so is Dave Welch. I shall miss them both sorely. The university is in terrible shape with five top administrators leaving. A sad thing. UNC could be a great place to work and has a great opportunity to make an important contribution but too many are missing the boat right and left.

7/27/97

Last Saturday I had a dinner party for 23 of my friends in the clubhouse here in the condo. A nice affair that gave me an opportunity for some of my friends to meet each other. It also celebrated my 85th birthday, although a bit delayed. What a rare privilege to have a group of close friends like these and how utterly lonely my life would be without them.

Dick and Mary Usher are back at their Allenspark cabin for a month and the girls and I went up there to visit them overnight. What great people! Once while at the cabin and again at their home in Kentucky, I had nights when I woke and spent three or fours hours kicking around new insights. This time it happened again! I slept on the floor in a sleeping bag and woke about 3 a.m. buzzing with ideas until folks got up at 7 a.m. For a few weeks I have been having more feelings that my world is closing in on me and have been mildly depressed. Lying there in the dark, totally relaxed and musing about such matters, I came to the conclusion that I am very lucky to be so mentally alive and awake and I need to appreciate that fact, spend less time thinking about aging and more time just keeping myself in good shape physically. I am in pretty good shape. I meditate daily, have a half hour of tai chi and setting up exercises, and try to walk two miles a day. Except for my blasted psoriasis,* and hearing and vision problems, I seem to be pretty normal.

Following that, I began to think about death in perceptual terms and came up with something like this. We are all organizations, like everything else in the universe, and we all participate in the universal need of organizations to find identity and to seek its fulfillment. This is really a figure/ground dynamic as the physical self and personal self rise into definition or differentiation from the ground of the field. From the field of the universe itself, life forms arise into figure as animals, plants, or human beings, become a force,

Editor's note: Although this is the first time Art mentions his psoriasis, it was a problem that had annoyed him for years. This is also the first time he mentions a hearing problem, although he began wearing a hearing aid in the mid-1980s after experiencing difficulties in hearing.

and return to the ground again at some indeterminate date after death. Thus we all come out of the stuff of the universe, rising into a figure or identity that we then seek to maintain or enhance.

In this process, time is an illusion, a handy device for helping us deal with the world but of no other consequence. And death? Physically, it is but the return of the body to ground as we go back to the matter of the universe from which we sprang. As for personality, the same thing holds: personal identity arises out of the field of awareness, and each person seeks maintenance and enhancement throughout his or her existence. The self organization, like all other organizations, exerts influence and it is that influence we refer to as a person's personality. What is more, that influence continues after an individual has physically expired. Having affected the physical world by its very existence and behavior, it changes the universe itself.

So is the world of human awareness affected by the nature and force of the personality, for experience is not a reversible process. Our spirit (personality, self, soul?) affects the world while we live and continues after we are physically gone. Over time it is diluted as the field expands, but it, too, is there forever. This has parallels in theology. If we think of the great force (field) of the universe as God, then, indeed, we are all the children of God and are constructed in her image. We are all continuous with the universe and the growth and decline of a person is but a rise into figure and return to the ground of the larger universe.

One significant addition to my thinking is the simplicity of a field view. I now see the nature of human persons as a function of two things. One is the basic character of organization for identity and its maintenance, which provides the force for growth and change. It is a given and not open to much influence. The other facet of personhood is contributed by the fact of awareness and its growth in human beings to high levels. Human personality is a consequence of the interaction of the basic need and the awareness of the organism. Awareness is a matter we can influence, but since it lies inside the organism and only exists as a field, to study and understand persons and behavior we must approach human beings from a field perspective.

Despite the inexorable narrowing of my physical world as aging creeps up on me, I am active, happy, and thankful to be so alert and excited with ideas. Lately, I have been musing upon the matter of connection and how long it took in my lifespan to reach the connectedness I currently feel. I experience a deep sense of oneness with the universe, a feeling of oneness in the human condition and compassion for persons in trouble, but also a sense of detachment in that I feel no great necessity to *make* things different beyond my immediate sphere of influence. I have a feeling it is enough to be who I am, that if I do that wholeheartedly with those I come in contact with, the outcomes will be good. If I be the best I can, wherever I am, I will simultaneously be doing what is best for me and for those I touch as well. There is so much more here than I can currently express, but this is the best I can do for now.

I also got to thinking of the therapeutic relationship in light of these insights. It is interesting that my clients rarely return for further therapy or express appreciation or thanks, etc., after leaving therapy. They seem to have a warm regard for me but no sense of indebtedness. It occurred to me that therapy is like a bridge that makes it possible for clients to get from point A to point B. Like a bridge, one passes over it matter-of-factly and feels no need to go back and pat the bridge for being there or take a piece along as a souvenir. I take no responsibility for my clients' actions. I respect and facilitate their struggles to find their own ways, share myself fully with them, but avoid their becoming dependent upon me.

Carl Rogers (1972), in his study of effective partnerships (marital, emotional, and living) found four basic characteristics in the successful ones: commitment to the relationship, intimate communication with few holds barred, no fixed roles or methods, and encouragement of and joy in the partner's growth. It strikes me that these criteria are likewise applicable to my relationships with my clients. When therapy goes well, we are both committed to the process (often very thoughtfully). I work very hard at communication by listening intently and making sure I am hearing correctly on the one hand and taking great care on the other hand to assure that whatever I say is clearly understood as I intended. I have no set roles for myself and no sense of applying methods or strategies to the process. I do what seems to me to be appropriate from moment to moment. Likewise, my clients behave in no set patterns or roles. Fourthly, I am always seeking to facilitate my clients' growth wherever it takes us with no judgments about what is good or right or necessary, and we are both genuinely happy for growth achieved. So, a good therapeutic relationship is parallel to other good human relationships in life. It is fascinating to me how all wholesome human relationships, whether leadership, teaching, counseling, parenting, loving, partnering, or governing, all keep coming back to the qualities of the four characteristics of healthy persons and the belief systems of helpers that I have been advocating and the person-centered characteristics Carl proposed.

9/9/97

Took Lynn off to college at the University of Missouri. Originally, Susan and [her partner] Anne were going to go with her, using two cars to carry all her stuff. Since at the last minute Anne could not go, I went and I am very glad I did. It was good that both of Lynn's parents were there. It will be a major adjustment for Lynn, but she is also very ready for the college experience and I am sure she will do well in a short time when she gets her feet under her. To Columbia, I rode most of the way with Lynn. Coming home, it was just Susan and me and we took two days for the trip instead of one. I was glad to see that I felt quite comfortable. I am long over the grieving process, able to accept the reality of our new relationship as interested and concerned parents, period.

3/1/98

I have sent the manuscript of *Being and Becoming* to the publishing arm of APA. I feel almost certain they will reject it but (perversely) I think I would win either way. If they accept it, I will feel a sense of vindication and be very pleased that psychology has at long last recognized the field view. On the other hand, if they reject it, I also feel vindicated, for I believe the field view is where psychology must go from here on and it will give me pleasure, when that time comes, to point out that APA rejected it when it was offered to them.

On the way out to Roy's ranch, Roy asked about my autobiography and I told him it was up to date. I also told him how I decided to do it as an indicator of one person's striving for health. He asked why I didn't publish it now. I told him I guess I don't believe I'm healthy enough yet. I said it as a joke, but afterward I got to thinking about that and realized the statement is true. I still have growing to do. Right now I'm looking forward to going to see Chuck and his family with the hope that I can resolve aspects of our lifelong separation by letting him know I truly love him and deeply regret our lack of closeness all these years. It is obvious to me that both Chuck and I have lived these many long years each believing the other wanted no part of him. After that, I will seek to do the same with my sister Dot. That's how it should be; no one ever achieves total health. Health is only something one can approximate—some more, some less, but there is always room for something more.

4/1/98

Long time since I last wrote. I have been busy working on finishing the *Being and Becoming: A Field Approach to Psychology* book. It's now done and I am seeking a publisher. Sent it to APA and it was rejected. First time I ever sent off a manuscript and was happy with the result either way. If they had accepted, I would have been pleased that at long last psychology is ready to look at a field approach. That they rejected it is all right too. I expected that and I now have the satisfaction of saying when it finally comes out that "APA turned it down." Ha!

I think the book is a good one and should make an important contribution if I can get it published. The leadership book I was doing with Kathy Whitaker and Ann Miser has been accepted by ASCD. It is about to go to press and I feel apologetic about it. It did not come out as I expected and I feel it is one of the poorest things I have done. But Kathy and Ann are excited about getting published so I am raising no questions and letting it go. I do not have the stomach to get involved in what a real revision would require. In fact, I have told myself I am through writing books when those on my plate are finished. I will write no more volumes. I'll stick to articles and to revising previously written manuscripts. After *Being and Becoming* is done I will revise the *Silent Revolution* book. That will leave this autobiography.

I do not plan to seek its publication but I am in the process of setting up a trust fund, known as the Field Psych Trust, designed to provide funds for publication of *Being and Becoming* and my autobiography after I am gone, receive any royalties from my works hereafter, and provide a source of funds to aid promising graduate students interested in field psychology. Anne Richards has agreed to act as trustee, for which I am deeply grateful. What a great lady!

At Christmas time I went to Susan's house for dinner with the girls, Susan, Anne (Susan's lover-partner?) and Anne's daughter and boyfriend. A nice time and I felt very comfortable. I must have. When I left, I hugged everyone, including Anne and her daughter! I feel good about that. Apparently I have pretty completely come to terms with the divorce, etc.

On the way home from Kentucky, where Lynn and I went for a surprise 60th birthday party for Dick Usher: a delightful three days with the Ushers, Richards, Welches, Shirley Avila, et al. Lovely people, lovely time! I feel so lucky to have such wonderful friends. I only wish I could see them more often.

On the way back to St. Louis, Lynn dropped me off at Chuck's home and I stayed for three days. I needed to let him know that I loved him and hoped we could find a new basis for our relationship. He is slowly and painfully recovering from a triple bypass and was quite weak. We spent some good hours reminiscing and getting reacquainted after nearly thirty years. I feel very good about our visit. I was pleased to meet his delightful

The day after Dick Usher's 60th Birthday Party (March, 1998) From left to right: Fred Richards, Art Combs, Mary Usher, Dick Usher, Shirley Avila, David Welch, Ron Chesley, Lynn Combs

wife, Gloria, and to spend some quality time together. An agenda that meant a lot to me.

Reminiscing with Chuck, I became aware of something I have not mentioned in my previous chapters discussing early days. Chuck said Mom and Dad had no friends, no one ever came to our house, and suddenly that hit me as very true. No one ever did! All they had was each other! Although they loved each other, I am sure, they could not avoid anger. Mom would pick at Dad, saying things like, "Well, I know better than that and I never went to college!" while Dad would take out his anger by clamming up. Many a meal was spent with no one talking to each other. I had forgotten. Chuck has made quite a study of the family tree* and included a great deal of information about the family that I have not included in my memoirs.

* Editor's note: After suffering a heart attack, stroke, and several health crises related to congestive heart failure followed by another heart attack and triple-bypass surgery (among other things), upon the request of some of his children, Chuck decided to put down in written form what he knew about his extended family, its roots, and its genealogy. Too often, Chuck believed, family members are aware of only two or three generations back, to the time of one's grandparents. In his twenties, he had become interested in family history to such an extent that while stationed in the Army in Europe and England he spent time in archives, churches, graveyards, and visits with people named Combs seeking to learn more about the family name and his ancestry. His 158-page document details this family history in considerable detail, and includes an account of his own life experiences as well as the experiences of others in his family.

I found it heartwarming (was deeply touched) on the trip from Kentucky to Chuck's house when Lynn said she loved traveling with me and could we go back to Florida one more time? What a thrill that my dearly beloved daughter would like to spend time with her old man! Such a nice feeling about the solidity and value of our relationship, something I have surely not always been certain about.

Life goes along swimmingly for me these days. I get up at 6:30, breakfast, and read the paper. This is followed by meditation, a half hour of calisthenics, and a two-mile walk around the lake. After that is lunch alone or out, a nap, and two or three hours work, counseling (I have two clients), writing, reading. Late afternoons I make myself dinner, or if Erin is with me that week, I rustle up something special that my vegetarian child can enjoy. So go my days.

I continue to be excited about the paradigm shift in science to relationships, ecology and self-regulating organizations. It feels so right, and of course, corroborates what I have been advocating ever since 1947. It is good to have this kind of support from another source. How slowly people change and how long it takes for a paradigmatic change to reach general acceptance!

I have a good feeling about where I am in life and what I have become. Lately, I have had a number of interactions in which people have commented about me in ways that imply that I am a calming influence, a source of stability, a person who conveys a sense of kindness, honesty, and authenticity. I ask myself if that is really true and I do believe it is. I think I have achieved a high degree of self-actualization. I am at ease with who I am and sure that that is a good thing for others with whom I come in contact. I feel comfortable and assured and have no ambition to try to be anything but who and what I truly am. That sounds rather self-glorifying as I reconsider what I've written down, but it is true for me and I do not feel it is an illusion. I am quite content with my life and who and what I am. About the only thing I miss is having a woman in my life. Even that, however, is not a problem so significant that I want to work at solving it. If it happens, fine, even great, but I have no particular motivation to make it happen. With Lynn gone off to college and Erin here only every other week, I have lots of time to myself, but I accept that and find things to do, e.g., reading, napping, watching the news and an occasional TV program. I am a happy man again, although I suppose some people reading the above would not believe it possible to be so serene with what must seem to others so very little. C'est la vie!

Two years ago, ASCD asked if I would be interested in an update of *Perceiving, Behaving, Becoming* and I was too busy to contemplate it, so they asked Jerry Freiberg to tackle it. The original volume [Combs, 1962] consisted of four papers by Rogers, Kelley, Maslow, and myself on what is a truly healthy person. The remainder of the volume was then devoted to the thinking of a wide group of front-line educators who asked, "If what these papers say is true, what does that mean for education?" They came up with some truly ingenious and innovative ideas. The book Freiberg has finally produced, written in typical academic journal style, is a series of scholarly critiques of each of the four original "expert" papers. I am appalled. Editing the original is one of the finest things I have ever done, but this revision seems to me a travesty. I objected to the direction it has taken, praised the contributors for their critical essays, and suggested they publish them as such. But ASCD has decided to bring out the book as is. I am sad about that and have asked that, at least, they give the volume a different title so people will understand it is not truly a redo of the original. At this point, they have not replied.*

4/30/98

SUNY Press has sent the manuscript of *Being and Becoming* out to readers. A good sign. Perhaps they will publish it. They will not be able to do as effective a job at marketing the project as a large commercial publisher might, but I have no stomach to spend a lot more time seeking a publisher. So if SUNY wants it, I will go with them.

The division of Humanistic Psychology in APA has named me for this year's "outstanding contribution" award to be presented at APA's annual meeting in August in San Francisco. I am pleased and will have an opportunity to make a 20-minute speech. I have just realized that this will be the first APA meeting I have attended since I left Syracuse way back in the '50s, except for the speech I made on the occasion of Carl Rogers's seventy-fifth year celebration that APA put on 10 years ago! In my Syracuse days, I went every year and enjoyed it thoroughly, but after the Syracuse experience I never returned. The rejection by psychology at Syracuse really cut deep and I so thoroughly enjoyed my acceptance by educators and counselors that I preferred to work with those groups. The transition to education was so total that I have often thought of myself not as an educational psychologist but a psychological educator, or educationist (?).

* Editor's note: The book described here, edited by H. Jerome Freiberg, came out in 1999, entitled *Perceiving, Behaving, Becoming: Lessons Learned.*

I continue to see indications of the degree to which this culture of ours imbues us all with the manipulation-of-forces orientation. We grow up learning that the way to deal with all problems is to make things happen. But human beings are not built for such coercive measures. As self-regulating organizations in a universe of organizations, change must come from within. The field of therapy is currently in serious trouble for failure to recognize that. Therapists want to produce changes in clients either by the client's "deciding" to be different or the therapist's suggesting or directing the client toward solutions. I am continually impressed with the way in which my clients automatically discover ingenious solutions to their problems when they have come to see themselves and their situation in different terms. They arrive at much better solutions than I could have proposed. Not surprising when you consider they live with themselves and their problems 24 hours a day while I see them only once a week. People with more data are very likely to find better solutions!

The culture we live in infuses us all with the idea that the way to cope with life is to control or buck the system. But, as the new paradigm in science helps us understand, we must learn to work *with* the world, not against it. So much of counseling these days is "solution-focused" or confrontational and therapists themselves get so caught up in the goal of *producing* that they give up facilitating. I, too, believe we should help our clients in the most efficient ways possible, but foisting solutions on clients before real change occurs in the perceptual field, if it works at all, results in symptomatic rather than holistic or authentic change. Our society has encouraged several generations of persons to spend their lives trying to make things, including themselves, be what they ought to or should be. Such persons are continuously acting instead of being, living an illusion instead of reality, and coping with life instead of expressing who they are. What a pity!

7/11/98

What do you know! Springer Publishing Co. wants to do *Being and Becoming*! I have signed a contract with them and will get the manuscript ready for delivery by August 15. I have canceled with SUNY Press. So all my book plans are finis. It will be interesting to see what sort of reaction this provokes from psychology. It's time someone wrote a beginning psychology book from a perceptual orientation. I don't have it in me, but I wish someone else would. What passes for introductory psych texts at the moment are pretty dreadful. An introductory course ought to be exciting and relevant but most beginning classes are dull as dishwater.

Lynn is doing an internship with Dottie Lamm's senate campaign to unseat Whitehorse Campbell. She's having a ball. If Lamm wins the primary, she is talking about delaying going back to Columbia till the second semester. Erin is working at a dry-cleaning shop. So both girls are into jobs and happy. Erin will be off, she hopes, to the University of Washington next year and that will leave me with no more chicks to raise. It will take some adjusting when they are both gone, but I have a good feeling about the kind of dad I have been. Not a world record-breaker, but a solid and loving performance.

My absorption with the paradigm shift in modern science continues and I am thrilled to find the parallels between what is happening in the hard sciences and at least my brand of psychology. Psychology desperately needs some kind of basic frame of reference to get restarted since the collapse of behaviorism. It seems so very clear to me that perceptual field psychology could provide that common base, but at this point, who besides me knows that? Maybe *Being and Becoming* will provide a catalyst. How slowly change comes about!

Last night as I lay awake I marveled at the idea that our bodies are organizations continuously involved in change in all their parts; cells keep dying and being replaced but the identity of the organization remains essentially stable. The death of cells is thus an essential part of the organism's maintenance and enhancement of self. A colony of bacteria every now and then sends off a troupe to explore new locations. Similar examples of sacrifice occur in ant and bee colonies. Loss is thus an integral process in the maintenance of the organization.* Applying this thought to the human community, the death of members is a necessity for the health of the community. For a person dying and for his or her friends, this is a sad event, but for the community it is an inevitable, even desirable, contribution to the maintenance and enhancement of the community, hence a cause for celebration.

This is a hard thing for individuals to accept but a vital necessity for the larger culture. Our efforts to keep people from dying by heroic measures is thus an aberration and a drag on society. Seen in this larger perspective, funerals should be occasions for celebration rather than times of great sadness, and for some cultures they are. Colorado governor Dick Lamm, calling attention to the enormous costs of keeping old folks alive, once observed that the elderly needed to move on to make way for society's progress. He was severely criticized for his "heartless" suggestion and called "governor gloom," but of course he was right.

* Editor's note: This is an understanding explained in considerable detail by Deepak Chopra (2004) in a chapter titled "Death Makes Life Possible" (pp. 161–177).

Our men's group is coming up on 10 years together. What a wonderful support group they have been for me! The longing for intimacy grows ever greater in this things-oriented society we have created. What a magnificent contribution it would be to find a way to sponsor such groups for men and women of all ages. A more person-centered society would find ways to do so.

7/12/98

Had a strange experience yesterday. After writing the above on the computer and saying goodbye to the girls as they moved over to Susan's house for this week, I wandered about aimlessly, then decided to walk to the lake across the street. The weather was so dreadfully hot that I walked to the park bench and sat for ten minutes or so and then came directly back home. I was suddenly so weary that I lay down on the couch, something I almost never do. I stayed there for quite a while with a feeling of not caring whether I ever got up. I think what I was feeling must be like what very old people feel when they decide to let go of life.

Then, lying in bed this morning, I thought, "No. It's not time yet. There is the APA session where I am to be honored in August and the Think Tank in Idyllwild in October followed by the Conflict Resolution Conference and Art Combs get-together in Charleston, SC.* Most important, I do not want to go until Erin is off to college. After that, I will be ready. Funny that seeing my books come out, or living into the millennium, excites no interest whatever. Only being around till Erin is out of the nest seems significant.

Throughout this autobiography I have been concluding each chapter with a recapitulation on the progress of my quest for self-actualization. I have decided not to do that for these last two chapters. I think it more appropriate for others to judge the end of my quest. I have therefore suggested to Anne that she write what she wishes and invite people like Dick Usher, per-

* What Art is referring to as a "Think Tank" in Idlyllwild was a dialogue held at the Gossamer Ridge Institute in Idlyllwild, CA, organized by Renate Nummela Caine and Geoffrey Caine of Caine Learning, for the purpose of discussing how best to design the future of education in light of recent developments in brain research, learning, and new sciences. Following that meeting, Art and Anne Richards had agreed to make a presentation with former doctoral student Will Neville about the significance of perceptual theory for mediation at the Conflict Resolution Conference held in South Carolina, and get together afterwards with colleague and friend, Walt Busby.

haps one of my kids, or members of the men's group to evaluate my progress. They know me very well.

8/23/98

Back home from San Francisco. The girls and I went to SF on Wednesday, took in a performance of Christopher Plummer in Barrymore, rode the cable car, ate dinner on the wharf, shopped and shopped and shopped. I took half a day to go to the convention and look up the folks from Springer Publishing. Impressive people. I'm glad they are doing *Being and Becoming*. Sat in on several meetings but found them so dry, academic, and dull that I gave up. At the award session, my talk went okay. I am not the soft-spoken, dynamic communicator I used to be. I do not have the confidence I once had because I sometimes have to fish around for words. All in all, it went quite well, however, and I was happy to have Lynn and Erin there. This is the first time either of them has ever heard me make a speech. They told me I made the best speech of the four in the session, so who cares what anyone else thought. What great kids! Kids? Young women!

The plaque that the Division of Humanistic Psychology presented to me reads: The Division "takes pleasure in presenting the Charlotte and Karl Bühler Award to Arthur W. Combs for his groundbreaking contributions to psychological theory, educational reform and research in the helping professions." I am, of course, honored to receive the award. It is nice to know that at least one branch of the profession recognizes my contributions after all these years. I am pleased at the award, but in a very quiet way. I have no sense of jubilation or urge to celebrate. I am far more enlivened by the ramifications and implications of the paradigm shifts in physical, biological, and psychological science from things to relationships. The program for the APA convention was the size of a telephone book and, for me, about as exciting. Leafing through it, I could not find much that struck me as being of vital significance. This may be a grossly unfair assessment, for I must admit I did not work hard at the task. As is the case with all institutions, I guess, most people's interest is in advancing their own special niche, housekeeping matters like insurance, standards, etc., and methodology—concern for the forms rather than the essence.

Having returned home from San Francisco, it has taken me three days to recover. I have slept long and hard and peacefully as a baby and I find I cannot do two miles each morning. Have had to cut it to 1½. And my naps run close to an hour rather than twenty minutes. Ah well! As the doctor says, "Well, Art, what do you expect for a man your age?"

In my acceptance speech for the award, I described how I had arrived at a perceptual view and suggested that humanistic psychology is in reality a perceptual frame of reference that could use further development. Have written an editorial calling attention to the paradigm shift of psychology from behaviorism to self psychology, humanistic psychology, phenomenological, etc. All are based on a common thread: a perceptual field view. I am suggesting the profession take steps to dialogue and explore perception as a basis for all psychology. Will do a similar thing for David Cain's book on humanistic psychotherapy.*

Have also done a piece for educators suggesting that the heart of the reform problem lies in the preoccupation with things, gadgets, gimmicks, and the manipulation of forces. Because education at every level is a people problem, we must adopt a person-centered frame of reference if true reform is going to occur. This is essential to bring about a fundamental shift in the assumptions from which we make decisions. I keep trying to clarify such issues in the hope that others may catch on. But oh my! How slowly people change and how resistant bureaucracies are! It would be interesting to come back in 50 years and see whether and where things have moved. To see change in institutions, a long perspective is needed.

In the news, a grandmother and developmental psychologist by the name of Judith Rich Harris (1998) has published a book in which she says that parents are not nearly so important in a child's development as our society seems to think. She maintains that, very early, children respond more to their peer groups than we have given credit for. The peer group, after all, is the world they must cope with, grow up with, and live the rest of their lives in. Small wonder that children are so strongly influenced by their peers. They do not have to live in their parents' world. Indeed, that would be a handicap. When I asked Erin if she thought it was true that the peer group was more important than family, she said, "Well, of course, Dad!"

---

* *Editor's note: Art, along with a few other prominent humanistic psychotherapists, was invited by David Cain to write a commentary on the field of humanistic psychotherapy for a book he edited with Julius Seeman (2001), *Humanistic Psychotherapies: Handbook of Research and Practice.* David reports that Art wrote an incisive and perceptive commentary. Unfortunately, because of page restrictions imposed by the publisher, the Commentaries section of the book had to be deleted. However, David did present some of Art's most seminal contributions in his introductory chapter reviewing the basic concepts, history, and evolution of humanistic psychotherapies (pp. 36-38). David wishes to note that he considers Art to be one of the under-appreciated giants in the fields of humanistic psychology, education, and psychotherapy. David reviewed Art's last book, *Being and Becoming,* and expressed his astonishment about the breadth and integration of his knowledge, not to mention Art's clear and engaging writing style (personal communication, September 1, 2005).

Thinking about that has given me a new perception of adolescence and an awareness of two matters:

1. How society has come to blame parents for so much that goes wrong and how many parents have bought that notion and live in guilt about being unable to communicate with, guide, or protect their children in the ways they are "supposed to." How many guilt-ridden parents I have seen in therapy!
2. If the peer group is so important, what a terrible job our society does in helping youth grow and mature. How little we do to provide places, facilities for youth to explore healthy ways of relating to each other and their own feelings, values, etc., and how little we do to facilitate the processes of developing satisfying relationships, a positive self-concept, a sense of oneness, or personal responsibility. Most of the things this society does for young people are designed to control them or channel their activities, rather than help them find themselves and work out more meaningful and uplifting relationships. Efforts are made to manipulate them because the process of self-discovery is so mistrusted.

9/3/98

When Susan and I first moved to Greeley, we lived on 15th Avenue just up the street from the Clutes, with whom we became very good friends. A year or so before we moved from there, the Clutes divorced and a year or so later Bonny Clute remarried and we rarely saw each other for a number of years. About four years ago, Bonny divorced her second husband, an abusive individual. Her son, Shannon, called and asked if I would go see his mother in the midst of her distress. I did so and began a delightful friendship that still continues. Bonny is a beautiful, sensitive, caring woman with a charming sense of humor. She is a marvelous second grade teacher and we have much in common to talk about. We have enjoyed each other's company, attending plays, concerts, the Greeley Philharmonic orchestra. One year we went to the opera series in Denver. We have also enjoyed trips to the mountains and to see the Ushers when they have been at their cabin.

About a year ago I realized I had fallen in love with her but also realized that the difference in our ages (28 years), along with my increasing signs of aging, made it unlikely we could ever be more than friends. Then, at my birthday bash in 1997, Bonny met Roy Wardell, my good friend the rancher from our men's group. They have been seeing a lot of each other lately and I have told each of them, "I love you and I think it would be great if you found happiness in one another." I am quite sincere in that wish but find it ironic to see Roy and Bonny engaged in intimacies I long for myself. What a twist of fate!

9/24/98

For some time I have been getting very short of breath when I exert myself bending over or climbing stairs. I went to see Tom Flower about it and he did a lot of blood work—no problems. Then he suggested an echocardiogram, which I had last Friday. I have today heard from Tom to add new medications to my current list because I apparently have a left ventricle that is not operating strongly. I have also made an appointment to see the cardiologist, a week from today! What an example of the medical profession's focus on the disease rather than the patient. For patients having their hearts checked, the period of not knowing what may be wrong is an anxious time. To be unable to get a conference with the cardiologist for two weeks is outrageous. The thought of taking two more medications disgusts me. I hate medications and I now have to take one for thyroid, one for thinning my blood, one to ease the strain on my left ventricle, and a diuretic. I hate it, but I guess there is nothing I can do about it.

This latest news makes me feel a bit uneasy. I am scheduled to go to California a week from Sunday for the think-tank at Idyllwild, then from there to Charleston, South Carolina for an appearance at a conference on conflict resolution and time for another "Art Combs Get-together." Nine days is a bit of a stretch. Hope things go well.

Finally got to see the cardiologist and it seems I have congestive heart failure, formerly known as dropsy, I understand. Apparently my heart is operating at only 30% efficiency. More medications!

I am having a great time with the advanced seminar I am teaching at UNC. Ten wonderful doctoral students, mostly from Educational Psychology. We are exploring *Being and Becoming* and asking, "If these ideas are true, what does that mean for me personally, professionally, and generally?" The group has coalesced into a truly responsive and exciting discussion each time we meet. What a thrill when teaching goes so well!

10/7/98

Took off on Sunday for Idyllwild. This area of California is terribly dry country and my psoriasis is in an uproar. In addition, I have to take things very slowly, as I get out of breath in a hurry. On Monday I made my appearance at the think-tank and for the first time in thirty years the audience responded with a standing ovation. Lovely feeling! After the speech I felt so exhausted, however, I had to leave the discussions and go to bed. Didn't get to sleep till 5 a.m. and got up feeling so rocky I decided I had better go home. So I canceled the rest of my trip and went back to Greeley. Tom Flower now tells me that in addition to my heart problem, I have the beginnings of pneumonia! More goddamn medications! All this gives me pause. I feel frustrated, angry, anxious.

On top of my physical woes, and in large part to deal with them, I found another condo up the street that is all on one level and placed a bid on it, which has been accepted. So now I have to arrange to move very shortly! I could use a little less excitement! Erin is very unhappy these days because Susan and Anne have bought a condo in Denver and are in the process of packing to move as soon as Susan can sell her house here. Erin feels betrayed because Susan had promised her she would not move to Denver until Erin was off to college. Now I am facing Erin with the necessity to move into my new place; a hard time for her. She seems to be taking it well, however.

10/17/98

Have further information about my condition today. It seems I may not have had pneumonia after all. Apparently the faulty left ventricle is not only reducing blood flow to my body, hence the frequent weariness. Instead of efficiently pulling blood from my lungs to pump around my body, it is actually pushing some blood back into the lungs so that X-rays show increasing fluid there. All this means to me that my days are numbered and my condition will get increasingly worse. The only escape from this prognosis is a heart transplant, a procedure I would never accept at my age. At first, all this was crushing to me. The thoughts of having to limit my activity and the dozens of additional things I can no longer do have been difficult to deal with. After leading an active life for so long, it is hard to accept that my body is letting me down. It especially worries me that I cannot get any kind of exercise and that is not good. Anyhow, I am over my initial despair and ready to concede all this and move on.

Here is where I am at this point. It is crucial that I maintain a home for Erin until she goes off to college. That is extremely important to me, probably more important than anything else. On the other hand, I do not want to suffer the indignities of hospitalization and the horror of existence with tubes running out of me in all directions. If I am going to deteriorate, I want to keep active as long as possible. So I have decided that I will do all I can to hang on until July 1 or so, then end my life on my terms. This will give Erin time to do some adjusting before leaving for college wherever she goes. This decision does not upset me. I find it straightforward, and in line with my beliefs. It maintains my integrity. The primary fear I have at this point is that hospitalization might cut me off from the means of accomplishing my goal. That would be horrid.

In the midst of all this, I have been deeply moved by the reactions of students and faculty to the news of my dilemma. My class on Wednesday was an outpouring of love and caring. That class amazes me. The 10 students have bonded with me and each other in a fashion I have not seen before. They have taken the book and each other to heart in all kinds of ways and every student is applying the thinking to his or her own life in directions that are truly therapeutic and growth-inducing—a beautiful thing to behold. Thank God the room is so small I can honestly say to folks who would like to come in and observe, "Sorry, we have only enough chairs for the class." It's just as well. I am afraid most faculty people would think what is going on in there is reprehensible and unscholarly. Yet these students are growing like mad and grasping the subject matter and applying it all over the place, even to their relationships with other faculty. What a group. I am scheduled to teach another course next semester, probably my last ever. I hope I make it through.

See you later. An interesting time with much to be experienced and thought about. Thank God my mind seems to be holding up well.

Little by little, it becomes clear to me that the sciences are going to have a hard time making the conversion to a paradigm that gives priority to organizations and relationships. I suspect they will fall into the trap that cognitive psychology has: namely, to hang on to the attempt to explain all things in terms of matter and mathematics. Fascinating idea.

11/23/98

I've been two weeks in my new home. Susan is moving to Denver today. Lynn is working two jobs until it's time for her to go back to Columbia. The house is comfortable and looks nice. I am still adapting to the requirements of my latest life style: taking it easy, getting plenty of rest, and trying to find ways to keep my body in shape without strenuous effort. Have been doing some tai chi as part of my daily regimen for some years and will now explore how to do more of that. As I adapt, I am finding somewhat more energy once again, but a far cry from what once was. This is my first time at the computer in a month and I seem to have lost a large dollop of my passion. I can easily just sit placidly and let time pass. I have no burning desire to write and I have started going to bed early and reading. I can easily sleep for ten or twelve hours if I let myself. Getting out of bed takes time and the days seem to pass by very quickly. I am in good spirits, however.

The men's group asked if I was afraid and I could honestly say, "Not at all." I fear only being trapped in a hospital, unable to care for myself, and I am very grateful that my mind is still functioning well.

Had the ultimate compliment this week. Erin is taking psychology at the lab school and her teacher asked if I would come to speak to the class. Erin felt two ways about my doing so: hoping I would do well and fearing that maybe I wouldn't. I enjoyed the experience. The kids responded favorably. Later Erin reported, "The kids liked you. They said they could listen to you all day. Remember the girl who sat next to you? She said you smelled nice!" Rarely have I had such enthusiastic response!

My graduate class at UNC continues to delight and amaze me. Most of those in the class are grad students in ed psych. Most of their previous experience has been strictly in academia. They have taken to the field view with verve and enthusiasm I can hardly believe. Until now, with trust and openness they have explored primarily what these ideas mean to them as individuals. Last week, they decided it was time they examined what this viewpoint means for the teaching of educational psychology and considered the possibility of writing a text for teacher education based on field theory instead of cognition and behaviorism!

One exceptionally bright member of the class asked me to serve on his doctoral committee and I agreed to do so. He is desperately trying to integrate field theory with his head full of objective, descriptive, philosophical, cognitive, etc., thinking. His struggle is almost painful to watch. His department is just beginning to recognize qualitative approaches to research and he is also contending with that. When I read his doctoral oral exam, I decided I had to beg off evaluating him. He is so entrenched in the academic approach that I could not even grasp what he was talking about half the time. It has been so long since I have had to deal with the traditional academic approach to psychology that it seems to me like a foreign language that I do not understand. [This student] is way beyond my level of comprehension and understanding and I am so out of touch with the academic life style that I met him today at lunch and withdrew from evaluation of his exam—not because of his incompetence, but mine. A new switch when the professor rates himself as incompetent rather than the student!

We had a good discussion and he still wants me to serve on his dissertation committee because he wants to do a study using a field approach. He reminds me so much of myself back in the late forties, torn between the traditional behavioristic psychology and my new awareness of field theory. I am also surprised at how far behind I have fallen from the behavioristic approach I once was so fluent in. It's like I used to teach chemistry when I was a high school teacher, but today's chemistry is so far advanced and so different it is almost incomprehensible to me now. I feel like that about traditional psychology and am amazed that it continues to be in the driver's seat.

Several months ago I wrote an article that I sent to the *American Psychologist:* a letter to the editor calling attention to the parallel paradigm shifts in science generally and in psychology particularly. I proposed a series of debates and symposia to explore the implications of such shifts in thinking. Today I get my rejection from two reviewers. One slapped down the whole notion in five lines; the other wrote five pages on why such ideas would be neither scholarly nor helpful! I begin to wonder: Am I a nut and a crackpot? Then I recall how counseling, education, and applied psychologists are increasingly finding perceptual-experiential thinking useful and am reassured.

Am reading a fascinating novel, *The story of B,* by Daniel Quinn [1996]. Quinn talks of a new vision and our culture's inability to understand or implement it because of its preoccupation with "programs." According to Quinn, if it's possible to save the world, this will only occur when people change their individual minds in some way(s) [pp. 48, 91, 155, 243]. When their minds change, individuals view the world with "new vision" and this in turn "propagates itself" [p. 155]. Sounds like my description of the difference between understanding the essence or the form. There are signs of movement in the world, but humanistic, perceptual, experiential thinking is treated like science fiction without relevance to the REAL world.

Heart-Warmers

Excerpts from cards, letters, and notes that Art preserved in a file bearing this title.

MARCH, 1996, *excerpted from student evaluations in PSY 331, Psychological Services, West Georgia College (now University of West Georgia)—after Art guest-lectured in the class*

. . .I enjoyed Dr. Combs's thoughtful discussion on helping relationships. . . . Because I sensed in him such a generous spirit, this led me to seek out his published works which I have enjoyed immensely and feel will be of more lasting benefit.

I . . . found what Art Combs said is something that I will want to keep with me for a very long time. I like his practicality in explaining his thoughts to us. What I mean is that he seemed to get down to the nitty-gritty about what he thought was a good way to help people, and he told it to us in order to help us. And maybe by helping us, we could learn how to be better helpers for other people. When he said that what we believe about people in general is how we will treat people in general, I saw truth in that. . . . More specifically, if you believe people have enormous capabilities, and are basically trustworthy, then they will be this way to you. On the other hand, if you believe the opposite, then it will seem this way to you also. I could not see myself helping too many people if I did not believe that people are basically good and trustworthy and friendly and worthy and capable. . . . Almost everything he said made sense to me. . . . I want to be the kind of helper that he has found to be a good kind of helper.

One of the most meaningful and significant speakers we had this quarter was Dr. Arthur W. Combs. One of the things that I liked or thought was interesting about him was his age. With his age, comes so much experience in the field of psychology. He had his Ph.D. before my father was even born. I thought this was interesting. I found myself wondering how much things have changed in the last fifty years of psychology. He has so much experience in this field. The most important thing he talked about to me was the line between good and bad helpers. . . . he said that it wasn't so much based on one's knowledge or methods, but rather on one's beliefs. . . . I learned how to be a good helper and that's meaningful to me and my work.

(Carrollton, GA)

APRIL, 1996

This is the last letter required as part of . . . this course. I have decided to write my last reaction on this class, Theories of Personality.

In my entire academic career I have not taken a class that has challenged my reasoning skills, my ability to synthesize information, my ability to formulate and analyze concepts, or question in depth my beliefs, origin, and self to the extent I have in your class. . . .

When I was first given the assignment to develop my own theory I toyed with the idea of playing it safe. I even thought about writing a generic one just using the theories of others and the comments made by those in my group. Then slowly it developed into a moral issue. How could I create a theory without developing it on the very basis of my existence? I struggled with my conscience and decided to make it my own, a theory from my soul. . . .

What I have learned in your class will be part of my life forever. (Greeley, CO)

APRIL, 1996

I wanted to tell you how much I enjoyed your class. This has been a learning experience unlike any other for me because this class has been an opportunity to become more self-aware concerning my beliefs about people. I feel I don't learn as much in classes that require rote memorization of material in order for it to be regurgitated back out on a test. I need practical application in order to learn. That is why I enjoyed writing my personal theory of personality. As I would write I would actually *feel;* if what I was writing fit. Sometimes I would start writing something that I thought I believed only to find myself questioning those beliefs. Writing my personal theory of personality made me do some deep thinking. (Greeley, CO)

OCTOBER, 1996

I want to thank you so very much for sharing at our Leadership Inquiry class last week. It became quite evident to myself and the individuals in the class that we were in the presence of a master with great wisdom. Your sharing left me hopeful for the future in education, . . . At the end of each class period, I have the students write a reflection of the class. I am sending you a copy of the reflections, as I'm sure you will enjoy reading them. They give tribute to the warm, articulate, authentic person that you are. . . . It was a delight to meet you, listen to you, and interact with you. Thank you for giving of yourself to us.

> I have not felt as inspired and hopeful about the future since Maya Angelou spoke at UNC a year ago. . . . I have to remind myself that my role is only a catalyst, to share knowledge, and it is not my responsibility for the outcome, to try and control it and make it "right" which is only my point of view, and not allowing choices when the decision is not for me to make, only the individual with whom I have shared knowledge and experience. I would love to have a videotape of him.

> The time listening to Art Combs was fascinating. . . . I especially liked his statement "When people are free they find their own best way." . . . we need people like Art Combs to guide and share their knowledge with educators.

> First, I have to tell you that I have admired Dr. Combs' work for over 20 years. While I was getting my master's degree in special education, his book [on the helping professions] was one of the required readings in my favorite class. . . . During that class I bought a tape that had a recording of Dr. Combs discussing his book before a large audience. I listened to that tape many times, included

quotes from his book in my thesis, and loaned the tape to many colleagues.

When I read that Dr. Combs was going to speak in our class, I was amazed. "THE" Dr. Combs right here in one of my classes? Speaking to us? Amazing!!!!!

During his presentation last night, I kept hearing him refer to information on the tape I used to own, and recalling his words from reading "Helping Professions. . . . I'm sure Combs must have thought I was stoned on some drug, because about all I could do was listen and smile. . . .

He had "it" then and he still has "it." In fact, as all great masters in all fields do as they mature in their area of expertise, Dr. Combs has taken his beliefs about people (and schools) to the next level—the spiritual level.

It was, and is, an honor to have been in Dr. Combs' presence, listened to him in person and even have him respond to questions from our class. It was exactly like being in the presence of a master martial artist, an enlightened young child or an awakened spiritual leader. . . .

85 years old—WOW—if I could be as bright, articulate, and informed as Art—bring on 55!

I am amazed at the energy and dedication that Dr. Combs has and has had in his 85 years. . . . "Any good thing you do [is not in vain and] will benefit the students." A good phrase to keep in mind as we head into the future.

Art Combs was profound. . . . His points about shifting educational reform and administrative activities from a "controlling forces" to "motivating people" orientation are especially poignant in our current time. My question is, how do we get this argument out in front of all the people—legislators, school boards, business people, parents—who are pushing the "controlling forces" bandwagons (DBE, SBE, back to basics, etc.)? They are the ones who are not being adequately challenged with the logic of Art Combs. . . . Art Combs exudes an interesting persona—quiet, warm, wise, and caring. It was a privilege & pleasure to listen and interact. (Greeley, CO)

OCTOBER, 1996

It was so wonderful being with you and our University of Florida colleagues for the retreat at Big Canoe. What an extraordinary legacy you continue to give us all. You have been an inspiration, a mentor, a colleague and a friend. We all hold you in the highest esteem for your professional accomplishments and we love you for what you have meant in our personal lives.

How wonderful to have an opportunity to thank you in person for the profound influence you have been in our lives. (Kennesaw, GA)

UNDATED LETTER FROM A CLIENT (1990s)

I appear to be changing in all types of ways. I don't do many of the things I [used] to do that caused me distress. Of the behaviors I still have that do cause me distress, I no longer seem to equate them to an evil me.

I am grateful today that my life is more open. I love at a deeper level and I can even allow myself to feel. It's strange, but the feelings I've run from all my life were not as bad as I thought. I'm finding that I can feel them when they come up. I've realized that I've been running from childhood feelings in an adult body. It seems that my limitations at this point are self-imposed. My beliefs concerning the core of my being leave me constricted and shut down. I feel like the old feelings I ran from in childhood are gigantic, and they are. Any child being rejected or told that he was no good would fear for his very life. That is what I did; I feared for my life. The problem in this lies in that I never gave up that belief. Now any time rejection, or what appears to be rejection, occurs in any way I fear for my life. I cling, push, and control. Just last night I tried to manipulate someone to get my own way. Luckily the person I was trying to manipulate told me that she felt manipulated. I felt horrible inside and I said, "Yes that is what I am doing." I should have felt wonderful for having caught myself and redirecting, instead I feared rejection for being caught as the manipulator.

I am a bit more relaxed today. I know it took me 36 years to dig myself in this deep. . . . Slowly the walls are coming down and I'm coming up for air. There is a long road of reconstruction ahead. [But this] emergence to a new, true self feels wonderful. . . . I thought emergence would kill me. Instead it has given me more life and vitality. . . . I've been in a lot of different therapies. All of them have treated the symptoms and I made lists of what to do. Now it really doesn't seem like I'm doing anything. Instead of me forcing myself to give up a bad habit, I more than ever want to give it up. The habit no longer seems to serve me.

I know I did some of the work, but I feel I owe this to you. You allow me to practice on getting close. You allow me to open up. I feel like I am worthy. These are things that are changing in my life. I am closer to people now. I have more warmth and care. I love. Thank you for this opportunity. (No known address.)

References

Becker, E. (1973). *The denial of death.* New York: The Free Press.

Chopra, D. (2004). *The book of secrets. Unlocking the hidden dimensions of your life.* New York: Harmony Books.

Harris, J. R. (1998). *The nurture assumption: Why children turn out the way they do.* New York: Simon and Schuster.

Quinn, D. (1996). *The story of B: An adventure of the mind and spirit.* New York: Bantam Books.

Meier, D. (1995). *The power of their ideas: Lessons for America from a small school in Harlem.* Boston: Beacon Press.

Richards, A. C. (1997). Metapsychology: Revisiting the past, confronting the present, serving the future. *New Ideas in Psychology, 15*(1), 17-33.

Rogers, C. R. (1972). *On becoming partners. Marriage and its alternatives*. New York: Dell.

Toynbee, A. J. (1957). *A study of history*. Two volume abridgment by D.C. Somervell. New York: Oxford University Press.

Wheatley, M. J. (1994). *Leadership and the new science: Learning about organization from an orderly universe*. San Francisco: Berrett-Koehler.

Wheatley, M. J., & Kellner-Rogers, M. (1996). *A simpler way*. San Francisco: Berrett-Koehler.

Arthur W. Combs, Gainesville, FL (February, 1999)

CHAPTER THIRTEEN

Counting the Days . . .

12/20/98

Anyhow—Wednesday I went to see Tom Flower and we talked some more about my heart condition and I left feeling quite good about holding the line. Then, that night I suddenly passed out while getting ready for bed. No warning and no after effects. I simply came to on the floor. I think the whole episode only lasted a few minutes. Next day, I talked about the experience in our men's group meeting. In the ensuing discussion I shared my desire to make it to July 1 so I could maintain a home for Erin until she is off to college. She has been accepted at the University of Washington, her first choice. Next day Tom scheduled me for a CAT scan, blood work, and a 24-hour Holter monitor. The CAT scan and blood work are all clear—no change. I may have to repeat the monitor because three of the patches came loose. My passing out has got everyone worried, including me, but for different reasons. Tom offered to talk with Lynn, Erin, and me on Saturday morning and the girls agreed.

Tom was wonderful at our Saturday morning meeting. He brought his charts and reviewed my status from the beginning to date. He made clear that this is irreversible and will get worse (how fast we don't know). I made it clear that I am accepting the facts, am increasingly unhappy with the shrinkage imposed on my life style, and reserve the right to end my life on my terms. Both girls accepted the information, sadly but very well. Tom indicated that my end would probably not be painful; at some time my heart would just give up. We talked about insuring that my desires will be met, reviewed my living will, and Tom gave me several hospital forms that would block CPR or other heroic measures: one to keep on the refrigerator and the other to carry with me.

Major concern at this point: Am I likely to begin blacking out or is the one episode I had a fluke or anomaly brought on by other factors? If I have to stop driving, that will be a hard thing. Lynn is now working in the governor's office in Denver and Erin is still in school. We talked some about my getting help during the day if that becomes necessary. Meantime, I am planning to go see Peter and Nancy on Saturday. The girls will be with me Christmas Eve and go to Susan's on Christmas day. Lynn will come back to have dinner with me and will take me to the airport the next day. I want very much to make this trip and another in February, when I would like to visit the Richards, Carol, Hannelore, and Shirley in Gainesville and Bob Blume in Flagler Beach. It is a little scary but if I pass out on the trips—so be it. To be painlessly cut down in the midst of an active life seems a very attractive way to go.

1/3/99

Had a good trip to Atlanta. Peter and Nancy were each coming down with colds so we stayed around home the whole time. I had no more blackouts, took long naps, and slept late. Coming home, I got through the airports okay, taking it very slowly. Bonny and Roy met me at the airport and drove me home. My energy level continues to drop. Yesterday while changing the sheets on my bed, I had to stop and lie down for a bit. Went out to lunch and a movie with Bonny to see *Patch Adams*—a great flick that should be seen by every medic! Coming out of the theater into the cold and riding home, Bonny was so caring that I lost it. Felt good and sorry for myself for a half mile or so, so choked up I couldn't talk. Erin was home and, bless her heart, listened to her dad with sympathy, love, and caring. Today went to the store and had to move very slowly. Lynn unloaded the car for me and pointed out that my hands were blue. Guess I'd better go back to see Tom tomorrow. I need to decide whether I can really make the February trip.

Have been reading three more books in the same theme as *The Story of B* above—Burke and Ornstein's [1997] *The Axemaker's Gift* and Daniel Quinn's [1992, 1997] *Ishmael* and *My Ishmael*. All make the same case that we are heading for catastrophe in our reliance upon the two-edged sword of technology. We love what technology brings us in the way of satisfactions and power over the world but fail to recognize or cope with the subtle changes it brings about in our world, including increases in population and interdependence that make us vulnerable to catastrophic collapse. A hard lesson! All this gives corroboration to my proposals in *The Silent Revolution*.

1/13/99

Lynn is off to college so now there is just Erin and me. Erin is very busy with her usual social life and has begun an internship in theater at UNC, which will keep her at rehearsals nights for the next month.

No change in my physical condition. Still get short of breath and have to move slowly and avoid exertion. Have taken to counting down the days to

July—my current target date—167 today. Each day seems like a minor triumph. I do not count on being around after that and the thought of suicide is not at all scary. Rather a date to look forward to. This may sound morbid to others but not to me. I do not feel at all depressed, only a sense of anticipation. Have lost my passion to write. By the time I dress, meditate, exercise, read the day's paper, check the computer, lunch, nap, visit the bank, go to the store or run errands, etc., the day just seems to melt away.

Met with Susan on Sunday and arranged to have her take over some of the financial matters for the girls. A good meeting.

Had lunch with Karen McGill, one of the students I had last semester, about the possibility of a volume of my best speeches and papers on education. I offered the possibility to ASCD but they turned it down because their readers "need more practical stuff"! Karen is about to complete her dissertation, has lots of experience in the classroom. She is beginning to grasp field theory pretty well and is a thoroughly lovely person. Hope she can handle it. If not, that is okay too.

The books I have been reading for the past month are simply fascinating as they trace our growth from tribal times to the things-oriented, manipulation-of-forces culture we now represent. I am especially struck by the corroboration it gives to my own thinking about the effects of culture upon the individual and where we seem to be going. I have been developing these notions for many years now, but only recently has the whole picture become so sharply in focus for me. *The Silent Revolution* manuscript deserves to be published. Unfortunately, it needs further work in the light of my current thinking, but I do not have the stomach to tackle the task. When I would urge Don Snygg years ago to write up an idea he told me about, he would reply, "No, Art. I need to solve these problems for my own sake. Others will come to them in time." I remember I used to think, "What a pity," but, I confess, now I am beginning to feel the same way. I don't need to push it out there. It is coming inevitably and who says it publicly is not important. Fascinating times and engaging new thinking are all around us. It's good to have been part of it, perhaps even to have kicked its tires or smoothed the way. When the time is ripe similar ideas occur to persons in widely separate places. I'm glad I helped. It's time now for a new generation.

2/3/99

For several weeks I have been feeling really bad—no energy, no feeling of being with it, hard to work up interest in anything. Went to see my cardiologist, then to see Tom for his report on Tuesday. It turns out I have been missing one of my medications (ugh). Having straightened that matter out, feel much better today. They are talking about putting me on a new drug when I get back from my Florida trip but hesitate to do it now because it has a bunch of side effects as one goes into it. I'm still counting the days to the neighborhood of July 1 as decision date. Down to 143 as of today. Last week I would have been happy to go immediately. I have now made further arrangements for an alternative way to go, but am content to wait until July. I still don't feel depressed, just accepting the way things are.

I am looking forward to my trip to Atlanta and Florida next week. It will be good to see so many of my friends once more, and may be the last time. I have decided to use a wheelchair through the airports to make sure of connections and to cut the strain on my ticker. My class at UNC is underway. Five good students. Am looking forward to the next session. The first two were pretty hard to get through. I'm hoping my current feeling of being more with it will continue from here on. When this semester is over, I will tell the university folks I'm through teaching for good.

2/21/99

Back from my trip to Atlanta, UWG [University of West Georgia] and Gainesville. Had some doubts when I set off about how well I would do. But I did fine. It was good to see Peter, Nancy, Jonathan [Buford] and my new great-granddaughter, Sierra; then on to Carrollton for two days with the Richards and the drive to Gainesville. Quite a crew at Shirley Avila's beautiful new home: Bob Blume, Walt Busby, Franz Epting, Hal Lewis, the Richards, the Ushers, Hannelore Wass. One day we went to see the manatees at Manatee Springs, then to dinner on the dock at Cedar Key. After that, two days with Carol and Russ [Topping].* I made it just fine and enjoyed myself much seeing these people probably for the last time. A new experience coming through the airports in a wheelchair (my self-concept slips another notch!). Before I went, I had a feeling this was kind of a farewell round-up, but in the process felt very good and relaxed. Looking back, it probably was a farewell, but that's all right too.

I find myself thinking often of suicide, not as something to be feared but as a matter to be embraced when the time is ripe. I feel like the star athlete who quits playing at the top of his form instead of sinking into a pitiful retirement. I certainly do not feel at the top of my form, far from it, but I am

* Editor's note: The second husband of Art's daughter Carol.

Arthur W. Combs, Anne Richards, Franz Epting, and Bob Blume Gainesville, Florida (February, 1999)

active and productive and have not yet slipped into embarrassments. I am still counting the days—126 today. For now, I look forward to it.

Franz Epting, David Cain, and Anne Richards have provided marketing comments for my new book, *Being and Becoming,* and I have sent them on to Springer Publishing. I am surprised and pleased with the whole-hearted, enthusiastic support they have given and only hope the work deserves it. I have a feeling the book will create little stir. I wanted it in paperback but the publishers want to see it succeed in hardback before committing to further printings. They want to make money. I want to see the broadest possible distribution. Not the first time I have been out of step with the current culture. Bob Blume is certain the message of *The Silent Revolution* needs to be published and I have given him the discs to see what he can do with them. I'd like to see it revised and published but I do not have the stomach for it. Maybe now that I am back and my income tax data is ready for the accountant, I will get back to writing some short pieces.

I feel so sorry for Dave Gonzalez and Sherri. Their baby girl was born just before I left for my saga. While I was gone, they discovered she has cystic fibrosis. Dave is quite sure they can find ways to control it but Sherri is devastated. If ever there was a couple more devoted to raising children and so completely absorbed in the process!! What a tragedy and what pain for these two wonderful people.

Bare the heart*:

I was surprised to get your package with a good start toward redoing *The Silent Revolution*. I did not realize how truly committed to the project you seem to be. I feel a need to let you know more precisely where I am these days.

First about my Florida trip. For some time I have been unhappy with the quality to which my life has sunk. So about six months ago I decided to set a date, to quit "while I was ahead" and set an approximate time for suicide. I began collecting what I might need, setting an approximate date, and taking steps to put my affairs in order. Part of that plan was to see, one more time, the people I love and who love me who don't live in Greeley. Hence my plan to visit my son and family in Atlanta, the Richards in Carrollton and my friends in Florida; namely, you, Walt, Shirley, Hannelore, and my daughter Carol. When I mentioned this projected trip, imagine my surprise and delight to find Hal Lewis might join the group and the Ushers would drive down from Nashville. Mirabile Dictu! They would all be included! And what a delight it was! I felt better than I have in months in close touch with people I love. No one knew or discussed (at least not with me) that this was a final farewell. But I knew and look back on it now as a glorious, heart-warming, fulfilling experience.

Now that I am back home, my condition continues to deteriorate and my doctors are trying new medications. Even with their help the quality of my life is in real jeopardy and I recognize that is not likely to change. I originally set a time after Erin's graduation and before she sets off to college. Lately, however, she and I have had some loving conversations in which she has become aware of the depths of my feelings and accepting of the possibility of my demise. I am deeply moved by her love and acceptance and also feel free to move up the date if I so desire. I have not done so but appreciate the option. I am not depressed by all this. I believe I am accepting the facts and getting along with my life as best I can under its new and increasing restrictions. I am not afraid of dying; instead it seems increasingly desirable.

3/12/99

Well, I am learning that deciding to take one's life is no simple matter. One would think one had a right to do what he pleased with his carcass, but I am finding it is a very involved process. First I thought I would go out in the garage when the spirit moved me and simply turn on the engine and go to sleep. But my house and garage are attached to another and it was pointed out to me that I could possibly take someone with me. So I turn to the use of

*Editor's note: In a letter dated 2-24-99, Art wrote this to Bob Blume as part of a longer letter that included his plans for *The Silent Revolution* manuscript, and asked him to send copies of it to the Richards, the Ushers, Walt Busby, Shirley Avila, and Hannelore Wass.

something I can take. Best bet there is potassium cyanide (what the spies use), but I can find no source for this. Next possibility is some form of sleeping pills, but no doctor will prescribe them. Then I discover that the digitalis I am taking is a powerful heart stimulant and will do the trick in doses three or four times normal prescription, so I have managed to accumulate that (I hope it proves enough). Next—go to motel, elsewhere?

So I make plans to go to a motel after Erin gets home from spring break in Cancun and Lynn arrives for her spring break from UMO, Sunday the 21st. Then things get complicated. When I tell Peter about this, we decide he ought to come and spend a day or two getting acquainted with what he will need to know about as executor of my will.

Editor's note: Art wrote nothing further in his autobiography after the above entry. Nine days later, he brought his life to an end.

Heart-Warmers

Excerpts from cards, letters, and notes that Art preserved in a file bearing this title.

UNDATED CARD FROM CLIENT

I used to fear that I would never "get things together" but I feel I have. I am happier than I have been in many years. You've made a big difference in my life, dear Dr. Combs, and I thank you. (No known address)

UNDATED, FROM STUDENT

I just want to thank you again for your support and the beautiful gesture of friendship.

When you walked in my defense a sense of security in my own inner strength was more realized—only because you validated me. You have that kind of people-power, Art. (Greeley, CO)

UNDATED

Third Zen Story. For Art—Whose Voice is Like Bankei's.

After Bankei had passed away, a blind man who lived near the master's temple told a friend: "Since I am blind, I cannot watch a person's face, so I must judge his character by the sound of his voice. Ordinarily when I hear someone congratulate another upon his happiness or success, I also hear a secret tone of envy. When condolence is expressed for the misfortune of another, I hear pleasure and satisfaction, as if the one condoling was really glad there was something left to gain in his world.

"In all my experience, however, Bankei's voice was always sincere. Whenever he expressed happiness, I heard nothing but happiness, and whenever he expressed sorrow, sorrow was all I heard." (No known address)

DECEMBER, 1998

I'm profoundly grateful that our paths crossed in this century. My personal and professional development have been enhanced beyond measure as a result of our meeting . . . and I'm just one among *thousands* who feel similarly. The world is definitely a better place, in various corners, as a consequence of your myriad contributions.

I'm pleased you are aware of the positive and significant impact you've had on so many as you come to terms with present and future life challenges. Didn't want the new year to begin, though, without reminding you of how much your existence and well-being are celebrated in *our* midst! (Carrollton, GA)

References

Burke, J., & Ornstein, R. (1997). *The axemaker's gift: Technology's capture and control of our minds and culture*. New York: Jeremy P. Tarcher/Putnam Books.

Quinn, D. (1992). *Ishmael: An adventure of the mind and spirit*. New York: Bantam/Turner.

Quinn, D. (1997). *My Ishmael*. New York: Bantam Books.

Photo by John Cleare

CHAPTER FOURTEEN

Epilogue

> Human life *is* a struggle—against frustration, ignorance, suffering, evil, the maddening inertia of things in general; but it is also a struggle *for* something, and for something which our experience tells us can be achieved in some measure, even if we personally find ourselves debarred from any measure that seems just or reasonable.
>
> JULIAN HUXLEY (1953, p. 162)

As he explained at the outset of Chapter 12, Art ceased writing Recapitulation sections for this autobiography around 1996, expecting persons who knew him well to draft these after his death. In June of 1998, he wrote me a letter discussing arrangements he was making on various fronts (e.g., travel plans, presentation ideas, plans to provide funds for the Field Psych Trust he was setting up) and informed me that he had discontinued writing Recapitulation sections. He thanked me for all I had done in editing other work of his, mentioned me among those who might take up the task of this sort of recapitulation, and added: "No one knows me and my work so well or is in a better position to interpret it." Despite this vote of confidence—or perhaps because of it—preparing this Epilogue has proven to be a daunting, difficult, and downright intimidating task for me at times. In part, I wasn't sure I was up to the task of clarifying for others how Art experienced everyday life in his latter years. We had visited together on several occasions, written one another fairly regularly, shared ideas and exchanged telephone calls, and collaborated on professional projects, but I wasn't living in close proximity to him. This left me feeling quite uneasy about summarizing his end-of-life path.

In developing this section, I thus immersed myself in an extensive research effort. During a six-year period, I interviewed family members, friends, and colleagues of Art's. I poured through the files, records, and earlier drafts of this manuscript as well as a variety of other documents that Art arranged to have passed on to me or that I was able to locate on my own. I sought out and read the books he mentioned in the text of this manuscript and those I recall his mentioning when we talked in the latter years. I also read books, articles, and dissertations on aging, death, and dying.

Persons reading this autobiography will undoubtedly be drawing their own conclusions as they reflect upon what they have already read and what they are about to read in this chapter and in Chapter 15. Each time I review this material, I discover facets or aspects that could have been further explored. And I expect we will all discover deeper meaning in the content of this volume as years go by. Whether a reader's views differ from or sustain the comments offered here, any insights or responses anyone reading this would like to share with me would be much appreciated. You can forward these to me by mail via the Field Psych Trust, 301 Dixie Street, Carrollton, GA 30117 or by e-mail via arichard@westga.edu.

Recapitulation

In terms of the theoretical frame of reference that made the most sense to Art over the course of his adult life, self-actualization or self-fulfillment is a function of at least four basic characteristics:

1. A positive view of self.
2. Acceptance or openness to experience.
3. Deep feelings of identification.
4. A comprehensive, available, and integrated or internally consistent belief system.

For over half his life—up to and including the moment he died—I believe Art was convinced these factors were central to the possibilities of a person's finding fulfillment in life (and death). These criteria were as fundamental to his professional legacy as they were to his personal understanding of the human condition and they clearly served as a compass for him in his final days. In what follows, I hope to convey the ways in which the meanings of events and life experiences in Art's personal history relate to these factors—at least as I understand these at the present time.

Positive View of Self

Between 1996 and 1999, Art's view of self was continuously under assault in a physical sense, while retaining strength and vitality at its core. During these years, Art contended with hearing problems, underwent cataract surgery that nearly cost him the sight in one eye, and became increasingly frustrated with entrenched psoriasis. As he described it, his physical world was becoming inexorably more narrow and restricted. By July, 1998, he had begun to experience such a loss of energy and shortness of breath at times that he came to understand what very old people feel when they decide to let go of life. Various medications were prescribed for his thyroid, to thin his blood and to ease the strain on his heart, etc. He was diagnosed with congestive heart failure and a faulty left ventricle that increased the amount of fluid in his lungs.

During his visits in Florida and Georgia, Art seemed to regain energy and strength. Upon his return to the higher altitude in Colorado, however, his condition rapidly worsened. He began sleeping more and more. He could no longer walk his routine two miles per day. He experienced marked shortness of breath. Beginning in March, 1999, he was attached to a portable oxygen machine virtually all day long. He had to quit teaching. He found all of these restrictions abhorrent, undignified, and signs that the days he would be capable of living a quality life were behind him.

After leading an active life for nearly 86 years, Art very slowly came to accept that his body was deteriorating—something he felt he could live with (albeit not happily), until he suddenly passed out one night while getting ready for bed. Although he experienced no other such blackouts, he began more and more to define his possibilities for future fulfillment in severely restricted terms due to a lack of basic physical resources. By March of 1999, when it became necessary for him to utilize a portable oxygen machine on a regular basis, he felt an increased sense of urgency to end his life on his own terms while he still had the capacity to control his own destiny. During this same period, however, he continued to view himself positively as a person, parent, friend, and contributing professional.

His positive views of self were reaffirmed many times over during these years, as parent, teacher, psychologist, and public speaker. Despite some vision problems, he continued to read, reflect upon, and be stimulated by new ideas. All of this was very gratifying for him. He experienced his brain and field of meanings as alert and capable of producing fresh and exciting insights. He was celebrated as a person and mentor by colleagues and former students at the gathering in Big Canoe, GA; he felt honored (though a bit unsettled) by efforts to capture some of his professional thinking and contributions on videotape. He was pleased to find publishers for book-length manuscripts he had written, quietly satisfied at being recognized by Division 32 of the American Psychological Association for his contributions to psychology, and moved by a standing ovation from a gathering of educators after a speech he gave in California.

Close friends, colleagues, and family rallied around him as his physical condition deteriorated. Learning about the changes occurring in his physical well-being, and uncertain of how much time they might have left to communicate with him in a lucid state, they began stopping by to provide support, address matters of consequence, keep Art company, and say their goodbyes in the event he suddenly took a turn for the worst.

During the weeks and months leading up to his death, he acknowledged being depressed at times, and found this natural. He especially agonized over the possibility that he might be letting his younger children down somehow by bowing out of their lives too soon. Once he felt assured that they could understand his reasoning for wanting to take his own life at a time of his choosing, he clearly felt positive about his capacity for negotiating this difficult matter.

George and Ann Rader Tate visited Art during the week before his death. They found him red-faced and atypically slow in walking. He was "not the vibrant Art" with whom they were accustomed to spending time. George said Art almost had an apologetic look, or seemed perturbed, over being seen by others in this debilitated condition. He told them he hated to present himself to them in such a state.

"The doctor told me I'm depressed," he said. "And of course I am." He also mentioned that a medical professional wanted to put him on Prozac, but he had refused, considering this inappropriate for a person at his particular stage of life. He explained that death was nothing to be fearful of in his view—that he had had a good life and could "hang it up with no regrets and no need to look back."

He knew he was loved, respected, and appreciated for who he was and honored for his experience and integrity. He was reminded on many occasions of how others appreciated him for honoring *their* experience and integrity. He wanted to experience himself as a person capable of directing the course of his own destiny to the very end, and this he accomplished. No one transformed him into a "thing" or a person incapable of determining the best course for this final chapter and the final choices of his life. In this sense I believe he saw himself in very positive ways at the time his life ended.

The Link between Behavior and Experience

Art spent the largest portion of his professional life seeking to help others grasp the vital relationship between human behavior and experience. Understanding human behavior from the point of view of the behaving person was of utmost importance to him. Time and time again he clarified why it was not enough to look to external, environmental factors, events, or circumstances that might have played a role in shaping behavior if one expected to understand what motivated the person behaving. Rather, to truly understand a person's actions, one had to take an insider's viewpoint, exploring, for example, how that person saw himself or herself, the world in which he or she lived, the challenges or threats to self he or she experienced, and the values that guided his or her choices in living.

Art recognized the importance of such understandings as early as the 1940s when he and Donald Snygg first formulated perceptual theory. A basic postulate of that theory, in its original version and all subsequent presentations of the theory, holds that human beings are motivated by a single need: *to maintain and enhance the self they experience*. Whether on the battlefield, in the depths of despair, or in everyday activities, individuals are "concerned solely with the preservation or enhancement" of their phenomenal or experienced selves.

Each presentation of the theory in book form (from the 1940s to 1999) also addresses the question of how suicide could be understood if such a fundamental need existed. The question seemed to arise naturally from the assertion that maintenance and enhancement of the perceived self was the primary motivating dynamic in life. As Snygg and Combs explained in 1949, persons aren't torn between a need or desire for self-destruction and a desire for self-preservation. In the last theoretical book he completed in the year prior to his death, Art put the matter this way:

> Looking at human behavior from an outsider's point of view, people seem to be motivated by an enormous diversity of needs. . . . Looking at behavior from the person's own viewpoint, . . . apparently diverse goals are quite harmonious. But what about suicide, one might ask. Is that not a denial of the need to maintain and enhance the self? Not at all. We must remind ourselves that the self we wish to maintain is not the physical self but the phenomenal self, the self that is perceived. Many a suicide has destroyed his body in order to avoid damage to the phenomenal self by remaining alive. So persons may take their lives today to avoid what seems like inevitable damage to the self tomorrow. (Combs, 1999, p. 11)

As a teacher of psychology at the college and university level for over thirty years, I had occasion to become acquainted with literature on suicide and suicide prevention. For my college-aged students, suicide was often best understood as "a permanent solution to a temporary problem" (Bolton with Mitchell, 1983, p. 109). It was most often associated with despair, depression, helplessness, hopelessness, isolation, and tunnel vision (an extremely narrow view) regarding one's prospects for ever experiencing success, happiness, or fulfillment in life.

Virtually every one of my students knew someone who had contemplated, attempted, or completed suicide. Many students shared ways in which failures and/or losses associated with the break-up of a relationship (their own or their parents'), abusive treatment on the part of peers, inability to be successful in a chosen career path, or a profound sense of being misunderstood, disrespected, wounded, or damaged in some way(s) as a person led to suicide attempts or to serious consideration of suicide as a means of coping with the overwhelming pain they were experiencing.

Suicide is often disturbing to us because it raises such questions as: Was pain and suffering involved? Was it messy? Did the person die at the wrong time? (Too young? Before fulfilling more of his or her potential?) Could more have been done "to prevent the fatal action, to help the individual through the crisis and on to a life-cherishing course?" (Kastenbaum, 1976, pp. 439–440).

Although suicide has long been recognized as a national problem among our high school and college-aged population, until doing some background reading for the writing of this portion of Art's autobiography I was not aware that suicide among the elderly has emerged in recent years as a significant concern as well, to the point where some even label it as having reached "epidemic" proportions (Bell, 2002; Weinreich, 1997).

A sizeable number of researchers have examined suicide among the elderly (including in more recent years Albright, 1994; Lewis, 1996; Weinreich, 1997; Lindberg, 1998; Bell, 2000; Malphurs, 2001; Brown, 2002), seeking to better understand what has been described as a "serious and rapidly growing public health problem" (Brown, 2002, p. 3), reported to have increased nearly 36% between 1980 and 1997 (Brown, 2002, p. 9). Most of these studies are aimed at identifying risk factors and warning signs so as to better educate the general public and professional colleagues in a position to take a preventive approach to elder suicide.

As important as these efforts may be to many among the elderly, I believe they fall short in addressing the nature and meaning of a death like Art's. For the most part, they fail to explore in any depth internal matters, focusing instead on external factors and circumstances in an individual's life. In so doing, they miss the person in the process. That, of course, would be the last thing Art would want done in his own case.

When he reached the age of 80, literary critic Malcolm Cowley (1980) wrote about growing old and experiences associated with the aging process. He opens his book with the cautionary statement: "To enter the country of age is a new experience, different from what you supposed it to be. Nobody, man or woman, knows the country until he has lived in it and has taken out his citizenship papers" (pp. 2–3). According to Cowley, "[a]s death comes nearer, it becomes less frightening, less a disaster, more an everyday fact to be noted and filed away" (p. 29). Aging, on the other hand, brings with it new fears. One of these, expressed by elderly persons he interviewed, "is that of declining into simplified versions of themselves, of being reduced from the complexity of adult life into a single characteristic. . . . It is frightening to think that one might end as a caricature of oneself" (p. 56). Another fear Cowley found to be sharper and more troubling to many of those with whom he spoke. It is a fear that can lead to suicide. As Cowley (1980) puts it, "Obviously the fear is not of death; it is of becoming helpless. It is the fear of being as dependent as a young child, while not being loved as a child is loved, but merely being kept alive against one's will" (pp. 56–57).

The Right to Die

On the national scene during the latter part of 1998 and the early months of 1999, impeachment proceedings were underway for then-President of the United States Bill Clinton. News stories associated with this process dominated the media. Almost simultaneously, another drama began unfolding that received lesser but notable national coverage. Dr. Jack Kevorkian, retired pathologist, was brought to trial for helping a man (Thomas York) suffering from ALS to die in September, 1998 by direct injection. Although ordered in April of 1997 to cease and desist from such practices, Dr. Kevorkian persisted in his efforts to respond to terminally ill patients who requested his services in order to end their pain and suffering. Kevorkian also recorded his actions on Mr. York's behalf and sent a videotape of the incident to CBS television. This tape aired in November, 1998 on the widely-watched program "60 Minutes." Three days later, the 70-year-old Kevorkian was charged with second-degree murder and use of a controlled substance (a lethal drug). His trial was scheduled for March 22, 1999.

Art was familiar with Kevorkian's work. He was also familiar with the work of the Hemlock Society, an organization in which he held membership for several years.* Derek Humphry's (1982) book, *Let Me Die Before I Wake*, published by the Hemlock Society, was in Art's personal library and he seems

* Editor's note: The Hemlock Society (now known as "Compassion and Choices"), founded in 1980, was able to verify that Art held membership in that organization from 1996–1999. Unfortunately, due to a database crash several years earlier, membership records of the Society prior to 1996 were lost (personal communication, May 30, 2003). Art's daughter Carol, a librarian, recalled his being knowledgeable about Hemlock Society publications as early as 1989 because he asked her if they were available in a Gainesville-area library when a former colleague and friend suffered a stroke.

Beyond the deaths of family members and close friends that preceded his own, Art also had opportunities to begin thinking about end-of-life issues as early as the 1950s, when he served as a lobbyist in the New York State legislature. At the time, the Euthanasia Society in New York was attempting to obtain state legislation to legalize a form of voluntary euthanasia. In addition, in 1971, when Art was still residing in Florida, the case of a Mrs. Carmen Martinez was brought to court by a doctor in Dade County, FL. Mrs. Martinez, afflicted with a fatal disease, was seeking the right to "a peaceful death" rather than having to undergo continued treatment which she described as "a prolonged life of physical pain and mental to have followed the "personal exit" strategies recommended in it and in Humphry's (1991) *Final Exit*. Paperwork found near his body specified the funeral arrangements he had made for himself several weeks in advance. A do-not-resuscitate order that Art had completed in his doctor's office in December of 1998 was also nearby.

In an opening statement describing the "origins and purposes" of his 1982 book, Humphry draws a distinction between persons "who are contemplating suicide because they are unhappy with life, or are suffering from a psychological affliction" and those who choose "the option of rational suicide," also known as "hastened death" or "self-deliverance" in the face of an advanced terminal illness or a serious incurable physical illness. In *Let Me Die Before I Wake*, Humphry (1982) writes that "[t]he only way to be reasonably certain of a good death is to plan it . . . when one is still in good health" (p. 7) and has control over his or her life circumstances. He also underscores the importance of taking decisive action "before becoming absolutely dependent on others" (p. 69) who could be charged with murder for providing assistance or simply couldn't bring themselves to take responsibility for aiding and abetting a loved one's efforts to choose the time and nature of his or her death.

As Art's physical condition deteriorated, more and more of the talks he had with his closest friends and family members revolved around how he felt about death and what might happen to his children, his estate, etc., after he was gone. Authorities on the aging process contend that one of the major tasks associated with responsible self-development and spiritual growth in the elder years is facing the reality of one's mortality and considering how best to prepare for both aging and death (e.g., Schachter-Shalomi & Miller, 1995, p. 113; Jecker, 1990, p. 168). As far as can be determined, Art was doing this mindfully, and, in fact, had been doing so for some time.

The Concept of Preemptive Suicide

Many of us apparently hope for a "quick and easy death," typically one that "comes softly and unexpectedly during sleep" (Kastenbaum, 1976, pp. 430–431). Of course, no one is guaranteed this type of final exit. And even when it does occur, it may actually be traumatic to those surviving us (e.g.,

anguish" (Humphry & Wickett, 1986, pp. 235–236). Judge David Popper ruled that "a person has the right to die in dignity" and that the patient in this case should not be "kept alive against her will." Mrs. Martinez was reported to have died comfortably 24 hours after Popper's ruling (Humphry & Wickett, 1986, p. 236).

when conflicts are unresolved, feelings of caring and concern have not been expressed, or the loss of a loved one has not been anticipated at that particular point). If persons arrive at a "ripe old age" and begin to question their prospects for achieving future well-being and a natural "good death," more and more apparently take matters into their own hands.

Kastenbaum envisions a form of suicide that would "not be regarded as crime, weakness, failure, or pathology" (p. 425), one that "strengthens rather than assaults the social fabric" (p. 439). In this type of suicide, "A person who has always valued independence, for example, might be considered [as] . . . taking responsibility for this final act" in a way that is characteristic of his or her life style (p. 437) and as giving others "an opportunity to reevaluate [their] relationship to the phenomena of self-destruction" (p. 439).

I am profoundly grateful to Prado (1990) for exploring this form of suicide in a very thoughtfully developed and carefully written book, entitled *The Last Choice: Preemptive Suicide in Advanced Age*. Although to my knowledge Art never knew of the existence of this book, I believe he would have found that it corroborated much in his independently arrived-at constellation of perceptions with regard to self and his decision to end his life when he did.

Prado focuses attention on a form of suicide he calls "preemptive," a rational form of suicide undertaken before a person deteriorates to a point where "meaningless survival" is all that he or she has left (p. 9).* Prado's aim was to provide an alternative to the prevailing idea in our culture that suicide is unjustifiable, "cowardly, driven, pathological, and *wrong*—not just in an ethical sense but as somehow contrary to nature . . ." (p. 197).

One of Art's former students, Katherine Ward, captures this idea very poignantly in a poem she wrote after learning of Art's death (see below). Katherine, who died unexpectedly on September 11, 2002 of an aortic dissection, considered Art a friend and mentor but was not in close communication with him in the latter years of his life.

LAMENT

(dated March 23, 1999—lament at learning of my mentor's death, a carefully designed suicide)

I wanted to celebrate your marvelous life
until

* Editor's note: Prado does point out, however, that our society honors persons who "give" their lives in battle "when circumstances warrant such action," as for example when "a soldier chooses to die rather than reveal vital information to the enemy" (p. 16). It is also "not hard to imagine a person committing suicide," writes Prado, rather than "be forced to do something that goes against everything she has lived for and that is of value to her"—as for example, in the case of Socrates (p. 51).

I heard you took it willfully away—
Now I puzzle,
haunted
by your strength and passion, so often
toasting Zorba-like, laughing
even when being sideswiped by surprises.
How then could you forcefully extinguish
your own enthusiasm—and mine—
taint the glory with presumed despair?
I need to know. I need to hear from you.
Who will tell me? What am I to think?
And what do I do with these confused
feelings for one I loved, who loved me?
If life is mystery, you have woven it with mine.

It is this sense of the mystery of a particular type of suicide that Prado seeks to unravel. For Prado, the concurrent increase in elderly suicides is related to "growing unwillingness by the old to endure the very mixed benefits of medically and technologically lengthened life spans" (p. 5). But such a conclusion is insufficient in his mind for understanding those who act upon this unwillingness by taking their lives. "For there to be adequate understanding [of self-inflicted death]," Prado explains, "it must be possible to give an account of what the potential suicidist intends to achieve in ceasing to exist, and also how the notion of achievement applies to a subject whose existence ends with the act in question" (p. 4).

Because he captures precisely and eloquently a line of reasoning that I think matched Art's own, I quote extensively from his work in the discussion that follows. Using female pronouns exclusively, but making it clear that his statements are fully applicable to males and females alike, Prado describes in compelling detail the experience of the *reflective aging individual,* someone "at least older than sixty-five who is perspicaciously self-aware, whose intellectual self-awareness shapes and defines her existence as a person and a social entity and who values her intellectual capacities enough to be seriously concerned that age may erode them in various ways. . . ." (p. 20). In quotations that follow, I've retained his exclusive use of the female pronoun to avoid the awkwardness of language in doing otherwise.

Prado goes on to say that

> at many points in our lives our conception of who and what we are, our self-image, is shaped and reshaped by adjustments we make to specific successes and failures. But in advanced age that image is reshaped by a global—though usually gradual—reassessment of our capacities. And the crucial point about this reassessment is that it cannot be preliminary to efforts at

> long-term improvement. The whole point is that the reassessment has to do with understanding what we are *becoming*, not with responding to something that has gone wrong, and can be set right. (pp. 24–25)

From the point of view of the person coming to this realization, changes perceived may be understood as "amount[ing] to the end of the being I am, even though they do not mark the end of me as a living organism" (p. 43). In light of this assessment, a person can simply accept that he or she will continue to experience new constraints on personal existence until death comes along, e.g., becoming increasingly dependent on others, losing more and more control not only over activities but over one's own body, etc. (p. 44). Or, he or she can take a course of action to avoid this happening.

Some hold religious beliefs that preclude the taking of their own lives. Some consider life to be so precious that existence itself is valued regardless of any other value. Others understand life as "the precondition of value," considering "the real interest in continued life as primarily an interest in still-attainable value—for which existence is a prerequisite" (p. 92). If the changes brought about by the aging process dissipate a person's interest in continued life to the extent "that what persists is only the *organism's* stake in continued existence" (p. 113) rather than the stake of the phenomenal or self-aware self, a person may well consider "whether to continue to exist as a *different* person or to cease to exist as herself" (p. 113).

Some may argue that bearing any adversity in life helps strengthen character and integrity. Art thought otherwise. As he often explained in books and presentations, challenges could indeed strengthen character and integrity if one believed one had adequate resources to confront them successfully. Threats, on the other hand, were another matter, because they had the potential to undermine or overwhelm the very core of a person's being. For Prado (1990), a "crucial" component of the reflective aging individual's value system is "*being* the person she is, and valuing everything *else* as the person she is. It is her very survival that now threatens these values" (p. 115). The individual's choice at this point becomes "one between dying now, as herself, or enduring . . . slow diminishment . . . and dying later as someone else" (p. 116).

Prado also clarifies effectively how timing is critical in preemptive suicide. The person who chooses this end to life has to weigh, consider, and assess the most reasonable time for taking preemptive action (p. 120). Clearly, this is not an easy task and can never be determined with precision. One has to have accurate and clear knowledge of one's present condition, have some sense of what the future will hold, yet not allow the debilitation of the aging process to go on to such an extent that "her deliberation is no longer reliable or she has lost the requisite autonomy to enact a suicidal decision" (p. 120).

Of course, a person choosing this path to death cannot know precisely how long it's possible to live "with as little risk of personal diminishment as possible" (p. 133) but is "prepared to relinquish somewhat more of her remaining viable life span than she actually would [have] to relinquish if her information about the future were complete" (p. 134). In this sense "preemptive suicide is an essentially *discretionary* act" (p. 136) and "there is an unavoidable measure of arbitrariness in the timing of [it]" (p. 137).

Understanding of this issue raises yet another "related temporal consideration" for Prado,

> about when in an individual's life that deliberation can be undertaken with full understanding of the consequences of suicide. It is probably safe to say that one must have lived to a mature age before such understanding is possible. A proper understanding of death presupposes a fully adult understanding of life. What is tragic about most adolescent suicides is that the suicidists have an incomplete understanding of what they are giving up. They have simply not lived long enough. For instance, they will not understand that time will eventually offer a new perspective on whatever prompts their suicidal thoughts, nor do they know enough about the compensations life undeniably provides for much of what we must endure. If there is to be a coherent preference for personal annihilation, one must have lived long enough to understand the nature of what is forfeited. (p. 131)

The rationale in preemptive suicide is that "it is better to die *as oneself* than to live as a lesser version of oneself" (p. 149). A person who commits preemptive suicide not only sees this as an effective means of "preserving identity from deteriorative influences," but also "as doing so in a fashion that *enhances* that identity by affirming the values which define it" (p. 161). Death is made "an act *in* life rather than letting it be only the end *to* life" (p. 161). For some individuals this seems a "fitting" or "good death," and one preferred to the uncertainties that are associated with continued life (p. 165). For Art in particular, I believe this was the case.

Acceptance or Openness to Experience

In describing this quality of a healthy individual, Art explained that it was characterized by an "open, 'all cards on the table,' kind of relationship" to both events occurring in the world and to perceptions of oneself (Combs,

1999, p. 167). Art approached the last years of his life straightforwardly, with a level-headed and common sense perspective that was characteristic of him.

Philosophers across the ages, authorities on human development, psychologists, counselors, and researchers working with the terminally ill as well as experts on death and dying have consistently asserted the importance of acknowledging one's own mortality and the inevitability of death (e.g., Moraglia, 2004; Feifel, 1969; May, 1958; Kübler-Ross, 1975). Persons unable to accept these realities are held to be in denial so far as their basic human nature is concerned.

Clearly, Art was open to the possibility of death and even had moments over these last few years where he welcomed meeting up with it. He read a wide range of books on the topic. During the period covered by this recapitulation, he came to accept that he wouldn't live to see his younger daughters pursue their adult dreams, and that his latest publications weren't likely to change the world or even change a host of individual minds. Yet he believed adequate progress had been made to support an inexorable shift in the directions he valued and championed.

He remained curious about others' perspectives and open to learning about new ideas despite visual difficulties that made reading more tedious now than in the past. To a considerable extent, Art accepted his lot and his limits and adapted to new challenges in everyday living. He was unwilling, however, to lead the kind of "death-in-life" that Moraglia (2004) refers to, found among persons who "hang on at all costs" to life (p. 341).

He acknowledged feelings of sadness, loss, despair, and disappointment—and was open to and accepting of feelings others shared with him. The Kevorkian case angered him. If he could have arranged a more optimal death, he would have wanted a knowledgeable professional to give him the proper dosage of an effective and reliable substance such as veterinarians do when an animal is "put to sleep." This way he could have drifted off surrounded by those he wanted with him at the very end of life. Based on his reading of Humphry's (1982, 1991) published writings, he accepted that the substances he had accumulated to take his life might not work as he hoped they would. He was not only prepared for this possibility, but prepared as well to use alternative means available to him as a backup plan if these turned out to be necessary. Despite his previously expressed hope that he might be able to use accumulated pills to simply slip away to death, Art was found with a plastic bag fastened around his neck with a rubber band, indicating that he had acted decisively and resolutely to achieve his desired outcome.

In his book entitled *Looking in the Distance: The Human Search for Meaning*, Richard Holloway (2004) has written: "A sentence is not finished til it has a full stop, and every life needs a dying to complete it. It is dying that finishes us, that ends our story" and death that "finally defines us" (p. 214). "Fortunately," adds Holloway, "life provides us with many opportunities to rehearse our own dying. As well as the death of relationships and the ending of careers, we are constant witnesses to the slow dying of movements and traditions" (p. 195).

Art had certainly gained experience along these lines as he moved through the eight decades of his life. Marc Ringel, a member of Art's men's group, discussed some of these with him in a conversation they had around 1996. Marc told him that he had noticed changes Art had undergone as a result, e.g.,

> to have reorganized his life without Susan and to have delved more explicitly into . . . spiritual issues that I perceived as the underpinnings of perceptual psychology. . . . As Art's physical world contracted (he used that word, contracted) he focused ever more on the boundlessness of the spirit and also of the mind. In the last few years of his life we had wonderful, far-ranging discussions about post-modern concepts such as chaos theory and self-organizing systems, as well as the Buddhist world view and how they all related back to the core beliefs that he began investigating in . . . perceptual psychology. He was always reading and always exposing himself to brand new ideas. He believed that the world was eventually getting around to a person-centered (as opposed to . . . thing-centered . . .) way of being and that therein lay our salvation. He was very happy to have contributed to the overall process of becoming a more person-centered civilization and saw all sorts of hopeful signs. On the other hand, he expressed no regret that he would not live to see the movement come to fruition. The *process* was what was important to him, another manifestation of his deeply spiritual view of life. Incidentally, he learned transcendental meditation in the late 1960s or early '70s and continued to meditate at the beginning of every day until the end of his life. He said that it gave the calmness and clarity that helped him in everything else he did. (personal communication, October 17, 1999)

Bob Blume visited with Art March 16–17, 1999 to discuss Art's hopes, wishes, and intentions for publication of *The Silent Revolution* manuscript.* They spoke of other matters as well, including their views of spirituality and how institutionalized religion had restricted various respectful and authentic expressions of spirituality. They discussed problems existing in our society

* Editor's note: This book was eventually published under the title *The Continuing American Revolution: A Psychological Perspective* (Combs & Blume, 2004). It provided an analysis of our culture along the lines Art describes in Chapters 11 and 12 and offered person-centered suggestions for better addressing problems found in families, child development, government, business and industry, health care, the legal system, and the helping professions.

along with potential and promising approaches for addressing these. Art recommended that Bob read Bartlett and Steele's (1992) *America: What Went Wrong* and Capra's (1996) *The Web of Life.*

Larry Kerrigan, a clinical psychologist, met Art in Greeley in the 1970s and had lunch with him on a regular basis over a ten- or twelve-year period. He addressed Art's capacity for acceptance or openness to experience by sharing the following:

> I don't think I've ever had a relationship with a male so absolutely uncompetitive and accepting. . . . It was total acceptance on his part that allowed me to be Larry Kerrigan in ways that I could not be with anybody else, certainly not with close male friends. . . . There was no dimension of myself I ever had hesitation to share with him. So often men get together and talk about high silhouette, humorous events. But Art was low key, not colorful in a typical male sense. At least when he was with me, he was so unjudgmental, so present.
>
> I didn't know in any specific sense about his plans to end his life. I knew he had this in mind, however, as we had talked about it at various times over the years.

Kerrigan noted that during the last year or so of his life, he thought Art "drove like an old man with visual problems and slower processing." He seemed "miffed," however, if anyone said something to this effect. In other areas of his life, Art seemed "unprotected" in his honesty. "I come from a close family," said Kerrigan, "but never married. . . . When I would be talking to Art [about this, he] would get a little bit teary" [and tell me how much he envied me for having this closeness].

He went on to explain that Art was typically "so serious." His first impulse was not one of humor.

> A friend and I used to meet on a regular basis. Most of our interactions were based on humor first and serious conversation second. This friend and I noticed one time that in past years our conversations seemed to revolve around libidinous-focused talking about women but now we were talking more about how our bowel movements were going. I shared this with Art. Art, twenty years older, said matter-of-factly, "Oh, I haven't come to that stage yet." (personal communication, June 25, 2002)

When he and Art met together, Kerrigan added, Art would often "ask me where I was at with regard to my belief system."

> I would touch upon the notion of *unicity* in life—not seeing myself as any more significant than my cat. Sometimes he would query me with regard to this. I got the idea we were on the same page in that regard. Western language makes it difficult to understand this concept. Oneness implies

> twoness. Unicity takes you away from oneness or unity which implies something of a dualistic nature. It's a sense of everything being tied together . . . that is just beyond human comprehension in every way.
>
> With Art, in the last dozen years, I don't think the term "belief" system is applicable in describing his mode of living, increasingly on a moment to moment natural basis. I feel as though "flow of meaning in life" captures better the human spirit of his being.

Some may wonder whether Art had ever gotten over the divorce from his second wife. Did he experience loneliness, feel keenly the loss of a life partner as he faced additional medical challenges? Find it difficult to go on without a special companion? One of Art's men's group members, Marc Ringel, addressed this issue in the following reminiscences (shared in a letter dated October 17, 1999).

> The divorce was devastating. We talked about it a lot in men's group. After not that long, as I recall six months to a year, [Art] decided that, though it was the last thing he wanted, it was better to make a clean break than to keep trying to patch things up because that wasn't what Susan really wanted. So he said, "Enough," and moved the breakup along. He rarely indulged in bad-mouthing Susan. I think we men in the group, who hurt for Art, were more critical of her than he was. Though he remained firm about keeping his distance, Art was never vindictive about it. All the while he talked with us men about where he was in his life. It took about three years before Art had reassembled his life . . . sans Susan. He had not yet given up on the idea of a female companion, but he had decided that he could get along just fine without [Susan].

Another member of the men's group, Roy Wardell, wrote that Art "used the men's group well in getting support while going through this very difficult time [of] separation, divorce and healing." And while "being without a mate surely made his last time (years) more difficult . . . he hadn't given up hoping to find female companionship" (personal communication, March 24, 2005).

Art's daughter, Erin, addressed the issue this way.

> Did dad ever fully recover from the divorce? Of course not. Mom was the love of his life, and . . . I'm sure he never quite figured out what went wrong or why. I don't think the shock of losing Mom ever quite wore off and who can blame him?!? He's human, after all. However, was Dad able to move on? Most definitely. Dad himself wrote about spending Christmas with us, Mom, Anne, and her daughter and son-in-law, and what a lovely time he had with everyone, even hugging Anne and Krista on the way out. Also, the week before Dad died I was in Mexico on Spring break and Mom came up to Greeley a couple nights and brought music, dinner, wine and they were able to spend some time together that I know was priceless to them both. (personal communication, October 30, 2004)

Feelings of Oneness and Identification

The theoretical perspective Art championed in his lifetime held that the achievement of personal fulfillment is related in part to "a person's success in developing mutually fulfilling relationships with other people" (Combs, 1999, p. 168). While Art considered himself an outsider and felt deeply rejected in his earlier years, over time he developed meaningful, sustaining, and mutually enhancing relationships with his children, students, clients, close friends, colleagues, and neighbors. In the latter years of his life, he also felt a sense of kinship with the farthest reaches of the universe, extending to the very nature of life itself.

He was mindful of these relationships as he moved through his latter days. He did his best "to make peace" with himself and with everyone he cared about. He arranged visits with friends, family, and ex-wives to clarify his feelings of love and respect for them, and to address unresolved (sometimes long-standing) differences. He had lengthy talks with his youngest daughter (who was still living with him) about both his experience and hers. Because Art was an integral part of a caring social network of friends and family, it was natural for him to consider the impact of his ending his life on those who loved him and whom he loved in return. He was concerned about the maintenance and enhancement not only of his own perceived self, but also about this dynamic in relation to the selves of those who constituted his circle of significant others. He was keenly aware that his remaining alive had value for others who knew him, even if this no longer held the same value for him.

Prado (1990) frames the situation this way:

> It is true that an elderly individual may be a source of strength for someone, perhaps even for many people. But all this means is that the potential suicidist has one more factor to consider in her deliberation. It does not mean that preemptive suicide is just precluded by the very existence of certain responsibilities. We cannot allow dependencies to tyrannize an individual who likely would pay a considerably higher price to remain alive than the dependent persons would pay to cope alone. (p. 195)

No one can have certain knowledge of the future so it is always possible for a preemptive suicide to harm self or others by an action intended to achieve other aims. It seems clear, however, from the lengths Art went to in clarifying his beliefs and values and giving others adequate opportunity to do likewise, that he felt deeply identified with others and sought to connect with them at highly personal levels as he moved, purposefully, toward his death.

According to the Tates, who visited Art in the week before his death, Art was his usual gracious self, still interested in others' lives, and they treasure the conversation they shared with both Art and Bob Blume on this occasion. Although Art initially said he could only visit for a few minutes, he remained in conversation with them for over an hour, stopping only briefly a couple of times when he began coughing. He told the Tates not to be worried about him. He mentioned how proud he was of his young daughters and how thankful he was that he had been in the world long enough to send them on their way. The Tates, who visited in order to buoy Art up during a difficult time, instead left with the feeling that his presence and spirit had inspired them.

For George Tate, Art's last act was "courageous" in nature. "Art blessed us with mercy, was merciful to those of us who knew and loved him," George said. "I would praise rather than condemn him for his not wanting us to suffer any longer, to not go through feeling helpless that we couldn't, somehow, save his life" (personal communication, June 21, 2002).

Art's daughter Carol didn't think the term *suicide* was a good fit for describing her dad's final act. He "felt like he had had his run," she said.

> He had sorted out his experience with several close friends and family members. This was an enormously moving experience for me—not at all macabre. He had many offers from others who invited him to come live with them, but he didn't want that.
>
> On the one hand, what he did can be seen as less a tragedy and more a fitting end of a very productive life. For me, it was most reminiscent of the death of Socrates—a courageous act. The day after he died I went out for a little walk. The news of his death had been in the Greeley papers at this point and a front page story indicated that it had been declared a suicide. One of his neighbors, an elderly man, approached me to ask, "How did he do it?" I explained that the medications he had taken apparently hadn't worked well for him and he had ended up using a plastic bag.
>
> "I hope I have the nerve to do the same," he said.
>
> In a conversation with my mother about my Dad's death, she also said she wished she had the courage to take matters into her own hands as Dad had done. And yet, on the other hand, because most adults hate the idea of dying with tubes or living out their last days in a nursing home, there's a sense in which it's braver still to abide with whatever comes along. (personal communication, June 12, 2004)

Art's son Peter said,

> My father went out with much grace. I can't say how glad I was he let us be with him the last few days. It was like a living wake. We really got closer

> with him while he was still alive. We had an extraordinary father and we know it. (personal communication, March 22, 1999)

Writing of the days and weeks leading up to her father's death, Art's daughter Erin shared the following:

> On our last trip to San Francisco, I can remember walking up the city street (anyone who has been to the city can appreciate the effort it takes for a person in perfect health to navigate the hills of downtown) and looking over at Dad just panting. We had to stop several times for him to catch his breath on the way back to our hotel. This is the first time I can remember Dad really showing signs of what we later found out was a serious heart condition. Dad was now 86 years old. Gradually, more and more warning signs showed up in his day-to-day life. He started taking long naps every afternoon. He had shortness of breath. Finally, his doctor diagnosed him with congestive heart failure in October of 1998. This was the beginning of a mind-boggling six months.
>
> Looking back, it is amazing to me how fast Dad's quality of living deteriorated. At the time, however, it seemed very gradual. To some degree, we were all in a state of shock, I think. He began to not have the energy to walk his routine 2 miles a day. He began sleeping more and more. He began to look almost old. Being the youngest of the four kids, I was the only one left in the house. Peter and Carol, of course, were both grown and lived across the country, and Lynn was in school in Missouri. I was a senior in high school at the time. This could account for why I didn't see an overnight change in Dad, although it may have seemed that way to many others. Somewhere, in the back of my mind, I knew that my dad was not going to live for much longer. During those last months with him, I spent as much time as I possibly could with him. Of course, we both had our own lives and it was as hard to find the time to spend together as it is for any high school senior parent, but we both knew it was important. Almost every night, this time came at the end of dinner.
>
> Something I will always cherish are the talks Dad and I used to have over dinner. For years and years, Dad and I would sit at the table and just talk about whatever was on our minds. Sometimes these talks turned into heated I-know-I'm-right-and-I'm-more-stubborn-than-you debates, and sometimes they were more humorous and light-hearted. As I got older, I was spending less and less time at home, and more time out with friends and so these dinnertime discussions became precious to both of us. Dad and I both treasured the time we spent getting to know each other.
>
> As Dad got sicker, more often these talks revolved around his death—what would happen to me, to the house, to his estate, etc., after he was gone. For the last month or two before his death, our dinnertime chats most often ended with both of us in tears. Even though it was painful, these times together were priceless. Understanding each other had become even more important than it had been just months before.

> I think somewhere in my subconscious I knew Dad would end his own life. There were numerous signs I just chose to ignore. But the night when he told me, point blank, that he intended to take his own life . . . I had to actually face the reality, rather than just the concept, that my father was not going to live forever.
>
> In all honesty, specific events and even the order of events in the months leading up to my dad's death are a blur. I had become numb to much of what was going on around me. I lost my father at way too early of an age. No child should have to go to their senior prom, high school graduation, or their first day of college without their proud father being there to witness it. Despite that, I would not ever, even for a moment, change anything about who my father is. He loved me enough to hand me the world, and then sit back and watch what I did with it. In return, I loved him enough to let him go. (personal communication, September 3, 2000)

Roy Wardell, a member of Art's men's group, had particular concerns about Art's dying alone in his final hours.

> In the years and months preceding his death, Art discussed in detail . . . his belief about and his plan for physically ending his life if certain circumstances occurred. I had known for years that if Art perceived his impending death would be preceded by physical incapacitation he would choose to end his life before that incapacitation happened, . . . and at his chosen time would go to a motel to orchestrate his death where he would not jeopardize anyone. I remember strongly objecting to that lonely (alone) scenario. I considered offering my home (where Art had been many times) as a friendly place to die. Other[s] . . . discouraged that, as it could perhaps be construed as "assisting" by legal authorities.
>
> At first Art objected to the suggestion that he die in the comfort and security of his own home. He thought his dying there might "contaminate" (I believe that was his word) the space for others to later occupy. I remember being rather surprised at this perception on his part given his seeming total acceptance of dying as an integral part of life. But as I write this it occurs to me he was probably, true to his principles, tuning in to what he would think to be the perception of others vis a vis death. (personal communication, March 24, 2005)

Dick Usher, whose more extensive reminiscences and reflections will be found in Chapter 15, shared the following:

> I have not written about Art's death nor his decision to take his own life. I have nothing to add. I simply feel the loss. I am not horrified at what he did and I am not disappointed in him for doing it. I am also not elated that he made some kind of important statement about life and/or death in his decision—I don't think he did. It was merely what seemed best for him and the

> circumstances of his family at the time. I see in his children, Lynn and Erin, and his friends in the men's group, that they are at ease with his final decisions and actions. That's good enough for me.
>
> It is perhaps significant that Art talked to me often in recent years about his aging and his concern for the well-being of his children. He confronted his physical limitations and spoke of them often. At the same time he did not talk much to me about his death—an occasional reference here, a veiled thought there, and a definite sense of what immortality could be. He probably realized that if he spoke directly about his own death plans to me I would have beaten a hasty retreat, made a funny remark, and changed the subject. He knew I didn't want to hear it. That's Art. Tuned in to the perceptions of others to the very end. (personal communication, June 6, 2000)

A Comprehensive, Available, and Integrated or Internally Consistent Belief System

As mentioned in Chapter 1, page 6, while writing this autobiography Art explained more clearly than ever before the meaning and significance of having an integrated or internally consistent belief system. A *comprehensive* belief system is one with sufficient depth and breadth to constitute an effective basis for successful interaction with the world in which one is living. By *available* Art meant that what persons understand, know, or believe is readily accessible to them when circumstances call for its use. For example, when taking a test, they can recall material they have studied; when making life decisions, they can utilize the full range of accumulated knowledge, wisdom, meaning, and perceptions of self for behaving in ways that are satisfying to both themselves and the social world they inhabit.

Sometimes at the moment of acting, knowledge of what we might do differently is not available to affect our behavior. Just as governmental officials in the United States failed to appreciate the threat posed by Al Qaeda prior to the terrorist attacks of September 11, 2001, we too can miss important signs or considerations that we later recognize should have been given greater significance.

As we attempt to put ourselves in Art's shoes, several questions may emerge. What might he have overlooked in his perceptual world before carrying out his final-exit plans? That he might have been able, somehow, to continue experiencing some significant measure of fulfillment despite reduced energy and physical disability? That a new regimen of medication might have improved his condition for an indefinite period of time? That he might have been able to move to a part of the country with a lower altitude that would have lessened pressure on his heart and lungs? That he might have come to enjoy living with any of the various friends or family who invited him to take up residence with them?

Sidney Jourard (1971), writing in his mid-forties, offered the insight that people who attempt or commit suicide may desperately want to end the way they are currently living but cannot imagine how to do this without ending their lives altogether. From this perspective suicide represents a failure of imagination or an inability to perceive more promising and uplifting ways of living (p. 96). As Jourard (1971) understood the dynamics of human consciousness, persons who experience a feeling of being trapped by life circumstances could potentially liberate themselves from this experience through a creative process of reinvention and reconstrual (pp. 92–100).

Here again, it is important to keep in mind that efforts to hasten death, if they occur at all, should be understood as highly personal ones that are embedded in the organization of meanings that constitute an individual's inner life. As Prado (1990) writes: "One aging individual might well decide that she will accept a high degree of mental and/or physical diminishment for the sake of continuing to live" while another " . . . may not be willing to tolerate even slight diminishment" (p. 125).

Morrie Schwartz, the subject of Albom's (1997) book *Tuesdays with Morrie* (which Art had read) discussed how difficult he had found it initially to adjust to or surrender to circumstances in which his disease had progressed to the point that he was no longer able to go to the bathroom, wipe his nose, or wash his private parts, and was dependent on others for nearly everything besides breathing and swallowing food. He said he felt a sense of shame at first "because our culture tells us we should be ashamed if we can't wipe our own behind. But then I figured, *Forget what the culture says. I have ignored the culture much of my life. I am not going to be ashamed.*" After this, Schwartz explained, "I began to *enjoy* my dependency. . . . It's like going back to being a child again. Someone to bathe you. Someone to lift you. Someone to wipe you. . . . We all yearn in some way to return to those days when we were completely taken care of -. . . . most of us didn't get enough" (pp. 115–116).

Art had already experienced what it was like to become similarly dependent on others (following the auto accident in 1995 when he broke both his wrists—see Chapter 11, pp. 267–269) and he did not find this an experience he wished to relive. Unlike Morrie Schwartz, Art, I believe, found this prospect most unappealing because of its inconsistency with a life-long value he had come to place on self-reliance.*

When Socrates was condemned to die and chose to take the hemlock, his students sought to talk him into some way, any way, of avoiding having to die just then. They wanted to assist him in escaping from prison. They thought of a number of places where he might find refuge and protection from harm. They attempted to reason with him, shame him, challenge him.

Socrates remained steadfast. When a man had reached his age, he said "he ought not to be repining at the approach of death" (Plato's *Crito*, 1952, p. 213) . . . and why, when a man is better dead, is he "not permitted to be his own benefactor, but must wait for the hand of another?" (Plato's *Phaedo*, 1952, p. 223). Most of all, Socrates chose not to "demean himself" (Plato's *Apology*, 1952, p. 208) in his eyes by pretending to be something he was not or by living in some inauthentic way. Instead, he faced a death sentence he considered unjust with dignity and hope—that death would be of such a nature that it would enable him to continue his search for truth and wisdom, and, if not—so be it. Similarly, I believe Art's final act can be seen as a reasonable and logical extension of a thoughtfully developed and well-integrated belief system. Whatever considerations might have surfaced in Art's field of awareness in the last days and moments of his life, they undoubtedly would have been weighed and considered in light of other established beliefs, concerns, assessments, values, sense of self, and understandings of personal integrity in his world of experience.

Months after Art's death, while organizing published and unpublished material he arranged to be sent to me, I discovered a transcript of an interview he had given in 1974 as part of an investigation of therapists' approaches to therapy, life, and the human condition carried out by John Fowler (1976).† This interview was conducted 10 days after Art's father's death and the day after the accidental and unexpected death of Sidney M. Jourard (see Richards & Schumrum, 1999, p. ix), one of Art's colleagues. Aware of these recent deaths, Fowler asked Art to discuss what death meant to him in light of these experiences. His response, articulated 25 years before his own death, was as follows:

* Editor's note: Two months prior to his death, Art gave a copy of *Tuesdays with Morrie* to one of the members of the men's group, Jim Fittz. After reading the book, Jim, who was out of the country at the time of Art's death, was struck by "the irony of his passing in the way he engineered it; . . . I was so looking forward to enjoying his last few months or even possibly years joining others in caring for him and sharing his experience of passing. I still feel bereft" (personal communication, June 8, 2005).

† Editor's note: Art's interview in this study was presented under the pseudonym "Bill Rose." Art identified himself as Bill Rose in a copy of this interview that he arranged to have sent to me after his death.

. . . we all have to live with the possibilities of dying, the possibilities of something in the world that could happen, that destroys what you are into, that could happen . . . I don't know. I don't know. [Given] what I've been through lately I think I have confronted the possibilities of death, perhaps with some consternation, but not real fear. I watched my father die. And I had a feeling of complete acceptance of his death, so much so that my sister-in-law said I was heartless. But I knew that indeed he wanted to die, to be out of it. And my own feeling about it is that I would not want to continue my life beyond a place where I knew I was possessed of my faculties. The thought of being a vegetable, filled up with tubes all over the place, and being kept alive would be absolutely foreign to me as it was to my father. And I think, and have consciously thought and believed, that I could commit suicide without any qualms. I am also aware, however, watching my father die, that there are three levels to this brain. The forebrain, which is conscious, the midbrain, and the medulla; and that damn medulla keeps you going. And my father was wanting to die but the primitive brain kept him breathing, kept his heart pumping. But all the while he was ready to move into death. So I don't think I take it lightly, but I think I've come to terms with it. But I'm also aware that that could be an illusion. I don't think so; I hope not. But I don't think anybody can really know. I don't know. That's just the best I can say. I know what I want and I know what I believe about it. . . . As I watched my father being willing and ready but the primitive aspects of this organism of ours which maintains its organization keeps it going. And I think that can be a terrible thing for people. It tends to keep them alive long after they would prefer death. But that too is a fact of life, I guess. I don't know. That's not a very good answer. I'm not very happy with it. I guess what I'm saying is that death is not for me the fearful thing for me that it is for many people. I think the fearful thing for me is not death but the possibility of human indignity associated with it. My experience for example in going to a hospital. It's a terrible thing for me. Because of the sense of giving yourself up completely into the hands of the nurses and the doctors is a difficult thing for me and every time I come out of the hospital I come out with a tremendous feeling and sigh of relief. So I think that's it for me, that's the best I can say; the fact of death itself doesn't bother me and I would be willing to do myself in if I reached that point—but that the indignity of it, and as I watched old people for example in old people's homes, suffering terrible indignities. The things we do with old people in our society [are] dreadful. I think I have come to terms with that because I still feel that. It's not the death but the indignity that really bothers me. . . . Of course, I also think . . . that the human spirit . . . goes on after a person dies. I've used this illustration before. We were talking with people about immortality once, talking about physical immortality which could be destroyed at any moment, you know, your kids being wiped out and that's the end of your physical immortality, or even . . . the immortality which the Church promises. But that, you know, they could be wrong. You can't be sure of it. And then there is the immortality you can always be sure of and the impact

> we have on the world in which we live. You will never be the same for having sat here and talked with me and I will never be the same for having talked with you. My god, I've gotten five new insights which came to me while we were talking and these will go on with me for the rest of my life and they will affect the ways in which I affect other people so this immortality is more in its impact on the world in which we live, the people we meet and the contacts that we have. [These] are the real immortality. And nobody can take that away from you. (pp. 10–11)

Summary

Feeling positive about having the physical and mental resources to control his death to the best of his ability in the context of a society that limited his legal options in choosing his most preferred way to die; accepting of the fact that the aging process had affected him in such a way that he would not find meaningful opportunities for enhancement in the future; feeling at one with the universe and with so many loving family and friends, and considering it a matter of personal integrity, Art chose to end his life on March 21, 1999.

In effect, he orchestrated an end to his life that occurred at a point when

1. he believed he was close to death's door;
2. he had the least amount of life left to lose but the most to gain by taking matters into his own hands (e.g., before any additional medical complications might have resulted in his being incapacitated and/or hospitalized);
3. he knew friends and family were nearby but not in his presence; and
4. he could end his life without subjecting others to the trauma of either witnessing his passing or experiencing possible legal jeopardy.

In sum, his death occurred in a manner Art undoubtedly sought to achieve and considered fitting, taking into account both his own need for self-fulfillment and his concerns for the experience and well-being of others he loved.

He had read Mitch Albom's (1997) moving tribute to his former professor, Morrie Schwartz, and I expect he would want us to keep in mind one of the important life lessons shared in that work:

> As long as we can love each other, and remember the feeling of love we had, we can die without ever really going away. All the love you created is still there. All the memories are still there. You live on—in the hearts of everyone you have touched and nurtured while you were here. (p. 174)

Knowing this doesn't necessarily make it any easier for those of us who knew him personally to deal with our loss, but, for those who didn't know him well, perhaps it offers a clearer sense of his life, his legacy or his leaving.

During the course of his professional career, Art spoke and wrote often of the "self as instrument" concept. As applied to teaching and counseling, he meant by this that professional workers should be seen not as technicians or automatons (applying methods in a more or less mechanical fashion (Combs, 1965, p. 8), but as unique, creative, and thinking human beings, capable of using themselves as effectively as possible for dealing with complex problems confronting them.

Art firmly and consistently believed that there was no one method or approach to teaching, counseling, ministering, doctoring, lawyering, nursing (and I would add living or dying) that, by its very nature, was good or bad, right or wrong for a particular individual. Instead, he believed that individuals would be best served by efforts to assist them in discovering their own best ways to accomplish meaningful aims and purposes and to find fulfillment in the context of their personal value systems and life circumstances. Whatever ways are chosen at any moment may have to be created on the spot to fit the complex realities of the situation in relation to a given personality. What works for or is appropriate for one person thus may not be acceptable to or appropriate for another. Such choices are always highly unique, individual matters.

In Memoriam

Speaking at a memorial service held for Art on March 26, 1999, I shared the following as a way of putting Art's death in the context of his life and his professional work. Over seven years later, it continues to capture my experience of Art, so I include it again here:

> Art very much appreciated the work of Margaret Wheatley (1994). On her own and in collaboration with Kellner-Rogers (1996), she wrote in recent years about life as a process of continuous self-exploration, self-organization and self-creation. In this view, even the most minute particles of living matter seek to be what and who they are and explore ever new possibilities for becoming something different, something more. Art's most recent book, titled *Being and Becoming* (1999) will be released next month. It reflects his understanding that self-organization is the capacity of life to decide what and how it will be, to invent and reinvent itself.
>
> Art read and enjoyed Elgin's (1993) book on *Voluntary Simplicity,* which discussed Toynbee's take on the rise and fall of civilizations. From this I

think he understood that traumatic breakdowns or collapses of organizations or systems are not inevitable. And stagnation is not inevitable—if one can find a transformational way to deal with the challenges confronting one. As Elgin put it, understanding such things we know we are not helpless in the face of challenges, "we are the only source from which the necessary creativity, compassion, and will can arise" (p. 194).

In his professional work, to name just a few of his contributions, Art developed a psychology more adequate to making sense of the human condition, one that went beyond the psychology of his day to a more comprehensive and more inclusive perspective. He pioneered an approach to teacher education which he and many others considered more adequate to the demands and requirements of this profession. In his marriage to Susan and his relationship with Lynn and Erin he worked on developing ways of relating and parenting that he thought were more adequate than the ways he had fallen into or come up with in his first marriage and family life.

In all of this work, Art resisted the notion of treating people as things or machines who were simply to be manipulated and controlled by persons with greater power and authority. Time and time again he asserted the right and responsibility of persons to choose their own best ways, to use their own best judgment, to examine their own fields of meaning and act as authentically as they could in light of what they found there. Art was consistent and persistent in his reiteration of these themes and in his pursuit of these principles. And, similarly, in coping with the challenges of aging and the inevitable approach of death, Art found sustenance and guidance in these same principles.

Art knew that death was inevitable; that none of us lives forever. We all die. And there is never enough time for human beings to share and experience love. He was no stranger to insecurity, rejection and suffering in his earlier years but thankfully enjoyed tremendous satisfaction and fulfillment in both his personal and professional life in his senior years.

He did much that was in his power to prolong his life. He exercised, meditated, ate mindfully. He engaged in meaningful and life-enhancing pursuits and relationships. But he also knew death as an ally, and a great teacher.

Art was an owl, a wise man in the sense Frank Rivers (1996) described in a book called *The Way of the Owl*. He knew death becomes our ally for rebirth of a larger Self when we let go of everything that no longer serves our journey, when we can die with grace not denying the pain or grief involved (Pearson, 1991, p. 143). "Many people avoid claiming their power because they fear the responsibility for the relationships they might have to leave, the people who might feel hurt, the damage to the status quo that the hero as transformer inevitably inflicts . . . [They simply] feel stuck in a world [they] did not create" (Pearson, 1991, p. 146).

Art was not a man content to be stuck or stagnant. He was a quietly heroic individual who envisioned a more promising psychology and sought not only to pass it on in his professional work but to embody it in his personal life. As Carol Pearson (1991) has written, knowing that "one's death lives within" can either "cripple or be transformative" (p. 141). "People afflicted with life-threatening illnesses," she says, "almost always give up attachment to what is inessential to them" (p. 141). They realize that often, "in order to open up to . . . something new," they "have to let go of the old" (p. 141). This is key to the hero's journey.

Art saw no need to suffer needlessly or to put others he loved and who loved him through needless suffering. Instead of viewing death as a terrifying or incomprehensible state, in the end I believe he considered that it might be an opportunity to reinvent himself, to become one with the great dance of unity, to unite with the larger whole of life. Art will surely be missed, but what a proud and life-enhancing legacy he has left us. I saw a card today that may capture the sentiments of many in this room. In part it read: "Those who have given so to others live forever within the hearts of those they have touched."

References

Albom, M. (1997). *Tuesdays with Morrie: An old man, a young man, and life's greatest lesson*. New York: Doubleday.

Albright, A. V. (1994). Counseling psychologists' and psychiatrists' attitudes toward suicide (Doctoral dissertation, University of S. California, 1994). *Dissertation Abstracts International*, *55*(08), 3561B.

Bartlett, D. L., & Steele, J. B. (1992). *America: What went wrong?* Kansas City, MO: Andrews & McNeel.

Bell, M. A. (2000). Losing connections: A process of decision-making in late life suicidality (Doctoral dissertation, University of Arizona, 2000). *Dissertation Abstracts International* *61*(10), 5232B. (UMI No. AAT 9992125)

Bolton, I., with Mitchell, C. (1983). *My son . . . my son . . . : A guide to healing after death, loss or suicide*. Atlanta, GA: Bolton Press.

Brown, L. M. (2002). Suicidal risk factors within an elderly population. Standard of care practices (Doctoral dissertation, Pacific Graduate School of Psychology, 2002). *Dissertation Abstracts International, 62*(11), 5364B. (UMI No. AAT 3034913)

Capra, F. (1996). *The web of life*. New York: Anchor Books/Doubleday.

Cowley, M. (1980). *The view from 80*. New York: Viking Press.

Elgin, D. (1993). *Voluntary simplicity: Toward a way of life that is outwardly simple, inwardly rich*. (Rev. ed.) New York: William Morrow.

Feifel, H. (1969). Death-relevant variable in psychology. In R. May (Ed.), *Existential Psychology* (2nd ed.) (pp. 58-71). New York: Random House.

Fowler, J. (1976). A two-way mirror: By interviews and personal encounter, a comparison and contrast of the styles of relating, perceiving and thinking of six "good" psychotherapists. (Project Demonstrating Excellence, Union Institute & University, Cincinnatti, OH, 1976). (UMI No. AAT DP10613)

Holloway, R. (2004). *Looking in the distance. The human search for meaning*. Edinburgh, England: Canongate Books Ltd.

Humphry, D. (1982). *Let me die before I wake: Hemlock's book of self-deliverance for the dying*. Los Angeles: The Hemlock Society.

Humphry, D. (1991). *Final exit: The practicalities of self-deliverance and assisted suicide for the dying*. New York: Dell.

Humphry, D., & Wickett, A. (1986). *The right to die. Understanding euthanasia.* New York: Harper & Row.

Huxley, J. S. (1953). *Evolution in action*. New York: Harper & Row.

Jecker, N. (1990). Disenfranchising the elderly from life-extending medical care. In P. Homer & M. Holstein (Eds.), *A good old age? The paradox of setting limits* (pp. 157-169). New York: Simon & Schuster/Touchstone.

Jourard, S. M. (1971). *The transparent self* (Rev. ed.). New York: Van Nostrand Reinhold.

Kastenbaum, R. (1976). Suicide as the preferred way of death. In E. S. Shneidman (Ed.), *Suicidology: Contemporary developments* (pp. 425–441). New York: Grune & Stratton.

Kübler-Ross, E. (1975). *Death: The final stage of growth.* Englewood Cliffs, NJ: Prentice-Hall.

Lewis, S. C. (1996). Suicidal thoughts in healthy seniors: An exploratory study (Master's of social work thesis, California State University, Long Beach, CA, 1996). *Masters Abstracts International, 34*(06), 2241. (UMI No. AAT 1380255)

Lindberg, E. (1998). Choosing death: A social psychological study of (un)willingness towards living (Doctoral dissertation, Uppsala Universitet, Sweden, 1998). *Dissertation Abstracts International, 60*(02), 278C.

Malphurs, J. E. (2001). Homicide-suicide in older persons (Doctoral dissertation, University of S. Florida, 2001). *Dissertation Abstracts International, 62*(03), 1560B. (UMI No. AAT 3009511)

May, R. (1958). Contributions of existential psychotherapy. In R. May, E. Angel, & H. F. Ellenberger (Eds.), *Existence: A new dimension in psychiatry and psychology* (pp. 37–91). New York: Basic Books.

Moraglia, G. (2004). On facing death: Views of some prominent psychologists. *Journal of Humanistic Psychology, 44*(3), 337–357.

Pearson, C. (1991). *Awakening the heroes within. Twelve archetypes to help us find ourselves and transform our* world. San Francisco: HarperSanFrancisco.

Plato. (1952). *The dialogues of Plato* (B. Jowett, Trans.). Great Books of the Western World, No. 7. Chicago: Encyclopedia Britannica.

Prado, C. G. (1990). *The last choice. Preemptive suicide in advanced age*. New York: Greenwood Press.

Richards, A. C. & Schumrum, T. (1999). *Invitations to dialogue. The legacy of Sidney M. Jourard.* Dubuque, IA: Kendall/Hunt.

Rivers, F. (1996). *The way of the owl. Succeeding with integrity in a conflicted world.* San Francisco: HarperSanFrancisco.

Schachter-Shalomi, Z., & Miller, R. S. (1995). *From age-ing to sage-ing: A profound new vision of growing older.* New York: Warner Books.

Weinreich, D. M. (1997). Late-life suicidal behavior: Complexity, descriptors, level of risk (Doctoral dissertation, University of Maryland, Baltimore, 1997). *Dissertation Abstracts International,58*(12), 4815A. (UMI No. AAT 9819192)

Wheatley, M. J. (1994). *Leadership and the new science. Learning about organization from an orderly universe.* San Francisco: Berrett-Koehler.

Wheatley, M. J. & Kellner-Rogers, M. (1996). *A simpler way*. San Francisco: Berrett-Koehler.

The Art Combs Memorial Deck, Allenspark, CO

CHAPTER FIFTEEN

Postscript: Reflections and Reminiscences

Carol Hole

[My father] repeats several times that he was absorbed by his work and left the kids to Millie, and that he deeply regrets that he didn't do more with his kids. . . . He often said the same to me in later life—he clearly felt guilty about it. Yet at the time I had no sense of deprivation. I always adored my father and felt he was accessible when I needed him. I felt his guilt was unnecessary—I had absolutely no doubt that he loved me very much.

As his first child, I was made to feel that I occupied a special place. When I went to Greeley when he died, I spent several nights sharing a room with Lynn and discovered that she felt the same way. In a sense, he had two "first" daughters," and we both worshipped him. If she is having trouble writing about that, I can understand why. It is so entwined in the core of my being that it is very hard to talk about.

By the time I was 8 or 9, I already realized that my father was a hero to many students who adored him. When he had parties or meetings at our house, some of them would ask me questions, such as "Does your Dad spank you?" They obviously wanted to know how the great psychologist was raising his children. In fact, for a while I got pretty bratty about it and would say: "I'm Art Combs' daughter and yes, I've been spanked!" when I met students. I blush to recall it! But I was terrifically proud of him and proud of being his daughter. And still am.

For a long time after he left my mother I resented him. I felt that he had "walked away whistling" and left me to take care of her—when she was his obligation. I loved my mother, but not with the fervor that I loved Dad. It also irritated me that Peter . . . didn't live in Gainesville and [didn't] have to be Mom's emotional support. It seemed to me that they were acting like all the men I knew who got away with leaving their wives for younger women. I really didn't get back together with Dad until after Susan left him. He came to Gainesville to tell me about that, and he was so miserable that I couldn't go on resenting him.

He often said to me in the later years, "You're very special to me" and that he felt "like I have my daughter back"—clearly that meant a lot to him, and to me, too. I know he often told me that when I was a preschooler I had "saved his sanity." He used to take me to the park and to visit the university farms, and apparently that was terrifically important to him in stabilizing his life. I suspect that is when our unshakeable bond was forged. Even when I was angry with him over my mother, still in my core I was my father's daughter and always will be.

He was one of the world's great fathers in my opinion and I think his other kids agree with me. We all know he wasn't perfect—but he was close enough. Maybe he was busy—but if you needed to talk to him he was emphatically "there" and of course the world's best listener. Everybody should have a nondirective therapist for a parent.

Something that struck me [in reading the draft of this manuscript] was that, if what he reports is true, he apparently made no attempt to use all those counseling skills on his own marriage. He makes it sound as if Mom was a totally inadequate person who didn't grow—but in fact she was extremely intelligent, interested in all sorts of things (anthropology for instance), was an excellent teacher, and was highly valued by the groups in which she participated—especially the League of Women Voters, who gave her a lifetime achievement award. She was also not nearly so timid as Dad seems to think.

It seems as if somehow he could not apply to her the skills he applied in counseling, which is common enough, but sad. I remember dinner table conversations when she would try to tell him something she knew from classroom experience, and he (who had never been an elementary school teacher and had not been a public school teacher in many years) would brusquely put her down and tell her that "research" showed she was wrong. She was not aggressive and would not argue with him for long—but I could see how unjust that was, even when I was in high school and even though I adored him (personal communication, November 1, 2004).

Expertise with Dogs

Some 75 years after Art shared responsibilities for work in his parents' kennels,* when visiting his daughter Carol in February of 1999, he observed her feeding her dogs one night. Carol recalls the following about that evening.

* Editor's note: Chuck Combs's family history recounts that when Art was growing up, his parents had a long and successful avocational interest in raising registered American Kennel Club show dogs. Beginning with collies, they eventually raised Shetland Sheep Dogs and later Afghan Hounds. The kennel operation (named ARTHEA for their two oldest children) had a constant dog population ranging from 30

"That's a lot of food for a dog that size," he commented when she began dishing out their food.

"Do you think she's too fat?" Carol asked.

Instantly, Art reached out a hand, briefly felt her back, and replied, "She needs to lose ten pounds."

The casual expertise he displayed boggled Carol's mind. She'd known he'd helped his parents in the kennels "but that simple gesture—which he did without thinking about it—said clearer than any words: 'I'm a pro.'" Elaborating, she wrote:

> It's hard to convey the revealing quality of that gesture, but it changed my idea of how dad had spent his youth. I felt the sudden lurch you get when an elevator stops too fast. It was like the feeling I had one time when a long-time friend began chattering away in a foreign language I didn't even know she knew. It was as if she'd suddenly dropped a mask and stood revealed as somebody I didn't really know at all.
>
> A couple of days after Dad died, Lynn and Erin and I were talking about him and I told them about that incident in the kitchen. Their jaws dropped. As far as they knew, their dad wasn't even interested in dogs—let alone an expert. They couldn't get over it (personal communication, June 12, 2004).
>
> He cared little about dogs as an adult [however]. He came to feel that his parents' obsession with them and the whole dog show world, was snobbish, and wasted on animals the concern that should have been kept for people. He didn't say this in detail but his bitterness occasionally came out. I think he felt that they cared for the dogs more than for him.
>
> They also made him spend a good part of his teen years going to dog shows every weekend, fanatically grooming the dogs, serving as handler in the ring, etc., etc. He told me more than once a story about how one weekend the dog he was handling ate his shoes. In the middle of the Depression shoes were hard to get, and apparently his parents didn't buy him replacements for them. (personal communication, November 1, 2004)

Other Reminiscences

On Saturday, March 20, 1999, [Dad and all of us children] went to lunch together. Reviewing the menu, Dad found something he thought he'd enjoy and then reconsidered, saying, "Oh no. I can't order that—too much cholesterol." As the irony of this statement struck him and others at the table, he

to 80 dogs at any given time. Art's father became a nationally well-known and respected American Kennel Club dog show judge in the "Working Breeds" and "Hounds" groups.

These kennels were located behind their home. Both Art and his brother Chuck were enlisted in the work required to operate the kennels and also were assigned responsibilities when it came time to take the dogs to dog shows. As children, Carol and Peter visited these kennels but had no idea their dad had been involved to any extent in the business when he was a child.

decided to go ahead and order what he wanted. Later in the day, he also enjoyed a pastrami sandwich, something he hadn't eaten since establishing healthy eating habits, but something he had enjoyed as a boy growing up in Newark, NJ.

I was struck [on reading the draft of this manuscript] that it makes him seem rather cold. Despite his tremendous empathy, the book has almost no praise for others, or insights into others. I believe that's because of the way he wrote it—as a description of his own inner journey—but it's unfortunate. The Heart-Warmers help. . . . They . . . provide a corrective to his strictly interior view of himself, showing how people saw him on the outside. (On the other hand, it struck me that a person who saved all those Heart-Warmers, was, as he says, badly in need of positive reinforcement. I have done a lot of speaking myself and received very nice notes too, but it never occurred to me to preserve them. But on the third hand, I had the advantage of being raised by a fantastic set of parents, which made me terrifically secure!)

Speaking of heart-warmers, the day after he died the four kids discussed who should call the long list of people [Dad] had asked to be notified. Nobody else wanted to so I volunteered. It took me three days, and as a result I spent three days positively being bathed in love and warmth and affection by people from all over the country. It was amazing! And a peak experience for me. I think it made the grieving process much easier (personal communication, November 1, 2004).

Peter Combs

When I was growing up, dad was working very hard to establish himself professionally. He wasn't there most of the time. I remember going fishing with him two times. One time it was just the two of us. There wasn't a lot of male bonding at that time—not a lot of family closeness. I hardly remember doing anything with either of my parents actually. Subsequently, he apologized for that on several occasions. We bonded more in later years than I did as a child. I love him. There's no doubt about that and I dearly miss him.

The trip out West was an important one for us—when he was struggling with the possibility of breaking up his marriage. It was the first time he shared what had happened between him and my mom. That was during a time I was living in Atlanta so we didn't have daily contact. I was in my "hippie" phase so he was also finding out who I was (personal communication, October 21, 2000).

I believe it is important that the way Dad decided to end his life be documented better. I believe the book should express the very human and thoughtful way in which he decided to die. The point is, the whole thing was a planned event with a set time and place that it would happen. He made his leaving this world a graceful exit that made it less traumatic on all those who were close to him. He sent me a letter a month before he planned to take his life and told me what he was planning. He asked that I fly out to be with him in his final days. He did the same with his other children.

After I got there we went out to breakfast the next morning. Dad was hooked up to oxygen and I had to wheel a small tank along with us wherever we went. I remember sitting down in the restaurant and wheeling the tank up next to him. In a rather disgusted voice he told me, "Put the damn tank behind me so I don't have to look at it."

In the days leading up to the set date, I went through all of Dad's files and other papers with him as he told me what to do with each: throw this out, send this to Anne [Richards], give this to Carol, etc. Dad was quite clear that he did not want a funeral. He had made prepaid arrangements to be cremated. Nancy [my wife] joked [with him at one point] that we would set his urn of ashes on the mantel and he replied, "Don't you dare." The remains were split between the four children and a couple of others who cared deeply for him. Some went to the mountains and my portion went to our lake place in Alabama.

On his last morning, Dad and his four children were sitting in the living room of his apartment. . . . We were all trying to act normal and carry on a conversation, but we weren't doing so well. Looking back, it is clear that none of us knew how to act. Dad surely didn't want a big scene with a lot of crying, but on the other hand we were sitting and talking with our father knowing that in a couple of hours he would be dead. Dad sensed the strangeness of the situation and near 9 o'clock he stood up and said it was time to say goodbye. We did so and left. As planned, I took Lynn and Carol to the mountains. We wanted to be in a peaceful place to wait it out. Erin went to the comfort of her mother's.

For me the whole thing was way beyond anything I had ever experienced. I had never had anyone close to me die before, nor had I even been to a funeral. I didn't know what to do or how I was supposed to act [in regard] to a planned suicide. I believe I handled it all badly. Dad had asked me if I wanted to stay . . . when he took the pills, but I declined. If he suffered horrible pain I didn't want to see him go through that. It was the wrong decision and I still regret not being there. As it turned out it was probably better that I wasn't there, however [because this might have looked suspicious to authorities].

I feel that the things I have told you here are an important part of my Dad's story and I hope that you use all of it in the book. I think the way that his "managed death" (suicide is a misleading description of what he did) was dealt with by those around him should also be included and I hope you will use the descriptions of my feelings. It was awkward, but graceful at the same time. It was sad, but good at the same time. It made it all so clear that society could do a lot to make our dying much more humanistic. I can only hope that I will some day go as gracefully as he did (personal communication, November 1, 2004).

Lynn A. Combs

For the past five and a half years, I have thought a great deal about what I wanted to contribute to my father's autobiography. I have realized that I know very little about my father's life outside of his role as my father. I am working every day to better understand my relationship with my father, and that is a process I expect to last for many years to come. My father was an amazing man, and I am very blessed to have been raised by him. Because my understanding of our relationship continues to evolve, I'm not sure that there is anything more that I am able to add to his autobiography [at this time] (personal communication, January 16, 2005).

Erin E. Combs

On His Profession

One point which sets myself apart from many others (I might even say *most* others) who knew my father, is the simple fact that I knew him personally, as opposed to professionally. Sure, I knew that my Dad was a psychologist, and an author, and a teacher, but as a young child this did not mean much to me. I remember one day when I began to realize how well known my dad was among his colleagues, and I informed my mom: "I think Dad is the most famous person I know!" This was a pretty impressive realization for a girl who was probably not more than seven at the time. When I got a little older and began to have a deeper understanding of my dad's work, I must admit I was impressed, and extremely proud. I always knew my dad was something special to me, but to know he was something special to others too was something I took much pride in.

On Age

My family was . . . well . . . to say the least, unique. My sister and I were the only ones in school with a father in his 80s, a brother and sister in their late

50s (older than Mom), a niece and nephew twice our age, and a mother who was 35 years younger than our father. For whatever reason, my sister and I took a great deal of pride in the uniqueness of our family, and delighted in amazing our peers and teachers with how distinctive our family was. To this day, I still find a certain amount of humor in telling new friends about my 86-year-old father, 60-year-old sister, and 30-year-old nephew.

Although Dad's age did distinguish mine from friends' families, it was also something I struggled with. Because I did realize how old my dad was, I grew up with the fear of something happening to him. For as long as I can remember, I was scared of my dad dying. As a result, I became fiercely protective.

This was not to say his age in any way hindered his ability to be a father to two young girls, even in his 70s and 80s. He was just as active, if not more so, than any father half his age with young children. (As a side note, I have pictures of Dad doing the "tuba-ruba"—a plastic tube you wrapped around your body and put a marble in one end then rolled and twisted around with the object of getting the marble to the other end!!) I have wonderful memories of trips with Dad to New York, Costa Rica, Boston, and many times to San Francisco and Florida.

In fact, I believe Dad's age was more positive than anything. Not only did it teach me about accepting diversity in families, he was able to give so much more to my sister and me than he would have if he had been younger. He was able to devote more of his time and resources to us than any of my friends' fathers. That was something I know he cherished, and I certainly did too (personal communication, September 3, 2000).

On Reading the First Draft of This Book

I feel very strongly that this is *his* story, and if I was writing it I would have a whole different take. I didn't write it though, and I don't really feel I am in a position to alter or change what Dad wrote. At times I just wanted to say to him, "Are you kidding me??" but in the end I also came around to it as his story to tell.

I think it might be that the Art I knew was a very different one than the Art in the book. I knew him as a Dad, and although he was highly revered in my eyes, it was for different reasons than those who knew him professionally. I knew him not as a saint, but as my father. There isn't anyone in the world I love more, or have a more special connection with. But I also knew the unsaintly part of him: the man who wouldn't get rid of anything if it wasn't broken, including a 15-year-old microwave, and a toaster oven that didn't work. I knew the man I used to fight relentlessly with about the proper disposal of banana peels, and leaving butter out on the counter. I knew him as stubborn, and bull-headed, and infuriating at times.

But again, this isn't my book, and it's not my story.

Death is a part of life, and Dad had a keen understanding of that. Even though those of us who are close to him still struggle with his death, or the manner in which he died, suicide is not what he will be remembered for; nor is it what he would want to be remembered for. I think the focus of the book should remain on his life—both professional and personal—rather than on his death. I believe it is his life, accomplishments, family, and influence that will be his legacy.

. . . I don't feel like [his death] is something that needs to be defended. It's simply the way he died. Period. It could have been a heart attack, or car accident, or stroke that stopped his heart from beating, but that doesn't really matter. Just because he ended his life before the heart disease did doesn't change anything about the 86 years leading up to that point (personal communication, October 30, 2004).

Roy Wardell

Art and I first met in 1990, when I attended my first meeting of a men's support group that had been meeting for a few months and of which Art was a member. This group of the same six men continued to meet through the time of Art's death in 1999.

My attempt to recall my early impressions of Art yields nothing profound—only the expected—an elderly man nearly my father's age (my father was still living) who seemed gentle, kind, open, and thoughtful. It was certainly a positive impression which was the beginning of a very strong friendship.

I think partly because Art and I came together without a lot of knowledge of each other's history—and yet had a lot in common—our circumstances were fertile for developing a very mutual friendship. (I am a rancher, having been a psychologist and then returned to my ranching roots.) We really, in the best sense of the word, became "buddies." Although I hadn't thought about it before, I'm sure Art's separation and divorce from Susan played an important part in our spending a lot of time together (I was also not in a significant relationship during most of the time I knew Art).

Our friendship included a full range of good-friend interactions, from just hanging out and playing together to being well-used consultants and counselors to each other about very personal issues—both in and outside of our men's group. I believe I used him most often to help me work on my personal and business relationships with my father and brothers. Art took a keen interest in my cattle-ranching business and often drew upon his early involvement with animals—particularly his family's dog kennel business and his brief stint as a major in pre-veterinary medicine when he started at Cornell. He visited me at the ranch quite often and, as a result, became my only personal friend who knew a lot about the day-to-day ups and downs of both my personal life and my work.

Probably the issue for which Art most often used me as a personal confidant was in his relationships with women. This was particularly true in the later phases of his getting to a practical, functional relationship with Susan as a co-parent of his kids. On at least two occasions after that he developed some romantic interest toward a woman. He talked a lot about the dynamics of those relationships and he very much wanted, if he got involved emotionally, for a relationship to be healthy, realistic and respectful without setting himself up to be hurt. I was probably a lousy consultant as his hope to have another loving, intimate relationship with a woman never happened.

One of the things I and other members of our group encouraged Art to do was to join and spend some time in some of the many varied senior activities in Greeley. He never would do that and on more than one occasion said he didn't want to spend time with a bunch of old people! I guess that might be an indication that there was a little chink in his integration and acceptance of his own aging. It may also have been at least partly due to some basic personal shyness which I think he usually masked pretty well. I really think if he had done that he would have found some fun companionship with men and women that could have made his life fuller and happier the last few years.

I think by the time it came to Art's final day and hour I had completely accepted what he had chosen to do. It is as if I knew him, his beliefs and his rationale so well that it made very good sense as I understood his big picture of life and death and no questions had been left unanswered. I was a little surprised at how clear and sure he was that this was his time and how calm and clear-minded he seemed.

My feelings on the day he died were probably more complex than I can know. Some I knew were:

- love and respect that felt mutual;
- a sense of awe in Art's clearness, confidence and calmness in his affirmation of his decision to end his life;

- a deep, but quiet sadness in losing a very good friend;
- a sense that he had given me all that he had for me without reservation.

My life is richer having felt loved by Art and for loving him. My experience in writing this about my relationship with Art, six years after he died, has strongly renewed his welcome presence in my life (personal communication, March 24, 2005).

Robert A. Blume*

I did not meet Art Combs until 1968 at the annual ASCD meeting, but I had heard him speak many times and I had read most of his writings by that time. I used his book, *The Professional Education of Teachers*, as a text in one of the college classes I was teaching. A year later, I became a colleague of his at the University of Florida, and have considered him to be my mentor ever since.

Many people did not know that, in addition to great success, Art had a troubled, mixed-up life in many ways. As a child he was somewhat neglected and rejected, but as an adult he was a successful teacher who earned his Ph.D., started a college career, and found success in developing a new theory of psychology. Behaviorists and other traditional, mainstream psychologists, however, failed to grasp its revolutionary importance. His professional successes included the presidency of ASCD and many other honors. He wrote prolifically and spoke at nearly all large organizations of teachers and school administrators, but paid a price at home because of all the travel.

He was divorced from his first wife of 39 years and almost simultaneously retired from the University of Florida in the mid-seventies. He soon met a new love, married, and moved to the University of Northern Colorado, where he became a Distinguished Professor of Education. He and his wife gave birth to two children who were more than forty years younger than his older two. While his wife worked, he totally retired and did the majority of the day-to-day childrearing, cooking, and housekeeping. He commented

---

* Editor's note: Robert Blume graduated from Ohio State University, Art's graduate alma mater. He subsequently earned a Ph.D. at the University of Michigan and became a colleague of Art's at the University of Florida. Arriving a year after the New Elementary Program [Childhood Education Program] began, Bob helped him develop the program and took over the leadership of it after Art retired from the University in Florida. They kept in touch over the years and became great friends, visiting in each other's homes and collaboratively writing and thinking. When Art learned his health was failing, he asked Bob to revise a manuscript he had written but never published, entitled *The Silent Revolution*. During the week before Art died, Bob visited with him to consult about how this book might be completed.

that he had neglected his older kids because of career-building excesses, and he was determined to do it right this time. He was a down-to-earth man who did not take his fame too seriously. I was visiting once when one of his middle-school-aged daughters came home and asked him why a neighbor had told her that he was a very famous person. "Is that true?" she asked. "Well, I guess a lot of people do know my name," he replied.

I found Art to be both a genius and a true friend. His theory of the centrality of perception in determining behavior is so simple and so profound that it changed my life as a young teacher trying to understand what made my kids tick. It almost miraculously explained to me what was going on in my own classroom. Many teachers must have had the same experience; how else to account for his success in reaching so many of us? Most of his lectures at education conferences were given standing ovations. He was able to connect with teachers as a teacher himself. When I visited with him only a few days before his death, I asked him why the psychology profession had not embraced his ideas like the teachers and administrators did. He said that the theory is too simple. They prefer to see something very complex and scientific-sounding. And they really do not understand the implications of it. Many people, including many psychologists, think Art is saying we should just be nice to people—that is all there is to it. He told me that if that is what he saw in this theory, he would reject it, too. But the point is not that. It is primarily an effort to underscore the importance of "reading behavior backwards," trying to see the world through the eyes of the behaver rather than looking at him [or her] from the outside as a rat running a maze. Like rats, people are animals, but people are infinitely more complex. To believe that they will behave in a desired way simply because you fill their food dish is a truly simplistic theory.

The other thing I want to say about Art is that he faced certain death calmly, bravely, and with a deep belief that this is nature's way, and therefore right. Those of us who are left with our tears are less sure that it was right for Art Combs to die when his message is so badly needed throughout this world. But I think the responsibility for getting that message out has now been passed to each one of us to explain it whenever we get an opportunity. Art would be very pleased about that (personal communication, March 16, 2000).

Richard H. Usher

Art Combs came to Owensboro, Kentucky, for an in-service workshop with teachers in 1961. He was president-elect of the national Association for

Supervision and Curriculum Development (ASCD), which was well established in the vanguard of progressive thought in American education. The 1959 revision of *Individual Behavior*, a masterpiece of understandable practitioner-oriented theory, was riding a crest of popularity and Art had previously accepted an appointment at the University of Florida, Gainesville in the Department of Foundations of Education. It was telling that a psychologist would accept an appointment in a college of education. It was a testimony to the currency and acceptance of his ideas in education and counseling.

Art had been invited to chair and edit the 1962 ASCD yearbook, and work was completed on that project which was published as *Perceiving, Behaving, Becoming*. The record of sales and printings of that yearbook later became a source of great pride for Art. Under Art's leadership, a committee of educators considered four seminal papers from eminent psychologists who were asked to write their own visions about the potentiality of human beings. The invited papers were from Abraham Maslow, Carl Rogers, Earl Kelley, and Art Combs. What can man become? became the primary question for consideration. And the question for the committee was: "If these four writings construct a vision for the potential of human beings, then what would schools look like if they were based upon such a vision?" These papers represent a sweet crescendo of thought in psychology that endeavored to approach human behavior from the standpoint of health rather than illness, from the view of what humans can become rather than how they can avoid maladjustment. They represented a positive psychology of hope that was just right for the boundless optimism following the aftermath of "the war to end all wars." American education was ripe for visionaries and these psychologists provided a vision of amazing promise. The 1962 yearbook was honored by ASCD in 1987, its 25th anniversary of printing, as the all-time leader of yearbook sales. It had sold more copies than all other ASCD yearbooks combined!

One of the teachers in that 1961 Owensboro in-service session was myself, Dick Usher. This was my second year as a teacher in the Owensboro system. I had come into teaching after a rocky experience in the public schools as a student. I was an idealistic young man who decided to become a teacher because I was inspired to make the schools better than they had been for me. I was 23 years old and involved in a special team-teaching project initiated by Owensboro Public schools. Since this was my second year as a teacher, I had already come to a slightly jaded view of teacher in-services. I had found them to be rather vacuous, curriculum- or method-centered, and largely irrelevant to my needs. Thus, when on this day I found myself in a large-group, "keynote-speech" situation in an auditorium full of fellow teachers and school administrators, I was prepared to endure the session and use the afternoon time to rejuvenate my classroom. The speaker/consultant was Arthur W. Combs and, although some of the school system leaders had spoken excitedly about Combs's contributions, I did not even know the name.

When Art began to speak, I found myself galvanized by the man and his message. To construct a vision of schools as an instrument of man's becoming—as a democratic institution commissioned to foster self-fulfillment in all students—came as a warm wind of transformation to this skinny son of the mid-South with his do-gooder mentality and naïve idealism. I was, as they say, blown away by it all! Here was a quiet, shy, soft-spoken man (much like how I remembered my own father who had died two years before) who brought big ideas of hope, inclusion, and the true promise of democracy into schooling. I was bathed in a stirring stream of inspiring and plain-spoken truth (in that moment I probably thought "Truth" with a capital "T," but later knew better). I was caught up in a fervor for the man and his ideas. I wanted more, more.

I was a very fortunate man at the time, for there were people of influence in the school system and in my life who knew my ideals and cared about me. These people introduced me later in the day to Art Combs. And since I was involved at the time with a new team-teaching experiment, and was teaching in the "showplace" school for the district, the chief administrators took Art to my school to show off the new octagon-shaped building with movable partitions and rolling bulletin boards and flexible cafeterium space. When they invited Art to see the innovative school, they also invited me to come along. It was a loving set-up, staged to bring the two of us into contact. And it worked. Art asked me to think about coming to the University of Florida to work with him as a graduate student.

The next year found me and my new wife, Mary, in Gainesville, and it was the beginning of a connection that lasted, and strengthened, until Art's death in 1999. The time was 1962. The program I pursued was an Ed.D. in psychological foundations with a minor in psychology and supporting area in counseling. It was a peak time of Art's popularity and influence in psychology, education, and counseling. Those three years of graduate study and work with Art were turning points in my life and in the life of my wife. The magnetism of Art and his work were powerful change agents for the lives of many and probably none was transformed more than I was. When I began my study with Art, I thought that if no one discovered my shallowness I might be lucky enough to complete a master's degree. It was testimony to the beauty and integrity of the people and the program and the perceptual point of view that I found myself headed for a doctorate without much reflection. It was assumed that I would make it by everyone around me, especially Art Combs. For a scared, skinny, and insecure kid from insular Kentucky, this was the ultimate life-changing time.

Art was my teacher, mentor, research director, and hero, sure. And he was more. There was the human side as well. Art suggested that he could loan my family some money if it was needed. How did he know? I took the money and would have been in dire straits if I hadn't. My wife and I house-sat for Art when he and his wife went on vacation. I had a research assistantship for the 62–63 academic year which was a part of the grant Art and Daniel Soper had to study self-concept in young children. This research showed, among other things, that self-concept inferences of kindergarten children provided more accurate predictors of success in reading than did all other variables, including past achievement and IQ scores. I was awarded a departmental teaching assistantship for the next two years, working with Art as a discussion leader in his graduate class in psychological foundations and eventually teaching an undergraduate class in child development.

During this time there were weekly meetings, usually at Art's home, to identify and discuss potential hypotheses for research to identify effectiveness of practitioners in the helping professions. It was there that I determined to do my doctoral dissertation applying effective helper dimensions to the study of college teacher effectiveness. My study later became a part of Art's publication, *Florida Studies in the Helping Professions* (Combs et al., 1969).

I left the Florida program in 1965 to take a position as an assistant professor of psychology, counseling and guidance at Colorado State College in Greeley, CO (later the University of Northern Colorado). This position was offered without a personal interview because of Art's influence. The chairman of the department, Arno Luker, was a strong Combs convert in his own professional life and was building a department to reflect his commitment to those ideas. He sent a telegram to me saying, "Combs recommended you!" And that was all it took for him to hire this new professor.

The Greeley, Colorado appointment for me was the beginning of a metamorphosis of the psychology department into "Art Combs West." An early student of mine, Dave Welch, made his way to the University of Florida to work on a doctorate and later, degree in hand, came back to the UNC faculty in psychology. During Dave's stay in the Florida program, he became good friends with Anne and Fred Richards. Anne was a student of Art's who, as an undergraduate, had worked with Abe Maslow at Brandeis University and Fred was an early spokesperson for the blossoming movement in humanistic psychology which was encompassing Art's work in perceptual psychology. Fred eventually completed his doctorate from the innovative graduate school "without walls," Union Graduate School [now Union Institute & University]. The fruits of his graduate study were published in a book called *Homonovus: The New Man* in 1973.

Eventually Anne and Fred Richards also came to Greeley, Anne as a faculty member in psychology and Fred as a consultant student and scholar as he was in the throes of completing his studies through Union. At one point in time, there resided in Greeley Dick and Mary Usher, Dave and Marie Welch, Fred and Anne Richards, Arno Luker, and George Tate, along with legions of humanistically inclined graduate students who were attracted to the ferment. Later there came Monte and Bonny Clute into Educational Foundations. Monte was the son of one of Art's longtime friends in education, Morrell Clute. Morrell was on the faculty at Wayne State University, having completed his degree under Earl Kelley, another of Art's longtime friends, supporters, and colleagues. Earl had written one of the most startling, parsimonious, and powerful statements of early perceptual theory, *Education for What Is Real*, in 1953. So it was that the Greeley connection was forged as Combs West. During this period, while still in Florida, Art underwent significant personal changes: divorcing his first wife, Millie, and engaging his son, Peter, in a self-reflective, soul-searching pilgrimage in a van. He came to visit Greeley as part of this trek. He spent long hours talking to me and Mary and all the other Greeley links to his ideas and ideals.

In 1976 Art and his new companion, Susan, came to settle in Greeley, Colorado—at least in part because Mary and I were there. This signaled the beginning of a deeper and more personal relationship between the Ushers and Art. Art and Susan visited often in our cabin, and when we moved to Kentucky in 1977 they rented the rocky mountain retreat for several years, leaving it open for our yearly summer stay. We welcomed Art and Susan for summer cabin visits and in turn visited them in their Greeley home. With the birth of their daughters, first Lynn and then Erin, the cabin became a more special shared retreat between our two families. The bond between Art and myself became more of a man-to-man, father-to-father, husband-to-husband centered relationship and less that of teacher-student and hero-follower. There were long talks about children, love, schooling, health, age, the future, and human fulfillment and fewer talks about universities, professors, and publications. Art delighted in our daughter Letitia, and saw in her some of what might be in store for him with his own. He remained an enthusiastic and loving supporter of Tish in all her life adventures.

The dissolution of Art's marriage to Susan further changed the nature of my relationship to Art. I became more of a confidant, supporter, listener, and perhaps a younger soul brother. And, over time, I began to realize that the relationship I shared with Art felt more and more like father-son. There were long-standing discussions between us about kids, male-female relationships, psychology, education, counseling, and fun. Art's two daughters were growing and developing and came often to enjoy our cabin in the mountains. I was always in awe of, and enthralled by, Art's kindness, depth of intellectual and social insight, writing, and ability to focus and concentrate. In turn, Art seemed to honor my personal stability, long-standing relationship with Mary, humor, and generally laid-back approach to professional and personal life. Art was buoyed by the relationship he saw shared by Mary and myself in all the years he had known us. He loved me and I loved him and for the first time ever it was openly expressed between us.

Art often told the story of when I came to his office at the University of Florida in 1965 to tell him goodbye and thanks for the all the support during my doctoral studies. I had accepted a position on the faculty at Colorado State College (now the University of Northern Colorado) and was off to the West for my first position in higher education. The goodbye was difficult for me—Art was still my mentor, teacher and hero. He had helped to open me to a world of big ideas. He had helped unlock my potential. He had nurtured, challenged and loved me. There were tears in my eyes as I moved to leave when Art said, "Dick, I love you!" With that, I made a hasty exit! Later, Art often told others of the experience, saying, with much laughter, "Dick practically ran out of my office." I thought, "Well, probably so."

What follows is a poem I wrote in rough form while we were at our Colorado cabin during the summer of 1999. It was our first summer there after Art's death in March. It was our first summer in the mountains without Art as a frequent guest since he and Susan came to Colorado from Florida in 1976. It was a sweet and empty summer of remembering our times together during the past 22 years. In this span of time Art had become a second father to me and now he was gone. The father-son sense I had about our relationship was unspoken between us. We were both aware that such a bond could be unhealthy and neither dwelled on it nor explored it. I felt it, though, and I believe he did, too. I suspect Art's comment that "nobody understands perceptual psychology and can explain it quite like Dick Usher," while often embarrassing to me and certainly frightening in its potential burden of expectation, was in reality a diffuse acknowledgment of the specialness of our relationship. Or, perhaps it is only my sense of our relationship and it never occurred to him. It doesn't matter, to me he became a second father.

There are no deep, dark implications here, simply my feelings for what seemed to be.

During the summer, Bonny Clute McNerney and Roy Wardell came to visit us and brought some of Art's ashes to be spread around the cabin. At first we mistook it for green chili and later I thought it was mix for the hummingbird feeder. We all had a big laugh and figured Art would love that.

My own father died in 1960. He was a quiet, good man who never raised his voice in anger. Sadly, his death came shortly before I graduated from college and he never knew for sure whether or not I was successful and happy in life. Thus, my poem, when it refers to "Son," is a reference to my father. Son was the name he was known by. That is who he was to all friends and family.

What's left then is the poem. The preceding background to the images of the poem is provided because I wanted you to know the nature of my relationship with Art. It is that relationship and its loss to which the poem speaks. There are Art and Son, two strong forks to my slingshot. A slingshot was called a "flipper" in my growing-up Kentucky years and it had a stock of two strong prongs merging into a sturdy and comfortable handle. Finally, there is the deck on the cabin. This past summer we completed a new deck, replacing the original upon which we sat with Art for many fine hours each year. We installed a plaque dedicating the deck in his memory. Since the 1970s we had sat, talked, watched the birds, drunk wine, and enjoyed each other's company on the original cabin deck. We joked often about the deteriorating condition of the old deck and about my ineptness as a carpenter in numerous attempts to shore it up. Once, it lurched precariously forward and downward as he sat while I was replacing some rotted lumber! He never let me forget it. I merely said, quietly, "Art, maybe you should move." If I hadn't said it, I think he would have simply trusted me to take care of it before there was a catastrophe.

I am a lucky person: his simple faith and trust in my abilities launched me on a journey to selfhood when I first met him and his ideas in 1962 and never wavered in all my contacts with him. And, this gift to me was much of the gift he gave to all who knew him personally, and, astonishingly, even to those who encountered him only through his ideas.

GREEN CHILI AND FORKED ELM

So, Art
part of you came to visit
in a ziploc
You masqueraded as green chili
We wanted to add water

for hummingbird feed.
We all laughed.
I'll bet you did too.

Where are you now, Art?
Everywhere? I breathe you in
out of the universe. I trespass your
Karma. I cultivate the ideas
we shared. I catch your
reflection in God's eye. I pet
your children.
So Art,
the Stellers fuss at the
Nuthatch's courage
You swept down with a ruby throat
and hovered in the low clouds
throwing widely spaced raindrops to explode
on the new deck—
The Art Combs Memorial Deck.

Where are you now, Art?
Everywhere? I trace you through
the woods path homeplace. I remember
your breathing. I taste the
barren barbecue. I watch your image
reflected in the locks. I pray
your health.

So Art
you and Son are
my fathers
You and he have grown me,
roots of kindness and depth
serve me well.
We are boy scout searchers—
We are joined at the handle

Where are you now, Art?
Everywhere? Maybe with Son.
He has been away so long and
so it will be with you
in the times to come. I search
for the perfect flipperstock. I let
it be a forked elm, just right. A
comfortable handle with
strong prongs to make me

a straight shooter
like you.
(personal communication, June 6, 2000)

References

Kelley, E. C. (1947). *Education for what is real*. New York: Harper & Row.
Richards, F., & Richards, A. C. (1973). *Homonovus: The new man*. Boulder, CO: Shields Publishing.

Publications of Arthur W. Combs

CHRONOLOGICAL LISTING

Publications of Arthur W. Combs*

1943

Pressey, S. L., & Combs, A. W. (1943). Acceleration and age of productivity. *Educational Research Bulletin, 22*(7), 191–196.

1944

1945

Combs, A. W. (1945). *An evaluation of the Thematic Apperception Test for the study of certain personality factors by comparison with autobiography.* Unpublished doctoral dissertation, Ohio State University.

*Combs, A. W. (1945). College counseling. *New York State APA Bulletin, 8,* 4.

Combs, A. W. (1945). Follow-up of a counseling case treated by the non-directive method. *Journal of Clinical Psychology, 1*(2), 147–154.

Combs, A. W. (1945). Some contributions of non-directive methods to college counseling. *Journal of Consulting Psychology, 9*(5), 218–223.

1946

Combs, A. W. (1946). Basic aspects of nondirective therapy. *American Journal of Orthopsychiatry, 16*(4), 589–607.

Combs, A. W. (1946). A method of analysis for the Thematic Apperception Test and autobiography. *Journal of Clinical Psychology, 2*(2), 167–174.

Combs, A. W. (1946). The school psychologist. In *PROCEEDINGS, Eleventh Annual Conference on Educational and Vocational Guidance* (held July 18–19, 1946),Volume 11 (pp. 13–20). Syracuse, NY: Published for the NY State Counselors Association by the School of Education of Syracuse University.

Combs, A. W. (1946). The use of personal experience in Thematic Apperception Test story plots. *Journal of Clinical Psychology, 2*(4), 357–363.

Combs, A. W. (1946). The validity and reliability of interpretation from autobiography and Thematic Apperception Test. *Journal of Clinical Psychology, 2*(3), 240–247.

*Combs, A. W. (1946). What is effective counseling? In *Proceedings: Annual Guidance Conference,* (pagination unknown). Muncie, IN: Ball State Teachers College.

1947

Combs, A. W. (1947). The case of Edith Moore. In W. U. Snyder (Ed.), in collaboration with C. R. Rogers, G. A. Muench, A. W. Combs, & V. M. Axline, *Casebook of nondirective counseling* (pp. 268–311). Boston: Houghton Mifflin.

Combs, A. W. (1947). A comparative study of motivations as revealed in Thematic Apperception stories and autobiography. *Journal of Clinical Psychology, 3*(1), 65–75.
REPRINTED in McClelland, D. C. (Ed.). (1955). *Studies in motivation* (pp. 89–101). New York: Appleton-Century-Crofts.

*Combs, A. W. (1947). Developing personality. In *Newsletter, New York State Council of Religious Education,* (April), 1–8.

Combs, A. W. (1947). Non-directive techniques and vocational counseling. *Occupations, The Vocational Guidance Magazine, 25* (February), 261–267
REPRINTED in Combs, A. W. (1948). Non-directive techniques and vocational counseling. *Work and Training. Vocational Information for Virginians, 8*(3), 3–4, 7–8.

* Editor's note: This is the most accurate and comprehensive compilation of the publications of Arthur W. Combs I found possible to produce at the time of publication. As explained in the Preface (see p. xvi), in cases where I was unable to secure or verify a given reference, this is indicated with an asterisk. If anyone reading this manuscript is in possession of copies of asterisked items, or knows how to locate any of them, I would very much appreciate being informed of this. Note also that inconsistency in references to non-directive therapy (i.e., appearing as non-directive or nondirective) reflects inconsistency in published literature, although more recent usage is consistent in the use of the term nondirective (without a hyphen).

*Combs, A. W. (1947). Some dynamic aspects of non-directive therapy. *The personal counselor, 2*, 12–21.

Combs, A. W. (1947). Some dynamic aspects of non-directive therapy. In *Current trends in clinical psychology. Annals of the New York Academy of Sciences, 49*(6), 878–888.

Snyder, W. U.(Ed.), in collaboration with Rogers, C. R., Muench, G. A., Combs, A. W., & Axline, V. M. (1947). *Casebook of non-directive counseling.* Boston: Houghton Mifflin.

1948

Combs, A. W. (1948). Phenomenological concepts in non-directive therapy. *Journal of Consulting Psychology, 12*(4), 197–208.

Combs, A. W., Wexler, M., & Hathaway, S. R. (1948). Psychotherapy and counseling: Summary of discussion [of Symposium on Psychotherapy and Counseling presented at the annual meeting of the American Psychological Association, September 12, 1947, Detroit, MI, pp. 65–87. Symposium speakers: R. Nevitt Sanford, H. F. Hunt, S. G. Estes, F. Wyatt]. *Journal of Consulting Psychology, 12*(2), 88–91. [Art's comments are on pp. 88–89.]

1949

Combs, A. W. (1949). A phenomenological approach to adjustment theory. *Journal of Abnormal and Social Psychology, 44*(1), 29–35.
REPRINTED in:
a. Millon, T. (Ed.) (1967). *Theories of psychopathology: Essays and critiques* (pp. 278–284). Philadelphia, PA: W. B. Saunders Co.
b. Morris, R. J. (Ed.). (1974). *Perspectives in abnormal behavior* (pp.58–64). New York: Pergamon Press.

Snygg, D., & Combs, A. W. (1949). *Individual behavior: A new frame of reference for psychology.* New York: Harper & Brothers.
Reference made to this work in
Mouly, G. J. (1960). *Psychology for effective teaching* (pp. 2–3, 22, 52–54, 491–496). New York: Henry Holt and Co.

1950

Combs, A. W., & Snygg, D. (1950). Implications of the phenomenological approach for the evaluation of psychotherapy. *The Psychological Service Center Journal, 2*(2), 96–102.

Cowen, E. L., & Combs, A. W. (1950). Follow-up study of 32 cases treated by nondirective psychotherapy. *Journal of Abnormal and Social Psychology, 45*(2), 232–258.

Landsman, T., Combs, A. W., & Peterson, K. (1950). The experimental application of psychotherapy as a learning technique.[Summary of program organized by Division of Clinical and Abnormal Psychology for 58th Annual meeting of the APA.] *American Psychologist, 5*(7), 323–324.

Snygg, D., & Combs, A. W. (1950). The phenomenological approach and the problem of "unconscious" behavior: A reply to Dr. Smith. *Journal of Abnormal and Social Psychology, 45*(3), 523–528.
REPRINTED in:
a. Kuenzli, A. E. (Ed.). (1959). *The phenomenological problem* (pp. 268–279). New York: Harper & Brothers.
b. Hamachek, D. E. (Ed.). (1965). *The SELF in growth, teaching, and learning: Selected readings* (pp. 79–87). Englewood Cliffs, NJ: Prentice-Hall.

1951

Combs, A. W. (1951). Mental hygiene and education. In *Proceedings: Sixteenth annual conference sponsored jointly by New York State Counselors Association, New York State Psychological Association, New York State Association of Deans and Guidance Personnel, New York State Regional Branches of the National Vocational Guidance Association, New York State Dental Hygiene Teachers Association, New York State School Nurse Teachers Association, New York State Department of Education & Syracuse University*: Vol. 16 (pp. 17–19). Conference held July 19–21, 1951, Syracuse, NY. Published cooperatively by the New York State Counselors Association and the School of Education of Syracuse University.

Combs, A. W. (1951). A report of the 1951 licensing effort in New York State. *American Psychologist, 6*(10), 541–548.

1952

Combs, A. W. (1952). Intelligence from a perceptual point of view. *Journal of Abnormal and Social Psychology, 47*(3), 662–673.
REPRINTED in:
a. Fullagar, W. A., Lewis, H. G., & Cumbee, C. F. (Eds). (1956). *Readings for educational psychology* (pp. 158–176). New York: Thomas Y. Crowell.
b. Fullagar, W. A., Lewis, H. G., & Cumbee, C. F. (Eds). (1964). *Readings for educational psychology* (2nd ed) (pp. 171–187). New York: Thomas Y. Crowell.
c. Hartley, E. L., & Hartley, R. E.(Eds.). (1957). *Outside readings in psychology.* (2nd ed.) (pp. 241–259). New York: Thomas Y. Crowell.
d. Hamachek, D. E. (Ed.). (1965). *The SELF in growth, teaching, and learning: Selected readings* (pp. 134–152). Englewood Cliffs, NJ: Prentice-Hall.
*e. *Professional Reprints in Education* (1965). Charles Merrill.
f. Hamachek, D. E. (Ed.). (1968). *Human dynamics in psychology and education: Selected readings* (pp.119–136). Boston: Allyn and Bacon.
g. Hamachek, D. E. (Ed.). (1972). *Human dynamics in psychology and education. Selected readings* (2nd ed.) (pp. 178–197). Boston: Allyn and Bacon
h. Frey, S. H., & Haugen, E. S. (Eds.). (1969). *Readings in classroom learning* (pp. 166–186). New York: American Book Co.
i. Brown, R. G., Newell, R. A., & Vonk, H. G. (Eds.). (1969). *Behavioral implications for curriculum and teaching: Interdisci-*

plinary readings (pp. 105–114). Dubuque, IA: Wm. C. Brown.
j. Good, R. G. (Ed.). (1972). *Science-Children: Readings in elementary science education* (pp. 206–224). Dubuque, IA: Wm. C. Brown.
k. Avila, D. L., Combs, A. W., & Purkey, W. W. (Eds.). (1971). *The helping relationship sourcebook* (pp. 363–383). Boston: Allyn and Bacon.
l. Avila, D. L., Combs, A. W., & Purkey, W. W. (Eds.). (1977). *The helping relationship sourcebook* (2nd ed.) (pp. 207–225). Boston: Allyn and Bacon.
m. Loree, M. R. (Ed.). (1959). *Educational psychology: Readings, supplementary text and study questions* (pp. 122–138). New York: Ronald Press.
n. Mouly, G. J. (1971). *Readings in educational psychology* (pp. 211–215). New York: Holt, Rinehart and Winston.

Combs, A. W., & Taylor, C. (1952). The effect of the perception of mild degrees of threat on performance. *Journal of Abnormal and Social Psychology, 47*(2, Supplement), 420–424.

Taylor, C., & Combs, A. W. (1952). Self-acceptance and adjustment. *Journal of Consulting Psychology, 16*(2), 89–91.
REPRINTED in:
a. Dulany, D. E, Jr., DeValois, R. L., Beardslee, D. C., & Winterbottom, M. R. (Eds.). (1958). *Contributions to modern psychology: Selected readings in general psychology* (pp. 269–273). New York: Oxford University Press.
b. Dulany, D. E., Jr., DeValois, R. L., Beardslee, D. C., & Winterbottom, M. R. (Eds.). (1963). *Contributions to modern psychology: Selected readings in general psychology.* (2nd ed.) (pp. 299–303). New York: Oxford University Press.

1953

Combs, A. W. (1953). *Human relations. Instructor's handbook including suggested discussion material.* Schenectady, NY: Technical Education Services, General Electric Co.

Combs, A. W. (1953). Child adjustment: Your job and mine. In M. Johannis (Ed.), *PROCEEDINGS: FOURTH ANNUAL CONFERENCE of the Southern Regional Association on Children Under Six* (pp. 10–11). April 16–18, 1953, Daytona Beach, FL.

Combs, A. W. (1953). Problems and definitions in legislation. *American Psychologist, 8*(10), 554–563.

1954

Combs, A. W. (1954). Counseling as a learning process. *Journal of Counseling Psychology, 1*(1), 31–36.
REPRINTED in:
a. Fullagar, W. A., Lewis, H. G. & Cumbee, C. F. (Eds.). (1956). *Readings for Educational psychology* (pp. 67–75). New York: Thomas Y. Crowell.
b. Fullagar,W. A., Lewis, H. G., & Cumbee, C. F. (Eds.). (1964). *Readings for educational psychology* (2nd ed.) (pp. 55–62). New York: Thomas Y. Crowell.
c. Farwell, G. F., & Peters, H. J. (Eds.). (1960). *Guidance readings for counselors* (pp. 361–369). Chicago: Rand McNally & Co.
d. Ito, H. (Ed.). (1962). *Readings in counseling psychology, [Kaunseringu no riron] Vol. II. Theoretical issues in counseling and psychotherapy* (T. Ueda, Trans.) (pp. 345–357). Tokyo, Japan: Shobo Publishing Co.
e. Dinkmeyer, D. C. (Ed.). (1968). *Guidance and counseling in the elementary school: Readings in theory and practice* (pp. 228–235). New York: Holt, Rinehart and Winston.

Combs, A. W. (1954). The psychology of the college student. In M. H. Luke (Ed.), *What should higher education be doing in 1954? The Thorne lectures* (pp. 31–35). Hempstead, L.I., NY: Hofstra College.

Combs, A. W., & Fisk, R. S. (Guest Eds.). (1954). Human Relations Training for School Administrators [Special Issue]. *Journal of Social Issues, 10*(2).

Combs, A. W., & Fisk, R. S. (Guest Eds.—Special Issue). (1954). Foreword. Human Relations Training for School Administrators [Special Issue]. *Journal of Social Issues, 10*(2), 2–4.

Combs, A. W., & Fisk, R. S. (1954). Problems and research needs in administration. *Journal of Social Issues, 10*(2), 49–58.

Combs, A. W., Fisk, R. S., Fine, H. J., Zimet, C. N., Wiberley, J. A., & Nesbitt, D. A. (1954). Part I: The Syracuse studies. *Journal of Social Issues, 10*(2), 5–24.

Mroz, E. J., Dahlquist, V., DeLany, C., DiIanni, P., Gardner, R., Overstreet, H., & Combs, A. W. (1954). *N.C.O. course in leadership and human relations: Instructor's handbook.* Geneva, NY: Sampson Air Force Base.

1955

Combs, A. W. (1955). How should we look at levels—from democratic practices. *Childhood Education, 32*(4), 160–163.

Combs, A. W. (1955). Why executives become frustrated. *Office Executive, 30*(4), 24–26.
Abstracted in *Proceedings of the American Society of Civil Engineers, Sanitary Engineering Division* (#9) under the title Tensions and frustrations in administration, April, 1956, pp. 7–11.
Digested in *Management Guide*—6K1, 6K2. Philadelphia, PA: National Office Management Association (n.d.).

Sanford, N., with Blos, P., Bone, H., Combs, A. W., Klein, G. & May, R. (1955). [Report]. The findings of the commission in psychology. In *Annals of the New York Academy of Sciences, 63*(Art. 3), 341–355.

1956

1957

Combs, A. W. (1957). A lobbyist's report. *Progressive Education, 34*(3), 119–123.

Combs, A. W. (1957). The myth of competition. *Childhood Education, 33*(6), 264–269.
REPRINTED in:
a. *Child-Family Digest* (1957), *16*(2), 38–46.
b. Rasmussen, M. (Ed.), with Sunderlin, S., & Martin, L. P. (Assistant Eds.). (1966) *Readings from childhood education: Articles of lasting value* (pp.40–47). Washington, DC: Association for Childhood Education International.
c. Combs, A. W. (1979). *Colorado Journal of Educational Research, 18*(4), 3–5.

Combs, A. W., & Soper, D. W. (1957). The self, its derivate terms, and research. *Journal of Individual Psychology, 13*(2), 134–145.
REPRINTED in:
a. Kuenzli, A. E. (Ed.). (1959). *The phenomenological problem* (pp. 31–48). New York: Harper & Brothers.
b. Turner, A. N., & Lombard, G. F. F. (Eds.). (1969). *Interpersonal behavior and administration* (pp. 184–193). New York: Free Press.
c. Reprinted as: "Teaching Case" by Harvard Business School (CC1A.1– reel 85–77–HP 573).

Soper, D. W., & Combs, A. W. (1957). Planning future research in education. *Educational Leadership, 14*(5), 315, 317–318.

1958

Combs, A. W. (1958). Adjustment . . . Through guidance and special services. *Educational Leadership, 16*(2), 89–92.

Combs, A. W. (1958). Good teaching creates change. *Washington Education, 69*(8), 14–15.

Combs, A. W. (1958). New horizons in field research: The self concept. *Educational Leadership, 15*(5), 315–317, 319, 328.

Combs, A. W. (1958). Seeing is behaving. *Educational Leadership, 16*(1), 21–26.
REPRINTED in:
a. Hass, G., & Wiles, K. (1965). *Readings in curriculum* (pp. 195–202). Boston: Allyn and Bacon.
b. Hass, G., Wiles, K., & Bondi, J. (1970). *Readings in curriculum* (2nd ed.) (pp. 210–219). Boston: Allyn and Bacon.
c. Frey, S. H., & Haugen, E. S. (1969). *Readings in classroom learning* (pp. 281–288). New York: American Book Company.
d. Froyen, L., & Pryzychodzin, J. (1967) *Teacher and child* (pagination unknown). Dubuque, IA: William Brown.
e. Revised as Combs, A. W. (1958). New patterns of behavior. *Resource, 2*(6), 16–19.
f. Mueller, R. J., Ary, D., & McCormick, C. (Eds.). (1974). *Readings in classroom learning and perception* (pp. 123–130). New York: Praeger.

Gordon, I. J., & Combs, A. W. (1958). The learner: Self and perception. *Review of Educational Research, 28*(5), 433–444.

1959

Combs, A. W. (1959). Personality theory and its implications for curriculum development. In A. Frazier (Ed.), *Learning more about learning* (pp. 5–20). [Papers and reports from the Third ASCD Research Institute.] Washington, DC: Association for Supervision and Curriculum Development, National Education Association.
REPRINTED in:
a. Resnick, W. C., & Heller, D. H. (Eds.). (1963) *On your own in college* (pp. 142–144). Columbus, OH: Charles E. Merrill Books.
b. Mills, B. C. (1972). *Understanding the young child and his curriculum: Selected readings* (pp. 239–252). New York: Macmillan.

Combs, A. W. (1959). Seeing is behaving (pp. 1–8). Knowing, Behaving and Learning (pp. 9–19). *Proceedings, Annual meeting, Puerto Rico Association for Supervision and Curriculum Development.* Rio Piedras, PR: University of Puerto Rico.

Combs, A. W., & Snygg, D. (1959). *Individual behavior: A perceptual approach to behavior* (Rev. ed). New York: Harper & Brothers.
EXCERPTS REPRINTED in:
a. Combs, A. W., & Snygg, D. (1964). Perception and its function. In C. G. Kemp (Ed.), *Perspectives on the group process: A foundation for counseling with groups* (pp. 286–289). [Reprint of pages 150–151, 153, 156]. Boston: Houghton Mifflin.
b. Combs, A. W., & Snygg, D. (1970). Perception and its function. In C. G. Kemp (Ed.), *Perspectives on the group process: A foundation for counseling with groups* (2nd ed.) (pp. 248–251). [Reprint of pages 150–151, 153, 156]. Boston: Houghton Mifflin.
c. Combs, A. W., & Snygg, D. (1960). The perceptual view of behavior. In J. C. Coleman with A. Marks (Eds.), *Personality dynamics and effective behavior* (pp. 466–474). [Reprint of pages 16–36] Chicago, IL: Scott, Foresman.

Combs, A. W., with White, J. B., Hill, T. J., Hilliard, P., & Lounsbury, J. H. (1959). The role of the laboratory school in teacher education. In A. W. Combs (Ed.), *Proceedings of Conference,* P. K. Yonge Laboratory School, November 23–25, 1958 (pp. 7–18). Gainesville, FL: University of Florida.

1960

Combs, A. W. (1960). Perceptual psychology. In *Western Washington College Bulletin: Proceedings of the 1960 Summer Conference; Intelligence, creativity and learning,* Bellingham, WA, *13*, 67–74.

1961

Combs, A. W. (1961). Knowing, learning, behaving. *The Instructor, 70*(6), 3, 88–89.

Combs, A. W. (1961). A perceptual view of the nature of "helpers." In A. W. Combs (Ed.), *Personality theory and coun-*

seling practice (pp. 53–58). Gainesville, FL: University of Florida.

Combs, A. W. (Ed.). (1961). *Personality theory and counseling practice.* Papers presented at the First Annual Conference on Personality Theory and Counseling Practice. Gainesville, FL: University of Florida.

Combs, A. W. (1961). Setting up the learning situation. In *Providing for diversity, Proceedings of the Annual Florida Community Junior College Conference, September 28–29, 1961, Gainesville, FL* (pp. 2–4). Tallahassee, FL: Florida State Department of Education.

Combs, A. W. (1961). What can man become? *California Journal for Instructional Improvement, 4*(4), 15–23.
REPRINTED in:
a. Hamachek, D. E. (Ed.) (1965). *The SELF in growth, teaching, and learning: Selected readings* (pp. 561–576). Englewood Cliffs, NJ: Prentice-Hall.
b. Strom, R. D. (Ed.). (1971). *Teachers and the learning process* (pp. 153–166). Englewood Cliffs, NJ: Prentice-Hall.
c. Day, C. A., & Ward, W. D. (Eds.) (1968). *Studies in developmental psychology* (pp. 357–371). Berkeley, CA: McCutchan.
d. Avila, D. L., Combs, A. W., & Purkey, W. W. (Eds.). (1971). *The helping relationship sourcebook* (pp. 397–412). Boston: Allyn and Bacon.
e. Avila, D. L., Combs, A. W., & Purkey, W. W. (Eds.). (1977). *The helping relationship sourcebook* (2nd ed.) (pp. 240–253). Boston: Allyn and Bacon.

1962

Combs, A. W. (Ed.). (1962). *Perceiving, behaving, becoming: A new focus for education, Yearbook 1962.* Washington, DC: Association for Supervision and Curriculum Development.

Combs, A. W. (1962). A perceptual view of the adequate personality. In A. W. Combs (Ed.), *Perceiving, behaving, becoming. A new focus for education, Yearbook 1962* (pp. 50–64). Washington, DC: Association for Supervision and Curriculum Development.
REPRINTED in:
a. Brown, R. G., Newell, R. A., & Vonk, H. G.(Eds.). (1969). *Behavioral implications for curriculum and teaching: Interdisciplinary readings* (pp. 95–102). Dubuque, IA: Wm. C. Brown.
b. Muse, M. (Ed.) (1970). *Selected readings for the introduction to the teaching profession* (pp. 30–41). Berkeley, CA: McCutchan.
c. Freiberg, H. J. (1999). *Perceiving, behaving, becoming. Lessons learned* (pp. 119–135). Alexandria, VA: Association for Supervision and Curriculum Development.
With responses by
H. H. Marshall, What does recent research say about the "truly adequate person"? (pp. 136–147) and B. L. McCombs, What role does perceptual psychology play in educational reform today? (pp. 148–157).

Combs, A. W. (1962). Psychological factors in college learning. In R. M. Cooper (Ed.), *The changing disciplines in higher education: Report of the Florida Higher Education Conference held November 23–24, 1962* (pp. 21–30). Tampa, FL: University of South Florida.

Combs, A. W. (1962). The self in chaos. [Review of the book *The self concept: A critical survey of pertinent research literature*]. *Contemporary Psychology, 7*(2), 53–54.

Soper, D. W., & Combs, A. W. (1962). The helping relationship as seen by teachers and therapists. *Journal of Consulting Psychology, 26*(3), 288.

1963

Combs, A. W. (1963). Perception of self and others in the helping relationship. In J. M. Seidman (Ed.), *Educating for mental health: A book of readings* (pp. 243–247). New York: Thomas Y. Crowell.

Combs, A. W. (1963). The perceptual orientation of personnel workers. In *New Concepts of Human Potential, Proceedings of major presentations and summary of discussions, State Conference of Project Directors, National Defense Education Act Title V-A, October 10–12, 1962* (pp. 31–63). Sacramento, CA: Sacramento City Unified School District in cooperation with the California State Department of Education.

Combs, A. W. (1963). The self-actualizing person: What kind of people do we want? *YWCA Magazine, 57*(7), 11, 34.

Combs, A. W., & Soper, D. W. (1963). The helping relationship as described by "good" and "poor" teachers. *Journal of Teacher Education, 14*(1), 64–67.
REPRINTED in Bradley, R. C., & Halstead, F. E. (1974). *The beginning elementary school teacher in action* (pp. 297–302). Wolfe City, TX: The University Press.

Combs, A. W., & Soper, D. W. (1963). The perceptual organization of effective counselors. *Journal of Counseling Psychology, 10*(3), 222–226.
REPRINTED in:
a. Adams, J. F. (1965). *Counseling & guidance: A summary view* (pp. 44–49). New York: Macmillan.
b. Adaptation in Combs, A. W., with Soper, D. W. (1969). In A. W. Combs, with D.W. Soper, C. T. Gooding, J. A. Benton, Jr., J. F. Dickman, & R. H. Usher, *Florida studies in the helping professions. University of Florida Social Sciences Monograph #37* (pp. 21–27). Gainesville, FL: University of Florida Press.
c. Koziey, P. W. (Ed.) (1970). *Selections for an introduction to guidance* (pp. 159–166). Berkeley, CA: McCutchan.

Combs, A. W., & Soper, D. W. (1963). *The relationship of child perceptions to achievement and behavior in the early school years.* Cooperative Research Project No. 814. Washington, DC: U.S. Office of Education, U.S. Department of Health, Education and Welfare.
REPRINTED excerpts from General Conclusions section reprinted as: Combs, A. W., & Soper, D. W. (1965). The

relationship of child perceptions to achievement and behavior in the early school years [Summary of Project No. 814]. *Chronicle Guidance Professional Service.* Moravia, NY: Chronicle Guidance Publications.

Combs, A. W., Soper, D. W., & Courson, C. C. (1963). The measurement of self concept and self report. *Educational and Psychological Measurement, 23*(3), 493–500.

1964

Combs, A. W. (1964). Can we measure good teaching objectively? Objective measurement is impossible. *National Education Association Journal, 53*(1), 34–36, 73.
REPRINTED in Hass, G., Wiles, K., & Roberts, A. (Eds.). (1970). *Readings in secondary teaching* (pp. 206–210). Boston: Allyn and Bacon.

Combs, A. W. (1964). Helping young people discover commitment. *Educational Leadership, 22*(3), 164–169.
REPRINTED in:
a. *Chronicle Guidance Professional Service* (1965). Moravia, NY: Chronicle Guidance Publications.
*b. *Professional Reprints in Education, #8203* (1965). Charles Merrill.
c. Combs, A. W. (1969). Helping young people discover commitment. *Iowa Personnel and Guidance Bulletin* 8(4), 9–14.
d. Allen, W. R. (Ed.). (1972). *Teacher aides: A process description* (pp. 32–36). Program site: Southwest Minnesota State College, Marshall, MN. Minnesota Department of Education.
e. Bradley, R. C., & Halstead, F. E. (1974). *The beginning elementary school teacher in action* (pp. 519–526). Wolfe City, TX: The University Press.

Combs, A. W. (1964). An observation on humanism and existentialism in American psychology. *Phoenix: Newsletter of the American Association for Humanistic Psychology, 1*(2), 1, 4.

Combs, A. W. (1964). The personal approach to good teaching. *Educational Leadership, 21*(6), 369–377, 399.
REPRINTED in:
a. Beckner, W., & Dumas, W. (Eds.).(1968). *Readings in secondary education: A foundations approach* (pp. 334–344). Scranton, PA: International Textbook Co.
b. Brown, R. G., Newell, R. A., & Vonk, H. G.(Eds.). (1969). *Behavioral implications for curriculum and teaching: Interdisciplinary readings* (pp. 252–258). Dubuque, IA: Wm. C. Brown.
c. Froyen, L., & Pryzychodzin, J. (Eds.). (1967). *Teacher and child* (pagination unknown). Dubuque, IA: William Brown.
d. Funk, H. D., & Olberg, R. T. (Eds.). (1971). *Learning to teach in the elementary school: Introductory readings* (pp. 9–20). New York: Dodd, Mead.
e. Hyman, R. T. (Ed.). (1971). *Contemporary thought on teaching* (pp. 257–267). Englewood Cliffs, NJ: Prentice-Hall.
f. Read, D. A., & Simon, S. B. (Eds.). (1975). *Humanistic education sourcebook* (pp. 249–261). Englewood Cliffs, NJ: Prentice-Hall.
g. Stone, J. C., & Schneider, F. W. (Eds.). (1965). *Readings in the foundations of education: Commitment to teaching* (Vol. II) (pp. 97–107). New York: Thomas Y. Crowell.

1965

Combs, A. W. (1965). *The professional education of teachers: A perceptual view of teacher preparation.* Boston: Allyn and Bacon.
REPRINTED excerpts reprinted as:
a. Combs, A. W. (1970). The teacher's purposes. In M. Muse (Ed.), *Selected readings for the introduction to the teaching profession* (pp. 118–123). Berkeley, CA: McCutchan.
b. Combs, A. W. (1970). The personal discovery of ways to teach. In M. Muse (Ed.), *Selected readings for the introduction to the teaching profession* (pp. 190–201). Berkeley, CA: McCutchan.

Combs, A. W. (1965), Some basic concepts in perceptual psychology. [Mimeographed transcript of speech presented April 14, 1965, Minneapolis, MN, pp. 1–8]. Washington, DC: American Personnel and Guidance Association.
REPRINTED in:
a. Avila, D. L., Combs, A. W., & Purkey, W. W. (Eds.). (1971). *The helping relationship sourcebook* (pp. 117–126). Boston: Allyn and Bacon.
b. Hass, G., Wiles, K., & Roberts, A. (Eds.). (1970). *Readings in secondary teaching* (pp. 116–124). Boston: Allyn and Bacon.

Combs, A. W. (1965). Teachers too are individuals. In D. E. Hamachek (Ed.), *The SELF in growth, teaching, and learning: Selected readings* (pp. 457–463). Englewood Cliffs, NJ: Prentice-Hall.

1966

Combs, A. W. (1966). Curriculum change and the humanist movement. *Educational Leadership, 23*(7), 527–530.

Combs, A. W. (1966). A forward look. Presentation in the ASCD Board of Directors, *1966 Conference Program, San Francisco, CA* (pp. 1–9). Washington, DC: Association for Supervision and Curriculum Development.

Combs, A. W. (1966). Fostering self-direction. *Educational Leadership, 23*(5), 373–376.
REPRINTED in:
a. *The Education Digest.* (1966). *31* (9), 5–7.
*b. *Education Gazette,* South Australian Education.
* c. *Education, 18*(20), (San Juan, Puerto Rico).
d. Hamachek, D. E. (Ed.). (1968). *Human dynamics in psychology and education. Selected readings* (pp. 564–568). Boston: Allyn and Bacon.
e. Jarvis, O. T. (Ed.). (1969). *Elementary school administration: Readings* (pp. 282–286). Dubuque, IA: Wm. C. Brown.
f. Nelson, L. N. (Ed.). (1969). *The nature of teaching: A collection of readings* (pp. 319–323). Waltham, MA: Blaisdell Publishing.

g. Howes, V. M. (Ed.). (1970). *Individualization of instruction. A teaching strategy* (pp. 30–36). New York: Macmillan.
h. Funk, H. D., & Olberg, R. T. (Eds.). (1971). *Learning to teach in the elementary school. Introductory readings* (pp. 181–185). New York: Dodd, Mead.
i. Ryan, K., & Cooper, J. M. (1972). *Kaleidoscope: Readings in education* (pp. 342–347). Boston: Houghton Mifflin.
j. Ryan, K., & Cooper, J. M. (1975). *Kaleidoscope: Readings in education* (2nd ed.) (pp. 170–173). Boston: Houghton Mifflin.
k. Trusty, F. M. (Ed.). (1971). *Administering human resources. A behavioral approach to educational administration* (pp. 81–85). Berkeley, CA: McCutchan.
l. Combs, A. W., with response by V. S. Fisher. (1967). *The Church of the Brethren Leader, 10*(3), 23–26.
m. Avila, D. L., Combs, A. W., & Purkey, W. W. (Eds.). (1971). *The helping relationship sourcebook* (pp. 244–249). Boston: Allyn and Bacon.
n. Avila, D. L., Combs, A. W., & Purkey, W. W. (Eds.). (1977). *The helping relationship sourcebook* (2nd ed.) (pp. 144–148). Boston: Allyn and Bacon.
*o. *Pacific Speech Journal.*

Combs, A. W. (1966). Teacher education - A problem in becoming. In E. B. Smith, H. C. Olsen, P. J. Johnson, & C. Barbour (Eds.), *Partnership in teacher education* (pp. 211–227). Washington, DC: The American Association of Colleges for Teacher Education, The Association for Student Teaching.

*Combs, A. W., & Gordon, I. J. (1966, February). Attitudes and behavior of biological sciences curriculum study special methods classes. *Florida Curriculum Study Directory.*

1967

Combs, A. W. (1967). Foreword. In F. T. Wilhelms (Ed.), *Evaluation as feedback and guide* (pp. v-vi). Washington, DC: Association for Supervision and Curriculum Development, NEA.

Combs, A. W. (1967). Foreword. In R. R. Leeper (Ed.), *Humanizing Education: The person in the process* (pp. v–vi). Washington, DC: Association for Supervision and Curriculum Development, NEA.

Combs, A. W. (1967). Humanizing education: The person in the process. In R. R. Leeper (Ed.), *Humanizing education: The person in the process* (pp. 73–88). Washington, DC: Association for Supervision and Curriculum Development, NEA.

Combs, A. W. (1967). Self concept as an objective self-concept. In G. Nelson (Ed.), *Education for the culturally disadvantaged: Proceedings of the National Conference on Educational Objectives for the Culturally Disadvantaged,* September 7–8, 1967, Hot Springs, AR.(pp. 36–66, includes commentaries by J. E. Peters [pp. 54–57], J. B. Jones [pp. 57–61] and W. T. Chase [pp. 61–66]). Little Rock, AR: South Central Region Educational Laboratory.
*REPRINTED 1987 by Ministry of Education, Port of Spain, Trinidad, Tobago. (T) file.

Leader in education. (1967). *Education, 87*(6), cover, 374.

1968

Combs, A. W. (1968). A curriculum for learners. In W. M. Alexander (Ed.), *The high school of the future: A memorial to Kimball Wiles* (pp. 119–128). Columbus, OH: Charles E. Merrill.

Combs, A. W. (1968). Preface. In W. M. Alexander (Ed.), *The high school of the future: A memorial to Kimball Wiles* (pp. vii-ix). Columbus, OH: Charles E. Merrill.

*Combs, A. W. (1968). *The humanizing process: Three addresses.* Honolulu, HI: Hawaii Association for Supervision and Curriculum Development.

1969

Combs, A. W. (1969). An intellectual conversion. *Theory Into Practice, 8*(5), 298–299.

Combs, A. W. (1969). The human factor in the current curriculum. In H. L. Jones (Ed.), *Curriculum development in a changing world* (pp. 57–70). Syracuse, NY: School of Education, Syracuse University.

*Combs, A. W. (1969). *Maintaining a supportive social environment for man: A world wide problem.* Washington, DC: Association for Supervision and Curriculum Development.

Combs, A. W. (1969). Book review: Methods of teaching elementary school mathematics by W. Olson. *Educational Leadership, 27*(1), 95, 97.

Combs, A. W. (1969). What can man become? In S. M. Grobman, J. L. Kennedy, & J. R. Frola (Eds.), *Great speaker series 1968, Title V, ESEA* (pp. 47–60). Harrisburg, PA: Pennsylvania Department of Public Instruction.

Combs, A. W., with Soper, D. W., Gooding, C. T., Benton, J. A., Jr., Dickman, J. F., & Usher, R. H. (1969). *Florida studies in the helping professions. University of Florida Social Sciences Monograph #37.* Gainesville, FL: University of Florida Press. REPRINTED excerpt reprinted as:
a. Combs, A. W. (1971). An overview and next steps. In D. L. Avila, A. W. Combs, & W. W. Purkey (Eds.), *The helping relationship sourcebook* (pp. 289–298). Boston: Allyn and Bacon.
b. Combs, A. W. (1977). An overview and next steps. In D. L. Avila, A. W. Combs, & W. W. Purkey (Eds.), *The helping relationship sourcebook* (2nd ed.) (pp. 19–27). Boston: Allyn and Bacon.

1970

Combs, A. W. (1970). An educational imperative: The human dimension. In M-M. Scobey & G. Graham (Eds.), *To nurture humanness: Commitment for the 70s, 1970 Yearbook*

(pp. 173–188). Washington DC: Association for Supervision and Curriculum Development, NEA.
REPRINTED excerpt in: Alexander, W. M., Saylor, J. G., & Williams, E. L.(Eds.), (1971). *The high school: Today and tomorrow* (pp. 414–415). New York: Holt, Rinehart and Winston.

Combs, A. W. (1970). Can education be relevant? *Colorado Journal of Educational Research, 9*(3), 2–8.
REPRINTED in Saylor, J.G. & Smith, J. L. (Eds.). (1971). *Removing barriers to humaneness in the high school* (pp. 30–42). Washington, DC: ASCD Council on Secondary Education, Association for Supervision and Curriculum Development.

Combs, A. W. (1970). The human aspect of administration. *Colorado Journal of Educational Research, 9*(3), 9–15.
REPRINTED in:
a. *Educational Leadership.* (1970). *28*(2), 197–201, 203–205.
b. **The Quarterly, N.J. Council of School Administrators, 6* (1976).

Combs, A. W. (1970). On becoming teachers. [Keynote address]. In *Proceedings of Annual Conference, September 25–26* (pp. 12–14). Winston-Salem, NC: North Carolina Kindergarten Association.

Combs, A. W. (1970). The perceptual approach to the helping professions. *Journal of the Association for the Study of Perception, 5*(2), 1–7.

Combs, A. W. (1970). Sensitivity education: Problems and promise. *Educational Leadership, 28*(3), 235–237.
REPRINTED in Read, D. A., & Simon, S. B. (Eds.). (1975). *Humanistic education sourcebook* (pp. 192–195). Englewood Cliffs, NJ: Prentice-Hall.

1971

*Combs, A. W. (1971). Ein innovations-program fur die professionelle ausbildung von grundschullehern. In A. Schuller (Ed.), *Lehrerrolle im Wandel.* Pädagogisches, Zentrum Veroffentlichungen (pp. 35–39). Reihe, C. Band 21, Berlin: Verlag Julius Beltz.
REPRINTED as: An innovative program for the professional education of elementary school teachers. In A. Schuller, (Ed.), (1971), *The role of the teacher in educational change* (pp. 19–23). (Report of international conference held in Berlin, Germany, October 10–November 1, 1968). Berlin: Pädagogisches Zentrum.

Combs, A. W. (1971). Foreword. In V. C. Raimy, *The self-concept as a factor in counseling and personality organization* (pp. vi–ix). Columbus, OH: Ohio State University Libraries.

*Combs A. W. (1971). Humanism and classroom management (mimeo). *Teacher Education Advisory Council,* Clearwater, FL.

*Combs, A. W. (1971). A humanistic approach to supervision. *Proceedings,* Indiana University.

*Combs, A. W. (1971). Lehrerbildun als sozialisation process. In A. Schuller (Ed.), *Lehrerrolle im Wandel: Pädagogisches Zentrum Veroffentlichungen* (unknown pagination). Reihe, C. Band 21. Berlin: Verlag Julius Beltz.

Combs, A. W. (1971). New concepts of human potentials: New challenge for teachers. *Childhood Education, 47*(7), 349–355.
REPRINTED in Palardy, J. M. (1975). *Teaching today: Tasks and challenges* (pp. 124–131). New York: Macmillan.

*Combs, A. W. (1971). The personal approach to teaching. *Proceedings: TTT [Training of Teacher Trainers] program,* Miami, FL.

*Combs, A. W. (1971). Report and comments on humanistic and behavioral studies in basic programs. In *Steps toward excellence in teacher education: Reports from around the country* (unknown pagination). Washington, DC: American Association of Colleges for Teacher Education.

Combs, A. W. (1971). Some basic guidelines for the training of "helpers." *Proceedings: National Faculty Development Conference, Community College Mental Health Worker Programs, August 26–29,* Louisville, KY (Orange paper, pp. 1–22). Atlanta, GA: Southern Regional Education Board.

Combs, A. W., Avila, D. L., & Purkey, W. W. (1971). *Helping relationships: Basic concepts for the helping professions.* Boston: Allyn and Bacon.
Translations:
German translation: *Die Helfenden Berufe,* Ernst Klett Verlag, Stuttgart, 1975.
Dutch translation: *Hulpeverlening en Psychologie, Eigentijdse in zichten getoetst aan de praktijk van de helpende relatie.* Basisboeken/Ambo/Baoion, 1977.

Avila, D. L., Combs, A. W., & Purkey, W. W. (Eds.). (1971). *The helping relationship sourcebook.* Boston: Allyn and Bacon.

McLaughlin, F. (Ed.) with Jourard, S., & Combs, A. W. (1971). Conversation: Two humanists. *Media & Methods, 8*(4), 24–29.

1972

Combs, A. W. (1972). Administration and the adequate personality. *Colorado Journal of Educational Research, 12*(1), 24–27.

Combs, A. W. (1972). *Educational accountability: Beyond behavioral objectives.* Washington, DC: Association for Supervision and Curriculum Development.
*Korean translation: *New Education.* Seoul, Korea, 1973.
**New Mexico School Review* (1974–75).
EXCERPTS REPRINTED as:
a. Combs, A. W. (1975). Humanistic goals of education. In D. A. Read & S. B. Simon (Eds.), *Humanistic education sourcebook* (pp. 91–100). Englewood Cliffs, NJ: Prentice-Hall.
b. Combs, A. W. (1974). Humanistic goals of education. In I. D. Welch, F. Richards, & A. C. Richards (Eds.), *Educational*

accountability: A humanistic perspective (pp. 227–243). Fort Collins, CO: Shields Publishing.
c. Combs, A. W. (1977). Humanistic goals of education. In F. Richards, I. D. Welch, A. L. Sanders, H. Moore, M. B. Scalice, & K. Ernst (Eds.), *When students grow. A humanistic look at educational accountability* (pp. 137–153). Carrollton, GA: Foundation for Person-Centered Projects and Research.
d. Combs, A.W. (1978). Humanistic goals of education. In I. D. Welch, G. A. Tate, & F. Richards (Eds.), *Humanistic psychology: A source book* (pp. 253–268). Buffalo, NY: Prometheus.

Combs, A. W. (1972). Helping teachers change their values. In J. A. Phillips, Jr. (Ed.), *Developing value constructs in schooling: Inquiry into process and product* (pp. 19–27). Papers and reports from the ASCD-OASCD Curriculum Research Institute, January 23–25, 1972. Columbus, OH: Ohio Association for Supervision and Curriculum Development.

Combs, A. W. (1972). Some basic concepts for teacher education. *The Journal of Teacher Education, 23*(3), 286–290.
REPRINTED in Mueller, R. J., Ary, D., & McCormick, C. (1974). *Readings in classroom learning and perception* (pp. 5–11). New York: Praeger.

Combs, A. W., & Pennypacker, H. S. (1972). Pennypacker/Combs dialogue. [Arranged and recorded by L. W. Nolting & T. Fauquet.] *New Voices in Education, 2*(4), 7–14.

Avila, D. L., Combs, A. W., Olson, W., Packer, A., & Shea, J. (1972). The Florida experimental program in elementary education. *Improving College and University Teaching, 20*(2), 148–149.

1973

Combs, A. W. (1973). Affective education - or none at all. In R. B. Sund & R. W. Bybee (Eds.), *Becoming a better elementary science teacher: A reader* (pp. 41–50). Columbus, OH: Charles E. Merrill.

Combs, A. W. (1973). Educational accountability from a humanistic perspective. *Educational Researcher, 2*(9), 19–21.

Combs, A. W. (1973). The human side of learning. *The National Elementary Principal, 52*(4), 38–42.
REPRINTED in:
a. Carswell, E. M., & Roubinek, D. L. (Eds.). (1974). *Open sesame: A primer in open education* (pp. 244–248). Pacific Palisades, CA: Goodyear.
b. Read, D. A., & Simon, S. B. (Eds.). (1975). *Humanistic education sourcebook* (pp. 123–129). Englewood Cliffs, NJ: Prentice-Hall.
c. LaMonica, E. L (Ed.). (1979). *The nursing process: A humanistic approach* (pp. 479–484). Menlo Park, CA: Addison-Wesley.
d. Hamachek, D. E. (Ed.). (1977). *Human dynamics in psychology and education: Selected readings* (3rd ed.) (pp. 18–22). Boston: Allyn and Bacon.

Combs, A. W. (1973). Transcendent man: New goals for human striving. In R. C. Gardner (Ed.), *Collected papers—Inter-institutional seminar in childhood education* (pp. 1–14). Ogden, UT: Weber State College.

Wass, H., & Combs, A. W. (1973). *A follow up study of on-the-job behavior of elementary teachers trained in an innovative and a traditional program of teacher preparation* (Final report, U.S. Department of Health, Education and Welfare. Project No. 2–D-028, Grant No. OEG 4–72–0016). Washington, DC: U.S. Department of Health, Education and Welfare.

1974

Combs, A. W. (1974). An ogre by profession. *Educational Leadership, 31*(4), 363.

Combs, A. W. (1974). Humanism and accountability. In I. D. Welch, F. Richards, & A. C. Richards (Eds.), *Educational accountability: A humanistic perspective* (pp. 113–123). Fort Collins, CO: Shields.
REPRINTED in Richards, F., Welch, I. D., Sanders, A. L., Moore, H., Scalice, M. B., & Ernst, K. (Eds.). (1977). *When students grow: A humanistic look at educational accountability* (pp. 67–77). Carrollton, GA: Foundation for Person-Centered Projects and Research.

Combs, A. W. (1974). Human rights and student rights. *Educational Leadership, 31*(8), 672–675.

Combs, A. W. (1974). Humanistic approach to learning of adults. In R. W. Bortner, S. S. Dubin, D. F. Hultsch, & J. Withall (Eds.), *Proceedings of Conference: Continuing Explorations: Studies in Continuing Education. Adults as learners* (pp. 51–62). University Park, PA: Pennsylvania State University.

Combs, A. W. (1974). The self concept of learning. In *The 1973–1974 Jennings Scholar Lectures* (pp. 89–106). Cleveland, OH: Martha Holden Jennings Foundation.

Combs, A. W. (1974). Why the humanistic movement needs a perceptual psychology. *Journal of the Association for the Study of Perception, 9*(2), 1–13.
REPRINTED in Avila, D. L., Combs, A. W., & Purkey, W. W. (Eds.). (1977). *The helping relationship sourcebook* (pp. 58–72). Boston: Allyn and Bacon.
REPRINTED in edited format in Combs, A. W. (1975). Needed: A perceptual psychology for the humanistic movement. *Thresholds in Secondary Education, 1*(1), 12–18.

Combs, A. W., & Kinzer, S. M. (1974). The University of Florida's childhood education program: An alternative approach to CBTE [competency based teacher education]. In W. R. Houston (Ed.), *Exploring competency based education* (pp. 173–188). Berkeley, CA: McCutchan.

Busby, W. A., Combs, A. W., Blume, R., Avila, D., & Oberlin, L. (1974). Can teacher education use the "self as instrument" concept? *Educational Leadership, 31*(6), 516–520.

Wass, H., & Combs, A. W. (1974). Humanizing the education of teachers. *Theory Into Practice, 13*(2), 123–129.

Combs, A. W., Blume, R. A., Newman, A. J., & Wass, H. L. (1974). *The professional education of teachers: A humanistic approach to teacher preparation* (2nd ed.) Boston: Allyn and Bacon.
Spanish translation: *Claves para la formacion de los profesores: Un efoque humanitica.* Madrid, Spain: Biblioteca de cencias de la education, 1978.

Wass, H., Blume, R. A., Combs, A. W., & Hedges, W. D. (1974). *Humanistic teacher education: An experiment in systematic curriculum innovation.* Fort Collins, CO: Shields.

1975

Combs, A. W. (1975). The development of self-concept: A humanistic approach to education. In T. Lickona & S. Dalziel (Eds.), *Educational alternatives: A sourcebook: Vol. II Education for the development of the person.* Proceedings of the 1973 and 1974 Conferences on Open Education (Nos. 1 & 2, pp. 1–11). Cortland, NY: State University of New York College at Cortland.

Combs, A. W. (1975). The educational researcher: A need for humanism. *CEDR (Center on Evaluation, Development and Research) Quarterly* [Phi Delta Kappa International], 8(1), 7–11.

1976

Combs, A. W. (1976). Affective-humanistic learning. In K. H. Hansen (Ed.), *Learning: An overview & update* (pp. 109–112). Report of Chief State School Officers 1976 Summer Institute held July 29–August 6, 1976, San Diego, CA. Washington, DC: U.S. Office of Education, Department of Health, Education, and Welfare.

Combs, A. W. (1976). A contract method of evaluation. In S. B. Simon & J. A. Bellanca (Eds.), *Degrading the grading myths: A primer of alternatives to grades and marks* (pp. 70–73). Washington, DC: Association for Supervision and Curriculum Development.

Combs, A. W. (1976). Fostering maximum development of the individual. In W. Van Til (Ed.), *Issues in secondary education: The seventy-fifth yearbook of the National Society for the Study of Education, Part II* (pp. 65–87). Chicago: National Society for the Study of Education.

Combs, A. W. (1976). Personal approach to teaching and learning. In *The roles of parents, teachers and administrators in programs for the deaf-blind.* Proceedings of Study Institute held August 24–29, 1975, San Jose, CA (pp. 21–29). Sacramento, CA: California State Department of Education.

Combs, A. W. (1976). Self-actualization and the teaching function of counselors. In G. S. Belkin (Ed.), *Counseling: Directions in theory and practice* (pp. 43–53). Dubuque, IA: Kendall/Hunt.

Combs, A. W. (1976). What we know about learning and criteria for practice. In S. B. Simon & J. A. Bellanca (Eds.), *Degrading the grading myths: A primer of alternatives to grades and marks* (pp. 6–9). Washington, DC: Association for Supervision and Curriculum Development.

Combs, A. W., Richards, A.C., & Richards, F. (1976). *Perceptual psychology: A humanistic approach to the study of persons.* New York: Harper & Row.

1977

Combs, A. W. (1977). A choice of futures. In D. D. Nevill (Ed.), *Humanistic psychology: New frontiers* (pp. 3–19). New York: Gardner Press.

Combs, A. W. (1977). Humanism in the middle schools. In J. C. Basile II & R. E. Shockley (Eds.), *A report on the proceedings of the West Virginia Conference on Middle Schools and Middle Childhood Education* (pp. 6–12). Charleston, WV: West Virginia Department of Education.

Combs, A. W. (1977). Reflections of a humanistic psychologist: An evening with Arthur Combs. In T. M. Nelson (Ed.), *New concerns and directions in mental health: The 11th annual Mark P. Farrell Emotional Crisis Workshop* held July 19–22, 1977 (pp. 197–219). Greeley, CO: University of Northern Colorado.

Combs, A. W., Popham, W. J., & Hosford, P. L. (1977). Behaviorism and humanism: A synthesis? *Educational Leadership, 35*(1), 52–53, 55–58, 60–63.

Avila, D. L., Combs, A. W., & Purkey, W. W. (Eds.). (1977). *Helping relationship sourcebook* (2nd ed.) Boston: Allyn and Bacon.

1978

Combs, A. W. (1978). Assessing humanistic objectives: Some general considerations. In A. W. Combs, D. N. Aspy, D. M. Brown, M. J. Clute, & L. H. Hicks (Eds.), *Humanistic education: Objectives and assessment—A report of the ASCD working group on humanistic education* (pp. 17–27). Washington, DC: Association for Supervision and Curriculum Development.

Combs, A. W. (1978). Humanism, education, and the future. *Educational Leadership, 35*(4), 300–303.
REPRINTED in *The Education Digest.* (1978). *43*(8), 17–19.

Combs, A. W. (1978). Teacher education: The person in the process. *Educational Leadership, 35*(7), 558–561.

Combs, A. W., Avila, D. L., & Purkey, W. W. (1978). *Helping relationships: Basic concepts for the helping professions* (2nd ed.) Boston: Allyn and Bacon.
Japanese translation: H. Osawa, translator. Tokyo, Japan: Tuttle-Mori Agency, 1978.

Combs, A. W., Aspy, D. N., Brown, D. M., Clute, M. J., & Hicks, L. H. (Eds.). (1978). *Humanistic education: Objectives and assessment—A report of the ASCD working group on humanistic education.* Washington, DC: Association for Supervision and Curriculum Development.

1979

Combs, A. W. (1979). Humanistic education: Hope or hazard? *The Educational Forum, 44*(1), 115–116.

Combs, A. W. (1979). Humanistic education—need or nonsense? *Journal of Humanistic Education, 3,* 1–5.

Combs, A. W. (1979). The myth of competition—twenty years later. *Colorado Journal of Educational Research, 18*(4), 5–7

Combs, A. W. (1979). *Myths in education: Beliefs that hinder progress and their alternatives.* Boston: Allyn and Bacon.

*Combs, A. W. (1979). Some observations on self concept research and theory. *Proceedings: Conference on Self Concept.* Twin Cities, MN: University of Minnesota.

1980

Combs, A. W. (1980). A personalidade adequada. *Proceedings: 6th Congresso Brasileiro de Orientação Educacional* (Z. C. Guenther, Trans.) (pp. 27–51). Belo Horizonte/MG, Brazil: Fundação Mariana Resende Costa (FUMARC)/Pontifical Catholic University of Minas Gerais.

Combs, A. W. (1980). Auto-realização e a prática da orientação educacional. *Proceedings: 6th congresso Brasileiro de Orientação Educacional* (Z. C. Guenther, Trans.) (pp. 65–83). Belo Horizonte/MG, Brazil: Fundação Mariana Resende Costa (FUMARC)/Pontifical Catholic University of Minas Gerais.

Combs, A. W. (1980). Earl Kelley and the humanist movement. *Urban Educator, 5*(1), iv–viii.
*REPRINTED in *Education Digest.* (1980). *46,* 7–12.

*Combs, A. W. (1980). Novas perspectivas para as profissões de ajuda. *Proceedings: 6th Congresso Brasileiro de Orientação Educacional* (Z. C. Guenther, Trans.) (pp. 41–63). Belo Horizonte/MG, Brazil: Fundação Mariana Resende Costa (FUMARC)/Pontifical Catholic University of Minas Gerais.

*Guenther, Z. C., with Combs, A. W. (1980). *Educacao de pessoas* [Portuguese]. Belo Horizonte/MG, Brazil: Fundação Mariana Resende Costa (FUMARC)/Pontifical Catholic University of Minas Gerais.

1981

Combs, A. W. (1981). Humanistic education: Too tender for a tough world? *Phi Delta Kappan, 62*(6), 446–449.
REPRINTED as: Why humanistic education is urgent and necessary. In S. Hoffman & C. Fehrle (Eds.), (n.d.), *Issues in early childhood education* (pp. 1–16). Columbia, MO: University of Missouri.
Also REPRINTED in:
*a. *Education Digest, Annual Edition (1981/1982).*
b. *Oregon English, 3,* 10–13 (1981).
c. Johnson, B. D. (Ed.). (1982). *Dealing with social problems in the classroom* (pp. 43–50). Dubuque, IA: Kendall/Hunt.
d. Colangelo, N., Dustin, D., & Foxley, C. H. (Eds.). (1985). *Multicultural nonsexist education: A human relations approach* (2nd ed) (pp. 19–27). Dubuque, IA: Kendall/Hunt.

Combs, A. W. (1981). What the future demands of education. *Phi Delta Kappan, 62*(5), 369–372.
Digested in *The Education Digest, 46*(7), 7–11.
REPRINTED in Avila, D. L., & Combs, A. W. (Eds.). (1985). *Perspectives on helping relationships and the helping professions. Past, present, and future* (pp. 156–166). Boston: Allyn and Bacon.

*Combs, A. W., Pietrofesa, J. J., & Hall, B. (1981). An interview with Arthur Combs, educator and humanist. *Urban Educator, 5,* 5–11.

1982

Combs, A. W. (1982). Affective education or none at all. *Educational Leadership, 39*(7), 494–497.

Combs, A. W. (1982). *A personal approach to teaching: Beliefs that make a difference.* Boston: Allyn and Bacon.

1983

1984

1985

Combs, A. W. (1985). Achieving self discipline: Some basic principles. *Theory Into Practice, 24*(4), 260–263.

Combs, A. W., & Avila, D. L. (1985). *Helping relationships: Basic concepts for the helping professions* (3rd ed.). Boston: Allyn and Bacon.

Avila, D. L., & Combs, A. W. (Eds.). (1985). *Perspectives on helping relationships and the helping professions: Past, present, and future.* Boston: Allyn and Bacon.

1986

Combs, A. W. (1986). ASCD and the humanist movement. In W. Van Til, *ASCD in retrospect* (pp.63–68). Alexandria, VA: Association for Supervision and Curriculum Development.

Combs, A. W. (1986). Bibliography of the works of Arthur W. Combs, 1943–1986 inclusive. *Person-Centered Review, 1*(2), 221–229.

Combs, A. W. (1986). On methods, conditions, and goals. *Person-Centered Review, 1*(4), 378–388.

Combs, A. W. (1986). Person-centered assumptions for counselor education. *Person-Centered Review, 1*(1), 72–82.

Combs, A. W. (1986). What makes a good helper? A person-centered approach. *Person-Centered Review, 1*(1), 51–61.

1987

1988

Combs, A. W. (1988). Is there a future for humanistic or person-centered education? *Person-Centered Review, 3*(1), 96–103.

Combs, A. W. (1988). New assumptions for educational reform. *Educational Leadership, 45*(5), 38–40.
REPRINTED in *The Education Digest.* (1988). *54,* 3–7.

Combs, A. W. (1988). Some current issues for person-centered therapy. *Person-Centered Review, 3*(3), 263–276.

Combs, A. W. (1988, November 26). The risk of "a nation at risk." *Rocky Mountain News, p. 61.*
Adaptation in Combs, A. W. (1988). The risk of a nation at risk. *Journal of Humanistic Education, 13,* 7–8.

Combs, A. W., Richards, A. C., & Richards, F. (1988). *Perceptual psychology: A humanistic approach to the study of persons.* Lanham, MD: University Press of America.
Japanese Translation: Tokyo: Tuttle-Mori Agency, 1988.

1989

Combs, A. W. (1989). New assumptions for teacher education. *Foreign Language Annals, Journal of the American Council on the Teaching of Foreign Languages, 22*(2), 129–134.

Combs, A. W. (1989). *A theory of therapy. Guidelines for counseling practice.* Newbury Park, CA: Sage Publications.

1990

Combs, A. W. (with P. Lawrence & C. Nussbaum, interviewers). (1990). Looking at basic assumptions: An interview with Arthur W. Combs. *Texas Association for Improvement of Reading (TAIR) Newsletter, 33*(2) 3, 10.

Combs, A. W. (1990). Toward a viable psychology of meaning. *Person-Centered Review, 5*(4), 449–463.

Arnett, R. C., Bowen, D. W., Bozarth, J. D., Brodley, B. T., Combs, A. W., Gaylin, N. L., Raskin, N. J., Solomon, L., Thorne, B., & Wood, J. K. (1990). Roundtable discussion: (1) What are the greatest contributions of client-centered theory and practice to the field of psychotherapy? (2) What modifications in client-centered therapy and practice are most essential to the evolution and effectiveness of client-centered psychotherapy? *Person-Centered Review, 5*(4), 464–477.

1991

Combs, A. W. (1991). El movimento humanista en la psicologia y los sistemas de pensamiento abierto (E. S. Ramirez, Trans.). *Revista Mexicana de Pedagogia,* Año 2(5), 25–30.

Combs, A. W. (1991). *The schools we need. New assumptions for educational reform.* Lanham, MD: University Press of America.
REPRINTED (1994) by Save America—Educate Our Children, Denver, CO.

1992

*Combs, A. W. (1992). America 2000: New hope for reform. *Changing Schools, 20,* 8–9.

Combs, A. W. (1992, October 18). Vouchers aren't the answer to what ails education. *Greeley Tribune,* p. A-15.

*Johnson, S. (1992). A personal conversation with Art Combs. *Destinations, 2*(3), 8–13.

Richards, A. C., & Combs, A. W. (1992). Education and the humanistic challenge. *The Humanistic Psychologist, 20*(2–3), 372–388.
REPRINTED in Wertz, F. J. (Ed.). (1994). *The humanistic movement. Recovering the person in psychology* (pp. 256–273). Lake Worth, FL: Gardner Press.

1993

Combs, A. W. (1993). Educational reform and the need for new assumptions. *Kentucky Council of Teachers of Mathematics Journal, 5*(1), 1–6.

Combs, A. W. (1993). Perceptual-experiential therapy. *The Family Journal: Counseling and Therapy for Couples and Families, 1*(1), 81–82.

1994

Combs, A. W. (1994). Los mitos en la educación. *Revista Mexicana De Pedagogia* (E. S. Ramirez, Trans.). *Año 5*(18), 25–28.

*Combs, A. W. (1994). Los mitos en la educación. *Revista Mexicana De Pedagogia* (E. S. Ramirez, Trans.). *Año* 5(19), pagination unknown.

Combs, A. W. (1994). Los mitos en la educación. *Revista Mexicana De Pedagogia* (E. S. Ramirez, Trans.). *Año 5*(20), 4–7.

Dolliver, R. H., & Patterson, D. C. (1994). An interview with Arthur W. Combs. *Journal of Humanistic Education and Development, 32*(4), 150–161.

Combs, A. W., & Gonzalez, D. M. (1994). *Helping relationships. Basic concepts for the helping professions* (4th ed). Boston: Allyn and Bacon.

1995

Combs, A. W. (1995). A search for personal meaning. In M. M. Suhd (Ed.), *Positive regard: Carl Rogers and other notables he influenced* (pp. 156–173). Palo Alto, CA: Science and Behavior Books.

1996

1997

Combs, A. W., with introduction by Epting, F. R. (1997). Being and becoming: A field approach to psychology. *The Humanistic Psychologist, 25*(3), 237–243.

1998

1999

Combs, A. W. (1999). *Being and becoming. A field approach to psychology.* New York: Springer Publishing Co.

Combs, A. W., Miser, A. B., & Whitaker, K. S. (1999). *On becoming a school leader: A person-centered challenge.* Alexandria, VA: Association for Supervision and Curriculum Development.
Chinese translation: Beijing, China: China Astronautic Publishing House, 2000.

2004

Combs, A. W., & Blume, R. A. (2004). *The continuing American revolution. A psychological perspective.* New York: iUniverse, Inc.

Some Publications and Audio/Visual Materials About Arthur W. Combs and his Legacy

Russell, J. T. (1969). *The Snygg-Combs phenomenological theory of perception and its implications for adult theory and practice.* Doctoral dissertation, Indiana University, Bloomington. (UMI No. 6922037)

Print, M. N. (1978). *The application of Arthur Combs' theory of teacher education to the preparation of teachers in Western Australia.* Doctoral dissertation, Ohio State University, Columbus, OH. (UMI No. 7819655)

O'Roark, A. M. (1999). Correction and comment: "Becoming a consultant: The real stories" (Leonard, 1999). *Consulting Psychology Journal: Practice and Research, 51*(2), 135–136.

Siu-Runyan, Y. (2000). The teacher is what matters, not silver bullets and magic formulas: An interview with A. W. Combs. *The Colorado Communicator, 24*(1), 6–17.

Wright, J. D. (2006). Exploring the relationships among dispositions associated with teacher effectiveness and indicators of student learning: A perceptual psychology theory approach. Doctoral dissertation, University of West Georgia, Carrollton, GA (UMI No. pending)

Videotapes:

Welch, I. D., & Breier, C. (Interviewers). (1997). Interviews with Dr. Arthur W. Combs. Theory, Part 1 (32 minutes); Theory, Part 2 (21 minutes); Contributions to Education, Part 1 (33.09 minutes); Contributions to Education, Part 2 (22.42 minutes). Available from the University of Northern Colorado, Greeley, CO 80631.

Audiotape:

Arthur W. Combs: A Life Celebrated. (1999, March 26). Available from Greg Heinbecker, Squidwerks, 117 17th Street, Greeley, CO 80631 (970–353–7447).

Other sound recordings and papers available from the Department of Special Collections, Davidson Library, University of California, Santa Barbara
(*http://www.library.ucsb.edu/speccoll/speccoll.html*), Collection number HPA Mss6.

References

Leonard, H.S. (1999). Becoming a consultant: The real stories. *Consulting Psychology Journal: Practice and Research, 51*(1), 3–13.

Index